CISTERCIAN FATHERS SERIES: NUMBER FIFTY-FIVE

BERNARD OF CLAIRVAUX:

the parables & the sentences

CISTERCIAN FATHERS SERIES: NUMBER FIFTY-FIVE

BERNARD OF CLAIRVAUX:

THE PARABLES

Translated, with an Introduction,
by Michael Casey

&

THE SENTENCES

Translated by Francis R. Swietek
Introduction by John R. Sommerfeldt

Edited by Maureen M. O'Brien

CISTERCIAN PUBLICATIONS
Kalamazoo, Michigan
2000

This translation has been made from
S. Bernardi. *Opera*. Vol. VI, 2. Edited by J. Leclercq OSB and H. Rochais.
Rome: Editiones Cistercienses, 1972.

Cistercian Publications
Editorial Offices
Institute of Cistercian Studies
Western Michigan University
Kalamazoo, MI 49008

Available from

Cistercian Publications (Distribution)
Saint Joseph's Abbey
167 North Spencer Road
Spencer, MA 01562–1233

and

Cistercian Publications (UK)
Mount Saint Bernard Abbey
Coalville, Leicester LE67 5UL

The work of Cistercian Publications
is made possible in part by support from Western Michigan University
to The Institute of Cistercian Studies

Library of Congress Cataloguing available upon request.
ISBN 0-87907-155-9 (hc)
0-87907-755-7 (pb)

Printed in the United States of America

TABLE OF CONTENTS

The Sentences

ABOUT THE AUTHORS

BERNARD OF CLAIRVAUX left his father's castle near Dijon to enter the struggling 'New Monastery' Cîteaux in 1120. With him he took thirty of his friends and relatives. This alone gives some idea of the persuasiveness and organizational abilities of this remarkable man, who three years later became the first abbot of Clairvaux— the 'valley of light'. Over the next forty years he composed works of theology and spiritual reflection, became the counselor of kings, nobles, popes and scholars, the articulated advocate of a strong, reformed papacy and, in general, the spiritual leader of the early twelfth-century european Church. He was canonized some twenty years after his death in 1153.

MICHAEL CASEY is a Cistercian monk of Tarrawarra Abbey in Australia. He holds degrees in theology from the Katholieke Universiteit te Leuven and from the Melbourne College of Divinity. In addition to numerous articles, he has written *Athirst for God: Spiritual Desire in Bernard of Clairvaux's Sermons on the Song of Songs* (Cistercian Publications, 1988) and *Towards God, a History of Meditation in the Western Tradition* (Collins-Dove).

FRANCIS R. SWIETEK is Associate Professor of History at the University of Dallas. He holds degrees in Humanities from St. John's University, Collegeville, and in History and Classics from the University of Illinois, Champaign-Urbana. In addition to his authorship of numerous articles and reviews, he is co-author of *Two Studies on Venetian Government* (1977) and co-editor of *Studiosorum speculum: Studies in Honor of Louis J. Lekai, O. Cist* (Cistercian Publications, 1993).

the parables

1. the story of the king's son

INTRODUCTION

THE FIRST OF ST BERNARD'S parables is a good illustration of the *genre* as a whole. The story itself is readily accessible. It is told with a keen dramatic sense and a wealth of imaginative detail. At the same time, the transference to a spiritual meaning is easy. Its message is both immediate and profound and relates naturally to the general lines of St Bernard's thought and teaching.

The reader is challenged to take the story seriously. It is not simply an entertaining narrative with an artificial moral message appended. It is quite clear that the message is the cardinal element; the story has been carefully constructed in all its details to serve as a medium for practical spiritual teaching. It is not like an allegorical interpretation of scripture in which the text is already given and the explanation appears both laboured and fanciful. Here the spiritual message is primary. The story serves the purpose of making it communicable.

Here we have to remember the sort of readership for which the *Parables* were intended. Many of those who were attracted to the Cistercian ideal in the lifetime of St Bernard were young men of the rank of knight. They were not children: they had some experience of adult life and came to monasticism in a movement of conversion from the ways of the world and of the flesh. In the *Parables* Bernard offers them a teaching which enables them to situate their own experiences within the perspective of general spiritual theory. At the same time he is able to predict routine problems and give advance notice of difficulties yet to come. In this way the possibility of their becoming discouraged by an apparent lack of progress is anticipated and lessened. He makes the spiritual pursuit seem as exciting and deserving of their youthful energies as the more carnal imaginings which had, until recently, filled their thoughts.

Bernard may have intended the *Parables* as a very early stage of monastic instruction, since very little is demanded of the reader. There are few arcane technical terms to be mastered. The scattering of neologisms throughout the series may be an indicator that the stories were originally composed for telling in the vernacular.

At the same time there is much here for the advanced. Whether consciously or not, Bernard has constructed his stories by weaving together themes from the Scriptures, following Origen's mode of interpretation, by seeing the events of salvation history as archetypes which throw light on the experiences of the Church and of individual souls. Thus the stories serve as a painless introduction to the biblical and monastic theology of the spiritual life and prepare their readers to appreciate the more theoretical presentations found in Bernard's other writings.

In this first parable we see the struggles of the individual soul set against the backdrop of Bernard's theological anthropology: the theme of Creation and Fall, the *Regio dissimilitudinis*, the Exodus, the Prodigal Son. This wily teacher opens our understanding of life to the wider patterns of revelation and the abounding sense of hope and confidence which they imply.

The imagery predominant in several of the *Parables* is that of spiritual warfare. The soul is presented as the soldier of Christ who has, for various reasons, fallen under the power of the enemy. God then initiates a series of events to extricate him from his predicament and to bring him home. Since we are all on this homeward road, it becomes possible to see our own past and our future equally mirrored in the narrative.

The Notion of Progress

The most obvious point that Bernard is making concerns the experience of development in monastic life. The monk's life with

God is not monochromatic. It goes through a sequence of phases which are more or less general, beginning far from God and ending in eternal closeness. The notion of spiritual growth is very familiar to us. We do not realise that the concept of development is relatively recent, its vocabulary appearing only in the sixteenth and seventeenth centuries. Bernard is attempting to come to grips with a very important element in the human experience of spirituality without the help of a developed conceptual system. Instead he uses images to signify that our relationship with God changes qualitatively in the course of a lifetime and that what is appropriate at one stage has no guarantee of universal relevance.

In general there are three phases distinguished by Bernard: a beginning, a middle, and an end. The beginning of the spiritual life he situates at the level of emotion: It is marked by salutary fear, hope and desire. The middle phase is one of practical virtue, in which the monk progressively gives himself to the performance of the whole range of good works and to the cultivation of the various virtues. The final stage is that of perfect charity and union with God.

In several *Parables*, fear is the agent sent by God to effect the sinner's conversion. Fear makes him see the extent of his own degradation and motivates him to cast off the shackles of evil habit.[1] Fear puts all enemies to flight.[2] Fear rouses the captive and liberates him from confinement.[3] Fear breaks down the bars of bad habit.[4] Fear is the beginning of contemplation.[5] Fear motivates the acceptance of discipline.[6] Although fear has a necessary role throughout life, it is of paramount importance in getting things started. Later fear may become a restraint upon progress and need to be offset by more positive forces. But at the beginning fear serves an irreplaceable function.

The opposite of fear is mindlessness. The role of fear is to make the sinner aware of the full implications of his situation and of

1. Par 1.3.
2. Par 2.1.
3. Par 3.3.
4. Par 5.6.
5. Par 6.
6. Par 7.

the danger in which he is placed. It is bad news: it shocks. But it is the only means by which an individual can be shaken out of deadly inaction and motivated to take practical measures to avoid total destruction.

Fear's work is incomplete. Hence there is a need for the addition first of hope and then of desire. If the situation is perceived as hopeless then even the sudden realisation of its gravity is unlikely to spur effort. So the harsh blows of dread and anxiety are supplemented by the soothing consolations of hope and the primal energy of desire. Thus some change for the better becomes possible.

As the former sinner begins to make progress towards God he is, by God's provision, instructed in the various virtues. These operate in concert to ensure that the work begun is brought to a felicitous conclusion. In the various *Parables* Bernard makes use of different systems of classifying the virtues. It seems that he was not particularly interested in the details, at this point; he simply wants to give the impression of a life lived according to the complementary demands of the whole range of Christian virtues. And so the monk makes progress, eventually taking up his abode with Wisdom.

At the end of the road is Charity in all its glory, which unites the monk with God.[7] Charity plays different roles throughout the series of *Parables*: sometimes it seems very active in doing battle with the enemy; at other times its triumph is serene and stately so that at its advent hostile forces fall back dismayed. In line with the doctrine of John Cassian and St Benedict, Bernard realises that Charity begins to bloom only after a lifetime of exercise in lowlier virtues.

In the last paragraph of the present *Parable* the sequence is clearly spelled out. After enslavement there is a phase of struggle and flight in which the agenda is determined by the nature of the past from which one is escaping. As the distance between the past and the present increases, a plateau is reached in which good living becomes quasi-habitual, but progressively one's energies become unfocussed. The third stage, that of fearful assailment causes one to look beyond the enemy, to transcend oneself and to take one's cue more and more from one's ultimate destination. The final stage is dominated

---

7. Par 1.6, 2.7.

by a progressive awareness of God and an accelerated movement towards him.

The Unexpected

Bernard's language and imagery is powerful enough to sustain the reader's interest. In several of the *Parables*, however, there is something more. The author gives a twist to the story which comes as something of a surprise to the reader. Instead of proposing a simple progression, he warns his monks that there are unexpected elements to be found in spiritual development. They are not to lose heart when their anticipated progress ceases and decline sets in.

So Bernard introduces into the homeward journey a period of regression. In the first story, the son once rescued and established in wisdom is subjected to a new wave of attacks.[8] In the second, the former captive is resting in the castle of justice when it is beseiged.[9] In the third, the captive is one who has already fought in the ranks of the just.[10] The stories of Ecclesia held captive in Egypt[11] and of the Ethiopian woman[12] are reminders that the Church has always battles to fight. In *Parable* 5, the city ruled by Faith, Hope, and Charity is overrun and lost.[13]

In all these cases deliverance is only by an act of God. The monk does as much as he can to return to his Father and the result is that he ends up in worse trouble than he began. He is absolutely unable to save himself, even with the help of the ordinary means of improving his position. He is direly and utterly helpless. In this extremity a new dimension is added to his life. Faith and prayer are what is called for. Bernard notes that in a time of such great upheaval, prayer is difficult to find.[14] But when prayer does go forth in the stillness of the night[15] the effect is immediate. God intervenes by sending Charity and all is well.

---

8. Par 1.6.
9. Par 2.5.
10. Par 3.2.
11. Par 4.
12. Par 6.
13. Par 5.5.
14. Par 1.6.
15. Par 2.6.

So there is a second journey to be made, a new manner in which total dependence on God is experienced, since all the achievements of the previous phase have been wiped out. Bernard wants his monks to experience this new development positively. Far from losing their nerve, they should realise that this destruction of all that had been built up at such expense is necessary for the emergence of genuine reliance on God; once such all-embracing confidence in God appears, growth becomes exponential. A completely new phase of relationship has been entered.

The Sequence of Virtues

One of the components of the *Parables* which is worthy of study and reflection is the interrelationship of the virtues as they appear in the various phases of the narrative. Here it is possible only to indicate schematically the elements of such investigation.[16]

The sequence is clearly defined by Bernard but there is no tight causal connection between its elements. The impression is given that for each different situation which emerges there is an appropriate virtuous response and that the way which leads to wisdom, charity and God is characterized by a growing proficiency in learning the different skills demanded by changing circumstances. The ragged continuity and the differences in emphasis from one parable to the next are, perhaps, further indications of the oral style adopted in these compositions. The looseness also gives the narratives an easier flow, since the author obviously does not feel constrained to interrupt his discourse with detailed comments to satisfy the pedants.

This parable contains substantial spiritual teaching. It is worth reading in a relaxed, uncritical way, allowing one's emotions to run with the narrative; letting oneself be formed by St Bernard's benign pastoral wisdom and allowing oneself to grow in appreciation of

---

16. See Figure 1.

	VIRTUE	FUNCTION
1	Fear	To destroy complacency and give a sense of urgency
2	Hope	To console by remembrance of the Father's goodness and power
3	Desire	To carry towards God
4	Pietas	To soften the impact of the journey
5	Good example	To prevent stumbling
6	Prudence	To restrain precipitate haste
7	Discretion	To subject desire to guidance
8	Temperance	To control the energy of desire
9	Fortitude	To do battle against the enemy
10	Boldness	Part of Fortitude
11	Joy	Part of Fortitude
12	Justice	To lead and direct
13	Wisdom	Almost to anticipate the welcoming arms of the Father
14	Humility	
15	Obedience	
16	Profession	
17	Prayer	To contact God in times of trouble
18	Faith	To be the means by which Prayer is transported to God
19	Praise	To reach heaven
20	Hymns	To penetrate heaven
21	Charity	To bring about the victory of God and to bring home the wanderers

Figure 1

the kindness of God who causes events to conspire so as to bring us all to everlasting life.

THE PARABLE

The Story of the King's Son

ONCE UPON A TIME, there was a rich and powerful king, God the almighty. And he caused Man, whom he had created, to become his son. And because he was a delicate boy, he delegated Law and the Prophets to be his guardians, and he gave him other tutors and masters during the predetermined time which preceded his adulthood. He issued instruction to him and cautioned him. He established him as the master of Paradise, showing him all the treasures of his glory and promising them to him if he remained faithful. And lest any benefit should be lacking, he endowed Man with free will so that his choice of good should be voluntary rather than forced.

With the possibility of good and evil before him, Man became dissatisfied with the good things which were his and he was incited with a desire to experience evil as well as good. So he left the paradise of good conscience. Until then he had knowledge only of good things; now he sought novelties beyond his experience. He left aside his Father's laws and guardians, and rejecting his Father's prohibition, he ate from the tree of the knowledge of good and evil.

Unhappy now, he hid himself and fled from the face of the Lord. The silly boy began to wander through mountains of conceit and through valleys of curiosity; through fields of indiscipline and woods of sexual excess; through the dark groves of fleshly delight and through the rough seas of worldly cares.

2. Observing the wanton wanderings of the boy, now without guide or guard, and far from his father's house, the ancient villain drew near to him. Full of wicked wiles, he handed him the little apple of disobedience. And then, having won his consent, he turned against the poor boy. He threw him down to earth and to the level of earthly desires. To prevent his getting up, he bound his feet (that is, the affections of his mind) with the stout chains of worldly concupiscence, and did the same to the activity of his hands and to the eyes of his mind. He set him in the ship of false security and with the powerful aid of the strong wind of flattery he conveyed him to the distant Region of Unlikeness.

When the boy arrived in this land which was not his own he was offered for sale to all who passed by. He learned to tend pigs and to eat their husks. He unlearned all that he had previously learned and he had to learn to do the work of slaves, of which he had no knowledge. He was crushed in that prison of despair where the wicked walk round. In that mill where the wicked wend their ways he was forced to work, with his only gain a bad conscience. Alas!

3. Meanwhile, where was the Father who was so powerful and kind and generous? Could he forget his own son? Never! Never! He did not forget him; he pitied him and grieved and mourned for his son's absence and loss. He instructed his friends and begged his slaves and roused them all to make a search for him.

Now, one of the slaves, whose name was Fear, following the fugitive's traces according to his Master's instructions, found the King's son in a deep dungeon. He was covered with the prison dirt of sin and held fast by the bonds and chains of evil habit. He was unhappy, but unmindful, and though badly treated he was still secure and smiling. With words and with blows Fear urged him to get out and return, but he so upset the poor boy that he fell to the ground, lying there as one near death.

On the heels of Fear came another slave whose name was Hope. Hope, seeing that the King's son was stunned but not saved by Fear, cast down and not helped, gently came forward. From the dust he lifts up the lowly; from the dunghill he raises the poor.[†] He raises the boy's head and wipes his eyes and his face with the cloth of consolation. 'Alas', he says, 'how many servants in your Father's house have more bread than they need, and here are you dying of starvation. Rise up, I beg you, and go to your Father and say to him: "Father, make me one of your servants" '. At this the boy finally began to return to himself somewhat. 'Who are you? Are you Hope? How is it that Hope is able to find entry into the ugly depths of my despair?' The other replied, 'Yes, I am Hope. I was sent by your Father to be your help, and not to leave your side until I bring you to your Father's house and into the room of the one who conceived you'.

And the boy said to Hope: 'O pleasant lightening of labours and gentle relief for the unhappy, you are not least among the three who attend the royal chambers. But see how very deep my dungeon is. See the chains which remain, even though most of them were broken and unfastened at your approach. See the vast number of my captors and how strong and swift and clever they are. But what is this place to you?'

Hope replied: 'Do not be afraid. He who helps us is kind; he who fights on our side is all-powerful. There are more for us than for them.[†] Moreover, I have brought for you a horse which your Father

Ps 113:7; only the more significant biblical references are given.

2 K 6:16

sent, a horse named Desire. Astride this horse and with my guidance you will advance, safe from all of them'.

Having said this, Hope covered the horse named Desire with soft rugs of holy devotion and gave it the shoes of good example. Then he put the King's son upon it. So hurried was their flight that there was no bridle. The horse left that place wildly, with Hope leading the way and Fear bringing up the rear, urging the horse on with blows and threats. Seeing this, the chieftans of Edom were dismayed, trembling seized the leaders of Moab, all the inhabitants of Canaan were in turmoil; terror and dread fell upon them. Through the might of your arm they stayed still as stone, as your son, O Lord, went past, the son whom you had made your own.† Borne along in headlong flight, they escaped; but danger remained, for they left without measure and without counsel. Ex 15:15–16

4. Because of this, Prudence, who was one of the most important officials of the palace, ran up, sent by the Father. With her was her friend Temperance. She restrained their haste. 'Slow down', she cried, 'please slow down. As Solomon says, "One in a hurry goes off the path".† If you keep running in this way you will go off the path, and if you go off the path you will fall. If you fall you will be giving back the King's son to his enemies, although you are trying to set him free. For if he falls, they will seize him'. Pr 19:2

Saying this, Prudence restrained the ardor of the horse named Desire with the bridle of Discretion, and gave the reins into the control of Temperance. And when Fear, from his rear position, began to talk about the nearness and might of their enemies and the slowness of their flight, Prudence said, 'Get behind, Satan, you are a source of stumbling. For

Cf. Mt 16:23;
Ex 15:2

it is the Lord who is our strength and our praise;
he has become our saviour'.†

And lo, Fortitude, the Lord's military champion
appeared. He surged through the fields of Bold-
ness, wielding the sword that is Joy. 'Do not be
disturbed', he cried, 'there are more for us than

2 K 6:16

for them'.† But Prudence, the seasoned counsellor
of the heavenly court, replied: 'Please be careful.
As my servant Solomon says, "If at the beginning
you hasten toward your inheritance, then at the

Pr 20:21

end there will be no blessing".† Let us, therefore,
advance prudently and without haste. If it happens
that our enemies are not on our path, then it is
likely that they will leave obstacles at the inter-
sections and cross-ways and at the bends in the
road. Therefore I shall go in front. If you remain
firmly on the road of Justice, then we will quickly
conduct you to the camp of Wisdom, for it is not
far away. For about Wisdom it was said, "If you

Si 1:33

desire wisdom then learn justice" '.†

5. In this manner they advanced. Fear added
urgency. Hope attracted. Fortitude strengthened.
Temperance controlled. Prudence kept watch and
gave instructions. Justice led and directed. The
King's son drew near to Wisdom's camp. When
Wisdom heard of the new guest's arrival, she anticipated his coming and ran outside joyfully letting
herself be seen in the streets by him who had so
much desired her.

The camp itself was surrounded by a trench of
deep Humility. Above it reared the mighty splendour of the wall of Obedience which reached
to the skies and was wondrously adorned with
painted histories of good examples. The wall was
constructed with bulwarks and a thousand shields
hung from it, each of them the equipment of a
brave man. The door of Profession stood open to

all, but a gatekeeper stood at the threshold, inviting those who were worthy and turning back those who were not. And there was a herald stationed above the gate and he cried out: 'If anyone loves Wisdom let him turn to me and he shall find Wisdom. And when he has found her, happy is he who keeps his hold on her'.† Pr 9:16, 3:18

To this place the King's son was brought. Wisdom went out to meet him and conducted him back, even carrying him in her arms. Confirmed by the homage of the ruling family, he was brought to the stronghold in the middle of the city, where Wisdom had built herself a home and had cut seven pillars† subduing peoples under her and, by her Pr 9:1 own might, trampling on the necks of the proud and haughty. Here he was placed in Wisdom's own bed, surrounded by sixty of Israel's mightiest, each with a sword at his side,† and David was there with Sg 3:7–8 timbrel and dance and with strings and pipes. With him were all the other companions of the heavenly courts rejoicing and celebrating more for the one sinner who had repented than for the ninety-nine in no need of repentance.† Lk 15:6

6. And lo, a whirlwind springs up from the north, and flashes of fire shake the whole house. Wisdom's camp is in upheaval. Pharoah has come forth with his chariots and horsemen to pursue Israel in its flight. They conspire with a single mind and make common alliance against him, the camps of Edom and Ishmael, the camps of Moab and Hagar, Gebal, Ammon and Amalek, foreigners joining with the dwellers in Tyre; Assyria, too, that great destructive devil, is their ally.† How numerous Ps 83:6–9 they are! The city is besieged. The devices of temptation are brought forward and the enemy presses in on every side: a dragon in deceit and a lion when it comes to open fighting. He drives his allies

forward. The walls are breached. Firebrands are
thrown into the city. Battles rage and ambushes are
sprung. Repeatedly he threatens the destruction of
the entire city.

Inside the city are fear and anguish. At the
onset of such a violent and unforeseen attack from
their enemies, they all staggered and reeled like
drunken men and all their skill was gone. Then
they cried to the Lord in their distress.† There was
a rush to Wisdom's stronghold; the bad news was
broken and counsel sought. Prudence, returning
to herself, asked Wisdom what was to be done.
Wisdom said that Prudence must hurry and seek
the help of the Supreme King. 'But who', she said,
'will go for us?' Wisdom replied, 'Send Prayer. And
so that there is no delay let him ride on the horse
named Faith'.

For a long time a search was made for Prayer.
So great was the upheaval that he was found only
with great difficulty. Prayer mounted the horse
named Faith and rode along the heavenly road
not stopping until by Praise he reached the Gates
of the Lord and entered his courts by Hymns.
Like a familiar servant, Prayer boldly approached
the throne of grace and explained the precarious
situation.

When the King heard of the danger his son was
in, he turned to Charity, his royal consort, and said:
'Whom shall we send and who will go for us?' She
replied, 'Here am I. Send me'.† And the King said:
'Victorious shall be your conquest; you shall set
them free'.

The whole heavenly court accompanied Charity, the Queen of Heaven, as she went out from
the face of the Lord. When they made their way
down into the camp, all who were inside were
enlivened by the joy and strength of her presence.

Ps 107:27–28

Is 6:8

Turbulence subsided and upheaval came to rest.
Light returned to these unhappy people and bold-
ness came back to those who were cowed. Hope,
who was on the point of running away, returned,
and Fortitude, who was almost overcome, revived.
Wisdom's whole army became firm once more.

Meanwhile the enemies who were besieging the
city said: 'What is happening? Why is there such
rejoicing in the camp? Yesterday and the day before
there was no such rejoicing. Woe upon us! God has
come into their camp. Woe upon us! Let us flee
from Israel, for the Lord is fighting on their side'.[†]   1 K 4:7–8 modified;

As the enemies fled away, a torrent of divine   Ex 14:25
grace gave joy to God's city, and the Most High
made holy the place where he dwells. God is
within, in cannot be shaken; God will help it at
the dawning of the day. Nations are in tumult,
kingdoms are shaken. He lifts his voice, the earth
shrinks away. The Lord of Hosts is with us; the
God of Jacob is our stronghold.[†]   Ps 46:5–8

Queen Charity gathered up God's young son
and carried him to Heaven and gave him back to
God his Father. The Father came to meet him,
full of mildness and gentleness. 'Quickly', he said,
'bring out the best garment and put it on him. Put
a ring on his finger and shoes on his feet. Go and
get the fatted calf and kill it. We must have a feast
and rejoice, because my son, who was dead, has
come back to life. He was lost and now is found'.[†]   Lk 15:22–24, 32

There are four stages to be noted on the boy's
return to freedom. Firstly, repentance, though not
well grounded; secondly, flight, but rash and un-
thinking; thirdly, the battle terrible and frighten-
ing; and fourthly, victory in all its strength and
wisdom. You will find that all who flee from the
world pass through all these phases. At first they
are weak and silly; then, with better times, they

become precipitate and rash; when troubles come, they begin to be fearful and lose heart; and finally, when they arrive at the kingdom of Charity, they are far-seeing, experienced and made perfect.

2. the story of the feud between two kings

THE SECOND PARABLE, like the first, communicates in narrative form some of the rhythms of the monk's ascent to God. The soul is taken captive by the enemy and has to be rescued. Once liberated he then has to be conducted along the dangerous routes through which his homeward journey wends. He has to be protected by God's intermediaries from his own mistakes as well as from the malice of the enemies. Finally, more through the action of God than by his own achievements, the captive receives the gift of charity and all ends well.

The Cosmic Canvas

One of the characteristic features of many of the parables is the fact that the skirmishes in which the individual is involved are clearly located within the context of the more fundamental conflict between good and evil. Perhaps St Bernard felt that young monks too easily become obsessed with their own problems and come to the conclusion that nobody else ever had to fight as they do. This may be so, but the fact remains that the war which impinges so distinctively on individual experience is yet a cosmic combat. Nobody struggles alone. All are involved in the universal warfare against the powers of darkness.

Thus Bernard begins the story with a ringing declaration: 'Between Babylon and Jerusalem there is no peace, but continuing war.' The consequence of this is that struggle is the normal experience of the Christian endeavor. Peace and security belong to that time when the warfare is over. Here, the soldiers of Christ must be prepared to fight. For Bernard it was a real combat full of dangers and traps where the imprudent and the lazy are constantly exposed to mortal peril. Only those who know how to draw on all available resources have any chance of coming home securely.

There is another important corollary to this. Whatever troubles the soldier of Christ endures, he should be aware that he is more a victim of war than a malefactor. The scope for blame and guilt is limited. No doubt he makes mistakes and fails; but the misfortunes and unhappiness which he causes are sufficient punishment in themselves. God's attitude to him is not one of censure but a matter of active compassion. In fact nobody undertakes a war expecting to sustain no damage. The negative consequences of a prolonged campaign are inevitable and therefore more to be pitied than blamed. Battles will be lost and wounds inflicted. There will be serious reverses and days on which all is dark. This is to be anticipated in fighting a war. They will succeed who accept these realities and labour patiently until the tides begin to turn in their favour and the action of God brings about the victory.

Bernard draws a useful lesson from military tactics. If a battle is unavoidable, it is better fought in advantageous territory. So Bernard counsels the new convert, so recently freed from bondage, to hasten to the high ground of justice which is a secure refuge from which a feasible defence may be mounted. Better to cultivate virtues and good habits when the going is easy so that when things become difficult, there will be some means of resisting the attack. The new convert is exhorted to the unexciting practice of good works, because these will stand him in good stead on the day of testing.

The battle of the individual soul is a microcosm of a larger conflict. In the last analysis it is not the individual soldier's war, but God's. Because God is the principal combatant then it must follow that victory is inevitable, so long as faith and fealty are not lost. The way to avoid defeat is to link one's destiny firmly with God's, to reach out to him in trust and prayer and in the confidence that he and he alone will triumph. The warfare is God's and so will be the victory.

The Sequence of Virtues

There are two nuances which are proper to this parable. Fear has a far more prominent role to play throughout the process of salvation and greater emphasis is given to the intellectual components of spiritual growth.

It is to fear that the release of the captive is entrusted. The condition of captivity is precisely the opposite of fear: it is a blend of unawareness, complacency, false security and in general a lack of any motivation which might energise the soul to do good and avoid evil. So fear has a necessary role in beginning the process of spiritual growth. In this parable fear maintains a presence throughout, pointing out dangers, making preparations to repel attacks and finally fighting fiercely against the foes. Though less successful in battle than charity, still it is to fear's credit that even in the ultimate combat he kills his thousands.

Bernard signals some unfortunate consequences that can follow fear. The first is sadness. Fear presents a gloomy picture and portrays the imminent danger in great detail. The intention is to spur the new convert to a more sustained effort. Sometimes the weary struggler is overwhelmed by an excess of negativity and becomes the prey of depression and despair. Therefore Bernard, throughout his teaching, constantly reminds his readers that there is also scope for hope and despair and joy, that the remembrance of sins needs to be counterbalanced by happy reflection on the promises of God. This is clearly spelled out in this parable; it is stated more emphatically in one of his *Sermons on the Song of Songs*:

> Therefore, my advice to you, friends, is to turn aside from troubled and anxious reflection on your own progress, and escape to the easier paths of remembering the good things which God has done; in this way, instead of becoming upset by thinking about yourself, you will find relief by turning your attention to God. Sorrow for sin is, indeed, a necessary thing, but it should not prevail all the time. It is necessary, rather, that happier recollections of the divine bounty should counterbalance it, lest

the heart should become hardened through too much sadness and so perish through despair.[1]

The second potential problem inherent in a response totally dictated by fear is that one's forward movement becomes precipitate. One's actions are governed by a strongly felt experience of dangers to be avoided and so one's practical decisions are dominated by immediate dangers so that urgency takes precedence over long-term and maybe more significant measures.

It is at this point that Bernard introduces the notion of supplementing fear by the other cardinal virtues, particularly prudence. Again it is possible to represent the sequence of virtues schematically.[2]

Again the logic of the sequence is not tight. The various skills and habits of virtuous living are called forth as demanded by the flow of the narrative. The message is that it takes more than a simple initiative to last the distance which separates the new convert from the ultimate state for which God has destined him. He needs the whole range of virtues in all their complementarity.

Fear has been given a more prominent role in this parable. To ensure that the journey does not become a dread-filled flight characterised by extreme anxiety, Bernard attaches equal importance to the role of prudence, which we know from his other writings, was one of his favourite virtues. To prudence is given control of the whole operation. With prudence is reason to lead the way to justice.

Bernard was no rationalist, but he appreciated the necessary role played by understanding in ensuring that the emotional energy necessary for the spiritual enterprise did not get out of hand. Good will is not enough; it needs to be supplemented by good understanding.

As in the previous parable we see the homeward journey proceeding well when an unexpected setback is experienced. Once settled within the castle of justice, the soldier of Christ is subjected to a very serious attack. It is at this point that he makes the discovery of his own minimal resources. It is only through being reduced to such an extremity that he is forced to have recourse to the agency of

---

1. SC 11:12; SBO 1:55:12–19.
2. See Figure 2.

	VIRTUE	FUNCTION
1	Fear	To release the captive, to add a sense of urgency, to take precautions
2	Hope	To offset the effects of sadness
3	Desire	To carry the captive home
4	Happiness	To combat sadness
5	Memory of promises	To sustain the sense of attraction
6	Memory of sins	To ensure continuing progress
7	Prudence	To take charge of the journey
8	Temperance	To ensure that due moderation is observed
9	Discretion	To subject desire to guidance
10	Caution	To prevent falls
11	Confession of sins	
12	Recall of judgement	
13	Patience	
14	Humility	
15	Justice	To provide security
16	Reason	Armour-bearer of Prudence
17	Prayer	To contact God in times of trouble
18	Charity	God's champion
19	Joy	Charity's entourage
20	Peace	
21	Patience [bis]	
22	Longanimity	
23	Benignity	
24	Goodness	
25	Meekness	

Figure 2

prayer. Charity along with all the fruits of the Holy Spirit comes to him by God's goodness; once this happens victory is assured. The individual cannot generate this happy outcome by his own works. The most he can do is to get into trouble and then to send forth his tearful prayer for deliverance. Salvation is of God alone.

THE PARABLE

The Story of the Feud between Two Kings

BETWEEN BABYLON AND Jerusalem there is no peace, but continuing war. Each state has its king: Christ the Lord is the King of Jerusalem and the devil is the King of Babylon. The first king is pleased to rule in righteousness, the other in evil. And the King of Babylon, through the agency of his servants, the unclean spirits, constantly tries to lure those citizens of Jerusalem whom he can into becoming more and more slaves of wickedness and thus to draw them to Babylon.

Mercy is the spirit who has been appointed as a watcher on the walls of Jerusalem. When she perceived that one of her fellow-citizens was being drawn away, she gave the king the news that he had been taken as spoil to Babylon.

The King of Jerusalem calls to him the spirit Fear, a soldier proficient in such matters. To him he says, 'Go and retrieve the captive'. Now Fear is always ready to do what he has been commanded, so he loses no time in pursuing the enemies and soon catches up with them. Without any warning there is a sound in their ears like the rush of a mighty wind.[†] Fear thunders over their heads and at the voice of his strength all the vigour of the foe begins to quake and they turned about and fled. Fear did not pursue them further, but snatched his fellow-citizen away from them and began to bring him back to his own place.

It happened that one of the hostile party was absent when Fear set upon them; this was the spirit of Sadness. When Sadness saw all his companions in headlong flight, he quickly came out of the

Ac 2:2

ambush where he was concealed and flew to them.
They told him, 'All this has been accomplished by
Fear alone and all of us have become a reproach'.
But Sadness replied, 'Do not be afraid of Fear. I
know what is to be done. I shall go and, as a lying
spirit in the bends of the roads, pretend that I am
Fear's friend. I understand humans; to deal with
them you need cunning, not force. Wait and see
for yourselves'.

Sadness did as he said and, taking a short cut,
got ahead of Fear. Then, going back along the road
by which Fear journeyed, he met the man and
engaged him in friendly though malign conversation and thus began to lead him astray. Fear was
unaware of what was happening and so followed
him in good faith.

Now they were very near the place where Sadness could cast his victim into the pit of despair, but
the watcher on the walls told the king what was
happening. The king ordered that another of his
soldiers, named Hope, be sent for and he instructed
him to hurry to the assistance of Fear taking with
him the horse of desire and the sword of happiness.

This loyal soldier went out as the king commanded, and when he arrived at the spot he bran-
dished the sword of happiness and put Sadness to
flight. He seated his liberated fellow-citizen on the
horse of desire. He himself walked in front, leading
the horse by the rope of the promises and Fear
followed after, urging him on with a whip made
of the residue of sins.

2. The horse made its way willingly, since it
was both pulled from the front and pushed from
behind. It travelled so quickly, however, that it left
itself open to attack.

Seeing this, the Babylonian soldiers held a con-
ference. 'What shall we do', they said, 'about this
one whom we so safely held captive who is now

making good his escape? Hell's celebration has been changed into gloom and by the work of only two soldiers great joy has been wrought in heaven over the liberation of their fellow-citizen. How has it happened that all the cunning of diabolical deceit has come to nothing?'

One of the company who was more wicked than the rest and more experienced in wrongdoing offered his unholy counsel. 'You know nothing', he said, 'and you are not using your heads. Now it will be easier than ever to make the capture and, once done, it will be even more difficult to extricate him. The rest of you, follow at a distance. I shall transform myself into an angel of light so that I may deceive those pilgrims and strangers who do not know the way, by pretending to give them information'.

The watcher on the walls gave to our king the news of this deception. She told him that there was a man coming on the horse of desire and that he was going too fast, since he was without bridle and saddle. 'The enemies are following him at a distance', she said, 'but there are others who have grown old in evil-doing, who are taking a short cut. Now I can see one whose armour bears our insignia, but who is not one of us. Someone must be sent out to challenge him with the question:

Jos 5:13 "Are you one of us or are you of our adversaries?" '†

3. Then the king, whose entire energy is devoted to the care of souls, sends two counsellors to him: Prudence and Temperance. Temperance places on the horse the bridle of discretion and persuades Hope to advance at a more moderate pace. Prudence rebukes Fear, condemns the lack of discipline and gives a warning about the future. She places on the horse the saddle of caution so that the rider does not fall off. Instead he is supported

from behind by the confession of past sins and in
front by reflection on future judgement; on the left
by patience and on the right by humility. Fear and
Hope give two spurs to the rider: on the right foot
the expectation of reward and on the left the dread
of punishment.

4. And it came to pass that as evening came and
the day declined, the enemy gathered together in
great numbers to do battle with them. Fear was
afraid and Hope hurried them up, but almost immediately Temperance, on the advice of Prudence
restrained them. And Prudence addressed these
words to them: 'See how the day has passed and
night is at hand. Whoever walks in the darkness
does not know where he is going.[†] Moreover, there Jn 12:35
remains ahead of us a considerable journey and the
enemy is numerous. But there is a military man
loyal to our king whom I know, named Justice,
whose castle is nearby. This dwelling is solidly
established because he has built his nest upon a
rock. My suggestion is that we turn aside to it,
since it will be good for us to be there'.

This idea met with the approval of all and so
they began to look for someone who could guide
them on their journey. Then Prudence said: 'It is
Reason, my armour-bearer, who is the one to go
ahead of us. He is familiar with the route and is
already known to Justice, since they are kinsmen'.
So Reason went ahead and the rest followed. On
arrival, Reason greeted Justice and announced the
coming of guests. Justice sought to know who they
were and whence they came and inquired about
the purpose of their coming. When he heard the
facts, he rose and went to meet those who were
in flight with a cheerful mien, offering them food
and welcoming them like a noble mother. Having
done this, he helped the soul to dismount from

the horse and led the fearful one into the inner chambers of his house.

5. The enemy army was in pursuit and laid siege to the castle. Like a lion seeking someone to devour,† it pressed forward from every direction, probing to see whether any entry was open. Then, finding that all was secure, the enemy pitched tents and posted sentries to ensure that none could enter or come out. Come morning, siege machines would be readied so that the walls could be breached and those inside them overwhelmed.

But Fear, meanwhile, who was made careful by being afraid, was not sluggish in his concern. He never took things for granted. Instead he roused up his fellow-soldiers and discussed with Justice the fortifications of the place and sought information about the state of unpreparedness in weapons and—lest they lack food—in provisions.

Justice replied thus: 'The place itself, as you can see, is solid rock and inaccessible, so there is no fear of damage either by weapons or by the enemy's machines. On the other hand, it is an arid area, whose few inhabitants subsist on dry barley bread. At the moment only five barley loaves and two fishes are available for us'. To this Fear replied: 'What is that among so many?' At this point Fear began to be greatly afraid and he became dispirited and he set to blaming the soul for dismounting from the horse of desire. The thought often came to his mind that the last state of that man would be worse than the first.† For the horse could have made a swift and unimpeded flight to the city, whereas now they were left with the leadership of Reason alone. And he said: 'See for yourself whether you would not have been better off then than now'.

6. At this stage, Fear was close to rising up against Hope, who viewed things differently, but

1 P 5:8

Mt 12:45

Temperance called on Prudence to intervene. Once summoned, Prudence rebuked Fear for his panic. 'O Fear, your sword has lost its edge against your adversaries. Do you not know that our king is the king of strength—the Lord, the mighty the valiant, the Lord, the valiant in war.[†] Therefore let a messenger go forth who will inform him of the plight and ask for aid and request a helper'.

Ps 24:8

And Fear said: 'Who is able to go forth, since darkness covers the land and a vast multitude of our foes besieges the walls? And we ourselves are as unfamiliar with the roads as we would be in a foreign country'.

So they called Justice, their host, to them and said to him, 'Help us if you can'.[†] He replied: 'Be of good heart.[†] I have a loyal messenger who is well known to the king and to the court. His name is Prayer. He will go forth secretly in the stillness of the night, traversing hidden pathways known to him and so obtain entrance to the inner courts of heaven. He will have access to the king's chamber and there he will use his experience to bend the king's resolve with an appropriate importunity. He will make heart-rending supplication so that the king may provide the help he usually gives to those in trouble. He can go if you approve for, behold, he stands ready'. And they all replied 'Yes!'

Mk 9:21
Ac 27:25

Prudence, at the instigation of Justice, gave Prayer instructions concerning what he should suggest to the king so that he would carry out the mission and not return empty-handed. The others, especially Fear, wished him Godspeed and let him out through a secret exit in the walls.

Prayer safely passed through the enemy lines and faster than any bird, in an instant, in a blink of the eye,[†] he arrived at the city gates of the new Jerusalem. Finding them closed, he knocked; nor was he afraid to upset the gatekeepers by filling the

1 Co 15:12

nocturnal silence of the city with his unwelcome
shouts and even being a nuisance to the king. He
persevered in his knocking and cried out even
louder: 'Open to me the gates of righteousness

Ps 118:19
and I will enter and confess to the Lord King,† for
Ps 94:19; Ps 109:30
in my heart are many afflictions.† These are the
gates of my king. Justice sent me to you so that
you might lead me to the king, for I have secret
matters to discuss with him'. While Prayer thus
made loud lamentation, the king awoke and said
to the soldiers who were with him: 'The voice of
Sg 2:12
the turtle-dove is heard in our land'.†

7. When the king realized that this was a messenger from Justice, he gave orders for his admission. Prayer entered, made obeisance and said,
'Long live the king!'. He replied: 'Does all go well
with your lord and with his affairs?' 'Very well,
My Lord, thanks to you. However, one thing is
Lk 10:42
necessary.† On the king's command, your servant
has been saved from the horns of the unicorns. He
then made a detour and came to my lord, your
loyal soldier. But, My Lord, that south land is arid
and is without food. May the Lord give his blessing
Ps 85:12
and the earth will yield its fruit.† Furthermore, the
enemies are gathering a great force to fight us and
we do not know what to do, and there are other
Ps 60:11
problems as well. Give us help in our troubles,† for
there is none other who fights on our side except
you, our God. See how the one whom your hand
snatched powerfully from the princes of darkness
now cries out to you from the bottom of his heart.
With many sighs and sobs and tears he pleads that
you may send him help from your holy place.
Hear, O Lord; Lord, be gracious; receive this prayer
Dn 9:19
and act.† Send him a liberating champion lest the
enemies say: "Where is his God?" and carry off
into a captivity worse than before, the one whom

your own right hand once saved. What purpose is there in the shedding of his blood while he sinks into decay? Save him, O Lord, so that he might confess your holy name and exult in your glory, for in the underworld no one gives you praise'.

The king, whose nature it is to be kind, was moved by these tears and said: 'Whom shall we send?' Charity replied: 'Here am I, O Lord, send me'. The king made inquiry about companions, but Charity responded that the members of the household would be sufficient.

And so Charity went forth, accompanied by a noble entourage—Joy, Peace, Patience, Longanimity, Benignity, Goodness and Meekness. With such a distinguished retinue did the leader set out. Certain of victory, they unfurled their triumphant banner and passed through the first and second guard-posts of the enemy. And when they reached the gate, it opened for them.

High jubilation marked their entry into the town. Then, when Joy prompted all to give voice and cry out, such a great shout resulted as to cause terror in the camps of those outside. 'What is that?' they said. 'There comes to our ears the sound of rejoicing in the camp of Israel. It was not so yesterday and the day before. Perhaps help has come to them and they are about to overwhelm us. Let us flee from Israel, since God fights for them against us'.[†] Ex 14:25

Meanwhile Charity, impatient with dallying, set the army in battle array, opened the gates and gave the order to set off in pursuit of the enemy, openly proclaiming, 'I shall go even unto the gates of hell!'.[†] Is 38:10

In one vast flood the whole army swept out, with Charity at its head. The Babylonians could do nothing to staunch its flow, nor could those who fled escape. A thousand fell on the side of Temperance and ten thousand fell, on the right, to Prudence. Fear killed thousands and Charity tens of thousands.

3. the story of the king's son sitting on his horse

INTRODUCTION

tHE IMAGE OF THE HORSE has already figured in the preceding two parables. In both cases it was used to indicate something of the strength and speed with which desire is able to carry us towards God.

Bernard was aware that the very qualities which make the horse successful in this task can sometimes be counter-productive.[1] So, in the third parable, the horse is identified with what the author of *The Cloud of Unknowing* would later term, 'boisterous bodiliness'—that reserve of physical and emotional energy which is largely related to organic appetites and which does not easily permit itself to be subdued by reason. Thus it is the horse which gets its rider into trouble by precipitating him into situations with which he does not have the skill to deal. The horse will cease to be a hindrance and become a positive asset only when the rider is in control. Bernard is evoking the common theme of the *ordinatio caritatis*.

It should be observed that Bernard's does not regard the body as dangerous in itself, but only in so far as it acts as an agent independent of rational control. In *De diligendo Deo* he makes it quite clear that the natural emotions of love are the source from which a

---

1. Cf. Sent 2:150.

spiritual love of God eventually evolves. They are the beginning; it is necessary that they be transcended, but there is no way that they can be avoided.

In the story the soldier of Christ, who is also the king's son, is so self-assured that he despises the rest of the army for their circumspection. He is determined to make a name for himself and to win the admiration of his peers. Notwithstanding the recency of his own conversion he presses forward, unaware that the energy which drives him is carrying him to destruction.

Warnings went unheeded. The dictates of prudence and discretion were ignored. Pride, vainglory and the dream of great achievement impelled him to go faster.

Almost before he knows where he is, the young man finds himself trapped in the very heart of enemy territory with no hope of escape. He has been lured into Babylon. The energies that carried him thus far are revealed as being less noble than he had assumed. His forces are depleted and gluttony and fornication reign supreme in his body. His former enthusiasm was no more than a lack of discipline; he has been landed in a highly dangerous situation without the personal resources necessary to deal with it. The body, once subdued, responds to its surroundings by wholeheartedly embracing the ways of Babylon.

So the soldier of Christ becomes a plaything of all the passions. Progressively he gives himself to greater and greater degradation. Not for him 'honest vices' but only those which were foul and repulsive. It is at this point that the spirit of fornication makes an appearance. Although he had planned the whole entrapment, until this point he had remained hidden; only when the youth is totally dominated by his passions does he become overtly ensnared by lust.

There is no doubt that the captive is not enjoying himself. The picture Bernard paints is of one who is unwillingly enslaved and dishonoured by the vices, one who is made utterly miserable by his condition. He cannot escape because he is bound by bad habits and unable to resist any suggestion of evil, no matter how revolting.

For most of us this would be a situation with which we would deal with by harsh recrimination. We would point out to the young man how he had ignored his elder's advice and where he had gone wrong and the extent of his aberration. We sometimes attribute the same judgemental attitude to God. Bernard, by contrast, portrays God as one overcome by grief and sorrow at the suffering which his son has brought upon himself. Like the father in the parable of the prodigal son, he has no time for blame. Instead he begins to take positive steps to reverse the unfortunate situation.

So he sends fear to rouse the youth and set him free. Since he needs the horse to make the homeward journey, obedience accompanies fear with the task of teaching the king's son how to control his appetites so that they lead him to his goal and not away from it. This is an interesting view of the role of obedience. It appears almost as a temporary measure which prevents the instincts of self-gratification from governing life until such time as alternative sources of interior guidance are solidly established.

The agents delegated by the king to involve themselves in the youth's formation are, in fact, the seven gifts of the Holy Spirit. Bernard pictures the former captive passing from one to the next and receiving from each the instruction necessary if he is to continue moving towards God. *Pietas* consoles him and soothes the residual wounds left by his experience of enslavement. Knowledge helps him to penetrate to the meaning of his own experience so that he can learn from it how to avoid similar pitfalls in the future. Fortitude builds up his reserves of strength so that he is able to continue the lifelong journey. Counsel forms in seeking the right path through the practice of taking counsel with others, being willing to seek advice and accept the guidance given. Understanding elevates his mental grasp of reality by raising it up so that he begins to comprehend something of the mind and the plan of God. Finally, wisdom gives him a taste for the things of God, a delight in unseen spiritual realities and progressively initiates him into the life of contemplation.

Thus Bernard depicts the youth's fall as utterly horrendous and entirely his own fault. Yet God's response to him is one of over-whelming pity. Not only does he extricate him from his immediate troubles, but he submits him to a process whereby he is brought to spiritual maturity and so protected from the possibility of a repeat performance. All is the work of God. He is the one who releases his son from prison and then has him passed willy-nilly from one tutor to another until his education is satisfactorily complete.

Bernard thus views monastic life in very positive terms as a lifetime of being formed to divine realities—irrespective of the liabilities which the new recruit carries with him. The whole enterprise is God's doing. The monk's sole task is to co-operate with the process, trusting in God's providence in his own regard, and allowing himself to profit from his experiences in the way that God intends.

This being so he can look forward to a reward which is certain and worth all the labour. Entering into the joy of the Lord he will be called to celebrate a sabbath of sabbaths.

THE PARABLE

The Story of the King's Son Sitting on His Horse

I N THE WAR BETWEEN JERUSALEM and Babylon, the lines are drawn up for battle. On the one side, David courageously leads forth the ranks of the virtues, drawn up in battle array and fearsome to behold. On the other side is Nebuchadnezzar of Babylon who, on behalf of the spiritual powers of wickedness, leads against him the rowdy army of the vices.

From the camp of David went forth a raw recruit. He had only recently been sworn into the king's army and had been equipped, by David himself, with the sword of God's word and with the spiritual armour and insignia. He went forth with enormous enthusiasm, but counter to the king's edict. For he was very impatient, not so much to conquer the enemy, as to win a name for himself. His horse was restive—this was his own body, still bubbling with worldly energy, ostentatious and lustful. And his soul within, whose banner it carried, was the same. Despising the discipline of his own ranks and holding his fellow soldiers in low repute, he attempted to make his mark by a display of solitary presumption, which far exceeded the performance of the others. For he burned and panted to make a name for himself.

When David saw his impetuous presumption, he sent a command under sanction by his son Solomon. 'Woe to the one who is alone; for when he falls he has no one to lift him up'.† Qo 4:10

The young man took no notice of his warning and continued to seek an occasion for demonstrating his great prowess either to himself or to others.

And so he laboured to bring about some outstanding achievement. From afar he spied, behind
enemy lines, one who was powerful in evil and
clever in doing wrong. He had fiery arms and his
hands were full of flaming darts. He had wounded
many, put those who were injured to death and
had trodden on the corpses of the slain. He was
one who was quick to seize and slow to let go. It
was the spirit of Fornication.

2. The young man, boastfully attempting to
demonstrate his outstanding strength in battle,
rushed toward him. And although his horse needed
no encouragement, he goaded it on with the whip
of fasting and the spurs of vigils. He was totally
given to the chase. From the rear Prudence called,
'Slow down!' and Discretion cried 'Wait!' and
the whole of David's army shouted after him. He
turned a deaf ear and disregarded them all, and so
the poor man was swept on to his doom, but knew
it not.

When Nebuchadnezzar saw what was happening, he growled, and began to prepare deceitful
tricks to bring him down. Two sisters, Pride and
Vain Glory, run up alongside him in his headlong haste, and pretended to applaud him, 'Bravo!
Bravo!' As a result, the poor boy, who was quite
gullible, gave himself fully to the pursuit, completely unaware of the traps which already surrounded him on every side. The spirit Fornication,
who was so vastly experienced in such attacks involving such people, pretended to run away and
thus, tricked the poor boy into following until he
had led him through the open gates into the centre
of Babylon, where he gave him over to be mocked
by his companions.

Gluttony and Fornication claimed the horse for
themselves and would permit its owner to exercise

no further rights over it. In fact, the horse was
very weak and so tired that it sought something
with which to amuse itself. While the fighting
was still going on, it had given way under the
knight and had, by its fall, grievously injured its
rider. However, the horse was soon restored by
the food of Babylon, and once it had eaten its fill,
it submitted itself to their service.

And so Anger, Envy and all the rest of the
vices banded together against the poor boy and
sinners boldly made play on his back.[2] At this
point Fornication, who until now had only been
seen from behind as he fled, stood up before him,
showing his face and mockingly confronting him.
He wounded him in the heart with a flaming
arrow, struck out at his neck with a sword and,
throwing him to the ground, walked all over him.
Then he gave him to Nabuzardan, the king of
Babylon's cook, and allowed his filthy youths to
make sport of him.[3] Nor was it permitted that
honest vices would have anything to do with him,
but only the filthy clowns from the king's kitchen.
This is to say that he was set up to become the sport
of vices which were foul and repulsive. And so it
came to pass that, having been thus caught by his
enemies, he was bound with the ropes of evil habit
and thus was plunged into the prison of despair.

3. But King David went about with his head
uncovered and mourned his son, saying 'Absalon
my son, my son Absalon, would that it were given

---

2. . . . *fiducialiter supra dorsum eius fabricaverunt peccatores.*
This is a quotation of the strange Vulgate rendering of Ps
128:3. To make some sense, I have been obliged to translate
the verb very loosely.

3. In the Septuagint, but not in the Vulgate, Nabuzardan is
wrongly described as *archimageiros*, the chief cook of the king
of Babylon. Cf. 4 K 25:8. It is presumed that Bernard obtained
this reading from a patristic comment on the Greek text.

2 K 18:33 to me to die in your stead, my son Absalon'.[†] Calling one of the royal entourage who was useful and well-tried in such affairs, namely Fear, he sent him off to fetch his son. And he gave orders that Obedience was to accompany him, so that once his son was safely released from prison, he might be entrusted to Obedience's guidance.

Fear, thus sent forth, found the poor boy and roused him. He released him from his chains and got him out of the prison, as he had been ordered. He gave him into the hands of Obedience and restored his horse to him, but the horse was wild and rebellious and would not recognize its master. But Obedience seized the horse and restrained it with an iron bit so that, although it struggled hard and kicked, it was subject to its former master. And Obedience gave instructions as to how to control its strength.[4]

4. And so Obedience, receiving the soldier of Christ from Fear, led him back to his own country by another road. First of all he made arrangements for him to stay with Loving-Care, so that the frightened feelings aroused by Fear, might be soothed by the loving care of a welcoming father. Then he stayed with Knowledge, so that he might come to know whence and by what means he had returned and also that he might learn to make use of both Loving-Care and Fear in such a way that loving care would not lead to a lack of humility and fear would not issue in disaster. Thirdly he stayed with Fortitude, who strengthened him so that he might continue his journey of return. After that he stayed with Counsel, so that, in the future, he might do all things with counsel and

---

4. *Mutare fortitudinem* seems to depend on the Vulgate Is 40:31. 'Control' represents a stretched translation here.

not allow himself to turn aside from the guidance
of obedience in anything. In the fifth place, he
stayed with Understanding so that he might begin
to understand, not on the basis of mere human
counsel, but on his own, something of the will of
the Lord, which is good and pleasing and perfect.[†]   Rm 12:2
The sixth stopping-place of the soldier of Christ
was with Wisdom, who escorted him with kindness and would not desert him on his journey so
that he might already taste the good things of the
Lord and so, like Moses on Mount Abarim, might
begin to contemplate what God has promised.[5] It
was from here that he arrived in Jerusalem, in the
kingdom and city of David, in the vision of peace,
where dwell those blessed peace-makers who are
God's children and all things are at peace, within
and without. And so, entering into the joy of their
Lord, they celebrate a sabbath of sabbaths.

---

5. Cf Nb 27:12: *Ascende in montem istum Abarim, et contem-
plare inde Terram quam daturus sum filiis Israel.*

4. the story of ecclesia held captive in egypt

INTRODUCTION

LIKE ITS PREDECESSORS, the fourth parable is designed to alert its readers to the dangers with which they will almost certainly have to deal. The focus is, however, different. Here the central character is Ecclesia, the Church, Christ's bride, loved by the king's son, wooed and won by him and then entrusted to the care of his followers.

Bernard reviews the ages of the Church in conventional terms. The one left alone by Christ is subjected first of all to persecution, then to the horrors of heresy and schism, then a period of mass infidelity with fornication, gluttony and avarice rife in the Church, with its funtionaries despoiling her inheritance for the purposes of their own self gratification. Finally there is the age of anti-Christ with Satan dazzling many by his radiance and luring them away from their loyalty to Christ.

Bernard locates the contemporary stage of the Church as somewhere between the third and fourth phase. This allows the reformist side of the abbot of Clairvaux—already evident in the *Apologia* and in certain passages of the letters, the advent sermons and the sermons *On the Song of Songs*—to come to the fore. The sentiments here expressed are completely appropriate to the century following the work of Gregory VII, but it is interesting that his diagnosis of the maladies of the church of his day is equally relevant for our own time. We have, he says, more or less, passed the age of persecution and the traumatic divisions of doctrinal differences. Our problem is one of morals. In particular we are more concerned with the gratification of our own carnal appetites and our need for possessions than we are for the advance of the kingdom of God. Progressively unaware of the actual meaning of our habits of behaviour we are establishing a distance between ourselves and the Church and so preparing the way for greater woes. Should Satan appear transfigured as an angel of light we who have lost contact with Christ's bride will be unable to recognise him for what he is and so will allow ourselves to be led astray. Once delusion sets in then the total abandonment of our loyalty to Christ begins to appear as almost inevitable.

The parable is not a happy one and its conclusion is left hanging. There is no felicitous outcome here, but simply poor Ecclesia stripped and despoiled, an object of derision for those whom she holds dear. The next step depends on the reader. Will he or she take steps to succour Ecclesia, to assuage her wounds and to restore her honour? There are few, Bernard laments, who concern themselves much with this—just a few persons who are members of the monastic and canonical institutes, a mere remnant.

The object of the parable is for the reader to be moved with pity and motivated to live a life of greater purity.

There is one beautiful and poignant image that may remain with the reader long after the book has been left aside. That concerns the utter fidelity of Ecclesia herself to Christ. In the opening sections we read of the mighty liberation from captivity and the extravagant bounty of the marriage itself. Everything is splendid and there is a fairytale quality about this ideal relationship. Yet when things change and the bridegroom is absent and everything is lost, the only stable factor is the bride's total self-giving to her husband. Even when others try to ease her lot by offering her friendship, she will not accept it. 'She will recognize no other.' Even in the darkest moments her faithfulness is complete.

Bernard warns that the mystery of iniquity is now at work in our midst and we are invited to participate in the constancy of Ecclesia, to wait for the coming of the Lord when our liberation from present evils will be effected. He ends with a fervent prayer: Come, Lord and set Ecclesia free, O Lord God of hosts, who live and reign forever and ever. Amen.

THE PARABLE

The Story of Ecclesia Held Captive in Egypt

tHE KINGDOM OF HEAVEN is like a king who celebrated the nuptials of his son.† As the day approached the father discussed with the son his choice of bride. The son replied that his choice was and had always been Ecclesia. To this the father responded, 'But she is held captive in Egypt and does forced labour there in clay and brick. She has been sold to sin. The heart of Pharaoh has been hardened in her regard,† and his grip on her has become tighter. He will not let her go unless a stronger hand forces him'.

To this the son replied, 'I shall do it, with your hand and with the arm of your strength. I shall enter Egypt with a strong hand and with outstretched arm and I shall set her free. And so that I may silence the mouth which speaks evil and redeem her from the calumnies of her enemies, I shall weigh in the balance the price for which she was sold to sin (that is, the pleasure of sin) and I shall set, as counter-weight, the price of my own blood. The former will be found wanting,† and so my judgement will have the victory'.†

'Clearly, that is so', the king replied, 'but the law of marriage demands that the bride gives her consent'. And the son said, 'It will be sought. I have found David, my servant, a man after my own heart.† I will send him with his lute to speak to her heart, to present my case to her and to soften her heart which has become habituated to the rotten ways of Egypt'.

And so David entered Egypt as an envoy, armed with his sweetest marriage songs. And he poured

(marginal references:) Mt 22:2; Rm 7:14, Ex 7:13; Dn 5:27; Jb 23:7; Ps 89:20–21; 1K 13:14

forth from the depths of his heart this good word:
'Listen, O daughter, give ear to my words. Forget
your own people and your father's house, for the
king has desired your beauty and he is the Lord,
Ps 45:10–11   your God'.† And Isaiah was ordered to follow on
his heels and this is what he said when he saw her
in her captive's chains: 'Arise, O arm of the Lord,
arise and be clothed in strength. Be lifted up. Be
lifted up. Arise, O Jerusalem, and cast the chains
Is 51:9, 17   from your neck, O captive daughter of Zion'.†

2. Then many others approached her, patriarchs and prophets, all proclaiming the same message. Finally, when she began to grasp something
of the grace of God, she rose from the dust and
said, 'O Lord God you have remembered me. You
have pity on whom you have pity, and whom you
pity you also show mercy'. Then she continued
with the words of wise Abigail: 'Who will give me
the chance to be a handmaid to the servants of my
Lord, so that I may wash the feet of the servants
Lk 25:41–42   of my Lord?'† And then, like Abigail herself, she
rose and mounted an ass, which is to say that she
brought her flesh into subjection and so followed
the servants of the king.

The bridegroom met her, of happy mien and
festive mood. Holding her right hand he willingly
showed her the way, receiving her with honour,
taking her into the capital of his kingdom and to
the very chamber where he was begotten. He set
her on the bed of his love and decked her out with
the ornaments of his grace. And with his left arm
under her head, he embraced her with his right.
'I adjure you, daughters of Jerusalem', he said, 'do
Sg 3:5   not rouse or waken the bride until she wills it'.†
And he placed sixty of Israel's strongest and most
experienced warriors around the bed; each with

his sword on his thigh against the terrors of the
night.† Sg 3:7-8

He kissed her with the kiss of his lips; then,
saying farewell, he set out for a distant land to
receive a kingdom,† and thence to return. And Lk 19:12
he gave her an order through the prophet Hosea:
'You will wait for me a long time and you will be
without priests and sacrifices'.† Ho 3:3-4

3. When the Egyptian Pharaoh realized that the
bridegroom had gone away, he called together his
army and said: 'Come with me. I will follow and
capture them; I will divide the spoil and my soul
shall be sated. I will unsheathe my sword and slay
them by my own hand'.† He arose with all his Ex 15:9
malicious militia and set in motion a persecution of
Ecclesia. Right away he advanced into her fort and
captured Peter and crucified him, together with
his brother Andrew. He beheaded Paul. John, he
sent into exile. Bartholemew he flayed, he stoned
Stephen and burned Laurence and Vincent. And in
the deaths of the saints he brought to completion
every sort of torment and death. They handed over
the bodies of the servants of God as food to feed
the birds of the heavens, and the flesh of his faithful
ones to the beasts of the earth. They poured out
innocent blood like water in Jerusalem and no one
was left to bury the dead.† Ps 79:2-3

When Ecclesia saw her defenders treated as
sheep for eating, she groaned and her bitterness
was exceeding great. But the land of Ecclesia was
rendered fruitful by the blood of the martyrs so
that, by a manifold growth, it returned a rich
harvest of the faithful. For each one cut down,
a hundred or a thousand resulted and so defeat was
turned into victory.

4. When this became apparent to the evil and
savage enemy, he became enraged and began to

make use of his notorious weapons of cunning. For the time being there was a lull in his persecution, he restrained his strength and called back his sword and changed his plans. 'Nobody', he said, 'is more dangerous than the enemy in one's household. Therefore I will pour forth contention among their princes and I will make them leave the path Ps 107:40 and wander from the way.† And when they say "Peace! Peace!" there will be no peace. I will stir up heresies and schisms among them and I will upset everything by a civil war fought in their very midst. It is easier if they die by their own swords than by mine'.

He said this and soon Ecclesia who, when drawn up in battle array was so fear-inspiring, no longer inspired fear, since her ranks were in disarray. They inflicted mutual wounds, falling on one another as enemies, whilst their foes stood afar off, laughing, mocking and taunting them. As for Ecclesia, she was afflicted by mourning and intolerable pain.

Her bitterness which had been great from the first now became overwhelming. She wept because she was being torn apart by the poisonous evil being done by her children. But when these saw that all the while the valiant soldiers of the Christian court were winning over the evil and trickery of the enemy, their spirits revived and they took hold of the weapons of faith and manfully drove the evil from their midst; Alexander and many others attacked Arius, Augustine fought with Manicheus,[1] and many more, and Jerome battled with Jovinian the Epicurean, while others set upon other heresies and schisms and either bravely slew them or prudently drove them away from the fort

---

1. Bernard seems to have considered that the founder of Manichaeism was Manichaeus; in fact it was Mani.

so that by their efforts peace and joy were restored to Ecclesia.

5. Alas! Alas! This life can no more be free of temptations than the sea can be rid of its waves. There can be no stable and lasting peace [for Ecclesia] except in her own country. When the sinner takes notice, he becomes envious and begins to be angry. He grinds his teeth and pines away. To prepare for new battles he turns to the weapons of spiritual malice. He calls together those distinguished leaders of his army, the spirit of fornication, the spirit of gluttony and the spirit of avarice. 'You see', he says to them, 'we are making no headway at all. The whole world is running after them. But they are yet to taste our strength even though they boast that they have already escaped and eluded my wiles'.

Having said this he sent them into the fort of Ecclesia, where it was night, and they found everyone asleep and drunk, for those who sleep, sleep at night, and those who get drunk, get drunk at night.† Immediately they disturbed everything. 1 Th 5:7 At once those who were lovers of themselves and seekers of what was theirs and not the things of Jesus Christ, claimed as their inheritance the sanctuary of God and defiled the temple dedicated to his name, not serving God in it but their own wills and pleasures, turning to their own use those things which were offered to God and holy.

The titles and functions of religion they took to themselves and made them into titles and justifications for avarice and elation and vanity. The seamless robe of charity, woven from top to bottom in one piece and the cloak of faith, dyed purple with the precious blood of the Lamb were the means by which the bridegroom covered the nakedness of the bride. These, along with the other adorn-

ments of religion, they ripped off the unwilling
and resisting Ecclesia. They stripped her of them
without clothing themselves. They left naked one
whom they should have protected, destroying her
quiet and, as far as it lay with them, trying to force
her to flee from the world.

6. Ecclesia was crying out and weeping because
she had been stripped and defiled and left naked as
at birth. She was reduced to tears because all her
secret and shameful parts had been exposed to the
mockery of everyone. She implored the children
of her womb, but they were pitiless. She beseeched
them and they spurned her.

With both hands and with all her strength, she
tried to wrap around her heart and her vital organs
some tatters of religious and monastic life, which
had barely escaped the hands of the spoilers. She
prayed that these, at least, should be left to her, but
her prayer was not granted. Even these, they who
were more bandits than protectors, tried to rip off
her, in the hope that unable to bear her nudity
she would either flee from the world or would die
among them, a victim of the cold of their malice.

Some of them pretended to have compassion
on her and tried to cover her with a garment
woven by the hand of hypocrisy from the sim-
ulation of virtues and dissimulation of vice. But
Ecclesia despised and abhorred it and would not
accept it. She would acknowledge no other than
the garment woven by the hand of wisdom, dyed
and hallowed by the blood of the Lamb, left to her
by her bridegroom and taken away from her by her
children. She would recognize no other, but would
throw it off and despise it. Thus she was scorned
and rejected and spat upon and held in contempt
by all.

7. These are our times, so perilous for Ecclesia,
in which peace has given way to an exceeding

great bitterness. Three woes have passed. There
remains a further woe in which the angel of Satan
will transfigure himself into an angel of light and
take his seat in the temple of God and exhibit
himself as if he were God. This mystery of in-
quity is even now at work; already its insulting
precursors surround Ecclesia saying, 'Behold he is
here and behold he is there'.† O bride of Christ,   Lk 17:23
give no credence to them, do not go. Wait for your
bridegroom who does not despise you, nor does he
forget you in time of trouble. He comes to them
at the fourth watch, walking on the sea.† Come   Mt 14:25
Lord, come and set her free, O Lord God of hosts,
who live and reign forever and ever. Amen.

5. the story of the three daughters of the king

INTRODUCTION

tHE FIFTH PARABLE REVERTS to the theme of the unending battle for the human soul. In this case the distinctive focus is on the manner in which freedom is lost and then, by the action of God, restored.

The picture Bernard evokes is of a serene city ruled by three royal daughters: faith, hope and charity. At the base of this simple image is one of the most important principles of Bernard's theological anthropology, namely that the human being is fully human only when he is subject to grace, when the spiritual is supreme, when God is king. Bernard has no two-tiered theory of the supernatural. The work of grace is to make us fully human and thereby fully receptive of the divine. It is not a superstructure on an existing totality. We are fully human with the fullness of free will only when the governance of faith, hope and charity are unchallenged.

The city is under the immediate stewardship of free will who is responsible for the operations of a varied range of virtues—some located in the reason (*rationabilitas*), some in the positive appetite (*concupiscibilitas*) and some in the negative appetite (*irascibilitas*). The ordering of these elements is as follows in Figure 3.

The literary and philosophic provenance of the tripartite division of the soul which Bernard employs here is a complex question

60

RULER	Faith	Hope	Charity
STEWARD	F r e	e W i	l l
CHIEF SERVANT	Prudence	Sobriety	Kindness
ASSISTANTS	Dispensation	Discretion	Purity
	Obedience	Continence	Exercises
	Patience	Constancy	
	Order	Humility	
DOOR-KEEPER	Discipline	Silence	Peace
LOCATION	RATIONALITY	POSITIVE APPETITE	NEGATIVE APPETITE

Figure 3

which merits a longer discussion than is possible here. I have given some brief indications in *Cistercian Studies* 20 (1985), pp. 23–27.

Once again, it is important not to try to construct a system out of the list of virtues. Bernard is notoriously fluid in such matters. It may, however, be observed that nearly all those listed in this parable have to do with the maintenance of standards. There is not much about an outgoing reaching out to the neighbour, but mostly what is at issue is a strong defence against possible sources of trouble. The end product of the whole complex is an ordered, disciplined life. One would endure reverses, avoid excess and perform all that seems virtuous with prudence and discretion.

There is nothing particularly evangelical about such a list; a Stoic philosopher would probably have been delighted with it. What is lacking is the specifically Christian experience of a God who acts beyond the pale of reason to bring salvation to those whom reason and reasonable living were unable to keep secure. Abstract virtues can readily win a notional assent; putting them into practice is another matter. For those who fail to do so through weakness, blindness and malice, all is not lost. In fact there is gain, since by their fall they come to the experience of what it is like to be saved by the intervention of God.

The plot of the parable concerns the inadequacy of free will in the absence of faith, hope and charity—even though they retain nominal control. Immediately practice begins to decline and small deviations are admitted into practical everyday living. No fundamental principles are challenged at this point; there is question only of minor imperfections. The point Bernard makes is that it is through the weakest link in the chain that the breakdown of the whole system begins. The city is infiltrated and gradually the swarms of contrary thoughts and impulses penetrate every cranny. Without the stimulating drama of a major battle, the city has fallen and all its resources are reduced to captivity.

Now is the time to see whether faith, hope and charity are really in control of their domain. Free will has proved inadequate to the task of maintaining the city in its integrity; will the rightful rulers be able to do any better? Faith, hope and charity do not intervene directly, rather they go post haste to their father, the king and by prayer seek his help. Again it seems that prayer is born of disaster.

God acts promptly and, as we have come to expect, sends fear to begin the process of recovery. Fear breaks the tyranny of bad habit and prepares for the arrival of grace. The opposition crumbles and the city is won. We note also Bernard's skill in portraying the celebration of the final triumph; how it stirs the emotions of the reader and causes at least a spark of joy and gratitude to break forth.

The moral of the story may be that the test of virtue is not a matter of resisting routine threats that are easily dismissed, but in coping with failure in doing good and avoiding evil, relying on God to accomplish what is so clearly beyond our own range of resources. Our task is to maintain our contact with God through faith, hope and charity and to call out to him in prayer when trouble strikes. To the extent that this happens we will be truly free and God will rule over our hearts and minds.

THE PARABLE

The Story of the Three Daughters of the King

a NOBLE AND POWERFUL KING had three daughters: Faith, Hope and Charity. To them he assigned a distinguished city: the human soul. In this city were three citadels: reason, positive appetite, and negative appetite. He gave the first to Faith, the second to Hope and the third to Charity. He put Faith in charge of reason because 'faith is not meritorious when human reasoning provides the proof'.[1] Hope was placed in charge of the positive appetite, since we are not to desire things that are seen but things which we hope for, and 'hope which is seen is not hope'.[†] Charity was placed in charge of the negative appetite, warmth to match warmth so that the warmth of nature might be controlled by the warmth of virtue, or rather so that natural warmth might be replaced by the warmth of virtue.

So the daughters entered their citadels and tried with all their might to govern and provide for their houses. As guardian of her house, Faith positioned Prudence in the reason, to safeguard her rights in it and to ensure that reason was ruled by the laws of Faith and remained within the limits fixed by Faith. Prudence was given Dispensation as an assistant,[2]

Rm 8:24

---

1. Gregory the Great, *Hom. in Ev.* 26.1; PL 76.1197c.
2. The Latin word *dispensatio* could almost be translated as 'management', since it was often used in the sense of the Greek *oikonomia*. It means the charge of ensuring that the written code is livable by making adaptations and changes and even, on occasion, suspending it altogether. It belongs to dispensation, as the deputy of prudence and governed by faith, to take practical measures to ensure that the law is conducive to its end in particular circumstances. In this way the beliefs and values of faith are effectively translated into practice. Cf. *Thesaurus Linguae Latinae* s.v. 'Dispensatio'; vol. 5.1, col. 1397–1399.

so that the lower family of acts and senses could
be well ruled and managed. So that Dispensation
could act without hesitation in the house, Obedience was added. So that Obedience could carry
on the work and put up with its laboriousness,
Patience was pressed into service. Then, following
the advice of the Apostle, Order was brought in so
that everything would be done appropriately and
in an orderly manner.† Finally, Discipline was put
to guard the house and to avert the curse, since
every house that lacks discipline is cursed.

1 Co 14:40

2. Hope placed Sobriety in charge of the house
of positive appetite to safeguard her rights in it and
to insist that the head of the house was always at her
service. To ensure that Sobriety was able wisely to
rule the lower family of acts of the will and acts of
pleasure, she gave Discretion as a subordinate. To
counter the lusts of the flesh she added Continence,
against the lust of the eyes she assigned Constancy,
and against worldly ambition she posted Humility.
Finally, Silence was set on the threshold to guard
the house and to prevent indigence from entering, since, as Solomon says, 'Where there is much
speaking, often there is indigence'.†

Pr 14:23

3. Charity's house was built on a north-south
line. She committed it to her friend Kindness and
communicated all her privileges to her. At her
service she placed, firstly, Purity of body and, then,
suitable Exercises, namely readings, meditations,
prayers and outpourings of spiritual feeling. And
so that Misery could not find entrance into the
house to disturb the happiness of the children of
God, who dwell at the seventh level and there, in
the house of Charity, play and rejoice in the fullness
of happiness, Peace was assigned to guard the gate,
since 'Happy are the peace-makers'.†

Mt 5:9

Thus establishing good order in all the houses,

Free Will was constituted steward, in charge of the whole city.

4. When this was done the royal ladies returned to their father's palace. Then, an enemy appeared on the scene and seeing the splendid orderliness of the city, he became envious and he began to plot its downfall.

Since he wanted to enter the city, he set about corrupting its two main guards, Discretion and Dispensation. In this way he was able to introduce his whole wicked army through the gates of reason and positive appetite. Free Will, who was in charge of the city and who was the guardian and judge of the whole city, since the owner had gone abroad and left his servants particular tasks, was bound with iron chains and thrown into prison.

Once the guardians of the citadel of reason were overthrown, Blasphemy rose up against Faith. Everything was upset by an onrush of contradictions, disturbances, disorders and a great crowd of that ilk, each defending whatever he liked so that no reason was left in reason. Once Discipline was removed as gatekeeper, there was ample opportunity for anything at all to pass in or out.

5. Meanwhile, in the house of Hope, Lady Lust has entered the positive appetite and appropriated everything, re-directing desire from the highest things to the lowest. She gave Continence over to be trampled underfoot and mocked by carnal desire, Constancy by the lust of the eyes and Humility by worldly ambition. Having removed Silence as gatekeeper, the gate lay open for anyone to come and go while Sobriety and her kindred virtues were killed, imprisoned or sent into exile.

Then the battle began for the upper citadel of the city. Having disposed of Peace, the gatekeeper and guardian of the highest happiness, Misery made its entrance. Not long after that Lady Pride made her entrance into the citadel, for the pride of those who hate you continually ascends.†

Ps 74:23

She wickedly unseated Kindness and condemned the whole household of Kindness and Peace to death or exile. Now anyone who wished might enter the Lord's sanctuary. Whatever was holy therein, whatever was reserved to the sons of Levi now became open and public. It was profaned, snatched up by enemies and carried off to Babylon. So now the vessels of the temple were used to serve wine to the concubines of the king of Babylon. Thus was the entire city seized and shaken so that its present shame matched its former glory.†

1 M 1:42

6. While everyone was in disarray, the sad news came to the three daughters that the city was lost. They were upset and cast themselves down at the feet of the father and implored his help. He, upon inquiry, put the blame on Free Will, its negligent guardian. His daughters said, 'But Father, what can Free Will do without the help of Grace?' He replied: 'Very well, I shall give Grace, but first I will send Fear. He will go before her and prepare her ways'.

Fear went out from the face of the Lord and so came to the city. In his hand was the rod of discipline. The gate of difficulty he found closed and secured with the bars of bad habit. The gatekeeper was an insolent rogue named Sexual Excess. He came to the gate and because he was very hostile to Fear, he tried to wear him down with insults and reviling. But Fear boldly thrust forward and broke the bars of bad habit. He knocked down the gates of difficulty and began to chastise that wretch, beating him to death with the rod of discipline which he carried.

Immediately Fear raised over the gates the flag

signalling the arrival of Grace and the whole city was filled with fear. Then Grace entered the city, bringing with her the entire army of the heavenly hosts. At once the forces of the enemy disappeared and the virtues resumed their previous positions. Then Discretion and Dispensation came forward, confessing their guilty error and begging for pardon. Free Will also, casting off his chains, hurried to greet Lady Grace, expressing the hope that he would indeed be free, henceforth, under her rule.

The houses were made ready for the king's daughters and appropriate meals prepared. On faith's table were placed the bread of sorrow and the water of distress, along with other penitential foods. Hope's table had strengthening bread and oil to make the face shine and other consoling dishes. Charity's table had the bread of life and the wine of gladness together with all the delights of paradise.

So the daughters returned and feasted and kept guard over the city, but if the Lord does not guard the city, then do they who guard it watch in vain.[†]   Ps 127:1

6. the story of the ethiopian woman whom the king's son took as wife

INTRODUCTION

N STYLE AND SPIRIT this parable is completely different from all the others in this series. There is no real story, just a series of moralising vignettes and images with wordy, self-conscious explanations of their meaning. Although there are linkages with other Bernardine compositions[1] and some overlap with the fourth parable, it is arguable that the internal indications for the *De Aethopissa* being an authentic literary production of the abbot of Clairvaux are less convincing than the external evidence.

There are two parts to the text: an introduction and the parable itself. Bernard's introduction develops a comparatively minor theme of the parable, that of the four ages of the Church. The ages he specifies are the same as those in the fourth parable, although he uses as images the dangers listed in Ps 90 (91) and the four horses of the book of Revelation. As in Par 4, the present age is one of false religion heading towards the age of anti-Christ. For each of the woes experienced by the Church an appropriate remedy is prescribed: one of the four cardinal virtues. What the present age needs is justice and prudence.

---

1. For example, SC 33 and QH 6.

The parable speaks of the nuptials of the king's son to a totally unsuitable bride. He loves her so much, however, that he effects her release from captivity, woos her and wins her heart and then makes up for her defects by showering her with precious gifts. In relatively short time Bernard covers the ground up to the time of Christ's leaving of his bride in the care of guardians. Whereas the apostles, martyrs and doctors each added to the bride's endowment in their own way, the Church of today despoils her. The parable ends on this plaintive note. If her guardians are so ready to bring her to penury and disgrace in order to enrich themselves, is it surprising that the common folk are no longer numbered among her friends.

The major part of the parable is taken up with a detailed, allegorical description of the bride's wardrobe. This is somewhat surprising, since Bernard is reputed to have exhibited little interest in clothing and a positive distaste for elaborate attire. Far be it from me to say that the symbolism is not particularly inspired; perhaps the reader may care to make a judgement on the matter.[2]

There is some moderately interesting material on the qualities of moral action which has resonances in other parts of the Bernardine corpus. The 'subjects' appropriate for contemplation will leave many disappointed, seemingly so dry and doctrinal. Neither treatment has the masterly touch one expects of Bernard of Clairvaux. Perhaps another has given literary development to a brief oral outline. Perhaps this text simply reflects a different aspect of the abbot of Clairvaux. Maybe St Bernard was not brilliant every day.

There are other images. The windows of contemplation.[3] The mule as an image of a Church formed of both Jews and Gentiles. The distinction between wool as being a painless product of the lamb and the lambskin, which requires its death. The colourful picture of the devil's bazaar. It will be for the reader to judge how typical these portrayals are of the style and thought of the abbot of Clairvaux.

This sixth parable does share with the other texts in the series the ambition of giving due warning to the reader to continue

---

2. See Figure 4.
3. Also in Sent 2.127, in a different sense.

WARDROBE	ALLEGORICAL DESCRIPTION
WOOLEN CAPE	Instruction in humility
LAMBSKIN	Mortification
PELISSE	Preaching
Ermine	on resurrection (joy and hope)
Sable	on passion (expressed in word, deed and feeling)
CORDOVANS	Separation from the earth
A pair	Two testaments, or Continence and charity
GLOVES	
Right hand	Activity
Five fingers	Uprightness
	Voluntariness
	Pureness
	Discernment
	Firmness
Left hand	Contemplation
Five fingers	Consideration of sin and hell
	Scorn for present life and future hope
	Judgement and the kingdom
	State of the glorified body
	Final beatitude
MANY-HUED GARMENT	The Holy Martyrs
White	Virgins
In-between colour	Married and widowed persons
Red	Christ's blood
SAMITE CLOAK	The lives of the holy doctors

Figure 4

making progress through the practice of a disciplined life of fidelity, eschewing all contrary attractions and being forewarned that we are constantly being drawn into alternative pursuits. To remain one with the bride of Christ we must participate fully in the gifts he has left her, not use them to serve our own interests and desires.

THE PARABLE

The Story of the Woman Whom the King's Son Took as His Wife

Introduction

tHERE ARE FOUR temptations which are universal in the Church but which are also found in particular form in every faithful soul. These are the following: adversity, prosperity, pretence or hypocrisy and being led astray by the enemy when he transfigures himself in to an angel of light.[†]   2 Co 11:14

Thus it is written 'You will not fear the terror of the night',[†] which is addressed to the faithful soul   Ps 91:5–6 to prevent its being afraid of adversities. 'Nor the arrow that flies by day', so that in time of prosperity it may be wary of vain glory which, like an arrow, comes from hiding to wound and kill. 'Nor the business which prowls in the darkness', to warn against being sold in the hiddenness of pretence. The hypocrite sees himself as engaged in a great and honourable business. Cleverly and skillfully he sells piecemeal what he has of good conscience for a mean price, be it for praise or for some similar reward. This business is carried out in the darkness, that is, in the hiddenness of pretense. It is said to prowl because no rank or order or person escapes this temptation. 'From attack' to warn against our falling or being led into temptation 'and from the noonday devil', to make us wary, lest we encounter the noonday devil who can transfigure himself into an angel of light in order to deceive the faithful. The noonday devil is said to transfigure himself for one of two reasons: either because of his spurious brightness, or because of the heat of his malice which burns especially fiercely when he advances for the final battle. So, it is usually at the end of one's life that one has to engage in this particular warfare.

Against the four temptations there are four guardians.[4] The first guardian is against adversity: fortitude. The second guardian is against prosperity: temperance. And the third is against hypocrisy: justice. The fourth is against the angel of Satan: prudence. This is the fourth watch of the night during which, if Jesus had not come to his disciples, the ship would have been endangered.[†] Even when he does come, he may be considered an illusion, unless through his power the deceiving spirit is crushed. When the power of this final temptation is felt, there is a reluctance to give further entrance to the counsel of truth.

These four temptations occur in the Church as a whole; they have done so in the past and will continue to do so. The 'terror of the night' is the fear experienced by the martyrs in times of persecution. The 'arrow that flies by day' is the bane of heresy which flew through the Church in the time of ease. The 'business which prowls in the darkness' is the hypocrisy which is everywhere so evident in our own time. The fact is that we are now in a period of pretence, in which we observe hypocrisy (that is, acting in darkness or simulating) making its way through the whole Church. Counterfeits along with the genuine articles are sold cheaply for human praise or human reward. The 'attack' of the 'noonday devil' is now not far off.

---

4. The Latin word is *vigilia*, there are four 'watches', hence the reference to the 'fourth watch' later in this paragraph. There is another discussion of the four watches in connection with Ps 91:5 in Sent 1.42; SBOp 6b.21.15–22, though the elements have been arranged differently.

Thence the four horses of the Apocalypse.[†] The Rv 6:2–8 first horse is white, that is, it is mild and placid and the one who rides it goes forth to win victory. In a time of peace he wears the crown of joy but against heresies he holds the bow of war, that is the weapon of holy preaching by which he shoots the warrior's sharpened arrows which are the efficacious words of the Holy Spirit. The second horse is red, the colour of blood. Its rider carries a great sword to banish peace from the earth and to kill, shedding the blood of the martyrs. The third horse is black and dark. Hypocrisy is its rider, carrying the scales of commerce, balancing one side against the other, as was noted above. The fourth horse is pale, being in the last extremity and close to death. Its rider is death with hell to follow.

Changing the order of events a little, since the time of persecution came first: the white horse signals a time of peace for the Church, the red horse a time of persecution, the black the age of hypocrisy and the pale horse the period of the Anti-Christ. These four seasons are better illustrated in the following parable.

The Parable

The Son of the king of the heavenly Jerusalem went abroad so that he might inspect the lower realms of his Father. Having looked around and seen everything, he returned to the Father and said, 'I have traversed all the territories of your realm and have taken note of what is happening in all of them. Even the cry of the inhabitants of Sodom, which rises up to you, I have found to be true and so I have inflicted upon them the appropriate punishment. It is now time, however, for me to look ahead to the future. I must marry, beget children and set up my own household. I have seen a bride whom I would like to have in the house of the king of Babylon. That king holds her captive, and to ensure that she cannot be recognized, he has clothed her with the filthy garments of a slave'.

The Father responded thus to the Son: 'May you never do this thing, my only Son, co-eternal and consubstantial with myself. This Ethiopian woman of whom you speak is unworthy of your rank and immensity'.

The Son said to the Father: 'I am determined. I wish to take a wife and I will marry none other than her'. 'If that is the case', replied the Father, 'because you are co-eternal and consubstantial and co-omnipotent with me, it is within your power to free her from the Babylonian captivity and to take her for your wife, as you wish'.

Immediately there appeared a multitude beyond counting of angels and celestial cohorts, making themselves ready to render service at the nuptials of the Son of the supreme king. One of these, the archangel Gabriel, was chosen as paranymph.[5] Once selected, Gabriel spoke thus to the Son of the supreme king: 'Behold, I am your strength. If you command, I am willing and able to snatch by force the woman you seek for yourself from within Babylon'.

The Son of the eternal king replied: 'That is not the way it is to be done. No violence is to be brought to bear on the Babylonian king. The woman is to be brought out of Babylonian captivity by counsels of stealth and by wisdom which is joined to me. Hence, you, Gabriel are secretly to carry the mystery of my plan to the virgin Mary,

---

5. The paranymph is the man's agent in dealing with the prospective bride and her family. Cf. Par 1.5.

of the lineage of David. With her, in her chamber, the celebration of my marriage feast is to begin'.

So the archangel Gabriel came down to Mary and faithfully carried out the task enjoined on him. However, the one who had sent him had already come to the virgin before the message was delivered. There began the celebration of this most sacred marriage feast.

Would such a groom come to his bride empty-handed? Never! He came bearing gifts and gave her what he brought. Because it was winter when he arrived the first things that he gave to his bride were winter garments—a pelisse and a cape, both products of the lamb. The wool for the cape is obtained without hurting the lamb, but the other is the skin (hence lambskin) and is only taken from the lamb by inflicting grave pain. Now, the bridegroom is himself the Lamb, as the Scripture attests. 'He is led like a lamb to the slaughter',[†] Is 53:7 and elsewhere, 'Behold the Lamb of God who takes away the sins of the world'.[†] This Lamb Jn 1:29 makes a cape for his bride from wool when, by words, he teaches humility: 'Learn of me for I am meek and humble of heart'.[†] He gives the pelisse Mt 11:29 when through fasts and vigils and other afflictions of the flesh he reveals to the bride the ultimate mortification of the flesh in the passion of the cross. The cape, which hides its wearer, signifies humility since whoever is Christ's bride keeps out of sight and refuses to be known by the world. The pelisse, which is made from dead animals, suggests the mortification of the flesh. So much for the season of winter.

At Eastertide he gives her an ermine pelisse trimmed with red sable at the neck, on the front and at the wrists.[6] This pelisse represents the holy preachers. They are white because they are the heralds of the resurrection accomplished in Christ and they proclaim the resurrection which will be realized in the future in the bride.

Because the preachers proclaim the passion of Christ they wear red sable about their necks. However, because there are some preachers who discourse of Christ's passion with the lips but feel nothing in their hearts, of whom Paul says: 'Some preach Christ without sincerity, thinking to advance themselves by the troubles of my chains',[†] it is important that those who preach the passion of Christ should feel in their hearts what they say with their mouths. So it would be improper if the pelisse had sable only around the neck and not coming down the front. Preachers also have sable at their hands since they communicate the sufferings of Christ through their actions.

Ph 1:17

---

6. The Easter pelisse is of white fur (ermine) with *gula* at neck, on the breast and at the end of the sleeves. *Gula*, which is preserved in heraldic English by the word 'gules' means simply red (perhaps associated with the colour of the gullet, since *gula* means this also). It is used of red fur used for the trimming of expensive garments; I am not sure whether this fur was sable or merely a more common variety dyed for appearance's sake. In the translation I have opted for the more expensive alternative. In Letter 42, to Henry, Archbishop of Sens (often printed as a treatise *De Moribus et Officio Episcoporum*) Bernard has a section on glamorous dressing. It includes the following passage: 'They draw back from the reddened fur of martens which are called *gulae*, not wanting them to surround their consecrated hands which have the power to consecrate the awesome mysteries. They do not want to have them on their breasts, which are more appropriately adorned with the jewel of wisdom. They are ashamed to have them about their necks which they might more honourably and more delightfully submit to the yoke of Christ. These are not the wounds of Christ which they, following the example of the martyrs, ought to bear on their bodies. They are the insignia of women, who make them for themselves to be as unusual and costly as possible, thinking of the things of earth, how they might please their husbands'. Ep 42:4; SBO 7.104.13–20.

To sum up: the bride's pelisse is made of ermine, which is white, to signify spiritual joy because of the hope of future resurrection. It is adorned at the neck, down the front and at the wrists with red sable because the passion of Christ which is proclaimed by mouth must also be experienced in the heart and witnessed by works.

During Eastertide Christ also gave to his bride a pair of cordovans. These represent the two testaments by which the affections of the bride are strengthened so that they do not cleave to the earth. Alternatively, they represent continence and charity which cover the two affections, one directed to her own flesh, the other to the bride's former vices. The affection which is directed to the flesh is fortified by continence which is restraint imposed under discipline. The affection which is directed to vices is extinguished by charity. These cordovans, however, will fall off the feet unless they are fastened by profession and obedience. We observe many people who, through charity, maintain continence of the flesh. This is to say that they take practical steps to live according to the two testaments. However, because they have not bound themselves by obedience and profession they have seriously fallen. The cordovans are, therefore, the two testaments or continence and charity, and the fasteners are profession and obedience.

Christ also gave his bride a pair of gloves. The hands of the bride are activity and contemplation. It is true elsewhere the left hand represents activity and the right hand contemplation, as in the text: 'His left hand is underneath my head and his right hand embraces me'.[†] Here, however, the left hand designates contemplation and the right activity. In this image we usually hold the left hand hidden Sg 2:6

beneath clothing, whereas the right hand is exposed for activity.

So the right hand is activity. The right glove is
divided into five sections to accommodate the five
fingers. This is because every good action must
be upright, voluntary, pure, discerning and firm.
That is to say that it must be upright in intention,
voluntary so that it is not due to fear or some
coercion, pure so that it is not rendered useless
by any hint of vanity, discerning that so that it
does not exceed due measure and firm so that it is
persevering.

The left hand, contemplation, likewise has a
glove divided into five, for there are five elements
in contemplation: the consideration of sin and
hell, scorn for the present combined with hope
for future realities, judgement and the kingdom,
the state of the body after the resurrection and
glorification and, finally, the human spirit and the
eternity with which it is to be united.

One who enters contemplation first considers
his sins: what crimes he has committed and how
frequently. Such reflection is not of much utility
unless he begins to experience a fear of being
punished in hell for them. Hence it is important
that he meditate not only on sin but also on hell.
On the other hand if one considers the nature and
variety of torments in hell without being mindful
of one's own sins, then the mind may think on such
things unabashed and unafraid because it does not
recall one's past offenses. For this reason the mind
given to contemplation should dwell on both sin
and hell so that from a consideration of both fear
may be born.

In a mind so possessed by fear arises a scorn for
present realities with which is associated a hope
for the things of the future. But to prevent this

hope from rendering the mind undisciplined, it is restrained by judgement, since it bears in mind that in order to arrive at the things hoped for one must pass through a judgement which is severe and fearsome. The fear occasioned by the thought of judgement is balance by the consolation which comes from the consideration of the kingdom. So, to the thought of judgement is added that of the kingdom in which we reflect on what we shall be: firstly on the condition of the body no longer subject to suffering and death, then on its glorification when it will assume a splendour and beauty which beggar description. As it is written: 'The just will be as resplendent as the sun'.[†]   Mt 13:43

After this the soul's beatitude is considered: the soul itself and God with whom the soul is to be united, which is the end and consummation of everything.

These five themes on which we reflect in contemplation are viewed through five windows.[7] A window is a space in a wall. If the wall is unbroken, there is no window. If there is only a space without a wall there is no window. A wall which contains a space is called a window.

Christ's humanity was like a wall which yet allowed the divinity to shine forth within that humanity. Therefore Christ is a window. Indeed five windows may be pondered on in him: his incarnation, his way of life, his teaching, his resurrection and his ascension. It is through these five realities that the things spoken of regarding contemplation are seen.

Through the incarnation of Christ sin and hell were revealed to many who had previously ignored

---

7. A different use of the image of windows in contemplation can be found in Sent 2.127; SBOp 6b.48.9–11.

them. His way of life clearly taught that we must
despise present realities and direct our hope to the
things of the future. In his teaching there is ample
treatment of judgement and the kingdom. In his
resurrection is demonstrated the condition of the
body and glorification, since those who belong to
him will be in the future, in their own small way,
what he is. In the ascension is revealed, however
slightly, how our spirit is to be united with God.
How was it that this human being, without any
conveyance and without the help of any created
thing, has been lifted up and taken to another place,
unless it was through the divinity which was united
with him.

So much for the gloves of the bride. The right
hand is action and its working must be upright,
voluntary, pure, discerning and firm. The left hand
is contemplation which considers first sins and hell,
then scorn for the present and hope for future realities, then judgement and the kingdom to which is
added the condition of the body and glorification
and finally the uniting of our spirit with God.

When Christ ascended he brought all this to
perfection in his bride and gave her to the apostles
to look after. He instructed them not to depart
from Jerusalem until they had been clothed in
strength from on high.† Ten days afterwards, on the
day of Pentecost, he sent from heaven a great and
strong army, that is, the Holy Spirit. He was the
one who brought them peace and joy and the other
fruits of the Spirit which the Apostle enumerates.†

Once this took place they became constant and
strong and so they attacked the enemy throngs and
Peter converted five thousand Jews to Christ on
one day and three thousand on another.†

When this was accomplished the apostles said:
Our mistress, Christ's bride, should no longer have

Lk 24:49

Ga 5:22–23

Cf. Ac 4:4, 2:41

to travel by foot. Let us seek an animal for her so that she can be conveyed more quickly and with greater dignity to wherever she has to go. It cannot be a horse because a horse is a proud and contentious animal. Neither can it be an ass, because an ass is foolish and unclean. Rather, let it be a mule so that the bride may travel surely and steadily. And so a mule was given to the bride, since the people who were converted to the faith were drawn from both Jews and gentiles. Just as a mule is descended from different animals, so the early Church was gathered from different peoples, that is from Jews and gentiles, from those who were too sure of themselves and from those who were becoming desperate. Christ has wondrously cured those labouring under different and even opposite infirmities with a single medicine, namely his cross. There were those who were overconfident and those who were despairing and there still are those who say: 'I am happy with my present situation', and 'I have never taken anything by violence', and such things, and 'Why should I despair of life and fear hell?' Let such persons take note that Christ, who did not sin, in whose mouth was found no deceit, nevertheless finished his life by a most foul death that is, on the cross.† Let them withdraw 1 P 2:22; Ws 2:20 from their pride and, shaken by fear, let them be converted to humility and to sharing in the sufferings of Christ.

There are some persons who are so defiled by their many serious crimes that they are reluctant to be generous with themselves. But if they consider that Christ endured not for himself but for sinners, then they gather hope and are healed from their despair. So we see that Christ by his cross brings healing to the overconfident because he suffered notwithstanding his innocence, and to the desperate since he suffered for the sake of sinners.

The Church, gathered together from different sorts of sinners, is the mule which the apostles prepared for the bride. To her who takes her ease thereon and who, by its means, makes progress to various places, the apostles give a spur, which is the love of the bridegroom by which she can compel those who belong to her to go forward. They also give her a whip, which is fear, which she strikes behind, to make them suffer for the evils they have done.

Holy Church has multiplied and grown. The apostles, having completed their struggle and fight, passed from this life and left the Church to the martyrs so that they might govern it. They fought manfully on her behalf and shed their blood in her defense. They said: The apostles made a gift to our mistress of one mule. It is right that we should likewise contribute something to her appropriate adornment. Since the heat of summer is already on us, she should not be loaded down with heavy coverings. Instead let us make for her something light and beautiful, a many-hued garment, covered with red and purple. This many-hued garment is made up of the holy martyrs. The white part represents the virgins whereas the in-between colours represent those who were widowed and the married.[8] On all of them red is superimposed, since they are spinkled with the blood of the slain Christ. At this period they courageously governed the Church, they made progress and multiplied.

When they died holy doctors and admirable confessors succeeded them, men like Ambrose,

---

8. Even among the martyrs marriage seems to run a poor third, after virginity and widowhood.

Hilary and Augustine.[9] It was at this time that the devil, perceiving that the open war which he had waged against the Church in the time of the apostles and martyrs was without effect, and that the Church had rather grown and made progress by its troubles, turned to fraudulent and stealthy means of persecution. He led some of its members astray and it was through them that he was able to carry out his evil business, more effective because it was unseen.

Arius, Pelaguis, Photinus[10] and others like them he instructed in his ways so that while they pretended to be Christ's ministers, they led the bride far off the track. When the holy doctors adverted to this they reacted, they became involved in controversies and rebutted the heretics and guided their mistress back to the way of truth. Once this was done, because her garments had been torn in the deserts of Arius and the detours of Pelagius, they made her a cloak of samite,[11] that is they adorned her with their own chaste lives and upright behaviour. In this manner was the enemy defeated both in open persecutions and in the hidden wiles of the heretics. Now the bride, with

---

9. Ambrose (339–397), Hilary of Poitiers (315–367) and Augustine of Hippo (354–430) were three of the most highly regarded western Fathers of the Church.

10. Arius (250–336) was condemned at the Council of Nicea in 325; Pelagius was a British ascetic and theologian who was condemned by the African bishops and the councils of Carthage and Milevis in 416. This was confirmed by Pope Innocent I in the following year and by Pope Zosimus in 418. The nature of Photinus' heresy is not clear. He was deposed and exiled in 351 and his followers were formally condemned by the Council of Constantinople in 381.

11. Bernard uses the middle French word *samit* although the Latin word *samitum* is attested. It is probably the same as *examitum*, which Bernard uses elsewhere, which is a transliteration of the Greek *hexamiton*, meaning six threads. The material referred to was a heavy silk fabric, often shot through with gold, used for ecclesiastical vestments and regal garments.

no more adversaries, went forward with many in
her company.

Still the twisting serpent attempts to bring her
to nothing. Because this is not possible while she
remains on the road, he prepares traps for her
beside the road. There he pitched his tents. Within
them he had his bankers sit with a great deal of gold
and silver on display. In another place were the
garment sellers with a wide range of rich apparel,
variously ornamented. In another place he located
those who sold various sorts of food and elsewhere
the taverns of those who sold wine and all sorts of
other drinks. In one place he erected triumphant
archways for the sake of those who boasted in
worldly pomp. And he put on display troupes of
girls and all sorts of incitements to lust.

The wise man who accompanies the bride stays
close to her and keeps to the bride's right path.
But those who are foolish and stupid leave the
road and take their pleasure in the devil's taverns
and never again return to the bride. In fact there
are many people today who leave the road and
take their pleasure in the devil's taverns. Some love
silver and are captivated by the beauty of gold;
preferring these things to Christ they pass their
time in the tent of the devil. Likewise those who
delight in costly clothing, exotic foods, honeyed
wine and other expensive drinks, in women, in
fun[12] and in worldly songs and who give these
things precedence over Christ are in the taverns
of the devil.

What can I say about those men who, although
they have the duty of governing the Church of

---

12. *Iocus* probably means more than 'jokes', so I have
translated it more broadly. Augustine uses it of theatrical
entertainment: *In Ps 38:2*, CChr Lat, 38.403. It also seems
to have been used of tournaments in the twelfth century.

God, depart from the path and are full of admiration for what they find in the tents of the devil; they look around and are filled with desire. Since they do not have the means to purchase what they lust after, they snatch the bride's adornments and foully use them to finance the gratification of their evil desires. So it is that the bride is lacerated round the shoulders and has scarcely any clothes to cover herself except for a few monks and some canons regular. When the bride thus suffers she keeps almost none of the other ranks of people.

7. the story of the eight beatitudes

INTRODUCTION

THE SEVENTH PARABLE can be broken into three sections. The first in a dialogue between Christ and the monk on the subject of the beatitudes; the central section the monk discourses on his own spiritual journey and how he came to acquire the beatitudes. The final section is an unflattering comparison of the four beatitudes of Luke with the eight beatitudes of Matthew, with Bernard concluding that the genuine monk has the full tally—the lukewarm monk has only the same number as the common folk who live on the plain and do not ascend the mountain.

The picture of the monk bartering with the Lord for the appropriate reward of his labours is imaginative and good-humoured. The Lord allows himself to be bludgeoned by his own words and so rewards the good monk disproportionately, giving him eternal and spiritual rewards in exchange for the relatively trivial items he has to offer. There is no question here of a system of strict merit—everything remains well in the sphere of the divine gratuity.

The Sequence of the Vices

In elaborating on his own itinerary, the monk speaks of his fall from grace in terms of the primal sin of Adam. As elsewhere in this series, Bernard is at pains to show that the path to total infidelity begins with relatively minor matters so that the greater sins creep up unawares. The moral of the story is to take measures to see that the downward decline is stopped while it is still possible. Better still, let it be prevented altogether.

The way back to God by means of monastic discipline is punctuated by different stages marked by the various beatitudes and/or gifts of the Holy Spirit. Here we see something of the clarity of Bernard's vision of monastic life. The purpose of all discipline and organisation is the growth in holiness of each monk through his being equipped to receive the gifts which God constantly offers.

Progressively as the monk matures spiritually he becomes less dependent on external authority and more able to live a good life under the guidance of interior principles, brought to fruition in him by the grace of God and the labour of decades. Here Bernard follows the end of St Benedict's chapter on humility in which the same progression is envisaged. The purpose of all external measures is to bring about interior change so that in time the monk begins to do naturally and enjoy what previously was an ill-understood burden for him.

It may be helpful to represent the progression schematically. Elements of it appear frequently in Bernard's other writings, where his views are given a complementary expression and somewhat nuanced. I have given a survey of some relevant texts in *Cistercian Studies* 22 (1987), pp. 37–45.[1]

The list appears a little unusual at first glance, but it repays reflection. It reinforces a notion that often appears in these parables which sees grave sin in terms of an antecedent omission to take ordinary measures to preserve intact the gifts of grace. Once a decline has begun, in Bernard's view, it becomes almost impossible to halt.

Here, as throughout the series, we can admire Bernard's facility with scripture; his skill with words and images and his playfulness in weaving solid spiritual teaching into a simple, attractive and moving narrative.

---

1. See Figure 5.

	VICE	REMEDY
1	Security	[ ]
2	Negligence	Fear of the Lord
3	Curiosity	*Pietas*, Goodness
4	Concupiscence	Knowledge
5	[Consent]	Fortitude
6	Habit	Counsel
7	Contempt	Understanding
8	Malice	Wisdom

Figure 5

In some senses the conclusion of this parable is a theme which predominates them all. For those who wish to receive what Christ has promised and what their nature desires, it is sufficient that they live well, according to the Gospels. The best way to do this is to become Cistercian monks, and once having made this profession, let them stay in their monasteries, let them do good and avoid evil. Do this and all will be well.

Simple clear teaching appropriate to new recruits and, for the rest of us, well worth meditating on.

THE PARABLE

The Story of the Eight Beatitudes

tHE KINGDOM OF HEAVEN is like a monk who is a trader. When he hears that a market is to be held in the near future, he gathers together his wares that are to be displayed there. He takes eight bundles, loaded on a beast of burden from the south.† Cf. Is 30:6

He met the Lord Jesus Christ who noticed his hard work and energy and said: Where are you coming from and where are you going?

The monk: I come from the monastery and I am going to the market to sell what you can see, if there is a buyer.

The Lord: There is a buyer already, if there is a seller. Open the first bundle.

The monk: The value of this merchandise will be clear to your wisdom, just as I am well aware of your omnipotent resources to make the purchase. See what the first bundle contains. You have said, 'Blessed are the poor in spirit'.† This bundle is Mt 5:3 made up of deprivation and indigence together with the sufferings and anguish of the deprived.

The Lord: Goodness me![2] What use is that?

The monk: A box of manure is very useful for putting about the roots of a tree.[3]

The Lord: Well said! What price are you asking for this first item?

The monk: The kingdom of heaven.

---

2. The exclamation *Papae!* is also found at Div 14.4; SBOp 6a.138.1.

3. The image of the box of manure being used for the roots of trees is also found in Augustine, *In Ps* 49:7; CChr 39.581. The context there is also the beatitudes, but for Augustine it signifies grief of heart and tears.

The Lord: The price is high, whereas the product is not much, unless one takes its consequences into consideration. Unload the second bundle. What is inside?

Mt 5:4

The monk: Meekness, for 'Blessed are the meek'.[†]

The Lord: Meekness is a noble reality and worthy of God. What price are you asking?

The monk: 'Pure gold cannot buy it, nor can its worth be weighed out in silver'.[†] I ask for the land. I do not want anything else in exchange for it, only the land.

Jb 28:15

The Lord: The land stretches from India to Britain. There is plenty of room and a need for cultivators. Take as much as you want, in whatever region you choose.

The monk: Never! That land is the land of the dead. It devours its inhabitants; human beings die in it. For my part, I desire the land of the living. 'I believe I shall see the good things of the Lord in the land of the living'.[†]

Ps 27:13

The Lord: All things considered, you will die without your willing it. But if you wish to live forever, then listen:

'Blessed are the meek, for they shall inherit the land'. And what does the third bundle contain?

The monk: Hunger, famine, thirst and utter penury.

The Lord: And what price is reckoned appropriate for the purchase of such merchandise?

The monk: Justice. 'Blessed are those that hunger and thirst for justice, for they shall have their fill'.[†]

Mt 5:6

The Lord: You will have your fill, then, and justice will come to you, so long as negligence does not interfere. What does the fourth bundle contain?

The monk: Tears, weeping and crying; streams from above and streams form below.†   Jg 1:15

The Lord: Normally lamentation and weeping are not goods to be purchased, but evils to be averted.[4] Nevertheless this also has a value since 'Blessed are they that mourn, for they will be comforted'.† And what is in the fifth bundle?   Mt 5:5

The monk: It contains a precious substance: mercy. I perceive that it is to your liking, so I will not dally. For mercy I want mercy. I want mercy which is eternal.

The Lord: I think you are not a fair judge in such matters. There can never be an exchange of temporal things for those of eternity. The only exception is when mercy itself acts as your intermediary. But let these matters be decided according to your faith and according to that saying, 'Blessed are the merciful for they themselves will receive mercy'.†   Mt 5:7 So, we now have an abundance of deprivation and weeping and troubles, mercy needed and mercy received. Bring out the sixth bundle, perhaps it might contain something better.

The monk: This one is certainly better, but it does not like being put on display. It can be viewed in secret, in the inner room and never in public. It is only under such conditions that its price can be determined.

The Lord: All right, we are inside. Now what is it?

The monk: Cleanness of heart. Here we have precious vessels of gold and silver: kindness, charity and joy in the Holy Spirit. Here precious fabrics will be unrolled: readings, meditations, prayers, contemplations. For 'the judgements of the Lord

---

4. . . . *non solent emi sed redimi.*

Ps 19:9–11

are true, made right in themselves. They are more to be desired than gold and many precious stones and they are sweeter than honey and honeycomb. This is why your servant keeps them'.†

Ps 19:9–11

The Lord: 'And in keeping them there is a great reward'.† Ask what you want.

The monk: The vision of God.

The Lord: 'Blessed are the clean of heart for they

Mt 5:8

shall see God'. Open the seventh bundle.†

The monk: Here it is. It contains peace.

The Lord: You want to sell me your peace?

The monk: It is not appropriate to my poverty or to your justice and your wealth that you should get anything from me for nothing. However, thanks to your generosity I now have enough, and more than enough, but I ask for the one thing that is lacking to me. I am a rough country man, not born of noble stock, but made from clay and moulded from the slime of the earth. My lack of nobility troubles me. I want no longer to be insulted with the saying, 'You are earth and unto earth shall you

Gn 3:19

return'.† Rather do I want it said, 'You are heaven and unto heaven you shall go'. I desire to have a portion with the sons of God.

The Lord: This is what I said about this in the past, a statement I cannot disavow: 'Blessed are those who make peace, they shall be called the

Mt 5:9

children of God'.† If you maintain the charity appropriate to such children then you will receive

Ep 5:5

the inheritance.† There is one bundle remaining. Open it up.

The monk: This contains only persecutions and troubles for the cause of justice.

The Lord: And what are you asking for that?

The monk: The kingdom of heaven.

The Lord: I have already made this over to you as the price or reward for poverty.

The monk: Yes, but month follows month and

week follows week.† I ask for a down payment. I   Is 66:23
want half of what is due this week and this month
and then I shall be prepared to wait until next week
and next month for the rest.

The Lord: I admire your prudence in doing
business. So now, 'well done, good and faithful
servant. Because you have been faithful over a few
things, I shall set you over many. Enter into the joy
of your Lord'.† 'You shall eat the fruit of your toil;   Mt 25:21
you are blessed, and things will go well for you'.†   Ps 128:2
Yet the whole world is full of those who would
profit from your skill in doing business and there
are so few who apply themselves as industriously
as you have. Therefore I would ask you to teach
them how to conduct their affairs so that perhaps
you might inspire some of your own kindred to
imitate your example.

The monk: Your wisdom which reaches to the
ends of the earth and disposes all things firmly
and sweetly† knows how I was created by God   Ws 8:1
the Father, how I became a new creature by your
baptism† and was placed in the paradise of good   2 Co 5:17; Ga 6:15
conscience so that I could work and maintain it. I
was to work by giving myself actively to goodness.[5]
I maintained it by guarding against the serpent's
cunning. Instead, however, I gave in to softness
and idleness and lay down on the bed of pleasure
in the bosom of my Eve, that is, of the fleshly
nature which was joined to me, which God gave
me as a helpmate to bring forth good works as
children.[6] I fell into the sleep of false security. In
this way I, a spiritual being, lost the first talent that

---

5. Goodness here translates *pietas*; sometimes this term
seems to have connotations of deeds done with reference to
God, at other times it reverts to the meaning of the affection
and kindliness practised by family members. I have opted for
a generic rendering.

6. Poor Eve is often reduced to serving as a symbol of the
flesh. Thus *carnis delectatio* in Sent 3.107; SBOp 6b.124.12.

was given to me, that is, reason. From security I fell into negligence, from negligence to curiosity, from curiosity into desire, from desire into habit, from habit into contempt and from contempt into malice.

The serpent was more cunning than all the beasts which God had created on the earth.[†] Once, when he was making his rounds, silent and slippery and full of guile, he found a chink of negligence in the surrounding wall. Without any opposition he entered into the paradise of my conscience. He found me inside, sleeping in the bosom of evil. Making his way to the ear of my Eve he hissed into it with the venom of persuasion to do evil. He raised her up from the sleeper's side and led her by way of curiosity to the tree of the knowledge of good and evil about which God had said, 'In the hour that you eat it, you will die the death'.[†]

The woman saw that the tree was beautiful to see and of pleasing aspect so she desired it.[†] She gave her consent and grew accustomed to it. She held in contempt the prospect of returning to her husband and seeking advice from him, since it was to her husband that she should have turned. In this matter she reached the point of malice, that is delight in committing sin and the defense of sin. And so she came to me, her husband, accompanied by the serpent, bringing with her the apple of disobedience.[7] While I was still asleep, she put it into my mouth and immediately we became, she and I, not one bone but one flesh, united as the old Adam, all flesh, the slave of sin, the servant of death and the offspring of perdition.

Gn 3:1

Gn 2:17

Gn 3:6

Augustine has the same usage, for instance, *In Ps* 48. sermo 1.6; CChr 38.556: *Eva nobis interior caro nostra est.*

7. Cf. *Par* 1.2; SBOp 6b.261.17.

The Lord was taking a walk in paradise, where he often used to stand and hold a conversation with me, as a man talks with his friend. When the breeze sprang up in the afternoon and the sun moved to its setting, the coldness of malice began to take hold of me. He cried out with a strong, impassioned rebuke, saying in the fierce breath of his anger, 'Adam, where are you?† Look, see where Gn 3:9 you are, because you are not in paradise where I placed you'.

And I answered and said, 'Lord, I heard your voice and I hid myself because I was naked. I have been stripped of the garment of righteousness of your grace and I have shame which is not of your making but of my own.[8] Cherubim stand before you, so I hid myself before your face'.

The Lord God was angry and threw me out of the paradise of good conscience. He made me a garment of skins,† that is, a monk's habit, the Gn 3:21 garment of mortification and a sign of penitence. He passed a sorry sentence on me, which I bear with love and patience, since it is my due. Having become a monk, I began to work the land, which is my flesh, cursed as it was by what Adam had done. I ate my bread in the sweat of my brow because the earth on which I laboured did not bring forth fruit but only thorns and thistles.

And when things were going badly for me, I turned my face towards the road along which I had come out of paradise. I sighed, as I remembered God's mercy, and found some relief. Then I caught

---

8. . . . *habens pudenda quae tu non fecisti sed ego mihi!* The next sentence, with its reference to Cherubim (which Bernard seems to regard as singular) connects loosely. It may be that some small emendation is necessary to make it read something like *ante te stare TERREBAR*, replacing the reference to Cherubim: I was afraid to stand before you.

sight of the cherubim which is the fullness of
knowledge, that is, the father of the monastery,
RB 64.9 learned in the divine law and in Scriptures.† He
brought forth from his treasury new things and
old and held in his hand the sword of discipline,
flaming to inspire terror and flashing to cut off
Cf. Gn 3:24 Vulgate spiritual and carnal vices to right and left.† God
had stationed him there to guard the way to the
tree of life.

Once I had grasped the fact that my return could
only be along this road I learned the discipline of
Pr 31:7 knowledge and, girding my loins with strength,†
I left myself completely open to the sword of
discipline. Thus if it touched my eye, my hand,
my right foot or my left, immediately I presented
it to be removed and cut off, preferring to enter
into the kingdom of heaven one-eyed or lame or
crippled than to be thrown into hell with all parts
Mk 9:42–47 intact.†

Once perfectly circumcised and cauterized by
the sword of discipline, I crossed the fiery torrent
by fighting against my vices and soon, thanks to the
help of obedience and counsel, I was ready to be
formed in virtue. After this, I was able to receive
understanding from the commandments of God.
So that I could understand for myself the ways I
trod, I was found worthy to receive the light of
understanding. Then I came to wisdom which is,
as she herself says, 'a tree of life to all who lay hold
Pr 3:18 of her'.† Like a poor serf, I grasped at her fruit
with all my best endeavours and it was sweet to my
mouth. I ate it with much appetite and afterwards
was found worthy to be restored by it. My past
evils slipped from my mind, my spirit revived and
I became aware of a hope for perpetuity. Already
the fear of the Lord, which neglects nothing, had
repaired the damage inflicted by my negligence,

goodness made up for curiosity, knowledge for concupiscence, fortitude for consent, counsel for habit, understanding for contempt and wisdom for malice since 'wisdom overcomes malice'.†   Ws 7:30

Indeed, I discovered that the extra help which I needed for my return was, in some way, doubled. For servile fear I received chaste fear. For goodness, real goodness which was at once more extensive and more enlightened. For knowledge I received that fullness of knowledge which is charity. I exchanged one fortitude for another, the first was fearful, the second was strong. Of the first it was written, 'You have made fear your fortress',†   Ps 88:41 Vulgate
but of the second, 'The Lord is my strength and my praise'.† In place of the counsel which comes   Ex 15:2
from obedience I have received the counsel which comes from understanding, the understanding of wisdom instead of the understanding of knowledge and even the gift of wisdom herself.

All of this was given to me thanks to that true tree of life which the Greeks call *panxulon*, that is, the universal tree. Through its help I have repaired many times over all the damage done previously when reason deserted me.

Even so, I still warmly desired to receive more profit from God. When I heard Wisdom giving a discourse on the mount of perfections on the subject of the eight beatitudes, I burned with desire to be called blessed and for that octave of which David sang in the Psalm, 'At the end: for the octave',† that is I burned with desire in the hope   Ps 6, 12
of that blessed resurrection, after the sabbath of quiet. I burned for love and cried aloud to the Lord and he heard me. At once, having found the treasure of beatitude in the field of poverty, I went off and sold all that I had and purchased that field. In this way I became poor in spirit. And

so for the other beatitudes. I gained poverty of spirit from fear, meekness from goodness and tears of sorrow from knowledge. For, 'whoever gains knowledge, gains also sorrow'.[9][†] Thus I continued with my bartering until I arrived at wisdom, which accords to those blessed peacemakers the capacity to become God's children. After much sweat and the labour of protracted business I gained all the beatitudes which I have displayed to you today, asking from you the reward or price which Truth promised for each beatitude.

The Lord: It would be a happy world for human beings if everyone worked so hard in such affairs instead of being caught up in the concupiscence of the flesh, the sight of the eyes and worldly ambition.[†] These shallow things and attachments take up their time and finally lead to nothing. Indeed, the memory of such things ought not to occupy the mind or concern the reason or affect the will. In that way the mind is not fragmented, the reason is not rendered blind and the will is not fouled. Thus one lives soberly with regard to oneself, justly with regard to one's neighbor and piously with regard to God.[†] In such a manner is the blessed hope and coming of the great God awaited with joy.

But what is this? Here is another trader carrying items for sale. He has only four bundles. To me he looks like a trader who is seeking fine pearls.[†]

The monk: Such is the case. He is one of many human beings for whom it is sufficient to make a bare living. He is a trader with few resources: a monk whose obedience is lukewarm. He dwells

(marginal references)
Qo 1:18

1 Jn 2:16

Tt 2:12–13

Mt 13:45

---

9. Bernard replaces the Vulgate *laborem* with *dolorem*.

only on the plains, together with that vast multitude from Judea and the sea coasts and from Tyre and Sidon.† He does not desire to go up the mountain of the Lord with the Apostles, nor to stand in his holy place, nor to hear Wisdom giving his discourse on the eight beatitudes. Sufficient for him to hear what is said on the plain, what he has in common with the multitude and with those who come to be cured of their disabilities.† He knows not this meekness. He is ignorant of mercy. He does not ponder on cleanness of heart. He cannot hear what is said of the peace which surpasses all sense. He has poverty of spirit, that is, he has humility and faith. He has the grief of penitence and the hunger for justice. And he has constancy and perseverance in all these things even despite persecution and the terrors of death. He is able to live on these things and without them he cannot live. His teacher is Luke, the Syrian physician who, because he is a physician, knows what is appropriate for him. But he does not reveal to him the delights and riches that Matthew, my tax-collector, prescribed, sitting at his tax desk, for he was devoted to making a profit in such matters and is a master and teacher in all such business.

The Lord: Well, of such is the kingdom of heaven. It is as Job said, 'Both small and great are there'.† To poverty of spirit is due the kingdom of heaven; to those who mourn, consolation; to those who hunger for justice, satiety; to those who persevere in times of trouble, an abundant reward in heaven. But tell me, I pray, O great trader, where did you do business? Where have you made these profits? Where have you gained these things?

The monk: In the monastery. In the cloister. In the discipline of the cloister. This is the place where such business is conducted, this is the means by

Lk 6:17

Lk 6:18

Jb 3:19

which such profits are possible. Nor can I ever recall having gained a profit by going out therefrom.

The Lord: O happy are those who live in that
monastery! I make you an apostle to your brothers.
Tell them for me not to take delight in going out
from the enclosure of that monastery often or in
being at a distance from it or in wandering abroad,
because in the monastery they have the possibility
of such abundant profit.

8. the story of the king and the slave whom he loved

INTRODUCTION

THE FINAL PARABLE consists of a single evocative image. Bernard reminds his monks that although monastic profession certainly has the possibility of making amends for their sinful past, this is dependent on their continuing fidelity. They do not have to fear punishment for what went before so long as they do not continue committing the same offences.

It is a sober, cautionary text which seeks both to forestall the possibility of presumption and to give solid warning about the dire consequences of falling again. It is solid moral preaching, not a considered dogmatic position on the possibility of further forgiveness.

What is, perhaps, most significant is the title. It is the slave whom the king loves—even though this slave has murdered his son. God's forgiveness is motivated by a single force, his immense love for the sinner, which obliterates everything in the past which could be an obstacle to its full expression.

THE PARABLE

The Story of the King
and the Slave Whom He Loved

a CERTAIN CITIZEN KILLED the king's son. When he was arrested to be punished, he began to plead with his judges as though he were seized by repentance. But just as he began to incline them towards mercy, he met another son of the king and slew him also. Who will have pity on him after that?

It is the same in the case of a monk who, when he was in the world, slew his soul through sin. To make up for his sin he has undertaken this life and made monastic profession. If he subsequently, by his negligence, scandalizes the souls of seculars and, as far as he can, slays them, then he cuts himself off from all hope of pardon. Indeed, for a double sin he will be awarded a double penalty.

the sentences

INTRODUCTION

BERNARD OF CLAIRVAUX AS SERMON
WRITER AND SENTENCE SPEAKER

by
John R. Sommerfeldt

ERNARD TOOK VERY SERIOUSLY
his abbatial responsibilities as teacher and
preacher. The ministry of teaching, he
thought, should be exercised by abbots primarily
through the example they give their monks:

> The prelate [whether bishop or abbot] should
> possess a pure heart[†] if he desires to do good 1 Tm 1:5
> rather than merely rule. He must not seek his
> own interests or worldly honor—or any thing
> other than what is pleasing to God and serves
> the salvation of souls. But, with a pure intention
> and an irreproachable life, he must be a model
> for the flock[†] and begin to do and teach.[*] As †1 P 5:3 *Ac 1:1
> the *Rule* of our teacher [Benedict] enjoins: 'By
> his deeds he must make it clear that nothing
> may be done which he has taught his disciples
> is forbidden.'[†] Otherwise, a brother whom he RB 2:13
> corrects may murmur quietly: 'Physician, heal
> yourself.'[1†] Lk 4:23

---

1. Abb 6; SBOp 5:292–93. The translations are mine;
when a good translation is readily available, I shall signal its
location. For Bernard's teaching on abbots and their responsibilities, see my 'Bernard of Clairvaux's Abbot: Both Daniel
and Noah', in Francis R. Swietek and John R. Sommerfeldt
(edd.), *Studiosorum Speculum: Studies in Honor of Louis J. Lekai,
O. Cist.*, CS 141 (Kalamazoo, Michigan: Cistercian Publications, 1993): 355–62.

The abbot must live for the welfare of his monks,
for their happiness,[2] and in this he must be a model
for his monks.

The abbot must also be a teacher, ready with
'useful teaching' for his sons.[3] Both in preaching
and providing guidance, Bernard's abbot must assume the roles of apostle and prophet. Bernard
bemoans the awesome responsibility of this dual
charge in his forty-second sermon on the *Song
of Songs*:

> I am neither prophet nor apostle, but, I must
> say, I act the role of both prophet and apostle.
> Though far beneath them in merit, I am caught
> up in similar cares. Even though it be a great
> embarrassment, though it puts me at serious
> risk, I am seated on the chair of Moses,† whose
> quality of life I do not claim and whose gifts I do
> not experience. But, then, should one withhold
> respect for the chair because the one sitting
> there is unworthy? Even though the Scribes and
> Pharisees sit on it, Christ has said: 'Do what they
> tell you.'[4]†

Mt 23:2

Mt 23:3

In his preaching and his teaching, the abbot
must exercise great discernment. In his tenth sermon on the *Song of Songs* Bernard tells us:

Sg 1:1

> We must return to the breasts of the bride†
> and show how both they and their milk differ.
> Congratulation yields the milk of encourage-
> ment, compassion that of consolation. As of-
> ten as the spiritual mother receives the kiss [of
> the Bridegroom], she feels both breasts flowing

---

2. SC 24.1; SBOp 1:151; CF 7:42.
3. SC 26.6; SBOp 1:174; CF 7:65.
4. SC 42.2; SBOp 2:34; CF 7:211–12. See also SC 42.4–5;
SBOp 2:35–36; CF 7:212–14.

with heavenly milk. You may see her nourishing her babes, suckling them with full breasts, from one the milk of consolation, from the other the milk of encouragement, according as she sees is the need of each.[5]

The burdens of abbatial motherhood are many. The burden of preaching is especially onerous for Bernard:

> See how she [the bride] yearns for one thing and receives another. In spite of her longing for contemplation, she is burdened with the task of preaching. Despite her desire to bask in the Bridegroom's presence, she is entrusted with the cares of begetting and rearing children. Nor is this the only time she has been so treated. As you may remember, once before, when she sighed for the Bridegroom's embrace and kiss, his response was: 'Your breasts are better than wine.'† And this made her realize that she was a mother, that her duty was to suckle her babes, to provide food for her children. . . . So now too, the bride, desiring and enquiring about the place where her beloved pastures his flock and rests at noon,† is given instead ornaments of gold studded with silver,† wisdom with eloquence, and committed to the work of preaching.[6]

Sg 1:1

Sg 1:6
Sg 1:10

' . . . No small effort and fatigue are involved in going out day by day to draw waters from the open streams of Scripture and providing for the needs of each of you . . .', Bernard acknowledges.[7] The greatest burden in preaching is that preparing

---

5. SC 10.2; SBOp 1:47; CF 4:61–62.
6. SC 41.5; SBOp 2:31; CF 7:208.
7. SC 22.2; SBOp 1:130; CF 7:15.

sermons distracts him from the meditation in
which he finds his greatest joy:

> How I wish that all had the gift of teaching!
> I should be rid of the need to preach these
> sermons! It is a burden I should like to transfer
> to another. Or, rather, I should prefer that none
> of you would need to exercise it and all would
> be taught by God.[†] Then I should have leisure
> to contemplate God's beauty.[8†]

But preach the abbot must. Like Paul, he has become ' . . . a chosen vessel to bring God's name
before gentiles and kings and the children of Israel. . . .'[9†]

And preach Bernard did! Twelfth-century cistercian abbots were enjoined to preach to their
communities at least twelve times a year, on the
greater feasts of the liturgical calendar.[10] Bernard
preached far more often than this and, in his tenth
sermon on *Psalm 90*, he offers this explanation:

> . . . You know that the great abbot [Benedict],
> father to you and me, assigned this time to
> manual labor,[†] not to be free for sermons. . . .
> Yet, if I preach to you many more times than
> is customary in our order, I do not do so out
> of presumption, but by the decision of my ven-
> erable brothers and fellow abbots. They have
> charged me to do what, nevertheless, they do
> not wish to allow indiscriminately to them-

Jn 6:45
Ps 45:11

Ac 9:15

RB 48

---

8. SC 22.3; SBOp 1:130–31; CF 7:15–16. See also Dil
27; SBOp 3:142–43; CF 13:119.
9. PP 1.2; SBOp 5:189; CF 53:100. See also SC 8.7; SBOp
1:40; CF 4:50–51.
10. *Consuetudines* 67; in Philippe Guignard (ed.), *Les mon-
uments primitifs de la règle cistercienne*, Analecta Divionensia 10
(Dijon, 1878): 161.

selves. They know it is another matter for me; there is a unique need—for I should not preach to you this often if I could work with you. Then, perhaps, my words would be more efficacious; they would at least be more acceptable to my conscience. Since this is denied me by my sins and, as you know, by the weakness of my burdensome body, as well as by the needs of the time, may I merit to be found the least in the kingdom of God, as one who says but does not.[11]† Mt 23:3

Bernard's response to this permission was overwhelming.

Bernard's literary output was massive—as the nine hefty volumes of the critical edition of his works amply testify—and much of Bernard's literary legacy is in the form of sermons. The critical edition by Jean Leclercq and his able aides contains some one hundred twenty-eight liturgical sermons,[12] four homilies in praise of the Virgin Mother,[13] eighty-six sermons on the *Song of Songs*,[14] nine miscellaneous sermons,[15] one hundred twenty-five sermons on various subjects (*De diversis*).[16] In addition, there are the eight parables[17] and the some three hundred fifty-eight 'sentences' translated in this volume. If my count is correct,

---

11. QH 10.6; SBOp 4:447; CF 25:198–99.

12. SBOp 4:161–492; 5:1–440. Some of them, the *Sermons for the Summer Season: Liturgical Sermons from Rogationtide and Pentecost*, have been translated in CF 53. The lenten sermons on *Psalm 90*, found in SBOp 4:383–492, are translated in CF 25:113–261.

13. SBOp 4:13–58. Translated in CF 18:3–58.

14. SBOp 1 and 2. Translated in CF 4, 7, 31, and 40.

15. SBOp 5:440–47; 6/1:9–55.

16. SBOp 6/1:73–406.

17. SBOp 6/2:261–303.

the total is seven hundred eighteen, and some of
Bernard's sermons are lost to us.[18] With the exception of the *Sentences*, Bernard's sermons—like all
his other works—exhibit a polished literary style
and, often, considerable philosophical and theological sophistication.

In describing the process by which Bernard
produced his literary masterpieces, Jean Leclercq
pointed out that

> the first sketch of a Bernardine writing was
> the result of a great art, but it did not satisfy
> the exacting requirements of its author. Bernard
> reread, listened anew, dictated corrections, and
> practiced that *emendatio* recommended by the
> literary tradition. . . . The variant readings of
> the successive and authentic collections of his
> works as they are preserved in manuscript form
> allow us to witness the author's labors and ap-
> preciate the improvements he made in his style.
> During the last years of his life, this elderly
> abbot, who was also a very active man of the
> Church, took pains to review his own major
> works, letter by letter, in order to prepare a
> revised edition.[19]

The composition of Bernard's sermons on the *Song
of Songs* consumed some eighteen years of his life;
the commentary was left unfinished at his death in
1153. This lengthy and laborious process produced
a literary masterpiece. 'From the treasury of Holy
Scripture', Jean Leclercq has written, '[Bernard]

---

18. See Jean Leclercq, *Études sur saint Bernard et le texte de
ses écrits* (=ASOC 9 [1953] fasc. 1–2) (Rome: Apud Curiam
Generalem Sacri Ordinis Cisterciensis, [1953]): 50–55.

19. Jean Leclercq, *Bernard of Clairvaux and the Cistercian
Spirit*, trans. Claire Lavoie; CF 16 (Kalamazoo, Michigan:
Cistercian Publications, 1976): 32.

drew ideas and, equally, words which his genius and grace caused to sparkle. The beauty of the *Sermons on the Song* explains their influence.'[20]

But Bernard's sermons on the *Song* were not heard by his monks. Like Bernard's other sermons, they were composed to be read, not heard. Jean Leclercq again:

> Seen as a whole, the text of the *Sermons* does not indicate oral delivery. The sermons are long. . . . One simply cannot imagine what period in the Cistercian horarium would have been available during which the monks could hear preached sermons, each of whose texts, if one either read it or delivered it in spoken word, would take up a full hour or more. Moreover, the text is not just long; it is hard to follow. The style is characterized by a great subtlety of phrase and thought in certain places. What audience could fully grasp the nuances? Even though he had prepared his theme by deep meditation, could Bernard himself have delivered, extemporaneously, talks whose expression and doctrine are so perfect in content, so closely reasoned and so precise?[21]

If he had preached the sermons we have, Bernard's monks would have been sent to sleep. Many a monk must have had difficulty reading them, though the medieval monk's familiarity with the classical rhetorical tradition would have better equipped him than us for the task. Indeed, many

---

20. Jean Leclercq, 'Saint Bernard écrivain', in his *Recueil d'études sur saint Bernard et ses écrits* 1 (Rome: Edizione di storia e letteratura, 1962): 351. Reprinted from *Revue Bénédictine* 70 (1960): 590.

21. Jean Leclercq, 'Were the Sermons on the Song of Songs Delivered in Chapter', the introduction to *On the Song of Songs II*, CF 7: xv–xvi.

of Bernard's present-day daughters and sons have complained to me about their father's prolix style.

Bernard's sermons demand an audience—or, better, readers—of great literary sensitivity. On occasion they demand considerable philosophical acumen and theological sophistication. Let one example suffice; it is from the eightieth of Bernard's sermons on the *Song*:

2 Ch 2:5

> Withdraw yourselves, my dear ones, withdraw from those who teach . . . that the greatness by which God is great,† and also the wisdom by which he is wise and the justice by which he is just, and, lastly, the divinity by which he is God, are not God. 'By divinity', they say, 'he is God, but divinity is not God.' Perhaps divinity does not deign to be God because it is what makes God what he is? But, if it is not God, what is it? For either it is God, or it is something which is of God, or it is nothing. Now you do not grant it to be God, and you do not grant, I think, that it is nothing. Rather, you indicate that it is so necessary for God to be God that, not only can God not be God in its absence, but also that by it he is. If it is something other than God, then it must either be less than God, or greater, or equal. How could it be less, if by it God is? There remains the necessity of acknowledging it is either greater or equal. But, if greater, it is itself the highest good; God is not. If it is equal to God, there are two highest goods, not one. Both of these the universal sense rejects.[22]

Bernard's monks certainly had a much better philosophical vocabulary and more dialectical training than do most moderns, but even they surely would

---

22. SC 80.6; SBOp 2:281; CF 40:152.

have found the preaching of such an argument beneficial only as a soporific.

Bernard preached often; but the hundreds of sermons we have from his hand were not preached —certainly not in the form in which we have them. How then are we to know how and what Bernard spoke to his monks at sermon time? The *Sentences* provide the best answer we have. In them the scholar can discover a good deal about the social and intellectual life of the ordinary twelfth-century monk. In them, the reader will recover a world and an idiom far different from those of Bernard's literary sermons; the language of the *Sentences* may well be more accessible to the reader. The *Sentences* are surely closer to the sermons Bernard actually preached than are the artificial and artful literary compositions which are labeled his 'sermons'.[23]

In the *Sentences* we find a stylistic simplicity and homeliness which assure us that Bernard's real sermons were 'warm and intimate little talks, none of whose texts have been preserved save in résumé in the form of a few sentences or "sermons in brief"'.[24] The simpler language which appears here, sometimes betrays the French which was the 'vulgar' language both Bernard and his monks had spoken at home.[25] The *Sentences* are often mere snippets, not treatises or well-constructed literary sermons. Some seem to be notes taken by Bernard

---

23. See Beverly Mayne Kienzle, 'Introduction' to *Sermons for the Summer Season*, CF 53:3–25, especially, 5–11. See, too, Emero Stiegman, 'The Literary Genre of Bernard of Clairvaux's *Sermones super Cantica Canticorum*', in John R. Sommerfeldt (ed.), *Simplicity and Ordinariness: Studies in Medieval Cistercian History* 4, CS 61 (Kalamazoo, Michigan: Cistercian Publications, 1980): 68–93.

24. Leclercq, 'Were the Sermons . . .', CF 7: xvi.

25. See the use of the gallic *guerram* for the Latin *bellum* in III Sent 87; SBOp 6/2:126, 15.

as he ruminated on Scripture, although some, especially in the third section of the *Sentences*, are
relatively well worked out and may be close to the
sermons Bernard actually delivered. Perhaps some
of them are notes and phrases jotted down by ap-
preciative monks after Bernard's talks.[26] Many will
find them edifying; some will find them merely
interesting. All of us can be grateful to Professor
Swietek for translating them so well into an English
which mirrors the original Latin so faithfully.

---

26. See Jean Leclercq, *Monks and Love in Twelfth-Century
France: Psycho-Historical Essays* (Oxford: at the Clarendon Press,
1979): 86–87.

TRANSLATOR'S NOTE

t HE PRESENT TRANSLATION of the *Sententiae* of Bernard of Clairvaux is based on the critical text in SBOp 6/2:7–255. When I diverge from that edition either in following a manuscript variant or by emendation, I have indicated the fact in the annotations which accompany the translation. In a single case (III Sent 39B) I have inserted into the body of the text a variant version of a *sententia* relegated to the critical apparatus in the edition. Otherwise, when substantial variants or textual additions of special interest occur in the apparatus, I have placed translations of them at appropriate points in the annotations.

A word about the translation itself. The *Sententiae* cannot be numbered among Bernard's more sophisticated works; many of them, especially in the first two series, are little more than snippets, and although the level of expansiveness and polish is somewhat greater in the third series, even there the texts do not approach the literary finish of his better-known writings. It would be misleading to translate the pieces in a falsely elevated style, and I have therefore attempted to maintain in the English the rather homespun character of the original. I have also tried to draw a balance between dogged literalism and a freer approach in order to effect a rendering which is accurate but which reads smoothly enough to afford some pleasure. I apologize for the inevitable instances in which the translation goes too far in either direction.

Most of the notes record parallels within the *sententiae* and comparable passages in other bernardine works; I make no claim to completeness in this regard, nor have I made any attempt to identify parallels in works of Bernard's contemporaries or the use of the texts by later writers. Some annotations offer brief literary or textual observations, but I have kept these to a minimum.

Information on the manuscript transmission of the *Sententiae* is provided in the brief introduction to the edition in SBOp 6/2:3–5. More detailed observations on this subject, as well as many valuable reflections upon the content of some of the texts, are found in two works by H.-M. Rochais: *Enquête sur les sermons divers et les sentences de saint Bernard* (=ASOC 18) (Rome, 1962), and 'Remarques sur les sermons divers et les sentences de saint Bernard', ASOC 21 (Rome, 1965): 1–34.

For his encouragement and advice throughout the preparation of this translation, I am deeply indebted to my friend and colleague, John R. Sommerfeldt. Of course, I bear sole responsibility for the errors which remain.

F.R.S.

The University of Dallas

1. the first series

tHERE ARE THREE WHO GIVE witness in heaven: the Father, the Son, and the Holy Spirit. There are three on earth: the Spirit, the water, and the blood.† Similarly, †1 Jn 5:7–8 there are three in hell. We read in Isaiah: 'Their worm will not die nor their fire go out'.† The †Is 66:24 worm and the fire are two evils: by the first the conscience is eaten away, and by the second bodies are burnt up. A third is added—despair, which is surely understood in the phrase 'will not die nor go out'. To those who are in heaven is given the testimony of beatitude; to those on earth, that of justification; and to those who are in hell, that of damnation. The first witness is that of glory, the second that of grace, and the third that of wrath.[1]

2. About the Holy Spirit, Scripture testifies that he proceeds,† he exhales,†a he indwells,†b he †Jn 15:26 fills,†c and he glorifies.†d He is said to proceed in †a Jn 3:8 †b Rm 8:11 two ways: from and toward. From what does he †c Ws 1:7 proceed? From the Father and the Son. To what? †d Rm 8:30 To creatures. By proceeding, he predestines; by exhaling, he calls those whom he has predestined;

---

1. Compare I Sent 41 and O Pasc 2.4–5 (SBOp 5:120–21).

by indwelling, he justifies those he has called; by filling, he heaps with merits those whom he has justified; and by glorifying, he enriches with rewards those whom he has showered with merits.†

See Rm 8:30

3. The Holy Spirit censures the world concerning sin, which it conceals; concerning justice, which it does not dispose when it ascribes justice to itself and not to God; and concerning judgment, which it usurps when it judges rashly, as much about itself as about other things.†

See Jn 16:8–11

4. Until today, a rushing of water—that is, a confusion of thoughts—among the Babylonians makes the earth barren and void.† For when all thought flows around the flesh, it is not possible to hope for any fruit of salvation† from it. And so let the waters be divided from the waters,† so that the soul, as is proper, might claim for herself a modicum of care and meditation. Indeed, let the waters beneath be restrained within certain limits, let them be held to definite channels, so that they might not go beyond the bounds of necessity, and so that those above might spread out more abundantly. As a result of this, the Lord rightly gives his blessing, and our soil will produce its harvest.†

See Gn 1:2
Si 1:22
See Gn 1:6
Ps 85:12

5. Although among the people of God some are carnal and others spiritual, the former still do not utterly lack a desire for eternal things, nor the latter a desire for temporal ones. But they differ in that they strive more intently after different things, and they are judged spiritual or carnal on the basis of those that they prefer. Thus it is that, in both the blessings of Jacob and Esau, the dew from heaven and the richness of the earth are mentioned,† but they do not occur in the same order in each blessing. Isaac says to Jacob: 'May the Lord give you dew from heaven and abundance from the richness of the earth',† but to Esau he says: 'Far from the richness of the earth shall be

Gn 27:28
Gn 27:28

your dwelling-place, far from the dew that falls
from heaven'.† What both of them prefer can be   Gn 27:39–40
inferred from their interests and concerns.

6. 'The death of sinners is the worst.'† It is bad   Ps 34:21
in the loss of the world, because they cannot be
separated without grief from that which they love.
It is worse in the destruction of the flesh, from
which their souls are torn by evil spirits. It is worst
in the torments of hell, when body and soul are
equally sentenced to endless fire. On the other
hand, the death of the good is surely the best, since
then there is rest from labor,† the joy of renewal,   Rv 14:13
and the assurance which derives from the eternal
character of their situation.[2]

7. 'An idler is like a lump formed from the dung
of oxen.'† The oxen are those who exert themselves   Si 22:2
energetically in God's work, who sow in tears but
reap in joy.† They consider whatever things are of   Ps 126:5
this world to be as dung.† But the idler—whose   Ph 3:8
enemies laugh, seeing his downfall†—is dishonored   Lm 1:7
by his enemies in his leisure, just as the hardwork-
ing oxen are honored in their labors† by God.   Ws 10:10
For when the evil spirits see an idler at spiritual
exercises, they rudely force mundane concerns into
his thoughts—as it were, forming lumps from the
dung of the oxen and stoning the idler with them,
just as he deserves.

8. 'Let him kiss me with the kisses of his mouth.'†   Sg 1:1
There are three kinds of kisses: those of reconciliation, those of reward, and those of contemplation.
The first kind of kiss is given to the feet, the second
to the hand, the third to the mouth. Through
the first is received remission of sins, through the
second the gift of virtues, and through the third a
perception of hidden things. Or to put it another

---

2. Compare III Sent 85 (at note 65).

way: they are the kiss of doctrine, of nature, and
of grace.[3]

Sg 4:5
9. The spouse has two breasts,[†] congratulation
and compassion, and there are two kinds of milk—
exhortation and consolation. There are three ointments: compunction, devotion, and piety. Compunction derives from the remembrance of sins,
devotion from recollection of blessings, and piety
from a consideration of the unfortunate.[4]

Sg 6:12
10. 'Turn away, turn away, O maid of Shulam,
turn away, turn away, that we may gaze on you.'[†]
Turn away first from unsuitable joy; secondly, turn
away from useless sadness; thirdly, turn away from
vainglory; and fourthly, turn away from hidden
pride. Vainglory is what comes forth from people's mouths; hidden pride arises within a person. When the soul has left behind all these vices,
her spouse will look on her. She ought to avoid
them, therefore, so that she might be worthy of
his glances. And so it is said to her: 'Turn away,
Sg 6:12 turn away, so that we may gaze on you'.[†]
See Lk 2:8
11. For shepherds to watch over their flock[†]
three things are required: discipline, watchfulness,
and prayers. Discipline is needed because of the
corrupt condition of nature, so that the flock committed to one may not drift off through its own
instability. Watchfulness is required because of the
devil's enticement, lest the flock be seduced by the
cunning of the enemy. Prayers are needed because
of the persistence of temptation, lest the flock be
overcome by timidity. In discipline is the strength
of justice, in watchfulness the spirit of counsel, and
in prayer a feeling of compassion.

---

3. Compare II Sent 164–164B; Div 87.1 (SBOp 6/1: 329–
30); and SC 4.1 (SBOp 1:18–19).
4. Compare I Sent 31; II Sent 168; Div 87.5–6 (SBOp
6/1:332–33); and SC 10.1–12.2 (SBOp 1:48–61).

12. The Creator of the universe has brought into being two creatures to understand him—human beings and angels. Faith and memory justify the human being, while understanding and the presence of God bless the angel. Because humans must somehow be brought to equality with the angels, it is necessary that in the meantime they be justified by faith, and through faith proceed to understanding. For it has been written: 'Unless you have believed, you will not understand'.† And so faith is the road to understanding, for the heart is purified by faith so that the intellect may see God. Similarly, the memory of God is the road to God's presence. For one who remembers his commandments here, so that he observes them, will also deserve someday to behold his presence. Let the angels, then, possess the understanding and presence of God in heaven; let us maintain faith in him and remembrance of him on earth.

Is 7:9, Septuagint version

13. 'We are, Lord, that portion of yours which you took from the hand of the Amorites with your sword and bow.'† Your sword is your living, active word,† and your bow is your incarnation. For in it, as if with the wood of your wisdom curved and your divinity bent in a clearly pious fashion, the sinew of the body is perceived as powerfully extended and humanity as unutterably enhanced. We are, therefore, your portion and the people of your choosing,† whom you have brought to yourself by the word of preaching and by the mystery of the incarnation.

Gn 48:22

Heb 4:12

1 P 2:9

14. In circumcision the sinew is not broken, nor is the bone shattered, so that both may be preserved unharmed, stronger and firmer. But the skin is opened, the flesh cut away, and blood spilled, so that our seductive softness may be punished. By flesh understand the sin which remains in the

body; by skin understand that which conceals it; and by blood understand the incentive to it. It is, therefore, a true circumcision in the spirit, not in the letter,[†] if you tear away the veil of excuse and dissimulation through compunction of heart and confession of mouth; if you cut away the habit of sinning through the correction of your manner of life; and if, as is finally necessary, you shun the occasions of sin and the catalyst of desire.

See Rm 2:29

15. 'They brought him gifts of gold, frankincense, and myrrh.'[†] Perhaps these seemed necessary by reason of the time and place: the richness of gold because of his poverty, the salve of myrrh because of the customary tenderness of an infant's body, and the sweet smell of frankincense because of the filthy condition of the stable. But since all of those factors no longer obtain, we offer him more acceptable gifts—the salve of myrrh in the form of our common life, the semblance of frankincense in the sweetness of our good reputation, and the splendor of gold in our purity of conscience. Through these we zealously seek not the friendly esteem which comes from a dutiful manner of life, nor the empty glory which comes from a favorable opinion of us, but rather the honor of God and the good of our brothers.

Mt 2:11

16. But above all let them be brothers without murmuring.[†] Perhaps some consider murmuring a slight sin, but not the one who warns that it must be avoided above all else. Nor do I think that he considered it a slight sin, who said to the murmurers: 'Your murmuring is not against us, but against the Lord. For who are we?'[†] Nor did it seem so to the one who said: 'You should not complain; some of them did, and they were killed by the destroyer'.[†] By that destroyer, indeed, who was appointed for this purpose—to keep murmurers

RB 34.6; 40.8, 9

Ex 16:8

1 Co 10:10

away from the boundaries of the blessed city, far from the limits of her to whom it is said: 'Praise the Lord, Jerusalem, praise your God, Zion, who has granted you peace on your frontiers'.† For murmuring and peace have nothing in common, nor do thanksgiving and slander, nor the bitterness of jealousy and the sound of praise.† So let the message in the mouth of these three powerful witnesses† remain strong, so that we will know full well that we must shun the plague of murmuring.

17. There are three with whom we ought to be reconciled—human beings, angels, and God. We are reconciled with human beings through open works, with angels through hidden signs, and with God through purity of heart. For of the works which are to be done in public, it has been written: 'Let your light shine in the sight of others, so that they may see your good works and give the praise to your Father in heaven'.† About the angels David says: 'In the presence of the angels I play for you'.† The hidden signs are groans, sighs, the use of haircloth, and other indications of repentance, which are pleasing to the angels. For, as is said: 'There is rejoicing among the angels of God over one repentant sinner'.† But to be reconciled with God, we need neither works nor signs, but purity and soundness of heart. For it is written: 'Happy are the pure in heart, for they shall see God',† and 'If your eye is sound, your whole body is filled with light'.†

18. 'The temple of God is sacred, and you are that temple.'† The temple of God is a cloister of religious. There are two walls to the cloister—the active and the contemplative, Mary and Martha, the inner and the outer walls. Two kinds of stone are required for the inner wall, namely, avoidance of the vices of sensual pleasure and curiosity.

Ps 147:12, 14

See Is 51:3

Mt 18:16

Mt 5:16
Ps 138:1

Lk 15:10

Mt 5:8

Lk 11:34

1 Co 3:17

Likewise two are required for the outer wall: that the monks not be deceitful and that they not be boisterous. This is why the Lord speaks of a faithful and prudent servant†—faithful, lest he be deceitful, and prudent, lest he be boisterous. The wall which joins each together with the other on this side and that are the prelates, along with those who faithfully go in and out,[5]† just as is written of the Lord: 'He has his rising on the edge of heaven, the end of his course is its furthest edge, and nothing can escape his heat'.†

Mt 24:45

Jn 10:9

Ps 19:6

19. A person learns for five reasons—to know, to be known to know, to sell, to build, and to be built. To learn in order to know is curiosity; to be known to know is vanity; to sell is simony; to build is charity; and to learn in order to be built is humility.[6]

19B. 'Those who were reared in the purple', that is, in spiritual delights, 'claw at the dung heaps',† that is, show concern for the stomach.

Lm 4:5

20. 'The beginning of wisdom is the fear of the Lord.'† This initial fear calls back those who are going toward death; it is followed by sadness over mundane things, but the hope of eternal life obviates this.

Ps 111:10

These two—Fear and Hope—take charge of the prodigal son as he sits astride the horse of desire, leading him through the plains of faith.[7] As they proceed Cunning follows them, encouraging them to go over a precipice or off the beaten path. For the world is put in the power of the Evil One.† Hope precedes the horse; Fear follows it.

1 Jn 5:19

---

5. Those 'who faithfully go in and out' are the obedientiaries of the monastery: see I Sent 26.
6. Compare III Sent 57; III Sent 108 (at note 124); and SC 36.3 (SBOp 2:5–6).
7. Compare Par 1.3–5 (SBOp 6/2:262–65).

Prudence is sent to temper Fear. But as Fear is diminished, Hope is increased, and she draws the horse of desire after her too quickly. Temperance is sent to prevent them from rushing over a precipice or off the beaten path by placing a bridle on the horse. And so those four lead the son of the king cautiously until they reach a castle whose name is Justice, where they are received as guests. Their enemies perceive that they are inside the castle and besiege the citadel, trying every device to break through; but they are prevented from doing so by the wall of Reason. For Reason is said to be the wall by which Justice is surrounded. The enemies assail the castle, but do not prevail.

At length those inside the castle realize that they will be prevented from leaving by the host of enemies, and consider among themselves which of them could escape secretly and take word to their king of the danger of their struggle. They conclude that one of their soldiers, whose name is Prayer, is best suited to undertake the task. For the prayer of the just man penetrates the heavens.† There can be no delay, they say; he should depart early in the morning, while the enemies are unaware of it. For 'the just person resorts at dawn and with all his heart to the Lord who made him; he prays in the presence of the Most High.'† When morning arrives, therefore, Prayer passes through the midst of the enemy and hastens right up to the gate of the royal hall. 'Open the gates of justice to me', he says, 'I will come in and confess to the Lord. This is the gate of the Lord, through which the just will enter.'† Having come in to the king, Prayer confesses to the Lord. After hearing this messenger, the king says to his men: 'Whom shall I send? Who shall go on our behalf?'† Whereupon Jeremiah, being put forward, replies: 'Look, I do

See Si 35:21

Si 39:6

Ps 118:19

Is 6:8

Jr 1:6
Is 6:8

not know how to speak; I am a child!'† Hearing
these words, Isaiah says: 'Here I am; send me!'†
In this man Charity is signified; and so Charity is
sent to assist the king's son. It is not enough for
Charity to rescue him; once he has been saved,
Charity rescues others through him. For Paul says:
'Who is weak, and I am not weak too? Who is
made to stumble, and I do not burn with anger?'†

2 Co 11:29

21. People often wonder whether love of God
precedes love of neighbor in temporal terms.[8] It
seems so, since we cannot love our neighbor for
the sake of God unless we love God first. Or
perhaps love of neighbor precedes love of God,
since it is written: 'How can a man who does
not love the brother whom he can see, love God,
whom he has never seen?'† Yet, we must realize
that the love of God should be understood in two
different senses—in its original form and in its
developed one. A person begins to love God before
loving his neighbor; but because that love cannot
be perfected unless it is nourished and expanded
through love of neighbor, it is necessary for him
to love his neighbor. Thus the love of God both
precedes that of neighbor in its original form and
is preceded by love of neighbor in terms of its
necessary development.

1 Jn 4:20

If perhaps there are some who come under
your governance, chastise them lovingly and correct them charitably, with an eye to their eternal
salvation, lest when you spare the flesh, the soul
should be lost. Do these things, even though you
will have to put up with many over whom you will
not be able to exercise proper discipline, because
they will not submit to your rightful jurisdiction.
Endure their threats and be confident, for God
shows mercy and justice toward all who are in-

8. Compare Ep 11.8 (SBOp 7:58).

jured;† he will be merciful toward you if you your-   See Ps 103:6
self have been compassionate. Thus be merciful, so
that the fact that you have suffered injury will not
go unpunished. 'Vengeance is mine,' says the Lord,
'and I will repay them.'†   Rm 12:19

22. 'Love your neighbor as yourself.'† Each per-   Mt 19:19
son ought to love his neighbor as himself, so as to
lead whomever he can to the worship of God—
whether through the consolation of kindness, the
instruction of right doctrine, or the power of discipline. One who chooses these things through
discretion alone is prudent; one who is not distracted from them by any misfortune is strong; one
who is not diverted from them by any pleasure is
temperate; and one who is not turned from them
by pride is just.

23. 'Praise is unseemly in a sinner's mouth',†   Si 15:9
but it is productive in that of a repentant sinner,
and beautiful in that of someone who has been
justified—just as it is not beautiful, but productive,
when fields are manured; it becomes quite beautiful when the crops are harvested.

24. There are four things which impede confession: fear that one may be lost; shame that one
may appear vile; the hope of honor or some other
earthly good if one is considered innocent; and
despair at acquiring such things if one is not considered innocent.

25. There are eight trinities. The first is that
highest and indivisible Trinity: Father, Son, and
Holy Spirit. The second is that which has fallen.
The third is that through which it has fallen. The
fourth is that into which it has fallen. And the fifth
is that through which it rises again, which itself is
divided into three trinities.

The trinity which has fallen consists of memory,
reason, and will. Memory symbolizes the Father,
reason the Son, and will the Holy Spirit, because

just as the Son is generated by the Father, so too
is reason generated by memory; and just as the
Holy Spirit proceeds from the Father and the Son,
will proceeds from memory and reason. Memory,
as it grows distant from the Father, is weakened
in three ways—that is, by thoughts which are either emotional, burdensome, or idle. Emotional
thoughts are those about our flesh, such as about
our parents. Burdensome thoughts are those about
our undertakings. Idle thoughts are those 'about
the king of the English'.[9] Reason is blinded in
three ways, because it often takes what is true for
what is false (and the reverse), or what is permitted for what is not (and, again, the reverse). The
will, moreover, is disgraced in a similar threefold
fashion: through the longing of the flesh, through
the desire of the eyes, and through an ambition for
See 1 Jn 2:16   worldly things.†

The trinity through which it has fallen consists
of temptation, pleasure, and consent. The trinity
into which it has fallen is made up of weakness,
vileness, and blindness. The trinity through which
it rises again consists of faith, hope, and charity.

---

9 Idle thoughts are exemplified by those 'about the king
of the English', presumably because royal matters generally
are beyond the control of ordinary people. Bernard might
also, however, be referring to the contemporary English ruler,
Stephen, with whom he himself had considerable difficulties
in the 1140s, particularly over a disputed election to the see of
York. For a brief account of the relationship between Bernard
and Stephen, including pertinent bibliography, see R.H.C.
Davis, *King Stephen*, 3rd ed. (London-New York: Longman,
1990): 96ff., with whose views I have taken issue in certain respects: Francis R. Swietek, 'The Role of Bernard of Clairvaux
in the Union of Savigny with Cîteaux: A Reconsideration', in
John R. Sommerfeldt (ed.), *Bernardus Magister: Papers Presented
at the Nonacentenary Celebration of the Birth of Saint Bernard
of Clairvaux, Kalamazoo, Michigan, Sponsored by the Institute
of Cistercian Studies, Western Michigan University, 10–13 May
1990*, CS 135 (Kalamazoo: Cistercian Publications, 1992):
290–92.

Faith is threefold; for there is a faith of precepts, a faith of signs, and a faith of promises. Hope, too, is threefold; for there is hope of pardon, hope of grace, and hope of glory. Finally, charity is threefold—with one's whole heart, one's whole soul, and one's whole strength.[†] We have, then, eleven trinities.[10]

See Dt 6:5; Mt 22:37; Mk 12:30; Lk 10:27

26. There should be two walls in any community—one inner, one outer.[11] The inner wall consists of those who are cloistered, the outer of the obedientiaries. The former should not be curious or filled with desire; the latter should be neither turbulent nor deceitful. But because there is rarely peace between the two, there is a third wall, running in the opposite direction, which joins them together. This wall is composed of the abbot, the prior, and the other spiritual brothers. Thus has the sacred foundation been designed.

27. Here is a comparison of the seven gifts of the Holy Spirit to the appearances of the risen Lord. First he appeared to the women, to whom the angel said: 'Do not be afraid';[†] here is the spirit of fear.[†] He appeared to Peter, who had denied him; here is the spirit of piety. He appeared also to a woman, to whom he said: 'Do not touch me, for I have not yet ascended to my Father';[†] this is the spirit of knowledge. He appeared to the eleven on the mount which he had selected, where he told them: 'All authority in heaven and on earth has been given to me';[†] this is the spirit of fortitude. He appeared to the two walking on the road to

Mt 28:5
See Is 11:2–3

Jn 20:17

Mt 28:18

---

10. The text refers to eleven trinities here, although the content (and the introduction to the passage) indicate eight. The difference arises from a calculation here of all the combinations of three touched upon in the text, which do in fact total eleven. Compare also III Sent 5 and Div 45.1–3 and 6 (SBOp 6/1:262–66).

11. Compare I Sent 18.

Emmaus, about whom it is written: 'He opened

Lk 24:45 their minds to understand the Scriptures';[†] here is
the spirit of understanding. And finally he appeared
to the apostles while they were sitting down to eat,
after which he ascended into heaven, because it
has been written of him: 'I, Wisdom, live in the

See Si 24:7 heights';[†] here is the spirit of wisdom.[12]

28. Grace is fourfold. There is the grace which
creates, the grace which redeems and shows pity,
the grace which gives, and the grace which rewards. We see the first in the words 'All things

Jn 1:4 were made through him',[†] the second in the phrase
Jn 1:14 'The Word was made flesh',[†] the third in the words
Jn 1:14 'full of grace',[†] and the fourth in the words 'and of
Jn 1:14 truth'.[†]

29. Peace is fourfold. There is peace toward
God, peace toward one's neighbor, peace in the
flesh, and peace in the spirit. In order that each may
be solid, a foundation must be placed beneath it—
temperance for the peace of the body, fortitude for
the peace of the spirit, prudence for the peace with
one's neighbor, and justice for the peace with God.

Lk 2:14 'Glory in the highest'[†] signifies peace with God;
Lk 2:14 'on earth peace to those of good will'[†] signifies
peace with one's neighbor; 'Peace be with you. . . .

Lk 24:36–39 Look at my hands and feet'[†] signifies the peace of
Jn 20:22 the body; and 'Receive the Holy Spirit'[†] signifies
the peace of the spirit.

Qo 10:1 30. 'Dead flies spoil a bowl of balm.'[†] The flies
are vanity, curiosity, and desire. Because they are
numerous in Egypt and around the sacrifices of the
Egyptians, we in Egypt cannot offer to the Lord

Ps 51:21 our God a 'sacrifice of justice'[†] and charity. And
so we go into the desert, that is into the solitude

Ex 5:3 of the heart, 'a three days' journey'.[†] On the first

---

12. Compare Res 3.6 (SBOp 5:109).

day the husband says to his bride: 'I have come into my garden, my sister, my promised bride'† — Sg 5:1 that is, into the nursery of good virtues. On the second day the bride grows bold and says: 'The king has taken me to his wine-chamber',† that is, Sg 2:4 into the delights of the Scriptures. The third day is the marriage-bed, the fullness of love, in which the husband and bride both delight in one another. Note well that opposed to vanity is the firmness of the virtues; to curiosity, the varied delight of the Scriptures; and to desire, the marriage-bed of that highest love.

31. Charity has two breasts, compassion and congratulation. From compassion one drinks the milk of consolation, and from congratulation the milk of exhortation.[13]

32. There are three things by which unity is preserved: patience, humility, and charity. The soldier of Christ should be armed with these. He should have patience as his shield,† which he bears and See Eph 6:16 turns against all adversities; humility as his breastplate,† which protects his inner heart; and charity See Eph 6:14 as his lance, with which, as the apostle says, one wages 'the war of God'† by encouraging all to a Ex 17:16 response of love† and making himself all things to See Heb 10:24 all people.[14]† It is also necessary for him to have the 1 Co 9:22 helmet of salvation,† which is hope, to protect and Eph 6:17 defend his head—which is the seat of the mind. He should have as well the sword of God's word† Eph 6:17 and the horse of right desire.

32B. Goliath must be killed with his own sword† See 1 S 17:51 —that is, vainglory must be destroyed through reflection on vainglory itself.

---

13. Compare I Sent 9; II Sent 168; Div 87.5 (SBOp 6/1:332); and SC 10.2 (SBOp 1:49).
14. Compare III Sent 38.

33. There are two 'last things'—death and life. We fly to these on two wings, fear and hope. We shoe our feet with two things, repentance of heart and confession by mouth, in accordance with the Scripture: 'Faith in your heart leads to righteousness; confessing with your lips brings salvation'.[†] We cover our head with two things as well, love of God and love of neighbor, for as the apostle says: 'If we seemed out of our senses, it was for God; but if we are being reasonable now, it is for your sake'.[15†]

Rm 10:10

2 Co 5:13

34. Note well that from fear comes compunction, and from compunction comes the renunciation of all things, and from that renunciation comes true humility. From humility in turn arises honest confession, in which there is a cleansing from all vice. From confession also comes a sprouting of virtue, and as the virtues increase they bring about purity of heart, in which reside true wisdom and perfect charity. Additionally, we must know that the spirit of fear[†] bestows fear, the spirit of piety compunction, the spirit of knowledge the renunciation of present things, and the spirit of fortitude true humility. Humility in turn overcomes all things. The spirit of counsel brings confession, the spirit of understanding leads to an increase in the virtues, and the spirit of wisdom effects perfect purity of heart and perfect love.

See Is 11:2–3

35. Note that there are four orders in the house of the Lord. For some fall to Jesus' feet, like the Ethiopians[†] and like Mary Magdalene, repentant and confessing her sins.[†] Others sit at his feet, like the same Mary listening to his words.[†] Still others lie on his lap, while some sit at his side.[†] The first

Ps 72:9
See Lk 7:38
See Lk 10:39
See Jn 13:23

---

15. Compare II Sent 134; III Sent 33; III Sent 92; and Div 123.2 (SBOp 6/1:401–402).

two orders live for themselves, the third for themselves and their neighbor—like the evangelist John,
who took and imbibed peace from his breast and
preached it to the people.† The fourth order lives   See Ps 72:3
for their neighbor, like the apostle, who wrote:
'I have fought the good fight to the end; I have
finished the course; I have kept the faith'.†   2 Tm 4:7
secure, he added: 'All there is left for me now is
the crown of righteousness'.† And so: 'I wish to be   2 Tm 4:8
gone and be with Christ, but for me to stay alive
in this body is a more urgent need for your sake'.†   Ph 1:23–24
Such persons do not fear to die, but neither do
they refuse to live.

36. One sort of pride is blind, a second is vain,
and a third both blind and vain. Pride is blind when
a person thinks there is in him what is not there.
It is vain when he glories in the fact that people
take him to be what he is not. And it is both blind
and vain when he glories inwardly and seeks the
respect of others for having a good which he does
not possess.

37. Humility can be either sufficient, abundant,
or superabundant. It is sufficient when a person
subjects himself to someone who is greater than
he and does not put himself above someone who
is his equal. It is abundant when he subjects himself
to someone who is his equal and does not put
himself above someone who is less than he. And
it is superabundant when he subjects himself to
someone who is less than he. Thus the Lord said
to John: 'Leave it for now; for it is proper that we
should fulfill all that justice demands'.[16]†   Mt 3:15

38. Whoever wishes to please God perfectly
should exhibit chastity as well as charity. Chastity,
moreover, is fivefold: it pertains to the senses of

---

16. Compare II Sent 28.

hearing, sight, smell, taste, and touch. Charity, on the other hand, is fourfold. As the apostle says, it trusts all things, so that it is not suspicious; it hopes for all things, so that it is not sluggish; it endures all things, so that it does not grumble; and

See 1 Co 13:7

it endures all things, so that it is not impatient.†
Note well these nine: he who perfectly possesses them is himself perfect, and he lives out his life on earth in accord with the nine orders of angels. Thus

Ph 3:20

the apostle writes: 'Our homeland is in heaven'.†
And, as I might say, a person living in the way I have described has greater merit than an angel who does so, because for a human being this is a matter of virtue, while for an angel it is a matter of office.

39. A holy soul mortifies her flesh from the foulness of vice when she renounces all the pleasures of the world in a spirit of moderation; and then she applies that moderation to the perishable body as though it were myrrh, so that after judgment the body will remain free of eternal corruption. And since she rouses herself to an ever-greater desire for celestial things and rigorously dismisses all extraneous considerations from the chamber of her heart, she makes her heart as it were a censer doing reverence to God. She collects virtues in the heart through her love, just as one puts coals in a censer; thereby the mind inflames itself with the fire of charity in God's sight. And when the soul sends pure, fervent prayers to God, it is as though she were drawing sweet-smelling smoke from a censer so that a pleasant scent may waft to the beloved one, and she may never cease from encouraging her neighbors toward the love of God through good deeds.

40. 'You must not boil a kid in its mother's

Ex 23:19

milk.'† The kid is a sinner, and the mother the first parents, from whom we have all been born. The milk signifies the vices which come from original sin. 'You must not boil a kid in its mother's milk'† — that is, a sinner cannot be permitted to remain in sin until the day of his death, but before his death he should be recalled to good works, lest he perish.

Ex 23:19

41. 'There are three who give witness on earth: the Spirit, the water, and the blood.'† At his coming the Lord put an end to circumcision and other forms of baptism. Indeed, he instituted the baptism in which he desired the three witnesses named above to be involved, giving, as it were, a testimony to Christianity here on earth. Listen to how the blood of Christ brings it about, and is a sign of the fact, that we should die to sin, as the apostle says: 'Do you not know that we who are baptized in Christ Jesus, were baptized in his death?'† The water which envelops the body like a tomb is a sign 'that we should no longer be slaves to sin'.† 'For through baptism in his death we were buried with him.'† The Spirit revivifies us† and brings it about that we who are buried in that element of water should rise again, renewed by the same Spirit, 'in order that as Christ was raised from the dead by his Father's glory, so we too might live a new life'.† And because 'these three'† work as one, 'they are one', in John's words.† They are one in mystery, not in nature. Thus the blood is the witness of death, the water the witness of burial, and the Spirit the witness of life. Ambrose says that the blood looks to reward, the water leads to purification, and the Spirit renews the mind.[17] The blood of the Lord redeems us, the water of the holy fount cleanses us, and the Spirit makes us, by adoption, sons of God.[18]

1 Jn 5:7–8

Rm 6:3

Rm 6:6

Rm 6:4
See Jn 6:64

Rm 6:4
1 Jn 5:7
1 Jn 5:8

---

17. Ambrose, *Expositio evangelii secundum Lucam* 10.48; in CCL 14:359.
18. Compare I Sent 1 and O Pasc 2.4–5 (SBOp 5:120–21).

42. 'In the fourth watch of the night he came toward them, walking on the lake.'[†] The first sleep is nocturnal fear,[†] that is fear of adversity; and the watch which follows is kept through prudence. The second sleep is 'the arrow that flies in the daytime'[†]—that is, the temptation which is brought about by success; and the watch which follows is kept through fortitude. The third sleep is 'the plague that stalks in the darkness',[†] namely vainglory; and the watch is justice. The fourth sleep is 'the noonday devil that wreaks havoc in broad daylight',[†] which is excess. It is at this point that the Lord comes toward them, walking on the lake. The Lord walks on the lake, but Peter sinks.[†] At first the Lord is thought to be an apparition,[†] but then he is recognized. The other disciples, who are fainter of heart than Peter but still men of faith, praise God in response to such extraordinary events.[19†]

43. Seven characteristics are required in prayers. For prayer should be faithful, in accordance with the Scripture: 'Whatever you pray for, believe that you already have it, and it will be yours'.[20†] Then prayer should be pure, after the example of Abraham, who drove the birds away from his sacrifice.[†] Third, it should be just; fourth, it should be heartfelt, since 'the heartfelt prayer of a just person works very powerfully';[†] fifth, it should be humble; sixth, it should be fervent (these last two characteristics you see in the mustard seed);[†] and seventh, it should be devout.

Mt 14:25
See Ps 91:5

Ps 91:6

Ps 91:6

Ps 91:6

See Mt 14:30
See Mt 14:26

See Mt 15:31

See Mk 11:24

See Gn 15:11

Jm 5:16

See Mt 13:31

---

19. Compare SC 33.11–13 (SBOp 1:241–43).
20. See Mk 11:24, as in *Communion Antiphon for the Twenty-Third Sunday after Pentecost.*

2. the second series

creature endowed with reason ought to love himself in order to be blessed and to love God through whom alone he can be made blessed. This creature's envious persecutor works to corrupt him in each of his qualities. Thus, he deeply perverts and depraves the creature's corporeal aspect through gluttonous desire and an inclination to self-indulgence, and with these two spurs he drives the steed of the flesh, maddened, down the precipice of death. Meanwhile the persecutor invades the invisible portion of the creature's being with spiritual weapons and corrupts it through a twofold pestilence, polluting it with the tumor of pride and the contagion of greed. Thus corrupting all the dough with the vile mixture of this yeast,[†] he snatches away from the human creature the beatitude which he has lost himself. See 1 Co 5:6–7; Ga 5:9

2. There are four things to which we give allegiance in this life: the flesh, the world, the devil, and God. We serve the flesh by subjecting ourselves to the snares of gluttony and by yielding to the stings of lust. We serve the world by panting with swells of avarice and striving for the height of honor. We serve the devil by envying the successes of good people and by swelling up in a spirit

of pride against God. We serve God by humbly
devoting ourselves to works of piety, and by strug-

See Eph 6:12 gling against the powers on high[†] through the
Rm 15:13 power of the Spirit.[†] Moreover, those four rulers
have their particular gifts. The flesh bestows upon
its recruits pleasure of brief duration; the world,
a passing exaltation; the devil, endless captivity;
God, boundless felicity. Only this last is of great
value.

3. It has been ordered by sanction of the Gospel
that on the road of this mortal life we should
See Lk 10:4 salute no one clinging to worldly attachments.[†]
But to those whom we perceive to be detached
from this life we should offer the joy of a cheerful
salutation. And so in the Gospel we find three
kinds of greetings—the Virgin Mary greeted Eliz-
†See Lk 1:40 abeth,[†] the angel greeted Mary,[*] and the Lord Jesus
*Lk 1:28 greeted the disciples after his resurrection.[†] When,
See Lk 24:36; therefore, we see those who had grown old in
Jn 20:19 the sterility of this life climbing the mountains of
confession to give birth to the fervor of penance,
like a child, in their heart, we should offer them
an exchange of greetings, and extend to them, in
the name of the Lord, the gift of forgiveness and
the grace of pardon. Moreover, to those whom we
perceive to be serving the Lord in holiness and purity we should, by encouraging them to still better
efforts, give certain assurance of an abundance of
blessing and grace. To those whom we see striving
to reach the pinnacle of apostolic imitation in the
enclosure of the secluded life, we should pledge,
with the ministry of our living voice, the double
security of peace and tranquility; they sense certain
foreshadowings of these even while they remain in
the body.

4. Three principal factors impelled, under the
direction of his will, the Lord Jesus Christ to undergo the humiliation of the cross and death. First

was his pure, filial obedience, through which he
rendered sacrifice for earlier disobedience.† Se- See Rm 5:19
cond was his profound and compassionate suffering, which prompted his inflexible sense of justice,
an iron rod,† to mercy. Heavy and grave was that Ps 2:9
misery which yoked the necks of men in a common condition of sin and death; it was public and
general, in that it bound the just and the unjust
equally under a similar sentence of damnation; and
it was continuous and perpetual, since unless the
grace of redemption had been effected through
Christ, it would have devoured the whole race of
Adam, trapped in incurable captivity, in the abyss of
damnation. Finally, the third element which drove
Christ voluntarily to death was the incredibly swift
and solemn nature of his triumph; as a result of
it, the inevitable power of the devil and of death
was done away with in an instant, gloriously and
absolutely.

5. The Lord lifts up our head† in three ways: by Si 11:1, 13
lifting our mind from worldly attachments, so that
we can spurn transitory things in the hope of heavenly ones; by conferring on us divine knowledge,
so that we can retain knowledge of those things
which do not appear in time; and by fostering our
love of heavenly things, so that, while we remain
in the flesh, we can nonetheless rise above the flesh
through the exaltation of divine love.

6. Human beings are capable of living in three
ways. One is not doing wrong, which is effected
by a servile fear. Another is not wishing to do
wrong, which a filial fear brings about. The last
is not being able to do wrong, which everlasting
beatitude alone bestows.

7. Four things are said to increase the grace of
our devotion: the recollection of our sins, which
makes a person humble in its presence; the remembrance of punishment, which encourages him to

act well; the consideration of his pilgrimage on this earth, which urges him to spurn visible goods; and the desire for everlasting life, which encourages him toward perfection and impels him to withdraw from worldly attachments by a change in his will.

8. The Lord teaches us about the dullness of our ignorance in three ways: through the generosity of the benefits granted to us, which softens the hardness of our mind and excites us to love; by severe and frequent punishment, which, by giving understanding to one who hears of it, strikes fear in us; and finally by the public contempt of wickedness, which, by covering our face with a look of disgrace, instills shame and modesty in us.

9. The agitation or excitement of our flesh arises from three causes: from the thought which precedes it, since when we draw illicit forms and images inside ourselves, we become agitated in thinking about them; from the fullness of our stomach, since, when the belly is swollen with an excess of food, our lascivious flesh is roused to the impulses of self-indulgence; and from the assault of the wicked spirit, because the more he reflects on his inability to conquer the just, the more vehemently he attacks them through the incitement of the flesh.

10. By the authority of Scripture, we are forbidden to think wrongly,† to speak wrongly,*or to act wrongly.† In thinking wrongly there is either impurity, when we recall vile and sordid things; or pride, when our spirit is aroused and becomes inflated, as though we were superior to our neighbors; or ambition, when at the devil's instigation we yearn for our neighbor's goods in violation of God's commandment. In wicked thought, one of these three elements must always be involved. In speaking wrongly, our words are either empty,

†See Mt 9:4; 1 Co 13:5 *See Rm 12:14 See Si 2:14; 3 Jn 3–4, 11

lacking reason and worth; or slanderous, lessening our brother's goods through the corrosive effect of envy and the power of hatred; or flattering, anointing someone's head with an application of false chrism. In acting wickedly there has to be either pretense, when we intend something other than what we indicate we are doing; or impiety, when we do harm to our neighbors; or shamelessness, when we disgrace ourselves in some other fashion.[1]

11. If we are going to ascend from the valley of tears, we must always strain and strive after higher things. The land is desert, inhospitable and arid.† Ps 63:1 But there are three kinds of deserts. One is just momentary vanity, which we should disdain by moderation of life. It behooves us to go up from this desert as it is written: 'Who is this coming up from the desert, rich in bounty, leaning on her beloved?'† We are rich in bounty when we abound Sg 8:5 in virtues. We lean upon our beloved when we attribute to God anything good we do. There is another desert—the humility of christian simplicity, which is called a desert because almost no one is an imitator of Christ, someone zealous in devoting himself to this good. It is necessary for us to go up through this desert. As it is written: 'Who is this who comes up from the desert like a column of smoke from incense?'† We go upwards like a col- Sg 3:6 umn of smoke from incense when, aroused by our zeal for and exercise of the virtues, we encourage our neighbors to emulate our good actions. There is still another desert, the simplicity or fullness of an even purer innocence. We ought to go up to this desert, because we should strive after true purity,

---

1. Compare II Sent 15.

1 Co 7:34
so that we may be holy in body and spirit.† And so let us go up from the desert of momentary vanity, through the desert of humble simplicity, to the desert of full purity.[2]

12. Our Lord has arrows that belong to him; with them he wounds his enemies, battling them Ps 89:10 'with his mighty arm'.† There are, then, three arrows with which he does them harm: one is the sting of lost wealth, because one is devastated when he remembers the loss of his means of living, and of the riches that served his pleasures. Then there is the curse of physical vexation, which torments even with bodily grief the one whom the Lord perceives to be rushing toward sinfulness, so as to block his way on every side. Finally, there is the hammer of the remembrance of hell, because when one reflects on how he is surrounded on all sides by the weight of corporal punishments, it directs his eyes toward that punishment which will be entirely without end, bringing the horrible furnace of Gehenna to his fearful consideration.

13. There are three other arrows with which the Lord wounds those whom he invites to taste the sweetness of his love. The first is chaste fear, which is so called because it compels the Lord's servants to fear him. It persuades the servant to refrain from forbidden things by reason of its continuous admonition regarding the Lord. The second is devout love, which, while it occupies the mind, enflames it totally with a fire of extraordinarily sweet love. The third is virtuous desire; when it blows over the breadth of the conscience like a gentle breeze, the mind, having forgotten those things which are past and eagerly desiring only the face of the Creator, pines away, because it seeks no end to its longing.

2. Compare III Sent 115 (at note 155).

14. The sacrifice of our thanksgiving which we offer up[†] should be threefold. It should be affective, so that our mind is one with our words.[†] It should bear fruit, so as to bring edification to anyone who witnesses it. And it should be gracious, in order to be pleasing to the Creator who has himself given so freely.

Ps 50:14

RB 19.7

15. We are admonished by the words and exhortations of the holy fathers continually to think well, to speak well, and to act well. Thinking well involves thought which is either honest, causing no impurity; or humble, knowing nothing prideful; or pious, seeking nothing harmful. Speaking well means speech which brings some benefit to its hearer; or which is humble, not teeming with the charms of eloquence; or which is truthful, exhibiting in its composition nothing veiled by deceitful embellishment. Acting well is action which is either pure, in that it exhibits integrity; or pious, in that it demonstrates mercy; or chaste, in that it does nothing to offend or injure the sight of those who behold it.[3]

16. It is customary and commonplace enough for this world to be referred to as Egypt by reason of its blindness and ignorance, because as often as we make progress through a change of will, three things surely assail us. There is the sting of desire, which, like the Red Sea, overwhelms our reasoning power with swelling, stormy waves of thought; and if the higher and lower waters are not parted by the rod of the prudent judge,[†] the flood will rush down and swallow us up. Then comes the great mass of temptations, which, overflowing the banks of its bed like another Jordan, will take possession of the territory of our body even more than usual, if the ark of the covenant—that is,

See Ex 14:16–22

---

3. Compare II Sent 10.

See Jos 3:1–17

See 2 K 2:14

the knowledge of truth—does not intervene to hold back its onslaught, drain it, and dry it up completely.† Finally there is the sting of troubles, which, when it falls upon us—once again like the Jordan, when it obstructed Elisha—requires the cloak of Elijah to be taken up and positioned against the waves,† so that whatever burdens us here in time can, after its taste has been changed through consideration of the Lord's passion, instead delight us with a new sweetness.

17. The roads which lead to death are divided by threefold reasoning. The first is full of hardship, the second full of labor, and the third full of delight. The hard path is for the poor who, in their poverty, swell up with a regal spirit and a passion for riches and are thus drawn from temporal poverty to eternal misery. The laborious road is for the greedy and avaricious, who, while wretchedly tormented in their anxiety over varied concerns, forget to seek

See 1 Co 7:34

those things which are God's† and, panting in their greedy frenzy, pass at the end of their life from temporal disquiet to the punishment of endless labor. The delight-laden route is for those luxuriating in their riches, who, nourishing both their bodies and their hearts with delights and pleasures, are carried down after their momentary joys and transient enjoyments to everlasting sorrows.

Mt 7:14

18. The narrow passage which leads to life† is also divided by a similar sort of reasoning. For one road is red, a second purple, and the third white. The red is for the martyrs, who wash the

Rv 7:14

outside of their bodies 'in the blood of the Lamb'† and, through their journey to martyrdom, attain a throne of triumphant height. The purple is for the confessors, who, in their self-restraint, show traces of the Lord's passion in their flesh and carry the stigmata of Christ's wounds on their bodies. The white is for the virgins, who have consecrated themselves in devotion to angelic purity and the virtue of chastity. Over this road of purity they happily take flight on the wings of virtue and speed to the marriage-chamber and the embrace of the true Spouse.

19. Forgetfulness is the death of the soul. One is aroused from this death in the following fashion: he feels through memory, hears through obedience, sees through understanding, smells through prudence, and tastes through love.

20. There are four kinds of human wills: the arid, the straight, the devout, and the blessed. The arid will is found in fallen and worldly people, whose hearts are not nourished by the dew of grace. The straight will is found among the initiates, who have left behind the crookedness of their prior lives and, with a changed will, rise toward the rectitude of good works. The devout will is found among those making progress, who are raised heavenward by the practice of assiduous prayer in their love of doing well. The blessed will is found in those who have been perfected, who think about almost nothing but God and situate the goal of all their desire in him. Between the arid and the straight will 'a great gulf has been fixed'[†]—namely, perverse intention—so that one Lk 16:26 who might wish to cross it cannot do so. Between the straight and the devout will lies our fixed habit. Between the devout and the blessed will is affection for the body. These three things are like huge stones opposing our progress along the road of our works; they impede our ascent from virtue to virtue.[†] See Ps 84:7

21. The trees[†] are all the just who have been See Ps 96:12 temporally planted in the middle of the Church.[†] Si 15:5 As long as they remain there, they ought to produce the fruits of life. Let each of them see to it, therefore, that he chooses for himself a well-

See Ps 1:3 watered spot, in which in his season[†] he can be productive and bear the fruit of life. There are,
Ps 1:3 moreover, three streams of water.[†] The first is the incentive offered by Scripture, which arouses an honest will in a person through threats and promises. The second involves the gifts of grace, which bring forth[4] the spiritual person from the animal, and, by shaping his foresight and care while
See Jn 16:13 teaching him the whole truth,[†] assist the fruitfulness of his works. The third consists of falling tears which, as they moisten and touch the veins of intention and design with their dew, nourish perseverance, so that the wood of perseverance will not wither away. One who has taken root beside these streams will produce fruit in each and every
See Rv 22:2 month,[†] and the leaves of his branches will assist the well-being of all peoples.

22. Those who become intoxicated do not all do so in one and the same way. For there is, on the one hand, a wine of vice, which comes
Dt 32:32 from the grapes of bitterness[†] and has its beginning with the devil, who gives the human race the bitterness of sin and death to drink. Those who become intoxicated from it become wicked, like him. Likewise there is the wine of difficulty. It comes from the wild vine of the human condition,
See Jn 19:29 which offered to its Lord the vinegar of iniquity[†] instead of wine. Whoever becomes intoxicated by this wine does so not unjustly but by reason of his sin, and in this way his endurance is tested by God. There is also the wine of grace, which comes from
Sg 1:13 the cluster of henna[†]—that is, from the generosity of the Creator. This is the new wine on which the
Mt 9:15 attendants of the bridegroom[†] are sated. It is put
Mt 9:17 into new skins.[†]

---

4. I follow the variant 'efficiunt' rather than 'effectum' of the critical text.

23. All of the elect are kings and priests, and it is appropriate for them to be christened with the oil of anointment.† That oil is, however, threefold. Ex 29:7, 21, etc. First is the oil of effusion, that is, the word of God, through which the elect are initiated so that, putting off the old man,† they can, like youths, Col 3:9 grow in love of the Spouse. The second form is the oil of purity, with which the flasks of our works ought to be anointed, because the fire of divine fervor ought to be nurtured continuously in the lamp of our heart. Third is the oil of exultation,† Heb 1:9 specifically the highest charity, which extends the mind which it has filled, so that, tasting how sweet the Lord is,† and sitting on the summit of justice, See Ps 34:8 the mind can rejoice and glory in God alone.† See 2 Co 10:17

24. Christians have taken their name from Christ. It is difficult but necessary that, just as they are heirs of his name, so too should they be imitators of his sanctity. There are three characteristics of Christ which should be expressed in us, and which we should practice with all our strength. The first is to reject firmly the vanity of the world, as Jesus did when he fled rather than be made king by the mob.† The second is intently to exercise patience, See Jn 6:15 since Jesus was cut down like a lamb.† The third is See Is 53:7 that we should honestly practice a twofold charity, just as Jesus prayed for his enemies.† See Lk 23:24

25. Humility has seven levels of descent. The first is the dismissal of things, in the fashion of the apostles.† The second is the rejection of garments, †See Mt 10:9–10; as in the cases of Elijah†a and John.5†b The third is Mk 6:8–9; Lk 9:3, the exercise of the body, after the example of Paul.†c 10:4; Ac 4:32 The fourth is sadness in the face of prosperity, †a See 2 K 2:13 like David, who was both pauper and king. The †b See Mk 14:52 †c See 2 Co 11:23–28

---

5. Bernard apparently follows such commentators as Ambrose, Chrysostom, and Bede in identifying the young man mentioned in Mk 14:52 as the apostle John.

fifth is patience in adversity, in the fashion of Job and Tobit. The sixth and seventh are to shun our own judgment and to despise the tendency of our own will.

26. The arms of virtue—which the weapons of negligence attack—are a full understanding of sin, which drives out the darkness of desire; the affliction of penance, which serves against the pleasure of carnality; a true and humble confession, which is effective against the destructiveness of wickedness; an appropriate and worthy fear, which works for the alteration of our original will; and a complete measure of perseverance, so that the full protection of sanctity might be attained.

27. Three things are necessary for penance. The first is abstinence, by which the pride of the flesh is tamed. The second is meditative reading, by whose fruit the spirit is nourished in order to be brought back to full strength. The third is prayer, under whose defense and protection the multitude of virtues is guarded.

28. The virtue of humility has these three elements: subjection to a superior, so that one is not seized by envy or by any ambition to be his equal; a refusal to be set over one's equal, lest one should seem to wish, through an impermissible longing, to become his superior; and a preference for being subjected to, rather than placed over, one's inferior, so that one's true humility may thereby be confirmed.[6]

29. All do not progress to God at the same pace. Some do so step by step, such as those deeply involved in the cares of the world, who hardly ever strive to remember the Lord. Others proceed at a moderate gait, such as those who are devoted to the service of the Lord and do indeed serve God,

---

6. Compare I Sent 37.

but still are too indulgent toward themselves. Still others make progress like the wind, at a rapid pace, such as those who perceive themselves beyond their flesh and, despising both themselves and all passing things, proceed quickly to God, desiring only to rest peacefully in him.† See Ps 4:8

30. There are three places: heaven, earth, and hell. Each has its own inhabitants: heaven, only the good; earth, good and bad intermingled; and hell, only the wicked.

31. The human race labors under a threefold disease—at the beginning, the middle, and the end; meaning at birth, in life, and at death. Its birth is impure, its life perverted, its death dangerous. Christ came, and against this threefold disease he brought a threefold cure; he was born, he lived, and he died. His birth cleansed ours; his life served as a model for ours; and his death destroyed ours.[7]

32. Three things await the elect in the future: abundance within, eternal delight, and joyous pleasure. About these it is written: 'The just rejoice',[8]† Ps 68:3 and so on.

33. The longing of the elect is threefold. The first part is to live harmoniously in the Lord, whence it is written: 'One thing I ask of the Lord, one thing I seek'.† The second is to obtain a victory Ps 27:4 over the world, whence it is said: 'Who will free me from this body doomed to death?'† The third Rm 7:24 is to be released and to be with Christ, whence comes the statement: 'I wish to be freed and to be with Christ'.† Ph 1:23

34. The fear proper to prelates has three aspects: that their splendid display should not disturb the spirits of those who listen to them; that their rather

---

7. See *Preface for Easter Mass.*
8. Ps 68:3, as in the *Alleluia Versicle of the Common Mass for Martyrs.*

extravagant style of life should not offend the eyes
of the inner judge; and that the punishment of
justice should not fall upon them in the present
life.

35. The grief of the saints is threefold: because
they have fallen from paradise, because they are
trapped in exile from it, and because they are
separated from the kingdom.

See Ps 68:16

36. On God's mountain of mountains[†] there
were two things for Christ: the bond of his passion
and the richness of his holiness.

37. We ought to sacrifice three calves to the

See Ex 24:5

Lord:[†] our disposition immediately after our conversion, which is like the new calf with horns

Ps 69:31

and hooves;[†] the development of reverence in us,

See Gn 18:7

which is the most delicate calf in the herd;[†] and
the resultant perfected virtue, which is the fatted

See Lk 15:23

calf.[†]

38. That which oppresses us is fourfold. The
first element comprises the difficulties of our cor-

Ps 18:4

ruptible corruption, which are the pains of death.[†]
The second embraces the troubles connected with

Ps 18:4

temporal ills, which are the fires of iniquity.[†] The
third involves the hidden snares of the secret enemy,

Ps 10.5

which are the sorrows of hell.[†] The fourth includes
the deceptive appearances of earthly glory, which

Ps 18:5

are the snares of death.[†]

Ps 18:8

39. Smoke[†] arises from God's anger, because
the elect are purified with respect to the wrath

Ps 18:8

of God. Fire comes from his face,[†] because the
elect are raised to love of him through knowledge

Ps 18:9

of his presence. A cloud is under his feet,[†] because
through his strict judgement the wicked are hidden
in the mists of desperation.

Ps 104:3

40. The Lord walks on the wings of the winds[†]
when the elect touch, even if only slightly, his

sweetness. He soars[†] when they experience noth- Ps 18:11
ing of his all-embracing being. Thus it is written:
'Hasten away, my beloved'.[†] The Lord has estab- Sg 8:14
lished a deep and profound darkness as a hiding-
place for his divinity,[†] pitched the tent of his flesh See Ps 18:11
in the sun of manifestation and labor,[†] and built See Ps 19:4
the dwelling-place of his mansion in the light of
purity and holiness.

41. There are two earthly gates through which
we enter the world: corrupt sensuality and impure
desire. Thus it is written: 'They approached the
gates of death'.[†] The gates of hell are blind des- Ps 107:18
peration and hard obstinacy. Thus it is written:
'The gates of hell will not prevail'.[†] The gates of Mt 16:18
heaven[†] are humble patience, which is the gate of See Gn 28:17
iron leading to the city,[†] and the harmony of love, Ac 12:10
which is the eastern gate.[†] See Ezk 40:6ff.

42. There are four kinds of recompense: two
in the present life and two in the future one. The
first two involve repayment for the prosperity and
wealth of the wicked. Thus it is written: 'They
have received their reward',[†] namely the reward Mt 6:16
of their disgrace and damnation. The second two
involve the reward of the fellowship and grace of
the just, of the sweetness of love and glory. There
are, moreover, two things which are rewarded: just
labor and purity of heart.

43. There are three lanterns: the example of
discipline in Christ, which is lit so that the lost
drachma might be found;[†] the beauty of the truth Lk 15:8
in the Gospel, which is placed on the lampstand;[†] Mt 5:15; Mk 4:21;
and purity of knowledge in a good heart, which is Lk 8:16
lit by the Lord.[9]

44. Our feet ought to be like those of the stags[†] Ps 18:33
and the calf.[†] Ezk 1:7

---

9. Compare II Sent 123.

Ps 18:45
1 S 2:12

45. Some are the foreign sons who lie;[†] others are the sons of Belial who do not know God;[†] and still others are the sons of Israel who do know God.

See Lk 8:5–8

46. Seed is of three kinds.[†] The first is the seed of truth and justice, which when sowed in the earth

Lk 8:8

produces a hundredfold crop.[†] The second is the seed of wickedness and ignorance, which is the

See Lk 3:7

brood of vipers.[†] The third is the seed of malice and error, which is the seed of Canaan, not of

Dn 13:56

Judah.[†]

47. The wisdom of God, like the partridge,

See Jr 17:11

fosters sons whom she has not herself borne;[†] and,

Mt 23:37

like the hen, takes her chicks under her wings;[†]

Dt 32:11

and, like the eagle, encourages her young to fly.[†]

48. Our garment has two parts: penitential anxiety, which is the cloak of widowhood; and religious maturity, which is the cloak of virginity.

See Gn 27:15
Gn 27:16

49. The clothes of Esau[†] are honesty of life and maturity of discipline. The skins of the kids[†] are the rejection of harmful sin and the mortification

See Gn 27:17

of one's will. The foods[†] are joyful obedience and humble patience. Father Isaac touches his son with his outstretched hand in order to secure proof of his

†Gn 27:21
*Gn 17:26
Gn 27:23

identity.[†] He kisses him* as a result of secret inspiration. He blesses him[†]because of his advancement in religion.

50. Three things are necessary to purity: fullness of action, simplicity of intention, and tranquility of devotion.

51. Purity brings three gifts: a spirit of freedom, a joyful assurance, and a secure charity.

See Ps 37:20

52. The wicked are sometimes like smoke,[†] because as they ascend they vanish. At other times

See Ps 1:4

they are like dust,[†] because they exude none of the moisture of charity. At other times they are like

See Ps 58:8

wax,[†] because they easily melt with heat, that is, under pressure of temptation.

53. The gates of Zion[†] are the sacraments, without which we cannot enter the Church. The gates of justice[†] are the intermediate virtues, which we practice in the temporal sphere. The eternal gates[†] are the principal virtues, which we will possess in the future life.

Ps 87:2

Ps 118:19

Ps 24:7

54. There are three things that make us subject to God's punishment. One is the seal of nature, because we are made in the image of God.[†] The second is the talent of faith, because through our good works we ought to restore it in full to God.[†] The third is the glory of our profession, by which we are bound to serve God through the bonds of our vow.

Gn 1:26

See Mt 25:14ff.

54B. God examines us in three ways: through the promulgation of his commandment, so that our obedience may be made apparent to ourselves; through the application of the whip, so that our patience may be revealed to our neighbors; and through the revelation of his mystery, so that the virtue of humility may exhibit itself to us.

55. Tribulation brings three gifts: discipline, lest love of virtue should grow cold through the tepidity of leisure; trial,[†] so that the strength of constancy may serve as an example to other people; and reward, so that one will receive a great weight of glory beyond the measure of his suffering.[†]

Rm 5:4

See 2 Co 4:17

55B. Three things should oppose adversity: the struggles and tribulations of the elect, which those who live piously suffer;[†] the sufferings and pains of our Redeemer, which the cruelest princes inflicted upon him; and the power of a controlling justice, whose height, like that of the rod of Joseph,[†] we should not dissipate, but adore. These are those three doors, bars, and boundaries, by which the Lord surrounded the sea of this world.[†]

See 2 Tm 3:12

Heb 11:21

See Pr 8:29

56. The discipline of the elect is threefold: austere fasting, by which the earth of the flesh is tended, so that it may bear fruit; assiduous meditative reading, by which the spirit is restored, so See Rm 7:22 that the inner person[†] may grow in fertility; and perseverance in prayer, through which the mind rises to a longing for heavenly things.

57. God, the author of miracles, worked three specific wonders in Mary. He marvelously instilled full purity in her, so that the ark of the covenant See Ex 25:11 could be covered with the purest gold.[†] He made her virginal purity flourish powerfully, so that the See Ex 3:2 burning bush could not be consumed.[†] He remarkably joined together the lowest things with the highest, so that, through the medium of Ja- Gn 28:12 cob's ladder,[†] earthly things could be linked with heavenly ones.

58. The fruitfulness of Mary benefits us in three ways. It takes away the yoke of our ancient captivity, turns aside the wrath of divine indignation, and effaces the mark of human iniquity.

59. The elect await three things in the future life: that what is mortal in them should be wholly See 2 Co 5:4 absorbed by life;[†] that they should be enriched by 2 Co 4:17 the reward of eternal glory;[†] and that they should See 1 Jn 3:2 contemplate God endlessly, just as he is.[†]

60. The wicked are said to hope for three things: that their bodily desires should be fulfilled to their satisfaction; that their momentary glory should suffice for their happiness; and that their characters and deeds should not be condemned by any judgment.

61. An imitator of Christ should do three things: cling to a sense of simple innocence, so that he may be made a child with Christ; love a common, humble mode of dress, so that he may be wrapped in the poor garments of the infant Christ; and walk

simply under discipline, so that he may be placed in the manger with Christ.

62. Some of the highest spirits are administrators[†] who are responsible for our salvation. Others are workers who are the actual instruments of human well-being. Still others are contemplatives who serve at the face of the divine majesty.[†]

See Heb 1:14

See Tb 12:15

63. The highest spirits are nourished by the vision of God, intoxicated by his sweetness, and filled with his love.

64. Those awaiting God ought to be uncertain about when he will come and doubtful about what he will bring them. They should be joyful, devout, and carefully prepared. They should also hope for three things in his coming: the presence of the Spouse, his intimate favor, and his free generosity.

65. There are three kinds of weddings. The first is the marriage of reconciliation through faith, in which there are three banquet courses: the remission of sin, the effect of grace, and the reformation of nature. The second is the marriage of adoption through devotion, in which are served the consolation of divine eloquence, the sharing of heavenly nourishment, and a libation of internal sweetness. The third is that of glorification through love, whose courses are eternal incorruptibility, true glory, and the endless vision of God.[10]

66. There are three kinds of horses: worldly pride, whose rider falls backward;[†] spiritual knowledge, whose neck is covered with a flowing mane;[†] and absolute purity, which the whole army of heaven, dressed in white robes, rides.[†]

See Gn 49:17

See Jb 39:19

See Rv 19:14

67. The words of God's consolation are the remission of guilt, the restoration of grace, escape from exile, the coming of the kingdom, an

---

10. Compare III Sent 115 (at note 156).

association with divinity, and the attainment of eternal life.

68. The faithful have three kinds of weapons: complete wisdom, which is the sling of David, from which the stones of judgement are launched; firm patience, which is David's staff, by which the rage of wolves is rebuffed; and full charity, which is David's purse, from which prayers pour forth.[†]

See 1 S 17:40

69. Prelates require three qualities: vibrant purity of faith and doctrine, so that they may all dwell 'in the same region';[†] studious determination to act well, so that they may keep watch with the shepherds;[†] and diligent concern for the well-being of those placed under them, so that they may guard their flock.[†]

Lk 2:8

See Lk 2:8

See Lk 2:8

70. The plowman needs two things: a pleasant voice, which can sweeten the effort of the laboring beasts; and a quick whip, which can drive sluggishness out of the lazy ones.

71. There are three kinds of penance. One is simulated and impure, of which we have examples in Esau[†] and Saul.[†a] The second is necessary but imperfect, such as existed in David.[†b] The third is useful and perfect, such as we see in Mary Magdalene[†c] and Zacchaeus.[†d] This last one has five elements: contrition of heart, confession by mouth, mortification of the flesh, chastisement in action, and perseverance in virtue.

[†]See Gn 33:4
[†a] See 1 S 15:24–31, 24:17–22, 26:17–25
[†b] See 2 S 12:13–14
[†c] See Lk 7:36–50
[†d] See Lk 19:1–10

72. We find three things in Peter: unity of faith,[†] true penitence,[†] and firm love.[*]

See Mt 16:16
[†]See Mt 26:75
[*]See Jn 21:15–17

73. There are three kinds of changes. The first is the change from the sublime to the humble, as when the Word became flesh.[†] The second is the change from the contemptible to the majestic, as when our Lord while in human form transfigured himself.[†] The third is the change from the transitory to the eternal, as when, having risen, the Lord ascended to rule in heaven.[†]

Jn 1:14

See Lk 9:29–31

Lk 24:50–52; Ac 1:9

74. The things that we do, we do either in light of the favor of other people, so that we may please them; or in light of our own favor, so that we may believe ourselves to be acting rightly—which is itself bad; or in light of the favor of God,[†] so that See Ps 89:15 we may humbly ascribe to him alone whatever good there is in us.

75. Three things undermine patience: the excessive anxiety which arises from grief; the just cause of an innocent person; and the baseness of his attacker.

76. One who separates himself from human society loses the consolation of companions. An unwillingness to accompany his confrères comes over him. In his wandering he easily strays off the proper path, and the ruin of his life frequently results.

77. The Pharaoh has three slave drivers:[†] a fer- Ex 1:11 vent desire for overwhelming luxury, a raging anxiety resulting from insatiable avarice, and a harmful longing for empty recognition.

78. There are in us three princes who must die in order that Christ may live: care over mundane affairs, which is represented by Joseph; eloquence in spiritual matters, which is represented by Moses; and an abundance of temporal goods, which is represented by Joshua.

79. There are three refuges for the wicked. There is a pattern of deception and deceit, which is the city of Pithom.[†] There is the defense of earthly Ex 1:11 power, which is the city of Rameses.[†] There is, Ex 1:11 finally, the false appearance of justice, which is the city of the sun.[†] It is Pharaoh who orders these Jos 19:41 three to be built.

80. There are three goblets which the Lord offers to us: the cup of penitence and grief, which is much diluted;[†] the cup of penitence and effort, See Ps 75:8

See Mt 26:42
See Ps 23:5

from which Jesus drank;[†] and the cup of benevolence and love, which is splendid and intoxicating.[†]

See Jg 4:7, 24; Ps 83:9
Jn 18:1
See Ps 110:7
See 1 S 17:2–6

81. There are five torrents. The first is that of
cruelty and malice, which is Kishon, where Jabin
was destroyed.[†] The second is that of philosophy
and eloquence, which is Kedron, beyond which
Jesus passed.[†] The third is that of suffering and
hardship, which is the stream from which Jesus is
said to have drunk on his way.[†] The fourth is that
of celestial wisdom, at which Elijah is nourished.[†]
The last is that of joy and gladness, from which the
elect drink.

82. We are renewed in four ways: in the flesh,
freed of original sin through the mystery of baptism; in the mind, freed from the vice of error
through an understanding of truth; in our action,
freed from actual wrongdoing through the curative
power of penance; and in the flesh and the spirit,
through the gift of resurrection.

83. There are four kinds of lands. The first is
marked by freshness and the flowering of temporal
goods, which is irrigated as paradise was.[†] The
second is characterized by usefulness of life and
the fellowship of the elect, from which comes
bread.[†] The third is marked by the sweetness of
the heavenly mansions, which flows with milk
and honey.[†] The fourth is the site of the infernal
regions, which is the land of darkness and misery.[†]

See Gn 2:10
See Jb 28:5
Ex 3:8
Jb 10:22

84. There are four kinds of deserts. The first is
the impassable anxiety of our earthly exile, from
which David came forth.[†] The second is the harsh
height of christian discipline, in which the sons
of Israel wandered.[†] The third is the delightful
expanse of the heavenly Jerusalem, in which the
ninety-nine sheep are left.[†] The fourth is the horrible, destitute space of hell, which is the desert of
solitude.[†]

See Ps 63:1–3
Dt 8:2
See Lk 15:4
Jr 12:10

85. There are four kinds of chariots. The first

is that of exaltation and power, on which Pharaoh was drowned.† The second is that of humility and zeal, in which the eunuch was seated.† The third is that of devoutness and submission, in which Joseph was seated when he met his father.† The fourth is the chariot of love and desire, in which Elijah was taken up.[11]†

See Ex 15:4

Ac 8:28

See Gn 46:29

2 K 2:11

86. The ascension of the Lord has three aspects. It is victorious, because he ascended beyond the clouds.[12]† It is splendid, because he ascended beyond the heavens.† It is glorious, because he ascended beyond the wings of the winds.†

Ps 68:5

Ps 68:34; Eph 4:10

Ps 18:10

87. Some take the kingdom of heaven by force,† such as the poor in spirit.† Others buy it, such as those who make friends through their riches, tainted though they are.† Still others snatch it, like the woman who touched the fringe of Christ's cloak.† And some are compelled to enter,† such as those poor in worldly things.[13]

See Mt 11:12

Mt 5:3

Lk 16:9

See Mt 9:20
See Lk 14:23

88. There are four things which bring us true humility: the meanness of our work; the constancy of our subjection to others; the comparison between us and those who are better; and the judgment of our Creator.[14]

89. There are three judgments: another's; our own; and God's.

90. Sometimes it is one's life that makes death precious,† as is the case with the confessors; sometimes it is the cause of death, as with the martyrs; and sometimes both one's life and the cause of death, as occurs in many instances.[15]

Ps 116:15

---

11. Compare II Sent 142 (at note 23).

12. The words 'super occasum', here translated as 'beyond the clouds' after the psalm, can also mean 'over death', strengthening the idea of victory.

13. Compare Div 99 (SBOp 6/1:365–66).

14. Compare III Sent 16 and III Sent 37.

15. Compare III Sent 85 (at note 64) and Div 64.1 (SBOp 6/1:297).

See Col 2:13
Dt 10:16
See Ex 6:12

See Jr 6:15

See Heb 7:16

See Rm 7:14

91. There are three kinds of foreskin that are cut off: the foreskin of the flesh in the Jew;[†] the foreskin of the heart[†] in the Christian; and the foreskin of the tongue[†] in one who is perfect.

92. There are four times: of prefiguring, of foretelling, of visitation,[†] and of redemption.

93. God comes to us in four ways. First, he comes through the publication of his commandment, for his commandment is both carnal[†] and spiritual.[†] Second, he comes with the harshness of the whip for five reasons: so that he may correct our iniquity; so that no one will be proud over the virtue he has achieved; so that the virtue of a person may be publicized through his floggings; so that he may restrain others through his example; and so that his crown may be increased and augmented. Third, God comes to us in the wonder of a miracle, which is both visible and invisible. Finally, he comes in his keen inspiration.

†See Gn 25:22
†a See Gn 25:27–
34; Gn 27:1–40
†b See Gn 30:25ff.
†c See Gn 32:24

94. Jacob wrestled four times: in the womb with Esau;[†] in his youth, again with Esau;[†a] in Mesopotamia with Laban;[†b] and in Bethel with the angel.[16†c]

See Ws 7:3
See Jn 11:35
Lk 19:41
†See 2 Ch 26:19
*See Ezk 9:4
See Ex 28:36–38
†See Jl 4:12
*See Mt 5:1
Is 6:1
See Ps 77:18
See Si 40:13

95. Jesus is said to have wept three times: at his birth,[†] for the human race; in the course of time, for Lazarus;[†] and finally in Jerusalem, over its impending destruction.[†]

96. On our forehead we sometimes carry leprosy,[†] sometimes the letter Thau,[*] and sometimes the golden plate.[†]

97. The Lord is seated sometimes in the valley of Jehoshaphat,[†] sometimes on the mount,[*] and sometimes on a high throne.[†]

98. Some thunder is accompanied by lightning,[†] some by rain.[†]

---

16. Compare III Sent 39–39B.

99. The prophet urges on his donkey with two spurs:[†] shame, that he may not be disgraced in this world; and fear, that he may not be punished eternally.[17]   See Nb 22:21ff.

100. Three things bind and restrain us, and can, as it were, be called belts: the recollection that we are going to die, which is the leather belt worn by Elijah[†] and John;[†] honesty[18] and becoming modesty, which is the belt which Aaron wore when he was going to God;[†] and the love of religion and justice, which is the golden belt which girds Jesus at the waist.[†]

See 2 K 1:8
See Mt 3:4; Mk 1:6
See Lv 16:4

See Rv 1:13

101. There are four virgins with whom we ought to join in marriage: philosophical eloquence, which is represented by Zilpha, Jacob's maid-servant; just judgment, which is represented by Laban; true innocence, which can be called Leah; and spiritual contemplation, which Rachel represents.[†]   See Gn 29–30

102. The bride has two eyes:[†] consideration of the things that pass away, which is like a fiery flame;[†] and a worthy estimation of the heavenly fatherland, in which the heart of the spouse is ravished.[†]

Sg 1:14

Rv 1:14

Sg 4:9

103. God's ministers have three common vestments: heavenly wisdom, which is the ephod[†] and covers the head; perseverance in justice, which is the alb[†] covering the entire body; and bodily chastity, which girds the loins.[†]

See Ex 25:7

See Ws 18:24
See Ezk 44:18

104. Three lampstands are found in the Scriptures. There is the obscurity of the law, which has calyxes and petals.[†] There is the subtlety of the   See Ex 25:31

---

17. Compare II Sent 150 (at note 25).

18. The edition reads 'probabilitas' here, which I have emended to 'probitas' for the translation as 'honesty'. If the original reading is maintained, the translation might be 'credibility'.

See Zc 4:3
prophets, which has two olive-trees at its top.† And
there is the truth of the Gospel, which has at its
See Rv 1:13
center a figure like the Son of Man.†

105. Three fortifications defend the soul: assiduous watchfulness, which is the enclosure; the
intercession of the saints, which is the strongest
possible palisade; and divine protection, which is
the wall defending the soul from the enemy's assault.

106. A tripartite reckoning defines and strengthens our hope. The first element is the humility
which derives from accumulated wisdom; its effect on hope may be compared to boiling an egg
in water. The second is the firmness of constant
patience; its effect is comparable to roasting an egg
over a fire. The third is the truth which comes from
hidden inspiration; its effect may be compared to
frying an egg in lard.

107. There are three means whereby God takes
vengeance on his enemies. There is the remedy of
a salutary washing, as when the Red Sea destroyed
See Ex 15:23–28
the Egyptians.† There is the exercise of appropriate
punishment, as when brimstone wiped out the sin-
See Gn 19:24–25
ners of Sodom and Gomorrah.† There is the harshness of the Last Judgment, which is like the fire
See 1 K 18:36–38
which consumed the sacrifice at the call of Elijah.†

108. There are three beds on which the soul re-
poses. First, there is the burden of bodily weakness,
on which the sick man made well by Christ had
See Jn 5:7–9
lain.† Second, there is the tranquility of a secure
conscience, on which a figure was put in David's
See 1 S 19:13
place when he fled Saul.† This is the bed, moreover,
for which two cushions are supplied—with respect
to the past, a full sense of confidence and assurance;
and with respect to the future, certainty of reward
and benefit. The pillow which supports the head
is the generosity of divine friendship and grace.

The third bed is the ability to achieve higher glory. This is the bed all green,† which sixty champions surround.† [Sg 1:16] [Sg 3:7]

109. There are three types of glass through which the sun's rays shower upon us. The first is complete charity, through which remission pours forth for the sinner.† The second is pure humility, through which heavenly grace came to Mary.† The third is subtle understanding, through which the ray of wisdom illuminates the heart. [See Lk 7:47] [See Lk 1:28, 30, 48]

110. Seven lamps shine upon the throne† of the elect mind: namely, the gifts of the Holy Spirit, which the prophet describes more fully.† While they consume the oil of glory, along with the wick of fear and infirmity in heavenly fire, they provide endlessly the light of truth. [See Rv 4:5] [See Is 11:2–3]

111. There are three types of flesh which are served to us as food. The first is in the fruit of penance: the kid† which Jacob brought to Isaac to be blessed.† The second is in a just act: the calf which Abraham assessed as proper food for the angels.† The third is at the apex of glory: the fatted calf, which the father is said to have killed at the return of his son.† [Jg 13:15] [See Gn 27:55ff.] [See Gn 18:7ff.] [See Lk 15:23]

112. The souls of the elect walk in three gardens. The first comprises the burdens of our corruptible earthly life, which is the orchard of nuts† in which Susanna bathed.† The second is the pleasure of exalted joy, which is the garden of delights in which Adam was put to work and to tend.† The third is the sweetness and splendor of the divine vision, which is that enclosed garden† in which Joseph of Arimathaea built for himself a tomb hewn out of the rock.† A clear conscience, by virtue of her diversity, draws all of these gardens into herself. [Sg 6:10] [Dn 13:15–17] [See Gn 2:15] [Sg 4:12] [See Mt 27:60; Jn 19:41]

113. Three tables are set to satisfy our hunger: the sacrament of the Law and the Gospel, on

See Pr 9:2-5

Lk 24:42

†See Lv 16:2
*Ex 25:30

Mt 6:19

Mt 13:44

See Jb 38:22

Jr 41:8

See Mt 2:11

†Ezk 4:12
*Ezk 4:15
†Gn 18:6 *Lv 2:4

Ex 27:1
Dt 27:5

Ex 20:24

Jg 16:4-21
1 K 21:1-16

Mt 14:6-11

which the feasts of wisdom are offered;† the mystery of catholic instruction, where the piece of roast fish and the honeycomb† are found; and the sanctuary of eternal fulfillment, which is beyond the veil† and which holds the bread of offering* and of life.

114. We ought to store up three treasures:† the desire for piety of heart, which is hidden in the field so that it may be purchased;† the teaching of truth in one's mouth, which is the treasure of snow and hail;† and constant perseverance in a person, which is the treasure comprising wheat, barley, oil, and honey.† These are the treasures of the magi, who brought gold, frankincense, and myrrh to the new-born Lord.†

115. Four different kinds of bread are found in the Scriptures, over which the varied miseries of the human race weep bitterly: there is bread baked over human dung;† bread baked over cow's dung;* bread baked over coals;†and bread baked in a pan.* The various dispositions of the human mind are formed according to these.

116. There are three altars on which we should place our sacrifices: the satisfaction of divine commands, which is made out of acacia wood in the desert;† the advocacy of many saints, which is made of stones which iron has not worked;† and the humble incarnation of the Redeemer, which is made of earth.†

117. Three women stir our senses: the softness of our flesh, which is Delilah, who tore out Samson's eyes;† the sweetness of worldly glory, which is Jezebel, who killed Naboth;† and despair of the future life, which is the daughter of Herodias, who carried off the head of the prophet.†

118. Priests are taken from two tribes: those of Levi and Judah, from which come Aaron, Christ,

and their successors. One can gauge how this is
fitting from an interpretation of their names.[19]

119. Three vultures gather beside the Lord's
body:[†] the enormity of lay power, which is a great   See Mt 24:28
bird with huge wings;[†] the misuse of clerical po-   Ezk 17:3
sition, which sets its nest in the heavens;[†] and the   Ob 4
spiritual acuity of the humble, which encourages
its young to fly.[†]   Dt 32:11

120. The priestly office has four aspects: to offer
up the living sacrifice of the flesh, which is the
duty of the Levites;[†] to offer up to God the gifts of   See 2 Ch 29:26–31
the virtues (that is, to burn incense), which is the
duty of the sons of Aaron;[†] to enter heaven with   See 1 Ch 23:13
a zeal for martyrdom, which means to go in with
the holy blood of the saints;[†] and to pour forth   See Lv 16:1ff.
vows of grace and prayer to heaven, which means
to offer bread and wine to God.[†]   Gn 14:8

121. Three fountains cleanse souls: the anxiety
associated with contrition, which moistens the face
of the earth;[†] the humility associated with con-   Gn 2:6
fession, which is located outside the town;[†] and   Gn 24:11
devout compunction, at which Jesus stopped and
sat down.[†]   Jn 4:6

122. Three kinds of bread nourish us in this life.
The first, which cleanses through its bitterness, is
the bread that the woman of Zarephath prepares
for Elijah during the drought.[†] The second, which   See 1 K 17:11–16
consoles with its sweetness, is the bread that the an-
gel brings to him while he is sleeping in the shade.[†]   1 K 19:5–6
The third, which strengthens one in courage, is
the bread that leads him to Oreb, the mountain of
God.[†] All are contained in the three aspects of the   1 K 19:8
Lord's body.

---

19. Jerome, *Liber interpr. hebr. nom.*, offers the following:
'Leui additus siue adsumptus' [CCL 72:68], 'Iuda laudatio siue
confessio' [CCL 72:67], 'Iuda confitens siue glorificans' [CCL
72:152], and 'Iuda confitens siue laudator' [CCL 72:157].

Lk 15:8

Mt 5:15

See Mt 25:1–13

See Mk 4:21

†See Jn 19:34

*See Mk 15:34

Heb 12:24

Jn 19:34

Is 22:11

Jn 5:2–4

Is 7:3

†Ex 2:17

*2 Ch 4:6

1 Co 3:12

1 Co 3:12

1 Co 3:12

See Ps 104:13

See 2 K 13:17

Ex 26:18

Ex 27:12

See Gn 2:10

Gn 2:13

Gn 2:14

123. Three lamps illuminate the night of this life: the power of understanding in the spirit, which is lit in order that the drachma may be found;† the splendor of wisdom in speech, which is raised aloft so that its light may be seen;† and exemplary justice towards one's neighbor, which is held before the bridegroom coming to the wedding† so that all the lamps can be placed on the lampstands.[20]†

124. Three saving streams flowed from the body of Jesus:† the articulation of grief,* which represents confession; the spilling of blood,† which signifies suffering; and the effusion of water,† in which one should understand compunction.

125. Three ponds are found in Scripture. The first is the ancient error, which is that pond between the two walls.† The second is carnal sensuality, which is the pond beside which the ill lie.† The third is cleverness of reason, which is the pond beside the Fuller's Field road.† In these three ponds sheep are given to drink† and sacrifices are washed.*

126. There are three causes of fire in us: the straw† of impure thought; the hay† of wicked speech; and the wood† of improper deeds. These will cause fire within us, unless they are put out by waters from on high.†

127. There are three windows for contemplatives: that which initiates contemplation, which is the window facing east;† that which directs contemplation, which is that facing south;† and that which brings contemplation to fulfillment, which is the window looking to the west.†

128. Four streams irrigate the garden of God:† sorrow over one's own wrongdoing, which surrounds the land of Ethiopia;† compassion for a brother's faults, which flows eastward toward the Assyrians;† reflection on the grace which has been

---

20. Compare II Sent 43.

bestowed on us, which cuts through the middle of Babylon;† and an eager attitude of charity, which surrounds the whole land of Havilah.† These streams embrace the upper pool and the lower pool,† and include the waters of the sea, of rivers, of springs, and of snow. See Jr 50:8, 51:6

Gn 2:11

Jos 15:19

129. There are three courses on God's dish: clearness of understanding, which will shine like the sun;† fullness of purity, which will be like the angels; and security of eternal life, which will be like God. Mt 13:43

130. There are three doors through which one passes to life: truthfulness of faith, behind which Sarah laughs;† stability of hope, which is on the side of the ark;† and firmness of charity, which the cherub guards with the flaming sword.† See Gn 18:10–12

See Gn 6:16

See Gn 3:24

131. The wine in God's cup takes three forms. It is red in the patience of the saints; this is the wine that made Isaac glad in his illness.† It is white in the reward of the just; this is the wine which intoxicated Noah.† It is black and harsh in the damnation of the wicked; this is the wine that Jesus tasted, but did not wish to drink.† Gn 27:25

Gn 9:21

Mt 27:34

132. The vestment which a priest ought to wear has three characteristics. It should exhibit coarseness in outer workmanship, as did the robe that Aaron wore in public. It should possess an appearance of spiritual holiness, as did the clothing which Rebecca took with her† and the robe which Aaron wore in the sanctuary.† It should also have the beauty of contemplative sweetness; such a robe is seamless, like that which Jesus wore.† Gn 27:15

Ex 28:35

Jn 19:23

133. We dress in three tunics. The first is that of chastisement, which subdues the body. It is made of skins, and Adam wore one.† The second has the length of constant perseverance. The beloved Gn 3:21

Gn 37:3   Joseph was clothed in this robe.[†] The third has the
           amplitude of the grace which rewards us. This is
Jn 19:23   the tunic which Jesus wore.[†]
Is 6:2   134. The seraphim have six wings.[†] Two are
           on their feet: shame for past deeds and concern
           regarding future ones. They fly with the two wings
           on their sides: fear, which presses them downward;
           and hope, which lifts them up. There are also the
           two wings on their heads: humility, which carries
           them forward; and charity, which perfects them.[21]
               135. God has two thrones: the substance of the
Is 6:1   angels, which is high;[†] and human nature, which
Is 6:1   is raised up.[†]
Ezk 1:5–6   136. Each of the four animals had four wings:[†]
Ezk 1:12   fear and patience, which covered their bodies;[†] and
           love and hope, which were joined to one another
Ezk 1:12   and flew.[†]
               137. There are six wings on the animals of
See Rv 4:8 the new law:[†] natural inclination, the instruction
           of the law, the declarations of the prophets, the
           command of the Gospel, the vision of the apostles,
           and ecclesiastical custom.
               138. Jesus' bed has three parts: the unity of
           the Testaments, which is, as it were, the virgin
           womb; the Church of the elect, which is like the
Lk 2:7, 12 manger;[†] and the conscience of those who have
           been purified, which is like the tomb hewn in the
Mt 27:60; Mk rock.[†]
15:46; Lk 23:53 139. There are three things which have been
           revealed to us in the saints for us to proclaim. The
           first concerns the outer appearance of the body,
Gn 18:6   which is made up of three bushels:[†] gravity of
           expression, shabbiness of clothing, and seriousness
           of manner. This is the bread of barley with which
Jn 6:9–12 five thousand were fed.[†] The second involves the

---

21. Compare I Sent 33; III Sent 33; III Sent 92; and Div
123.2 (SBOp 6/1:401–402).

interior quality of their spirit, also made up of
three bushels:[†] humility in prosperity, steadfastness   Gn 18:6
in adversity, and moderation in all things. This
is the bread of wheat with which four thousand
were fed.[†] Last is their higher beauty, similar to   Mt 15:37–38
that of God. The threefold nature of their love
toward God and humanity makes up its bushels. It
embraces friend and foe, and it loves on account
of God himself. This is the bread of corn which is
baked by the heat of the Holy Spirit and is called
the bread of angels.[†]   Ps 78:25

140. There are two houses of God: curiosity,
the outer attendant of things, which is the tabernacle over which God's glory comes and goes;[†]   Ex 40:32–36
and devout simplicity, emptying herself for God
and serving him, which is the temple from which
God does not depart.[†]   See 1 Co 3:16–17

141. There are two arks in the old law:[†] the   Gn 6:14
literal text of the narrative, which has both humans
and beasts in it; and the spiritual meaning of its
content, which holds the manna and the rod of
Aaron.[†]   Heb 9:4

142. Three chariots are found in Scripture. The
first is the arrogance of temporal power. Its driver
is the pride which comes from presumption and
audacity. Its horse is strong self-confidence, and
its wheels are the headlong motion of vanity and
a happy chain of prosperity. This is the chariot
of Pharaoh,[†] on which Ahab[22] died.[†] The second   Ex 15:4
chariot is the exaltation of conversion and of life.   1 K 22:34–38
Its driver is the word of divine warning. Its horse is
a vow to persevere, and its wheels are the terrifying
horror of hell's torments and the wondrous delight

---

22. The critical text reads 'Rechab', which I have emended
to 'Ahab' in accordance with the scriptural reference. This is
the sort of error which might easily have been made by a
scribe taking down words being delivered orally.

Ac 8:27ff.

of heaven's rewards. This is the chariot in which the eunuch read Scripture with Philip.† The third chariot is the loftiness of grace and contemplation. Its driver is the love of the heavenly fatherland. Its horse is the longing for eternal life, and its wheels are the condemnation of worldly glory and reverence for the divine majesty. This is the fiery

2 K 2:11

chariot on which Elijah was taken up to heaven.²³†

143. There are three altar-cloths. The first is the affliction of penance for our sins, which is sack-

Jdt 4:9

cloth.† The second is the great joy and happiness arising from our pardon, which is like sounding

1 Co 13:1; See Ex 27:2
See Ex 30:3

brass.† The third is the public joy arising from grace, which shines like gold.†

144. Three keys unlock hidden things for us. One is the harshness of our troubled time, which

Rv 9:1–2

opens the shaft of the abyss.† Another is the acuteness of our hope and expectation, which opens

Mt 16:19
Rv 3:7

the kingdom of heaven.† The last is the special character of true love, which is the key of David.†

145. Sinners bathe in two rivers: that of corruption and lust, and that of flattery and deceit. These are the Abana and the Pharphar, the rivers

2 K 5:12

of Damascus.† The rivers in which the just bathe are also two: that of reproach against insult and accusation, and that of the sweetness of consolation and grace. These are the Jordan and the Dan, the

2 K 5:10–14

rivers of Judea.†

146. There are four canticles of the faithful. The first is the canticle of victory, which is sung when

Ex 15:1–19

Pharaoh is drowned.† The second is the canticle of exhortation, which the Hebrews sang when they

Dt 32:1–43

were about to enter the Promised Land.† The third is the canticle of joy, which Hannah sang upon receiving her son.† The fourth is the canticle of

1 S 2:1–1

---

23. Compare II Sent 85.

fortitude, which David sang when he was saved
from the hand of Saul.[†]   2 S 22; Ps 18
147. There are four kinds of flowers in the
garden of God. The first is purity of body, which
is like the lily;[†] the second, the grace of spiritual   Si 39:19; Is 35:1
innocence, which is like hyssop; the third, a ready
eloquence in speaking the truth, which is like the
violet; and the fourth, persistence in acting justly,
which is like the rose.[24†]   Si 39:17
148. There are three sorts of martyrdom in
which blood is not shed. One is scarcity in the
midst of abundance, which is exemplified in David
and Job. The second involves generosity despite
one's poverty, which both Tobit[†] and the widow[*]   †Tb 1:19–20
exhibited. The third is chastity in one's youth,   *Mk 12:42–43
which Joseph practiced during his time in Egypt.[†]   Gn 39:7–20
149. We ought to walk on two feet: nature and
custom.
150. We are taken up to heaven on three horses.
The first is the grief which derives from repen-
tance. The serpent bites at its hoofs.[†] Its saddle is the   Gn 49:17
hopeful expectation that comes from our recogni-
tion that we have gained God's pardon. Its bridle
and halter are the consolation offered by Scripture
and the example provided by those who have preceded us. The spurs with which it is urged on are
the confusion which comes from the enormity of
our guilt and the fear that arises from our reflection
on the punishment we deserve.[25] The pitfall into
which it can stumble is despair. The second horse
is the fervor which comes from religion. It was
this horse that Mordecai rode dressed in the royal
robes.[†] Its saddle is the seriousness which comes   Est 6:8–11

---

24. Compare III Sent 122 (at note 185).
25. Compare II Sent 99.

from a sense of discretion, moderating our actions. Its bridle and halter are the unreliable habit of our flesh and the useful application of perseverance. Its spurs are the longing to act honestly and the desire for the well-being of our brothers. The pitfall into which it can stumble, however, is a lack of moderation. The third horse is the desire which derives from love. This horse is endowed with great courage and a flowing mane.[†] Its spurs are the recognition of the transitory character of things in this world and of the absolute eternity of things in the next. It is led forward by our striving to see God.

Jb 39:19

151. Three caves are found in the books of Scripture. There is the impiousness of our perverted will, which is the cave of thieves in which Saul relieved himself.[†] There is a firm, unshakable equanimity, which is made within the altar and is of one cubit.[†] There is finally the exercise of twofold piety, which is the double cave[†] in which the patriarchs are buried.

1 S 24:4

Ex 27:8; Ezk 43:13

Gn 23:17

152. There are four principal weapons which defend us: prudent and humble understanding, which is like a helmet covering the head;[†] temperance, which moderates conduct and practices frugality, and which, like a plate of armor, covers the breast;[†] constant and patient perseverance, which is like a shield protecting the right arm;[†] and justice, which pays others back equitably, and which is like the sword[†] which cuts on both sides to the point of division between soul and spirit.[†]

Eph 6:17

Eph 6:14

Eph 6:16

Eph 6:17

Heb 4:12

153. There are three sacrifices: pious contrition, which contains the butter of humility and the wormwood of indignation; worthy action, which contains the oil of discretion and the vinegar of confusion; and the action of grace, which contains the balsam of devotion and the poison of ingratitude.

154. Four things ensnare the soul: worldly wickedness; useless sorrow; vain glory; and hidden pride.

155. We are taken to three heavens. The first is the dignity of ecclesiastical purity, to which Elijah was taken up in the body.† The second is the truth 2 Co 12:2; 2 K 2:11
of angelic profundity, to which Ezekiel was taken in the spirit.† The third is the limitlessness of the Ezk 1:1, 37:1
highest godhead, to which the souls of the elect are taken.

156. There are six cities of refuge:† caution Nb 35:9–15
about forbidden transgressions, obedience in following God's precept, and the desire to propitiate the divine power (these three are in the land of Canaan†); and reflection on the maker of the world, Gn 11:31, 12:5
continuous thinking about the heavenly city, and preeminent consideration of the Word of God (these three are across the Jordan and are of the lot of the Levites).† Jos 21:1–3

157. There are three kinds of paradises. The first is the desirable sweetness of things that can be seen, which is watered like the garden of delights.† Gn 2:10
The second is the sincere purity of spiritual things, which preserves humanity within it. The third is the delicious truth of heavenly things, where Paul heard mysterious words.† 2 Co 12:4

158. There are four kinds of mountains: the mountains of Gilboa, where the shield of Saul was thrown away;† the mountains of Samaria, which 2 S 1:21
are raised up too high;† the mountains of Armenia, Am 3:9
atop which the ark rested;† and the mountains of Gn 8:4
Israel, which stretch forth their ridges.† Ezk 36:8

159. Two things call us back from our purpose: shame over what we have begun to do; and despair at maintaining our virtue. These are Rechab and Benaah, who killed Ishbaal in his bed.† 2 S 4:5–7

160. Four coverings conceal our nakedness. There is first the antiquity of our error and wicked-

Gn 3:7

Gn 24:64–65

2 K 2:8–14

Est 8:15

See 1 S 5:6

Rv 9:3
Nb 21:6

Ps 91:5

Ps 91:6

Ps 91:5

Ps 91:4
2 K 6:23

Lk 7:38

ness, which is like the loincloth of those who are afraid.† Then there is the newness of our conversion of life, with which Rebecca covered her face as she came down from the camel.† Third is the fullness of heavenly sanctity, which is like the cloak with which Elijah divided the Jordan and which he left behind for Elisha.† Finally, there is the brilliance of eternal life, which is the cloak of sapphire blue which Mordecai wore on the festal day.†

161. God is good, in that he generously bestows temporal benefits upon us. He is patient, in that he mercifully delays the punishment for sin. He is long-suffering, in that he shows kindness in inviting those who have done wrong to penance.

162. We surrender ourselves to three enemies: the impurity of our unclean desires, which is like the rats gnawing at our backs;† the foulness of our bodily passions, which is like the locusts that sting like scorpions;† and the obstinate perversity of our reason and sense, which are the fiery serpents.†

163. Four thieves steal our best possessions. The first is the foolishness of our dulled intellect, which carries away our knowledge of the truth. This is the thief who is called by the psalmist the plague which attacks in the dark.† Second is the unfettered lust of the flesh, which steals away our beneficial integrity, and is termed the demon that comes at mid-day.† Third is the whirlwind of flattery and boasting, which carries off the fullness of holiness, and is called the arrow which flies during the day.† The fourth is the love and desire for this life, which steals the reward of eternal bliss, and which is called the terror that comes in the night.† These are the thieves of Syria.†

164. There are three kisses: that of reconciliation, by which the two feet of the Lord, namely mercy and justice, are covered;† that of reward, by which the two hands of God, the work of the

just Creator and the manner of his perpetual governance, are grasped; and that of contemplation, which is given at the mouth[†] and which joins together humanity with the Word of God in a wondrous unity.

See Sg 1:1

164B. These kisses can also be called natural, when we are led to the good through the probity of our own will; doctrinal, when we are encouraged toward God by the admonition of another; and gracious, when we are drawn to act well by inspiration alone.[26]

165. There are three callings: the divine, as seen in Paul;[†] the human, as in the five thousand converted by the preaching of the apostles;[†] and the necessary, as in the case of Paul, the first hermit.[27]

Ga 1:1

Ac 4:4

166. Contemplation is called food in this life, where we feed on our bread in the sweat of our brow.[†] It is called drink in the future life, where it is taken up freely and without grief. It is called intoxication at the end, when the spirit will rejoice together with the body it has recovered. So it is written: 'Eat, friends', and so forth.[28†]

Gn 3:19

Sg 5:1

167. Some contemplatives rise and fall, like the beast which touches the mountain.[†] Others are seized and descend, just as Peter, after his vision, came down from the upper chamber.[29†]

Ex 19:12–13

Ac 10:21

168. There are two breasts: compassion, from which flows the milk of consolation, which nourishes the infirm; and congratulation, from which flows the milk of exhortation, which sustains those who are strong.[30]

---

26. Compare I Sent 8; Div 87.1 (SBOp 6/1:329–30); and SC 4.1 (SBOp 1:18–19).

27. See Jerome, *Vita s. Pauli* 4; in PL 23:20.

28. Compare Div 87.4 (SBOp 6/1:331).

29. Compare II Sent 187; III Sent 21 (at note 19); and Div 87.2 (SBOp 6/1:330).

30. Compare I Sent 9; I Sent 31; Div 87.5 (SBOp 6/1:332); and SC 10.1–2 (SBOp 1:48–49).

169. There are three ointments. One is the compunction which arises from the memory of our sins, which was poured over Jesus' feet.† The second is the devotion which comes from thinking about the benefits we have received, with which Jesus' head was anointed.† The third is the piety which results from our consideration of the unfortunate, which was prepared by the women to anoint the body of Jesus.³¹†

170. There are three staffs: that of Moses, which divided the Red Sea;† that of Aaron, which conferred the priesthood;† and that of the shepherd David, which drives away our adversary.†

171. The form of Jesus was threefold. It was common and despised.† It was brighter than the sun and totally splendid.† And it was spiritual and divine, yet moderated when presented to human eyes.

172. The foods of Israel were three: the unleavened bread of secular knowledge, which they had on their journey out of Egypt;† the manna of spiritual understanding, which they had in the desert;† and the palm-tree of triumphant victory, which they had in the promised kingdom.†

173. Three are cognizant of the divine secrets: the firmest possible adherent of his remembered faith; the one who is intent on tripping up the vices which attack humanity;† and the humble confessor of the grace he perceives that he has received. These are Peter, James, and John respectively.†

174. Three are freed out of the entire people: Noah, Daniel, and Job.†

175. Three are taken into the priesthood: Moses, Aaron, and Samuel.†

Margin references: Lk 7:38; Mt 26:7; Lk 24:1; Ex 14:16; Nb 17; 1 S 17:40; Is 53:3; Mt 17:2; Mk 9:2; Ex 12:8; Jn 6:49; Rv 7:9; Gn 27:36; Mt 17:1; Ezk 14:14; Ps 99:6

---

31. Compare I Sent 9; Div 87.6 (SBOp 6/1:332–33); and SC 10.4–12.2 (SBOp 1:50–61).

176. The thieves[†] rob us of the cloak of inno- See Lk 10:30
cence, stab us with the arrows of temptation, and
strip us of heavenly consolation.

177. Wrongdoers receive pardon from Our Lady,
the just receive grace, and the angels joy.

178. We ought to show our concern with what
is good in the sight of others[†] in terms of our dress, Rm 12:17
so that it will not be excessive; in our action, so
that it will not be reprehensible; and in our speech,
so that it will not be contemptible. We should be
concerned with what is good in the sight of God
with regard to our thought, so that it will be holy;[†] 2 Co 10:10
in our state of mind, so that it will be pure; and in
our intention, so that it will be right.

179. There are two generations in Christ: the
divine and the human. In the Holy Spirit there are
procession and grace.

180. The grace of the Holy Spirit works in
us sometimes for our own good, as in the case
of compunction, which removes our sins; or devotion, which heals our wound; or love, which
reveals heavenly things to us. At other times it
works for the benefit of our neighbor, as in the
case of the power to speak of doctrine,[†] or the 1 Co 12:8–9
office of healing,[†] and so on. 1 Co 12:28

181. There is a twofold danger: we should not
hand over to our neighbors those gifts which we
have received for our own sake, or keep to ourselves those gifts which we have received for our
neighbor's benefit. This is what is called the gift of
distinguishing spirits.[†] 1 Co 12:10

182. The door-keeper of memory is the remembrance of our profession. The porter of the
will is our memory of the heavenly fatherland. The
butler of our intention is our reflection on hell.

183. There are four ways of loving: to love the

flesh carnally; to love the spirit carnally; to love the
flesh spiritually; and to love the spirit spiritually.

184. There are three loaves for which the friend

Lk 11:5–6 coming along the road asks:[†] chastity, humility, and
charity.

185. Peace is of three kinds: it may be false, as in

Mt 26:49
Jn 14:27 Judas;[†] or confused, as in Adam and Eve; or true,
which is the peace that Christ left to his disciples.[32†]

186. Three sorts of people seek peace: those
who have been pacified, who possess their land in

Mt 5:4; Lk 11:21
†Lk 21:19
*Mt 5:9 peace;[†] those who endure, and in their patience
save their souls;[†] and the peacemakers,[*] who effect
peace.

187. Some contemplatives rise and fall, like

Rm 1:21 those who vanished in their own thoughts,[†] while
others are taken up and descend, of whom it is
written: 'If we seemed out of our senses, it was

2 Co 5:13 from God'.[33†]

---

32. Compare Div 96 (SBOp 6/1:364).
33. Compare II Sent 167; III Sent 21 (at note 19); and
Div 87.2 (SBOp 6/1:330).
A single manuscript adds the following here:
'Whether a tree falls to the south or to the north, there
will it remain (see Qo 11:3). The warmth of the south and
the gentleness one finds in Sacred Scripture have the same
beneficial aspect. For every sort of evil derives from the north.
Furthermore, one person beheld human beings as trees (see
Mk 8:24). Now a tree is cut down on a mount and will
remain wherever it has fallen because God will judge you at the
point where he finds you. One, therefore, will remain there
unchangeably and irrevocably. God can see where a person is
going to fall before the fall actually happens, but after one has
fallen God will not direct him to rise up (see Ps 41:8), nor
will he permit him to turn himself around.
'If you want to know where a tree is going to fall, examine
its branches. You should not doubt that it will fall in the
direction where the mass of branches is larger and heavier, if it
is cut down just at that time. Our branches are our desires. We
extend them toward the south if they are spiritual and toward
the north if they are carnal. The trunk of the tree indicates
which branches are heavier—the ones that weigh more bend
the trunk in their direction. Now our bodily trunk is situated
between the spirit, which it ought to serve, and those carnal
desires which war against the soul (1 P 2:11), or the powers
of darkness, as though it were a cow caught between a cattle

188. The stone is dressed:† it is dressed above,   Am 5:11
with the love of heavenly things; below, in the
dismissal of earthly things; to the right, by treating
good fortune as vile; and to the left, in enduring
unfavorable occurrences with equanimity.

---

thief and the farmer who owns it. No matter what threats the
thief makes, no matter what he intends to do, the farmer wins
if he does not steal away with the cow. So too, no matter how
much the evil one rages, no matter how dreadfully perverse
desires torture us, if the soul succeeds in claiming her bodily
vessel for herself, she must be understood to have triumphed,
so that—as the apostle says—sin cannot rule in our mortal
bodies (Rm 6:12), but rather, just as we have in the past put
our bodies at the service of wickedness and impurity, we can
now serve justice for our sanctification' (see Rm 6:19).
   Compare to this text Div 85 (SBOp 6/1:326–27).
   Two further points should be made about this passage. One
is that I have emended 'praeponderat', at line 10 of the critical
apparatus translated here, to 'praeponderant' for reasons of
sense. Second, there is a play on words toward the close of the
passage which cannot be conveyed in the translation, between
'vacca' (a cow) and 'vas' (a vessel, here the body).

3. the thiro series

THERE ARE FOUR CROSSES which point toward radically different outcomes in terms of their just deserts. The first is the cross of Christ—not that wooden cross on which he hung, but the cross of charity on which, then as now, he was outstretched as if to embrace us with his extended, loving arms. For although at the point of death one can be expected to breathe out nothing but a groan, when about to expire Christ said: 'I thirst.'† For what do you thirst, Lord? 'I thirst', he replies, 'for human salvation. And for this reason I have surrendered myself totally on their behalf, for while I have always loved them, in the end I loved them absolutely'.† 'And crying out with a loud voice, he gave up his spirit.'† What was this loud voice? A certain incalculable affection which no words could express, through which he commended us to God the Father. 'And crying out with a loud voice, he gave up his spirit',† because in that voice of reconciliation he turned over the soul which he had taken up for us into the hand of God the Father on our behalf, saying: 'Father, into your hands I commend my spirit'.† Suspended on this cross of charity both then and now, as we have said, he waits and longs for us to be crucified

Jn 19:28

Jn 13:1
Mt 27:50; Jn 19:30

Mt 27:50; Jn 19:30

Lk 23:46

Ga 2:19
Rm 6:6
2 Co 5:15

2 Co 6:5–6

Mt 16:24

See Lk 23:40–43

Ps 20:3; Ps 66:15

Ph 3:19

Mk 15:21

with him, so that each of us may say, along with the apostle: 'I have been crucified with Christ[†] so that we might no longer serve sin,[†] but rather him who has died for us.'[†] This is the cross of charity which we must bear by reason of the cross he bore. That means that we should serve him in vigils, in fasting, in a love free from affectation.[†] This is the cross which the Lord has instructed his disciples to take up.[†]

The second cross is that of penitence, the cross of the thief who hung at the right hand of the Lord.[†] If the matter is properly understood, that thief proved to be rich in penance, humility, confession, faith, hope, charity, and the other virtues. He prefigured those who, in penitence, recognize their own injustice and the justice of God, and who offer themselves with voluntary piety up to God on the cross of penitence as a sacrifice both fat and rich.[†]

There is a third cross, that of the thief on the Lord's left hand, which is without penance, without hope, without consolation. On this cross the other thief hung, totally wicked—suffering the same pains as the thief on the right, but not in a similar way. Full of grumbling, slander, envy, and pride, he represented those who bear the same burdens in the service of God as those who are truly penitent, but do so unwillingly, bemoaning their lot. Because they are not truly penitent, their end is death.[†]

The last cross is that of forced service, which that man carries whose name is Simon,[†] that is 'the obedient one'. To be sure, he instantly takes upon himself all the works of obedience, carrying all the things which belong to that cross just as he bore the cross of the Lord. He hastens forward and exerts an effort, because he has harsh taskmasters:

pride and vainglory. In the end, however, he lacks
the fruits of obedience, because he has been judged
not on the basis of his obedience, but according to
the purpose and intention behind it.[1]

2. On the eight beatitudes. 'Blessed are the poor
in spirit',[†] that is one whom the spirit of reason has
made poor by showing him his real self through the
revelation of his losses—demonstrating that he has
lost the kingdom of God which had been within
him.[†] That spirit which is the spirit of fear[†] effects
this poverty, and the soul touched by it merits a certain degree of illumination from the sun of justice.[†]
In this illumination, reason examines the memory
and, reflecting within itself, finds her to be corrupt
and impure, like an unclean rag.[†] Pondering in
wonder how and why—through what opening, by
what route, at what point—such drops of filth have
flowed there, reason discovers that it was through
the body, by means of the will, that they made their
way into the memory or conscience—through the
entrance provided by wicked suggestion, by way
of evil delight, and at the point of evil consent.
Groaning in sorrow over this discovery and seeking
consolation, reason finds none in the memory, or
in the body, or in the will. At this point an answer
comes to reason from God: 'Blessed are the poor in
spirit, for theirs is the kingdom of heaven'.[†] Hearing these words, reason incites itself to a condition
of poverty.

But since there are three kinds of poverty—
necessary poverty, voluntary poverty, and feigned
poverty—reason is made poor in spirit by correctly
distinguishing and choosing among them, rejecting false poverty, patiently enduring necessary

Mt 5:3

Lk 17:21 Is 11:3

Ml 4:2

Is 64:6

Mt 5:3

---

1. On the cross of Simon, compare Apo 1.2 (SBOp 3:82)
and Ben 6 (SBOp 5:5).

poverty, and embracing voluntary poverty. Thus
reason seeks the kingdom of God, which it had

Lk 17:21
held within itself but had lost.† It girds itself to
recover it. It orders the body into its service to
this end, because it was through the body that
foulness had instilled itself into the memory. And so
reason commands the body to fast, to keep watch,
and so forth. The will becomes disturbed at this,
since she was lying, ill and near death, on a bed
of idleness. The body, the servant of her misery,
is now, by order of reason, transferred to other
service, quite unsuited to her disease and habits.
Angered and disturbed by this, the will jumps up
and rages against reason: 'Why have you taken away
my servant? I had taken control of the eyes and
feet away from you so that they could serve my
curiosity, the ears and tongue to serve my vanity,
the nose and throat, the stomach and genitals, to
serve my desires, and the hands—rushing about
everywhere—and other limbs to serve me, each
in its own way. All of these were insufficient to
meet my needs in my illness. Yet now you have
taken them all away from me.' Hearing this complaint, reason becomes agitated and, sharing her
suffering, takes a place with her on the bed of
sloth, where it feels her pain and commiserates
with her. To reason, in this pain and consternation,
comes another divine response: 'Blessed are the

Mt 5:4
meek, for they shall possess the earth',† as if to
say: Master the will, and you will take charge of
the land which is your body. 'How', reason asks,
'will I master the will?' God responds: 'Through
piety.' Then reason, raising its head and wishing
to master the will through piety, finds itself blind
and impotent—blinded by the darkness of its ignorance, and impotent through of its corrupt nature
and evil habits. (For reason is undone first by the

corruption of nature and then by the corruption of habit which, according to those learned in natural philosophy, is a second nature.) As reason groans over its ignorance and impotence, another directive comes to it from God: 'Blessed are those who mourn, for they will be comforted'.[†] In this reason finds the ability, when it wishes, to proceed to the spirit of knowledge,[†] and, by applying knowledge, to make its way to grief[†]—since much cause of sorrow is at hand. 'Blessed', God repeats, 'are those who mourn, for they will be comforted'. Reason is uplifted, hearing an indication or promise of consolation through an application of knowledge and grief. It wonders, however, about the source of this consolation. It cannot be hoped for from reason itself, since reason is blind and impotent; nor from the will, which is weak and apathetic; nor from the memory, which is foul and dark; nor from the body, which is corrupt and disturbing to the soul.[†]

Despairing of help from all these sources, therefore, reason turns to the source of the promise, the sun of justice[†]—in whose radiance it had seen the light,[†] however little it had seen, and in which it had revealed itself to itself. From this source it begs the consolation needed to master the will— from the very source by whom that consolation is promised. Reason wails deeply, since it has so great a basis for its grief. And just as the sun of justice rose for Lot, as he was leaving Sodom, in Segor[†]— that is, in the humility of grief—so now, with the ever-greater illumination of his grace, he illumines reason through contemplation. He likewise invites reason into the spiritual paradise, into the garden of his delights, where the plants which are the virtues—the tree of chastity along with all the other trees of the spiritual paradise—flourish.[†] To

Mt 5:5

Is 11:2

See Qo 1:18

Ws 9:15

Ml 4:2

Ps 36:9

See Gn 19:23

See Gn 2:16

reason, engaged in contemplation, hungering and
thirsting, God says: 'Blessed are those who hunger

Mt 5:6 and thirst for justice, for they will be satisfied'.[†]

Hearing this, reason enters the garden through
Is 11:2 the spirit of fortitude[†] and takes up residence there.
It enters—that is, it hungers for such a condition—
and it takes up residence—that is, it is fulfilled
by the effect. Looking back on its illness, reason
wonders why will has not followed it. It rises to
lead her on, and by comparing the pleasures of
the flesh with the singular delight of the virtues,
by shouting, by entreating, it finally rouses will
from the bed of sloth. It urges her on although
she is reluctant and draws her forward although
she is tired and weak. Then it begins little by
little to introduce her to a hunger for justice and
to show her the refreshment prepared for those
feeling such hunger. Will proceeds cautiously. As
Ps 34:8 she begins to taste how sweet the Lord is,[†] however, her face grows more and more joyous with
Ps 104:15 the oil of chastity,[†] and she says: 'Alas, that my
habitation here has been delayed! I have lived with
the inhabitants of Kedar; my soul has lived there
Ps 120:5–6 far too long!'[†]

Soon the rational will, giving the body over to
the service of reason for the exercise of fasts, vigils,
and other such practices, takes up residence and
remains in the paradise of the virtues along with
reason. She says: 'It is good for us to be here; let
Mt 17:4 us make three tabernacles here:[†] one for me; one
for you, reason; and one for the memory.' Now,
through the mastery of the will, the territory of
the body is possessed by the meek, now blessed.
Now, after much grief and consolation of grief,
after the hunger and thirst, and after the fulfillment
of justice, all is well for humanity in the midst of
Gn 2:9 the trees of paradise.[†]

When one perceives, however, that what had
been implanted in his memory through the corruption of the body, brought about by the wickedness of his will, has not yet been effaced from the
memory, he grieves over the foulness of conscience
which derives from the sins of his former life.
He sighs and, looking back to God, sighs again.
The divine Word responds to him continuously
through the spirit of counsel:† 'Blessed are the Is 11:2
merciful, for they shall be granted mercy'.† 'But Mt 5:7
what', he asks, 'if there are faults in me?' 'I forgive
them. And blessed are those whose faults have been
forgiven'.† 'But what if there are sins in me?' 'Blot Ps 32:1
them out with works of mercy, and you will find
the mercy of my forgiveness; and you whose sins
are blotted out, and to whom will be imputed
no sin for past wrongdoing, shall be blessed. You
will be black but beautiful, like the tabernacles
of Kedar,† since the true Solomon will shape the Sg 1:4
formlessness of your darkness and adorn it with the
ornaments and beautiful garments of his grace.'

Now, with memory overjoyed, the will illuminated and comforted, reason in charge and the
body serving it, the rational human being begins
to live again and aspires to his origin. 'My soul',
he says, 'thirsts for God, the fount of life; when
will I go and see the face of my God?'† Rejoicing Ps 42:2
in the good things of the Lord and wishing to
contemplate the good itself intellectually through
the spirit of understanding,† he hears these words Is 11:2
from the Lord: 'Blessed are the pure in heart, for
they shall see God',† as if to say: Purify your heart, Mt 5:8
free yourself from all things, become a monk—that
is, become singular of heart. Seek but one thing
from the Lord, ask but for this†—stop and see that Ps 27:4
he is God.† When you have purified your heart Ps 46:10
through the spirit of understanding, you shall soon

Is 11:2 see God through the spirit of wisdom† and you will rejoice in God to the full.

Now tranquil both in himself and toward his neighbor and made pleasing to God, one is moved to placate him to whom he is pleasing, so that he may become a mediator and peacemaker between God and humanity. He takes upon himself both the name and the responsibility of the Son of God, the 1 Tm 2:5 mediator of God and humankind.† For 'Blessed are the peacemakers, for they shall be called the Mt 5:9 children of God'.† And because the blessed person is not one who begins something but someone who has brought it to fruition, who has held fast to all these things even to the point of persecution and death, to him will belong that which is within us, and that which has been described here, and See Mt 5:10 that which is in heaven—the kingdom of heaven,† which is promised at the beginning and restored at the end.[2]

Mt 5:3 3. 'Blessed are the poor in spirit'† who, because of their humility, do not desire to have power over others. But since this is not enough, there follows: 'Blessed are the meek' who wish always to be subject to others. 'Blessed are those who mourn' the pleasures of their old life, 'because they will be Mt 5:5 comforted'†—that is, they will not be destroyed by the harshness of their new life. 'Blessed are those who hunger and thirst for the justice' of Mt 5:6 the new life, 'because they will be filled'†—that is, they will detest the pleasures of their old life. Mt 5:7 'Blessed are the merciful':† now that the blessed person has learned to take pity on his own soul, Si 30:24 pleasing as he is to God,† he ought to take pity on his neighbor as well. He has learned well to love himself. Now he ought also to love his neighbor

---

2. Compare III Sent 3; III Sent 15; and Conv 6.9–22.40 (SBOp 4:81–116).

as himself.[†] After he has destroyed the remnants of disgrace in himself and the foulness in others, he begins to purify his eyes and raise them to the vision of God, and to love him with his whole heart, his whole soul, and his whole strength[†]— and 'blessed are the pure of heart, for they shall see God'.[†] 'Blessed are the peacemakers':[*] the one who has authority over others is now worthy to be a mediator and peacemaker between God and humankind.[†] For he is now able to placate God, to whom he is deservedly pleasing. 'Blessed are the peacemakers, for they will be called children of God'[†]—that is, those who by reason of their likeness to the Son of God are established as mediators between God and humanity. 'Blessed are those who suffer persecution for justice's sake, for theirs is the kingdom of heaven'.[†] Here the border is woven for the cloak[†]—that is: Blessed are those who fulfill all these things unto persecution and to the moment of death.[3]

4. How the soul is cleansed of the seven vices through sevenfold grace. Sinners are seized first by negligence concerning their own welfare, then by curiosity about things outside themselves which have no relevance to them, and then by lust for those things. Acquiescence follows lust, bad habit follows acquiescence, contempt follows habit, and malice—that is, an attachment to sin and delight in sinning—follows contempt.

Negligence retards us, curiosity impedes us, lust binds us, acquiescence ties us harshly down, bad habit drags us further along, contempt forces us headlong, and delight in sin locks us in the prison of despair, because a sinner despairs when he has arrived at the depths of evil.

Marginal references:
Mt 19:19, 22:39; Mk 12:31; Lk 10:27

See Dt 6:5; Mt 22:37; Mk 12:30; Lk 10:27
[†]Mt 5:8
[*]Mt 5:9

See 1 Tm 2:5

Mt 5:9

Mt 5:10
See 1 S 24:6

---

3. Compare III Sent 2 and Conv 6.9–22.40 (SBOp 4:81–116).

But the Holy Spirit approaches and enters our

Is 11:2–3 wretched soul through his sevenfold grace.† First
he grants her fear. Then he adds piety to fear, so
that piety's sweetness may console the misery of
fear. He adds knowledge to piety, in order that the
soul may know how to make use of both fear and

2 Co 2:7 piety and not be swallowed up by the great sadness†
which arises from fear, or be hurled headlong by
the baseless presumption which can derive from
piety. The Spirit then adds fortitude to knowledge
to serve against temptation, in order that the soul
can advance in goodness not only knowingly, but
courageously as well. He adds counsel to fortitude,
so that the soul will not trust too much in either
knowledge or fortitude, and to insure that all things

See Si 32:34 will be done advisedly.† He adds understanding
to counsel, so that within her heart the soul can
choose for herself not merely what people might
recommend, but 'what the will of God is, what

Rm 12:2 is good and pleasing to him, what is perfect'.† To
understanding he adds wisdom, so that what the
soul has learned up to this point through counsel
or understanding may now become her regular
disposition, with the result that now she tastes, by
the grace of God, through the medium of wisdom
itself, and whatever heretofore seemed tough and
unbearable may now be sweet and flavorful for her.

Note that the Spirit first places fear in opposition to negligence, because 'he who fears God

Qo 7:19 will neglect nothing'.† He places piety—which is
an attachment to God—in response to curiosity,
because piety, as the apostle says, 'is useful for any

1 Tm 4:8; 2 Tm
2:21 good work',† and it is utterly opposed to curiosity.
He places knowledge in opposition to lust, so that
the soul may know herself and not, wandering in
her own thoughts, stumble into a longing for the
world. He does this lest the soul should hear: 'If you

do not know yourself, O beautiful among women, go forth and feed your herd',[†] and so that she will Sg 1:7 know how empty and frail are the things which she desires. The Spirit sets fortitude against acquiescence, lest the soul be overcome at the point of giving assent. He puts counsel in opposition to bad habit, because when the soul arrives at the point of bad habit, there is great need for deliberation. He sets understanding against contempt, because, given that the soul now spurns the advice of other people, she is now close to plunging into despair, unless she can perceive on her own the danger she is in. He opposes wisdom to malice, because wisdom alone can conquer evil.[†] Ws 7:30

Thus the Holy Spirit through his sevenfold grace destroys the sevenfold misery in the human soul. In its place he builds within the soul a sevenfold blessedness.[†] Through the spirit of fear he Mt 5:3–9 makes the blessed poor in spirit. Through the spirit of piety he makes them meek. Through the spirit of knowledge he makes them mournful. Through the spirit of fortitude he makes them hunger and thirst for justice. Through the spirit of counsel he makes them merciful. Through the spirit of understanding he makes them pure of heart. Through the spirit of wisdom he makes them peacemakers, since wisdom conquers wickedness.[†] The peace of Ws 7:30 God,[†] 'which surpasses all understanding',[*] rises †Col 3:15; Ph 4:7 up in their hearts. This represents the perfection *Ph 4:7 of God's servants.[4]

5. How one who has fallen rises again and moves forward. We have been made in the image of God.[†] We cling to the Father through the power Gn 1:26 of memory, to the Son by means of our reason or understanding, and to the Holy Spirit through

---

4. Compare III Sent 19; III Sent 20; III Sent 89; and III Sent 98.

See 1 Jn 2:16

our will. But we have fallen away from this Holy
Trinity into another trinity, a foul one. We have
fallen into the lust of the flesh, the longing of the
eyes, and a craving for the things of the world.[†]
Our power of memory is thereby taken captive, our
reason disturbed, our will weakened. As a result
our mind is squandered, our reason blinded, and
our will defiled. But from this state we arise from
our affliction through another trinity promised to
us by God. We begin our restoration to wisdom,
that is to the Son of God, when our reason is
illumined by faith, and to the Father when our
memory is strengthened by hope, and to the Holy
Spirit when our will is purified by charity. Raised
from earthly concerns by the zealous exercise of
these three virtues, we come to realize that little
by little there arises within us a dining-room of
marvelous craftsmanship. About it the apostle says:
'Because we know that, if our earthly home is done
away with, we have in heaven a home not made by
2 Co 5:1 human hands'.[†] When we consider our end, we attend to what is lacking in us. We cannot, however,
attend to it unless we see what is available to us.
We did not perceive the help that was accessible to
us so long as we were enslaved to earthly concerns.
We obscured our origin with our worldly activities as though it were hidden underground. Our
memory was distracted by wasteful, demanding,
and passionate thoughts. Our reason, meanwhile,
was dulled by the heaviness of our flesh, by the
darkness of our bad conscience, and by the absence
of the light proper to it. Our will was defiled by the
enticements of temptation, by the effect of earthly
delights, and by the disordered character of our
choices.[5]

---

5. Compare I Sent 25 and Div 45.1–3 and 6 (SBOp
6/1:262–66).

6. Sin is a wound to the soul. The sorrow we feel for sin is the pain of that wound. Doing penance is the medicine for the pain, while the forgiveness of sin is the cure for the wound.

7. On the words of the apostle: 'We should live soberly and justly and piously in this life':† Tt 2:12 soberly for ourselves, justly toward our neighbor, and piously toward God.

We should live soberly in two respects: by repressing the desire of the flesh and our curiosity about the world. Thus the Lord says: 'Take care that your hearts should not be weighed down in debauchery and drunkenness and the cares of this life'.† Solomon says: 'The corruptible body presses Lk 21:34 down on the soul, and this earthly dwelling oppresses the mind, which is teeming with thoughts'.† Ws 9:15 Behold our fetters and our prison! The fetters, which are the concerns of the flesh, bind and restrain us. The prison, which is our curiosity about the world, closes in on us and ties us down.[6] One who overcomes the first of these, though walking in the flesh,† does not struggle according to the Rm 8:1 flesh. One who overcomes the second of them can say: 'Our homeland is in heaven'.† Ph 3:20

You should live justly in two respects as well. First, you should live so as to do harm to no one, and secondly, you should desire to do good to everyone. Thus it is written: 'What you do not want done to you, you should not do to another',† Tb 4:16; RB 61.14 and 'Always do to others all those things that you would have them do to you'.† Mt 7:12

We should live piously with regard to faith, which has two objects: the justification which justifies us in the present life; and the beatification which will make us blessed in the future one. God demands this faith from us: namely, we should

---

6. Compare III Sent 114 (at note 148).

believe that we will be justified by him through mercy; and that we will be made blessed through truth. He has promised that he will make the just blessed, for it is written: 'He has glorified those

Rm 8:30

whom he has justified'.[†] And so Christ said: 'If you do not believe me when I speak about the things of this world, how will you believe me when I

Jn 3:12

speak about heavenly things?'[†] My brothers, our justification in this life falls under the rubric of 'things of this world', while our beatification in the future life is among the things of heaven. As the apostle says: 'Our knowledge is imperfect, and

1 Co 13:9
Tt 2:12

our prophesying is imperfect'.[†]

Let us, therefore, live soberly[†] so that we may have a good conscience. Let us live justly so that we may be able to benefit our neighbor—for, as it is said, 'the wisdom which comes from above

Jm 3:17

is first of all chaste; then it makes peace'.[†] Let us likewise live piously, so that we may love God. All of these things ought to be done because of God.

8. On the words of Isaiah: 'Zion, city of our strength: our Savior is placed in it as a wall and

Is 26:1–2

a rampart; open the gates!'[†] The Savior, which means the self-control of our Savior, is placed in it as a wall, because we are taught through his example to hold ourselves back from the world and

See 1 Jn 2:17

its luxuries.[†] The rampart is his patience, because the inner effort of temperance is of little value unless we add to it the outer, the example of his patience in the face of every adversity.

A bridge must be added so that we can go

Jn 10:9

in and out and find the heavenly pastures.[†] The meaning of this is that one must maintain his body, because it is through the body that 'one goes to his

Ps 104:23

work, in which he engages until evening'.[†] But to prevent enemies from finding entrance through it, the body must not be built up with great effort.

Rather, it should be so placed and directed that it can survive in times of peace with little support, while in times of struggle it can be restrained with only light pressure from allowing the enemy to enter.[7]

9. Concerning the three and four crimes of Jerusalem: 'I will not alter my judgment regarding the three crimes and the four crimes of Jerusalem'.[†] See Am 2:4 Of these seven crimes, three are of the soul and four of the body.

The three which are of the soul are pride, vanity, and envy. These arise from the corruption of those three things which naturally reside in the soul: the ability to reason, the power of desire, and the ability to feel anger. When corrupted, the ability to reason is turned into pride, the power of desire into vanity, and the ability to feel anger into envy.

The four crimes which are of the body are curiosity in the eyes, garrulity in the tongue, cruelty in the limbs, and lechery in the loins. The body, after all, is made up of four elements. From fire, which by its nature always seeks the heights, it possesses the light of the eyes. From the striking and shaping of air it has the power of speech. From earth it has solidity. From water it has the fullness of the natural humors. From an excess of sight, however, curiosity is born, and from a lightness of the tongue, garrulousness. From the dullness which comes from corpulence arises roughness or cruelty, which is most evident in animals: the more they are given over to the body, the more brutish and cruel they appear. From the natural humors, moreover, comes the wave of lust. Thus, just as the three corruptions of the soul give rise to three

---

7. Compare III Sent 24 (at note 25).

vices, so do the four corruptions of the body bring about four more.

These are the three crimes and four crimes on account of which God's judgment on Jerusalem, Edom, and the other cities will not be changed.[†]

See Am 1:11
Rv 3:7

10. Obedience is the key of David;[†] a pillory; and the bronze altar outside the temple, before which animals were sacrificed.[†] Obedience is the key of David, and 'what it opens no one closes'.[†] It opens the hidden secrets[†] of God to us and makes us neighbors of God himself.[†] If anyone lacks it, it closes off those secrets of God to him, because all other goods assist him little or not at all in his labors.

2 Ch 7:7
Rv 3:7
Is 45:3
See Ws 6:20

Obedience is a pillory, because whoever desires to be perfect must be obedient as though in a pillory, since he has to struggle continuously against his desires.

Moreover, obedience is a bronze altar,[†] beneath which is a pit of perpetual fire.[†] The pit represents humility, the fire charity. On this altar the bull of pride, the lustful ram, and the foul-smelling kid are slain. We sacrifice the bull to God when we trample pride through humility. We offer up the ram when we restrain anger through patience. The nature of the ram is such that if it wants to strike somebody down, it first pulls back in order to collect its strength so that it can strike the one provoking him more fiercely. Thus the ram signifies anger, since anyone given to anger likewise pulls back at first so that he can strike the one provoking his anger more fiercely. So, while he turns his past and present injuries over and over in his mind, he hastens to return evil for evil.[†] Such anger as this is described by Saint Gregory as falling into four categories. He writes: 'There are those who become angry easily, and are placated slowly.

2 Ch 7:7
See Lv 6:13

Rm 12:17

There are others who become angry easily, and are easily placated. There are some who become angry slowly, and are placated slowly. And there are those who become angry slowly, and are easily placated'.[8]

The kid, which is foul-smelling, signifies lust. We overcome it through chastity, thereby sacrificing the kid to God. This sacrifice should in no way be made without salt,[†] because we are in the wrong if we make the offering properly, but do not wisely understand its meaning.[9]   See Lv 2:13

11. The angel Gabriel announced to Mary that she would conceive Jesus.[†] That signifies every preacher's pronouncement to every sinner. The sinner responds to the preaching when he determines to turn to God. Before he can accomplish this, however, he carries what he has conceived for nine months, which are as follows. The first month is that he should return anything he has taken from anyone. The second is that he should fulfill the law in accordance with justice. The third month is that he should reconcile to himself anyone whom he has harmed. The fourth is that he should make things right with the Lord. (Behold the fourfold payment of Zacchaeus![†]) The fifth month is his renunciation of the world, the sixth his approach to a monastic congregation, the seventh his selection of an order, and the eighth his choice of the location of his house. The ninth month is that, as a result of my fear of you,[†] O Lord, I will conceive and bring forth[†] the Spirit.   Lk 1:26–38   Lk 19:8   Ps 119:120   See Is 7:14; Lk 1:31

The new-born child is laid in a manger.[†] The child is our intention; the manger, our memory. The hay represents carnal desires and the nearby   Lk 2:7

---

8. Gregory, *Moralia in Job* 5.14.80; in CCL 143:278.
9. Compare III Sent 116 (at note 158) and III Sent 121 (at note 177).

animals the evil spirits. The clothes in which he is dressed represent our recollection of Christ's passion and the shedding of his blood.

The child is watched over for eight days, so that he may be circumcised on the eighth.[†] The first day is that of hope; the second that of truth, that is, of judgment; the third that of virtue; the fourth that of peace; the fifth that of justice; the sixth that of knowledge; the seventh that of wisdom; and the eighth that of charity. It is on the eighth day that the infant is circumcised, for as it is written: 'The man whose foreskin has not been circumcised will fall away from his people'.[†]

12. Within us we have a castle which is opposed to us[†]—that is, our own will, whose wall is obstinacy, whose tower is pride, whose weapons are our wicked excuses, and whose provisions are our perverse pleasures.

In this castle the ass—that is, obedience—is tied up, along with her colt, which is humility.[†] They are tied with the chains of sin, about which it is written: 'The ropes of sin have tightened around me'.[†]

Christ sends to the castle two of his disciples,[†] mercy and truth. Thus it is written: 'Mercy and truth go before you'.[†] Mercy loosens the chains, while truth draws the animals out and leads them to the confession of sin, which is signified by Bethphage. 'Untie them', Christ says, 'and bring them to me'.[†]

Mercy frees, and truth directs. So it is said: 'Belief in the heart leads to justice, and confession of tongue brings about salvation'.[†] Still further: 'The word in your mouth is near' for confession 'and in your heart' for believing.[†]

'And if anyone should say something to you',[†] and so on. There are some who are accustomed to

Lk 2:21

Gn 17:14; see Lv 7:25

See Mt 21:2

See Mt 21:2

Ps 119:61

Mt 21:1

Ps 89:14

Mt 21:2

Rm 10:10

See Rm 10:8

Mt 21:3

defend their actions, because their own ways seem
right to them, rather than the instructions of their
superiors. But it is written to the contrary: 'The
Lord has need of these',[†] namely of obedience and
humility, rather than of those things which arise
from one's own will. To explain it another way,
the ass represents simplicity, and the colt humility.
They are tied down by the three crimes and the
four crimes.[†] When it is said that 'The Lord has
need of these',[†] it means that anyone who desires
to be governed rightly by others has need of simplicity as opposed to cleverness, and of humility as
opposed to pride.[10]

13. 'Teach me goodness and discipline and
knowledge.'[†] These are the attributes that are
appropriate to a shepherd. Goodness attracts, discipline corrects, and knowledge nourishes. Goodness makes one worthy of love, discipline makes
him worthy of imitation, and knowledge renders
him capable of teaching others.[†]

14. 'Mercy and truth have met one another;
justice and peace have embraced.'[†] Mercy is that
which protects, truth that which teaches, justice
that which guides, and peace that which fosters.

15. How reason and will engage in a dispute on
behalf of the body. Reason determines to chastise
the body in penance and to subject it to servitude.
The worthless, lazy servant[†] complains to will,
which lies in a harmful languor, saying: 'Am I not
your servant? Have I not served you assiduously
since my earliest days? Have I not suffered many
great burdens and dangers on your behalf, and
am I not prepared to bear them still? I give you
threefold service for the threefold infirmity from
which you suffer. For my throat, nose, stomach,

Margin references:
Mt 21:3

See Am 1:3
Mt 21:3

Ps 119:66

See 2 Tm 2:24–25

Ps 85:10

See Mt 25:26–30

---

10. Compare III Sent 24 (at note 24).

and genitals serve your lust, my feet and eyes serve
your curiosity, and my ears and tongue serve your
vanity. My hands, since they move about freely,
serve you to all purposes on every side and carry
assistance to all the other bodily members. Will
you then patiently endure such shame and loss
by permitting reason to take away your servant so
brutally?'

Little old will gnashes her teeth. Her mind is
maddened; she grows voluble,† contentious,* and
loud.† She stalks out with her chest uncovered, her
hair a tangle, and covered with horrible running
sores. In such a state she accosts reason and shouts
at him with great indignation: 'Is this the kind of
faith you keep with me? The servant is mine. I
do not turn him over to you! He is mine. I still
have him and will keep him a long time!' Reason
soothes this angry viper, concealing what is going
to happen until she has quieted down.

Then reason introduces into the discussion matters other than those raised by will. 'I have seen',
he says, 'a pleasure-garden with beautiful trees, and
the sweetness of the place is beyond all delight.
Would that you could rouse yourself and go there!
After all, perhaps it is harmful for you to sit for
so long in this dungheap. It could help you to
walk about.' Will responds: 'You were right to
seek out such things on my behalf and tell me
about them, but I do not know whether I am
able. Still, I will try to go out and get to it.' Thus
reason, as though through a back-door, reveals to
her the beauteous tree of chastity, describing what
sort of goods it embraces. Likewise, he explains
how whoever enjoys it can be freed from great and
burdensome cares, what great joy her unfurrowed
brow could show among people, and how secure
her conscience can be before God. Adding many

other similar remarks about chastity and the other
virtues, reason prudently entices will to enter the
garden and gradually begin to taste its fruits until,
full of delight, she will shout: 'Nourish me with
flowers, restore me with apples, for I languish with
love'.[†] For she has been filled not with that jus-   Sg 2:5
tice for which one grows in desire the more of it
one consumes, but rather with those things that
she previously longed for so ardently that never
could the eye see or the ear hear them enough.[†]   Qo 1:8
Now she is filled with all of them, and they are
transformed into a cause of revulsion to her. She
even freely places her servant, the body, under the
rule of reason, and furthermore urges him to serve
justice.^{11†}   Rm 6:19

16. On the exercise of humility. Five things can
assist us to exercise humility. The first is love of
lowliness, so that one seeks out those circumstances
in which a position of humiliation seems to exist
for him. The second is a continuous practice of
subjection, so that one always wants to be with
someone whom he respects and fears, in order
that he may learn to break his own will. For a
branch which is accustomed to be straight will,
if it is bent but not held very long in the new
position, rise up even stronger than before. If,
however, it is bent and holds that position for a
longer time, it becomes more difficult—indeed
much more difficult—for it to be straightened than
it was for it to be bent in the first place. You will
find the same thing to be true in the soul. The
third aid in the exercise of humility is a comparison
with a better person, so that an individual should
always be a companion to one in whom he finds

---

11. Compare III Sent 2 and Conv 6.9–22.40 (SBOp 4:81–
116).

the grace which is lacking in himself. Forgetting those things he has left behind, he should always strain toward those which lie before him.† Fourth is continuous meditation on one's condition, so that this verse will at once occur to you whenever you feel exalted: 'What reason do dust and ashes have to be proud?'† The fifth aid is to remember the one who watches you secretly. For how can someone who frequently confesses to another concerning words that he has spoken out of arrogance help but be thrown into confusion if it should happen that he notices his confessor listening when he later says something of the same sort? Thus an individual who remembers that there is one who watches secretly, to whom one's very thoughts make confession,† will not be able to keep from being ashamed if he should engage in prideful thoughts. And so it is extremely beneficial, not only against pride but against all the vices, for a person always to realize that God is watching him, to give heed to his gaze in one's heart, and to consider what he should do and what he should decide and what he should think as if it were of concern only to God.[12]

17. About what is written in Revelation: 'They follow the lamb wherever he goes'.† Those who follow the lamb wherever he goes, follow him to redemption—just as all may do, since he died for us all.† They also follow him to his law, although all do not do so, because all do not obey the commandments. They further follow him to his counsel, about which it is written: 'Let anyone who can accept this'†—he was referring here to chastity, to which not all of the elect follow him— and to the example of his passion, of which Peter

Marginal references:
See Ph 3:13
Si 10:9
Ps 76:10
Rv 14:4
2 Co 5:15
Mt 19:12

---

12. Compare II Sent 88 and III Sent 37.

speaks in the words: 'Christ has died for us, leaving us an example that we should follow in his footsteps'.[†] Those who follow the lamb to these four destinations truly follow him 'wherever he goes',[†] because he revealed these four to us himself.

18. On the threefold mercy of God and the four types of compassion. 'Take pity on me, God, through your great mercy'.[†] Divine mercy is threefold. It can be lesser, intermediate, or great. God takes pity on a sinner according to his lesser mercy when he tolerates him so far through his patience.[†] He takes pity on him according to his intermediate mercy when he suddenly stings him to tears. God takes pity on the sinner according to his great mercy when he grants him the strength to restrain himself from sin and resist vice. The first mercy is called lesser because no one is saved through it alone. The second is called intermediate because through compunction one begins to be saved, but he does not arrive at salvation unless he continues to refrain from sin. The third kind of mercy is called great because through it alone can one be saved. It is for this reason that even the prophet prays that God should take pity on him.[†] Thus, with respect to his mercy, God takes pity on us in many ways. And thus that mercy, which is like the mother of the types of the Lord's compassion, arises, about which it is written (indicating the fact of their succession): 'Destroy my iniquity through the many forms of your compassion'.[†] As I consider this idea of the multiplicity of the Lord's compassion, four ways of his taking pity especially come to mind. For God takes pity on a sinner sometimes by removing an occasion of sin, sometimes by adding bitterness to it, and sometimes by giving the strength to resist it. He shows complete and perfect compassion

1 P 2:21

See Rv 14:4

Ps 51:1

See Rm 9:22

Ps 51:1

Ps 51:1

when he utterly does away with the desire to sin.[13]

19. About the seven gifts of the Holy Spirit and how they combat the seven vices. There are seven vices which the seven gifts of the Holy Spirit drive out of us: negligence, curiosity, acquiescence, lust, bad habit, contempt, and malice. The fear of God expels negligence; piety, curiosity; knowledge, acquiescence; fortitude, lust; counsel, bad habit; understanding, contempt; and wisdom, malice.[14]

20. 'Wisdom overcomes evil. She reaches powerfully from one end of the earth to the other and orders all things sweetly.'† From the highest heaven* wisdom with her power cast down the proud demon and ordered things sweetly by strengthening humankind in the good, as long as it remained obedient. On earth, wisdom conquered evil by powerfully smashing its instruments† and ordered things sweetly by liberating humanity through the sweet teaching of the Gospel. Moreover, through her power she freed from hell those whom she had chosen and sweetly placed them in eternal beatitude.

'Wisdom overcomes evil. She reaches powerfully from one end of the earth to the other.'† Another interpretation: from the inception of evil through its consummation, which means from negligence to malice. Negligence makes a person fall asleep, curiosity entices him, acquiescence takes him captive, lust despoils him once he has been captured, bad habit binds him, contempt casts him into prison, and malice bars the door. The fear which is the beginning of wisdom† drives away negligence, which is the beginning of evil;

†Ws 7:30–8:1
*See Dt 4:32

Mt 12:29

Ws 7:30–8:1

Si 1:16

---

13. Compare Div 13 (SBOp 6/1:131–33).
14. Compare III Sent 4; III Sent 20; III Sent 89; and III Sent 98.

piety keeps away curiosity; knowledge, acquiescence; fortitude, lust; counsel, bad habit; understanding, contempt; and finally wisdom overcomes malice.[15†] And 'she reaches powerfully from one end of the earth to the other'[†] by expelling the vices and sweetly bestowing the virtues. Ws 7:30 Ws 8:1

21. Concerning the son of the king sitting in his chariot. 'Blessed is the man who has not strayed'.[†] Adam 'strayed' by assenting to temptation;[†] he 'stood'[†] by defending himself;[†a] and he 'sat'[†b] by teaching others to sin. In straying understand human fickleness; in standing understand obstinacy; and in sitting understand pride. One strays in four ways. Some are dragged away unwillingly, while others are seduced to leave. Still others are enticed away without realizing it, and some depart willingly. Fortitude is needed by the unwilling, temperance by those who are seduced, prudence by those who are enticed, and justice by those who leave willingly. Justice alone, however, suffices for all. The other three virtues are her guardians and assistants. Ps 1:1 See Gn 3:6 †Ps 1:1 †a See Gn 3:12 †b Ps 1:1

'Through the counsel of the wicked.'[†] The wicked one was the serpent, who wanted to involve Eve in his evil.[†] Eve was wicked, because she desired Adam to join in her transgression. Adam was wretched, because he 'strayed through the counsel of the wicked'.[†] Thus 'Blessed is the one'—in truth, anyone, either Christ or any of the members of Christ—because 'he has not strayed through the counsel of the wicked'.[†] Piety is the worship of God, which consists of three elements: faith, hope, and charity. Wickedness opposes piety, also through three elements: vanity, curiosity, and Ps 1:1 See Gn 3:1–6 Ps 1:1 Ps 1:1

---

15. Compare III Sent 4; III Sent 19; III Sent 89; and III Sent 98.

lust. Those who are impious are the devil, the
flesh, and the spirit. These three, coming together
in opposition to the Lord and his servant,[†] say:
'Come, let us lie in wait for blood.[†] Let there be
one purse for us all.'[†] The purse is human memory,
into which the devil puts temptation, the flesh puts
delight, and the spirit puts acquiescence—such is
the talent that each of them contributed. Later
they sat down to dine together. The devil demands
blood, the body the worm that dies, and the spirit
the worm that does not die.[†]

'And has not stood on the road of sin.'[†] If we
understand 'sin' as 'sinners', then 'the road of sin' is
the world, which is full of sinners. One who wishes
to avoid sins should not stand on the road of sin,
that is, in the world. If, however, we understand
'sin' to refer to sin itself, then 'the road of sin'
symbolizes our will, through which sins come and
go and meet with one another in turn (and just as
is said of Babylon, demons, owls, hairy beasts, and
the other things that are mentioned in Scripture[†]
congregate there). Or 'the road of sin' can be
understood as obstinacy, over which the followers
of sin come and go on two feet, namely their own
counsel and their own will.

'And he has not sat on the throne of pestilence.'[†]
This throne, which is called the throne of pestilence because it not only is harmful to itself but
infects many others besides, has four legs: malice,
which is the love of evil; cleverness in accomplishing things; impudence toward God; and lack of
respect for others. The throne has, as it were at
its rear, a backrest or support on which one can
lean—worldly power. Its footstool is one's body,
which one tramples with feigned abstinence. Its
feet, which are the states of the soul, doze in vainglory upon this abstinence of the body. The throne

Ps 2:2

Pr 1:11

Pr 1:14

See Is 66:24; Mk
9:43, 45, 47
Ps 1:1

See Is 13:21–22

Ps 1:1

also has a small pillow, earthly peace or prosperity, on which one can sit and rest.

'But his will is in the law of the Lord.'† The servile law does not transform souls, but the law of the Lord does.† For the carnal law in itself is like an empty jar which is filled with the wine of grace and intoxicates the whole world. It is the law of the letter. When it is illumined by grace, charity is effected—the law of the Lord, which transforms souls.† In this law of the Lord is his will.* The will may be just or blessed. That will is just which wants to desire the good, while that is blessed which does desire it. Insofar as the will was created by God, it is good, but as a result of the corruption of the passions it strays from God into the region of unlikeness.[16] Insofar as it wants to desire the good, it is just. Insofar as it actually desires the good, it is blessed. But insofar as it does not want to desire the good, it is wicked and perverse. Likewise, insofar as it desires the wicked, it is filthy and wretched. For to desire the wicked belongs to us, while to desire the good belongs to both us and God. To wish to desire the good belongs to God, but not to wish to desire the good belongs to the devil.[17]

Note that opposed to 'straying'† is stability of will in the law of the Lord. Opposed to 'standing'† is meditation on the law of the Lord. Likewise, opposed to 'sitting'† is the tree situated near the running stream.† Meditation on this law is threefold, because one must meditate on charity constantly,

Ps 1:2

Ps 19:8

†Ps 1:2 *Ps 1:2

Ps 1:1

Ps 1:1

Ps 1:1

Ps 1:3

---

16. This is the first occurrence in the text of the phrase 'regio dissimilitudinis', the 'region of unlikeness', which is discussed at length by Etienne Gilson, *The Mystical Theology of Saint Bernard*, trans. A.H.C. Downes; CS 120 (Kalamazoo: Cistercian Publications, 1990): 33–53. Much used by Bernard and other cistercian writers, it indicates the territory of sinfulness, or simply the world as a place of exile for the soul.

17. Compare III Sent 60.

so that it may exist where it is not, grow where it is slight, and be strengthened and made more powerful wherever it is great.

Ps 1:2   'And on his law he will meditate day and night.'[†] The day signifies prosperity and the night adversity, or the day is contemplation and the night action. Note that he has put in the law of the Lord first will and then meditation. For spiritual individuals first stir up their hearts to zeal of will and then go on to meditation, while carnal individuals bypass zeal of will and try, first or merely, to engage in meditation, even though it is written: 'Wisdom will not

Ws 1:4   enter into the ill-disposed soul'.[†] But understand that one who first wills and then meditates—that is, who is progressing in the law—is, as it were, a ten-

Dt 28:56   der and delicate[†] son lying on the gentle blankets of grace in the chariot of the Gospel, spiritually longing after the delights of God's law, laughing and singing: 'Who will separate us from the love of God? Tribulation? Hardship? Poverty? Hunger?

Rm 8:35   Danger? Or the sword?'[†] He burns with the love of Christ so much that, for Christ, he desires even

Rm 9:3   to be cut off from Christ[†] and to be stricken from
See Ex 32:32 the book of life[†]—to be cut off from Christ and stricken from the book of life not with reference to love or justice but with reference to beatitude, in that one wishes not to be blessed for the sake of Christ or one's neighbor, even though one does not wish to be unloving or unjust.[18]

The son of the king, therefore, sits in a chariot whose wheels sometimes seek the heights and sometimes the depths—love and fear, joy and sadness—love when he has things and fear lest he lose them, joy over what he possesses and sadness over what he has lost. Or: hope about those things he

---

18. Compare III Sent 25.

will have, joy over the things he has gained, fear about the things he is going to lose, and sorrow over the things he has lost. Understand, moreover, that the two horses drawing the chariot forward with weariness and effort—indeed worn out with labor and almost collapsing from exhaustion—signify threats and promises, since the servile spirit is fixed upon threats and the mercenary spirit upon promises: for unless a servant feared punishment he would not work, and a merchant would not succeed if he had no hope of profit.

Note, finally, that in meditation on the law of God those who ascend fall, but those who are raised descend. Those who ascend through an assumption that their talent is sufficient fall because of their error, while those who are raised up through grace know how to descend through humility.[19]

22. On the words of Isaiah: 'He will eat curds and honey.' 'He will eat curds and honey so that he may know to shun the wicked and to choose the good'.† The curd is a richer, more healthful substance which can be extracted from milk. It is also more pleasing to the Lord than milk is. Actually the curd refers to the Old Testament and honey to the New. In fact milk is the Old Testament: it is the nourishment of the early Church. 'Everyone subsisting on milk is incapable of digesting the doctrine of righteousness, for he is still a baby'.† The curds gleaned from it represent the understanding of the spiritual law, for just as the thickness of curds is such as to float atop other liquids, so too the grace of the New Testament exceeds that of the Old. So Christ is said to be like 'a craggy mount of many

Is 7:15

Heb 5:13

---

19. Compare II Sent 167; II Sent 187; and Div 87.2 (SBOp 6/1:330).

peaks, a rich mount. How can you look down on
such craggy mountains?'[20]† Christ, then, eats the
curd; that is, he draws it to himself and into himself,† because after the unnecessary rules of the law
have been renounced and forced aside as though
they were superfluous liquids, in the spiritual sense
one's entire understanding is brought into obedience to Christ.† Honey still in the wax, moreover,
represents charity in one's observances of the New
Testament. Lest anyone think that these should be
ignored, after his resurrection Christ is said to have
eaten honey with wax, that is the honeycomb.†
Honey is separated from the wax in order to bring
it to the peak of its strength and sweetness.† So too
charity is set apart from observances of law in the
precious and pure vessel of the conscience, in order
to be offered to the Lord to taste. Freed from rote
observances as the honey is from the wax, charity
naturally develops into a more precious thing of
spiritual brilliance. It becomes the candle which,
when placed on the lampstand which is Christ,
shines equally on all who are in the house of God.†
This, then, is the dish which Christ eats or tastes
'so that he may know to shun the wicked and to
choose the good'.† Following the tasting comes the
flavor, or wisdom—the one who, once evil has
been shunned and good chosen, delights in, and
holds as sweet and savory, the good work of our
redemption, and returns the savor of his humanity
to God the Father. So now the Father will not say:
'I regret having made humanity to live upon the
earth',† but 'This is my beloved Son, in whom I
am well pleased'.† Christ effects that same savor
for us with his own body, so that we should sing
to him with great joy:† 'The earth will be filled

Ps 68:15–16

See Jn 12:32

2 Co 10:5

Lk 24:42

See Jg 14:14

Mt 5:15

Is 7:15

Gn 6:7

Mt 3:17

1 Ch 29:17

---

20. Compare Div 33.8 (SBOp 6/1:227).

with the fruit of your works, O Lord', up to the
words: 'Bread will strengthen the hearts of human
beings'.† Ps 104:13–15
23. On the recovery of the human race, which
was lost. As a result of Mercy's effort, an assembly
was held in the heavenly recesses of God to effect
the recovery of the fallen human race. In this
council Mercy and Truth met with each other.† Ps 85:10
When two people meet with one another, each
must approach the other in order that they may
meet; otherwise they do not come together. If
Mercy did not meet with Truth, she would be
not mercy, but misery. If Truth did not meet with
Mercy, she would be not verity, but severity.[21] So
here Mercy and Truth met with one another,† and Ps 85:10
Mercy discussed the damnation of the human race
with Truth. Truth said: 'The judgment has been
fixed. The human race is dead. For Adam was
told: "In the hour when you eat of it, you will
surely die."† He did not obey; he ate. He is surely Gn 2:17
dead.' Mercy replied: 'Must it be that one who is
sleeping will never rise again?† What if a human Ps 41:8
being without sin were created from the same
earth? Perhaps he could wipe out the sin of the
first human?' But Truth responded: 'Impossible.
For the earth is accursed in the work of Adam,† Gn 3:17
and it will yield him nothing but brambles and
thistles.'† Then Mercy said: 'Certainly, the earth is Gn 3:18
accursed insofar as Adam's work is concerned, but
is it in terms of ours? And so it may be possible
for a human being without sin to be created from
it.' 'Recall humanity and the angels', replied Truth.
'Remember that each of them has fallen, and recall
that, without exception, every human being is but

---

21. There are plays on words here between 'misericordia'
and 'miseria' on the one hand, and 'veritas' and 'severitas' on
the other.

a shadow.† How could it be that a single human being, to whom the role of saving the whole world will be given, would not simply prove impotent? For to save is a greater thing than to be created, and it must be feared that one who was not faithful in small matters† is unlikely to be found faithful in a great one.' Mercy responded: 'It is true, Truth, that every human being is but a shadow.† But if you, steadfast Truth, were willing to undertake this task, no hint of vanity could undermine your effort.' At this Truth exclaimed: 'Father, let this cup pass from me, if it is possible. Nonetheless, let it be not as I will, but as you wish'.† Justice, hearing these words, intervened, saying: 'Impossible. The scepter of our kingdom is the scepter of integrity.† In the realm of justice, no sin can remain unpunished. Mercy cannot join with truth, nor truth with mercy.' But Truth again exclaimed: 'Father, if it is not possible for this cup to pass from me unless I drink of it, let your will be done'.† Hearing this, Justice embraced and kissed Peace,† who had been standing at a distance,† fearful because she did not know what the outcome would be. And so peace was achieved for those who were near and those who were far away† in one man, Christ, the mediator.[22]* For Christ is the truth rising from the earth†—that is, from blessed Mary. He is the justice of the Father from heaven†—that is, from the highest reaches of his judgment. On earth he watched out for humanity and took care that anyone who could not be saved except in a just fashion, was justly saved. The truth has risen from the earth. The Lord has bestowed his kindness,† namely the grace of the Holy Spirit. Our earth, that is the body of our Virgin, has given forth its fruit.† Justice will

Ps 39:6

See Lk 19:17

Ps 39:6

Mt 26:29

Ps 45:6

Mt 26:42
Ps 85:10
Lk 18:13

†Eph 2:17
*1 Tm 2:5
Ps 85:11

Ps 85:11

Ps 85:12

Ps 85:12

---

22. Compare to the foregoing III Sent 120 (at note 173).

walk before him† who is that fruit, and he will, Ps 85:13
as a result, place his feet onto the road† of human Ps 85:13
salvation so that, as we have said, the human race,
which could not be saved except in a just fashion,
may be justly saved.

24. Concerning the castle where two disciples
are sent by the Lord.† On his way to Jerusalem, See Mt 21:1–2
the Lord arrived at Bethphage. From there he sent
two of his disciples to a castle situated opposite
to them, instructing them to free an ass tied there
and her colt and lead them back to him. Bethphage
means the house of the mouth.[23] It is a village of
priests. It signifies confession, at which the Lord
arrives because he comes to those who confess.
For he is far from those who do not choose to
confess their faults, but he rests in those who make
confession. From Bethphage he sends two of his
disciples—that is, the Scripture in two Testaments
or the preachers who are endowed with twofold
charity—to the castle which lies opposite them:
that is, into the mind which is given over to its
own desires. In that castle stands the wall which
is obstinacy, because a person of this sort resists
with an obstinate spirit all the things which are
enjoined on him. There are also weapons inside—
that is, harsh words with which such an individual
snaps—and he is often feared because of them and
defended by them lest anything be imposed on
him. The food in the castle is the fruit which
follows from this, since for his obstinacy and harsh
words he frequently gets some repose, because
at least it is gratifying for him to fulfill his own
will. It is in this castle that the ass is tied, along
with her colt—that is, humility and simplicity.
For one given to his own will sometimes knows

---

23. See Jerome, *Liber interpr. hebr. nom.*; in CCL 72:135.

what humility is. Likewise, he knows that he could possess simplicity, if he wished to. He also knows, however, that if he did so, he could not fulfill his own desire. So he has tied them up and put them away, not allowing them to appear. But when a person such as this is moved by the divine word, he tears down the wall of obstinacy, throws aside the weapons of harsh speech, and comes to regard the sustenance of repose which is wickedly sought to be of little value. He unties the ass and her colt, and hurriedly leads them to the Lord at Bethphage. In other words, he confesses that he has sinned in these matters and hopes henceforth to live humbly and simply.[24] What previously was a castle of the devil becomes 'the city of our strength, Zion:

Is 26:1

our Savior is its wall and its rampart'.[†] The wall is humility, the rampart patience. This city also has several gates—the ears, the eyes, and so forth. These should not always be open. They should be open to God, but closed to the devil. For the body is a drawbridge over which one ascends into the city. As such it should be raised and lowered, lowered so that it can provide support for the spirit, but raised so that it cannot be trodden by the vices or the devil. Thus entry into the city will be denied them.[25]

25. On the attachment of the apostle to his brothers: 'I hoped to be cut off from Christ for

Rm 9:3

the sake of my brothers'.[†] There are two things in Christ, love and beatitude. Likewise, on the part of his enemy there are the two things opposite to them, hatred and misery. Since it is better to wish to be just than to wish to be blessed, the apostle, out of his great attachment to justice, wanted to

---

24. Compare III Sent 12.
25. Compare III Sent 8.

be cut off from the beatitude of Christ and to be wretched (not, however, to be cut off from his love, which would be wicked and unjust) in order to make his brothers participants in the love of Christ, whom they ought to love and long for just as they all love him.[26] This is the highest form of justice, even though it cannot in fact be realized: the more we wish to be cut off from Christ's beatitude for the love of Christ—in order that we may make our brothers participants in Christ's love—the more we are found worthy of it. These are words describing disposition, therefore, rather than the actual result.[27]

26. On the three grades of obedience. There are three grades of obedience. When one fears that he may transgress, he exhibits an obedience which derives from timidity. Then, when one obeys out of a hope of reward, he exhibits an obedience which aims to be meritorious. Finally there is chaste and filial obedience, exhibited by one who trusts that all the things that belong to his Father are also his.[28†]   Jn 17:10

27. On the three matters for which we should render account to God. We are going to render account to God† regarding three things: as a result   Rm 14:12
of the fact that we are rational beings, that we have not received our soul in vain;† by reason of the fact   Ps 24:4
that we are Christians, that we have not taken the name of the Lord in vain;† and because we have   Ex 20:7
been called to some part of the duty of saints† in   Col 1:12
that we are called clerics or monks, that we have not received the grace of God to no purpose.†   2 Co 6:1

---

26. Compare III Sent 21 (at note 18).

27. There is a play on words here between 'affectus' ('disposition') and 'effectus' ('result').

28. Compare III Sent 92 (at note 94); III Sent 121 (at note 179); and Dil 12.34–14.38 (SBOp 3:148–52).

28. On the words of Solomon: 'Woe to anyone who is alone! Woe to anyone who is alone!';[†] that is, woe to one who hides his sins in the recesses of his conscience and does not want to have a colleague or confidant who can assist him if he falls. Or, 'Woe to anyone who is alone!';[†] that is, woe to one who in his arrogant isolation presumes to introduce innovations into the community.

Qo 4:10 (margin)

29. On discretion. In the paradise which is the cloister, there ought to exist that tree of the knowledge of good and evil[†] which is discretion. It should, however, stand in its proper place—that is, among the superiors. As far as those who are under them are concerned, whoever touches it will surely die,[†] because it is not proper for those who are ruled to make discretionary judgments, but simply to obey.

Gn 2:16–17 (margin)

Ex 19:12 (margin)

30. On the words of the apostle: 'I want to be gone.' 'I want to be gone and to be with Christ, but it is necessary for me to remain in the flesh for your sake'.[†] It is certain that Christ is with us, for as he said himself: 'Behold, I am with you even until the end of the world'.[†] For us to be with Christ is a blessed and glorious thing, whether it be in this world through contemplation, or in the next by reason of our beatitude. So love of God carries us upward, but love of neighbor presses us downward, hanging, as it were, from our neck. Thus, these words follow: 'It is necessary for me to remain in the flesh for your sake'.[†]

Ph 1:23–24 (margin)

Mt 28:20 (margin)

Ph 1:24 (margin)

31. There are four kinds of monks in every cloister.[†] It can be shown that in every cloister there are the four kinds of monks that blessed Benedict describes. There are cenobites, serving God in the common rule of their monastery and their common life of obedience to authority. There are anchorites, of whom it is said in the book of

See RB 1 (margin)

Job that 'they build lonely places for themselves'.[†] Jb 3:14
Although they are involved in a common way
of life with their brothers, they nonetheless, in
a praiseworthy fashion, devote themselves to private contemplation. There are also gyrovages of
the flesh, who are corporally enclosed within the
walls of the monastery, but wander about the entire
world in their hearts and their conversation. There
are spiritual gyrovages, who pass from meditative
reading to prayer and from prayer to work in a
lighthearted fashion. In nothing they do can they
anticipate the fruit that comes from stability which
is constant and devotion which perseveres. Rather,
in their mental sloth they think first this, then that,
to be better, and while they begin everything, they
complete nothing. There are also sarabites who
love themselves[†] and are interested in their own   2 Tm 3:2
welfare.[†] In any community there may be two or   Ph 2:21
three or four of them, always devising new ideas
and innovations, quite peculiar to themselves and
against the common rule of the monastery. Forming factions and cliques within the community,
they defend one another and the divisions created
by their unorthodox ideas, and do not cease their
disturbance of the Lord's flock.

32. On voluntary sacrifice. 'I will make sacrifice to you of my own will'.[†] A father has an ill   Ps 54:6
son, who cannot be cured without surgery and
cauterization. He asks his son whether he wants
to be bound in order to undergo the procedure.
The son, wanting to be well, asks to be tied down,
and for the surgery and cauterization to be done.
After he has been bound and begins to feel the fire
or the blade, however, he rages, shouts, and begs
to be released. But the father will not untie him
until he is cured. If, then, you consider the will
of the sick man, you will understand that he both

wants and does not want to be untied. On the one
hand he wants to be cured, but he does not want
to be operated on or cauterized. When, however,
he has been cured, he is glad to have been tied
and cut and burned, just as before he was bound
he wanted, because of his longing for health, to
be tied down and operated on and cauterized. So
it is with the monk who freely and knowingly has
bound himself to the monastic discipline. If during
his time of discipline, which will always have some
element of pain in it, he tries to break the chains
to which, joyously and of his own volition, he has
submitted, after this temptation he will rejoice to
have submitted to them. He will then be able to
sing with confidence: 'I will make sacrifice to you

Ps 54:6
of my own free will'.†

33. On the first, second, and third heaven and
the two seraphim. Paul was taken up into the third

See 2 Co 12:2
heaven.† The first heaven is one's initial position
in the Church of God, which is that of secular
but catholic persons. This heaven, like the earth,
is filled with the light of the sun, because there

Ps 19:6
is no one who can hide from its heat,† and God

See Jn 13:32
is glorified† in both their good deeds and their
wicked ones, in what they desire and what they do
not. The second heaven is the second position, that
of the religious. Just as air is filled with sunlight, this

Ml 4:2
status is filled with the sun of justice† in their hearts
and consciences. The third heaven is the third
position, that of the perfect who, just as the ether
burns with the very presence of the sun, themselves

Jn 5:35
burn and shine† with the heat and light of the sun of

Ml 4:2
justice†—with his most brilliant and clear presence.

See 2 Co 12:2
It was to this heaven that Paul was taken up,† and
from this heaven he burns. The seraph stands over

See Is 6:2
it†—that is, in it he has his essence and being—
burning totally from it.

Each of the seraphim has six wings.[†] They fly   Is 6:2
with two of them, cover their head with two,
and cover their feet with two[†]—their own feet,   See Is 6:2
I note, not God's. For those holy beings fly on two
wings—that is, fear and hope—when, according
to the counsel of wisdom, they are mindful in all
things of their ends,[†] that is, of heaven and earth.   Si 7:40
On the one wing, which is hope, they fly upward
to that fire so as always to burn with it. On the
other, which is fear, they fly according to the words
of Job, 'visiting their sheepfold lest they should
sin'[†]—that is, returning to themselves and descend-   Jb 5:24
ing beneath themselves into hell itself,[†] down into   Ps 55:15
that eternal fire.[†] Whenever they descend there, in   Mt 18:8
order to be able to step upon the burning coals
safely they cover and protect their feet—that is,
their affections—with those two wings which are
penance of the heart and confession of the mouth.
When they are carried back up on the wing[28b],
of good hope, they cover their head, that is their
mind, with the two wings which are love of God
and neighbor as they prepare to pass through the
powers of air which lie in ambush for them on
one side and the other. This is so that they cannot
be seen in their ascent by the one who looks on
everything with arrogance and is the king of all the
sons of pride.[29†]   See Jb 41:25

34. On the sevenfold bathing in the Jordan.[30]
Naaman, the leper, who represents any sinner desiring to be cleansed, came to the Word of God
and heard him say: 'Go, wash seven times in the

28b. I follow the variant 'ala' rather than the reading 'aliae'
of the critical text.

29. Compare I Sent 33; II Sent 134; III Sent 92; and Div
123.2 (SBOp 6/1:401–402).

30. Compare to this text III Sent 88 (at note 81) and Res
3.1–5 (SBOp 5:103–109).

2 K 5:10 Jordan',[†] and your soul will be cleansed. The name Jordan means 'descent',[31] that is, humility, which signifies the profession of the religious life. The sevenfold bathing in the Jordan is as follows: the first involves the outside of the body, which is the renunciation of external things; the second involves the area around the body, which is the change of attire; the third is within the body, which involves the binding and display of one's mem-
2 Co 10:5 bers in obedience to Christ.[†] Then there are two bathings of the tongue: to avoid boastful words in good times and to shun impatient ones in times of adversity. There are also two of the heart: to spurn one's own will and not to dare to make any defense of one's own opinion or judgment.

Note that all these are found in the Lord Jesus. We see the first in the words: 'Although he was
See 2 Co 8:9 rich, he became poor';[†] the second in 'She wrapped
Lk 2:7 him in swaddling clothes';[†] the third in 'Jesus began
Ac 1:1 to teach and act';[†] the fourth in 'He fled into the
Jn 6:15 mountains'[†] because they wanted to make him
Jn 8:49 king; the fifth in 'I am not possessed';[†] the sixth in 'I
Jn 6:38 have not come to do my own will' and so on;[†] and the seventh in 'Did you not know that I must be
Lk 2:49 about my father's business?'[†] —but although he said this, he did not persist in his view, but 'went down
Lk 2:51 with them and lived under their authority'.[32][†]

Through these seven bathings the leper is cleansed. In a similar manner a sinner is cured through the sevenfold grace of the Holy Spirit, which is found even in the Lord.

35. 'My people have committed a double crime: they have abandoned me, the fountain of living water, and have dug old cisterns for themselves,
Jr 2:13 cisterns which hold no water'.[†] In me they have abandoned the fountain which lies open for the

---

31. See Jerome, *Liber interpr. hebr. nom.*; in CCL 72:67.
32. Compare SC 19.7 (SBOp 1:113).

cleansing of sinners, the fountain of living water[†]   Jr 2:13
made available to all for the restoration of life and
justification. They have instead dug,[†] that is, made   Jr 2:13
for themselves at great labor, the cisterns[†] of their   Jr 2:13
observances and justifications. But anyone who
trusts in these more than in God is lost.

36. On the master, the servant, and the ill person. With the body and soul, it is as with a master
and a servant. Just as the master is in his house, so
is Christ in the mind. The servant is the spirit or
reason, and the body is like a sick person to whom
the servant ministers at the order of the Lord. But
care must be taken that the obedience owed to the
Lord should not be abandoned so that service can
be done to the one who is ill.[33]

37. Four things teach and strengthen humility:
the exercise of humility through the poorness of
one's clothing, food, and similar things; consideration of oneself; consideration of those better
than oneself; and consideration of the judgments
of God.[34] In the first place, vainglory lies in ambush
against the material poverty we have mentioned;
then love of self attacks the second, envy or vainglory the third, and despair the fourth.

38. On the three things which preserve unity.
We need three things to secure unity: patience of
soul, charity toward our neighbor, and humility
before God. Patience is the guardian of the soul, as
the Lord says: 'In your patience you will save your
souls'.[†] Patience is like a shield. If it is shattered,   Lk 21:19
we are protected by humility, which is like a breastplate. Peter denied Christ through impatience,[†] but   Mt 26:70
he wept over it because of humility.[†] Love is the   Mt 26:75
lance with which we strike out in all directions.[35]

---

33. Compare III Sent 65.
34. Compare II Sent 88 and III Sent 16.
35. Compare I Sent 32.

Gn 25:22

Gn 25:31–33
†Gn 30:25ff
*Gn 32:24ff

Gn 25:22
Gn 25:31–34,
27:1ff.
Gn 31:7

Gn 32:24–28
Eph 6:12

Jb 30:29

2 Co 11:14

See Is 9:5,
Septuagint version

Lk 11:8

See 2 Co 2:7

39. On the threefold wrestling of Jacob. We wrestle against the flesh, against the world or false brothers, against the devil, and against God. Jacob wrestled with his brother in his mother's womb,† and after a fashion he wrestled with him again when he took his birthright.† Then he wrestled with Laban,† and finally with the angel.* Laban, which means 'whitening',[36] signifies the devil.[37]

39B. Jacob first wrestled with Esau, in his mother's womb,† and a second time in his father's home.† He wrestled a third time with Laban, who altered his wages ten times in turn,† and a fourth time with the angel, who changed his name for the better.† So our first struggle is against flesh and blood,† when we have not yet been born to God. Our second is with those with whom we live in the religious life, for as is said in the book of Job: 'I have become the brother of jackals and the companion of ostriches'.† Our third struggle is with the devil, who is 'whitened'[38] because he disguises himself as an angel of light.† Finally we struggle with the angel, that is with Christ, the angel of great counsel,† who admonishes us urgently to persevere for as long as it takes for us to be filled with spiritual blessing.[39]†

40. On the person who is consumed by grief. Just as an infant will perish unless he is removed from the baptismal water, a sinner can be so consumed with grief over his sins† that he does not rise up to hope.

41. On the threefold question and injunction

36. See Jerome, *Liber interpr. hebr. nom.*; in CCL 72:68.
37. Compare II Sent 94.
38. See Jerome, *Liber interpr. hebr. nom.*; in CCL 72:68.
39. This text is a variant version of III Sent 39, appearing in several manuscripts. Though relegated to the apparatus in the critical edition, it seems sufficiently distinctive to warrant inclusion here. Compare also II Sent 94.

of the Lord to Peter. Three times the Lord said to Peter 'Do you love me? Then feed my sheep':[†] Jn 21:15–17 meaning feed them through your life, your teaching, and your prayer.

42. On the weapons of Goliath. The weapons of Goliath which David put in his tent[†] seem to 1 S 17:54 be those about which the apostle warns us, to the effect that we should not allow any of our bodily members to become unholy weapons used for sin, but should make them weapons fighting for justice.[†] The sword of Goliath is the emotion of anger Rm 6:13 which, when turned to a good purpose sought with zeal, passes into David's use and slices away not only the crown of pride,[†] but the members of ex- 1 S 17:51 cess as well. Thus it is written: 'My sword will feed on flesh'.[†] With this sword Phineas, striking out Dt 32:42 furiously against wickedness, restrained the anger of God.[†] The priest Abimelech kept this same See Nb 25:7–9 sword of Goliath wrapped <in a cloth behind> the ephod[40] in the tabernacle.[†] And Christ said to See 1 S 21:9 Peter: 'Put your sword back in its scabbard'.[†] Thus, Jn 18:11; Mt 26:52 the sword of the devil is transformed into the sword of Christ, so that that which once served sin may now serve justice.[†] See Rm 6:19

43. Concerning the tribute which David took from the Philistines as a means of controlling them. David took tribute from the hands of the Philistines as a means of controlling them.[†] As long as any- 2 S 8:1 one is a servant of sin,[†] he pays tribute to the Rm 6:17 Philistines—that is, to unclean spirits. If, however, he becomes just and strong of hand, when he restrains his vices he takes back the tribute from the hands of those whom he had previously served. For the very temptation by which the just person

---

40. I translate according to the scriptural reference, understanding the text to read 'involutum <pallio post> ephod'.

is instructed, so long as he does not give in to it, constitutes a great increase in virtue for him.

44. About the words: 'David defeated the Moabites, and he measured them off with a rope, making them lie on the ground'.[†] 'David defeated the Moabites, and he measured them off with a rope, making them lie on the ground'.[†] The Moabites are those proud, arrogant, puffed up individuals who have the devil for a father.[41†] Thus it is written: 'We have heard of the pride of Moab—it is an excessive pride. His pride and arrogance are greater than his courage'.[†] The true David strikes them from time to time when he subjects them to whipping. Shaken by grief over their punishment, they measure out the extent of their faults and, leaving the heights of pride behind, they are made to lie on the ground, as if to say: 'You know that we are dust',[†] and 'What have dust and dirt to be proud about?'[†]

From that divine flogging, however, some proceed to death and others to life. So it follows: 'He measured out two lines, one to be put to death and one to be left alive',[†] because 'The Lord scrutinizes the just and the unjust'[†] and 'He repays each and every one according to their works'.[†] Or we can put it another way, according to these words: 'The Lord gives death and gives life; he takes one down to hell and lifts another up'.[†] One can find much more in this vein: 'I will strike, and I will heal'.[†]

45. On the words of the Song of Songs: 'Eat and drink, eat and drink, drink deeply, my friends, my dearest friends'.[†] Some friends are dear, others dearer, and still others dearest of all. Those who are 'dear' eat, because those who are holy in this life take up or penetrate the word of God only

2 S 8:2

2 S 8:2

Jn 8:44

See Is 16:6

Ps 103:14
Si 10:9

2 S 8:2
Ps 11:5
Ps 62:12

1 S 2:6
Dt 32:39

Sg 5:1

---

41. Jerome, *Liber interpr. hebr. nom.* [in CCL 72:69] gives the meaning of 'Moab' as 'de patre', 'from the father'.

with difficulty. Those who are 'dearer' drink—
that is, they swallow without effort; these are holy
souls, stripped of their bodies and rejoicing in God.
Those who are 'dearest' drink deeply; these are
the holy angels or saints after the reception of the
solemn garment,† that is, of their bodies.[42]   Gn 45:22

46. On purity of heart, goodness of conscience,
and true faith. Anyone who wishes to possess charity should have a pure heart, a good conscience,
and true faith.† We owe certain things particu-   See 1 Tm 1:5
larly to God (for example, religious worship), and
certain others to our neighbor (like the duties of
fraternal charity), and still others to ourselves (for
instance, to serve our own needs in a holy fashion).
A person who, in a religious spirit, gives those
things which he owes to God and neighbor has a
pure heart, and if he is devout even in those things
that pertain to himself, he has a good conscience.
In each of these areas, moreover, he should have
perseverance, which means having true faith. For
there is a false faith, as is written: 'They believe for
a while, and in time of trial they give up'.†   Lk 8:13

47. On the three things that were announced to
Abraham. The three things announced to Abraham were suffering, respite, and glorification, for
as was told him: 'Know this for certain. . . . You,
however, shall go. . . . But in the fourth generation. . . .'†   Gn 15:13–16

48. On Peter's first and second guardposts. Peter
passed through a first and a second guardpost.†   Ac 12:10
The first guardpost is the desire of the flesh or
the world.† The second is that vainglory which   See 1 Jn 2:16–17
surrounds Peter and keeps watch on him. When
he has passed it by, he comes to an iron gate† —that Ac 12:10
is, death, which is harsh and weighty for mortals

---

42. Compare Dil 11.33 (SBOp 3:146–47).

Ac 12:10
and, since it is common and natural to all, is said to open of its own accord.[†] Having passed it, he beholds God face to face and says: 'Now I know for certain that the Lord sent his angel and snatched
Ac 12:11
me from Herod's hand'.[†]

Ac 12:10
1 Jn 2:17
1 Jn 2:16
49. On the same text. The first guardpost[†] is the desire of the world,[†] the second the desire of the flesh.[†] The latter we pass by with difficulty, because we can abandon worldly concerns more easily than
Ac 12:10
we can avoid the desires of the flesh. The iron gate[†] is vainglory or spiritual pride. It is iron because it is weighty and difficult for all to get through, and it offers no easy exit for travelers. Still, it is said to open on its own because when the faithful soul has gotten past the preceding guardposts through the grace of God, that same grace opens the gate for it as it were 'on its own', because in this case grace is far more abundant than in the other two. It is entirely proper that the individual who has labored through grace to get past the preceding guardposts should find God even more gracious in this final instance, so that he may rightly say: 'Now I know
Ac 12:11
for certain that God has sent his angel'.[†]

50. On the three stages in faith. Note that there are three stages in faith. The first consists in the natural knowledge of reason, according to the words: 'The invisible aspects of God are perceived through the understanding of the things
Rm 1:20
which he has made'.[†] The second stage is that which flesh and blood do not reveal, nor sense power or natural reason discover, but to which the Holy Spirit alone leads. For who can comprehend the mystery of human salvation, unless the Holy Spirit has revealed it to him? Thus it is written: 'You are blessed, Simon Bar Jonah, for it was not flesh and blood that revealed this to you, but my
Mt 16:17
Father who is in heaven'.[†] The third stage of faith

is far more difficult to grasp, since it is far more exalted and removed from the power of human comprehension.

51. On the Moabite Ruth. Ruth, the Moabite, represents the sinful soul which has followed her mother-in-law,[43] which is the Church, out of the region of darkness and arrived in Judea, the land of confession.† There, in the field of Boaz—that is, in Holy Scripture—she gathers up the sheaves which have escaped the hands of the reapers.† These are certain points untouched by the great doctors, which the law has ordained should remain as food for the widow, the orphan, and the stranger† following behind the reapers, so that in her thoughts the soul may not depart from catholic doctrine. The great reapers are Augustine, Jerome, Gregory, and certain others who have gathered great bales of insight from Scripture. They have left us traces of these in their writings, so that through the sheaves which we collect ourselves and those which we comprehend through them our soul can feed during time of famine and survive by dipping its mouth into the wine† of sorrow and consuming it along with the servants of Christ† — that is, regarding itself in humility among the least who are in the Church.†

Nor should one who has vowed himself to christian discipline reap any longer in another's field†—that is, immerse himself in secular studies. Beating his harvest with a rod (that is, with acute discernment), then, he discovers three measures,† which are the three kinds of understanding according to the measure of Christ's gift.† For on that very night (that is, in one's consideration of

See Rt 1:7

See Rt 2:3

See Dt 24:19

See Rt 2:14
See Rt 2:22

See 1 Co 6:4

See Rt 2:22

Rt 2:17

Eph 4:7

---

43. The critical edition reads 'nurum' ('daughter-in-law'), but I emend it to 'socrum' ('mother-in-law') as the sense requires.

the approach of death), while the true Boaz is win-

Rt 3:2–3 nowing grain on his threshing floor†—for the time
has come for the judgment to begin at the house of
1 P 4:17 God†—Ruth bathes herself, is anointed with oil,
Rt 3:3 and puts on fine clothing,† in accordance with the
Ps 6:6 words: 'I will soak my bed with tears every night',†
Ps 45:8 and 'Myrrh and aloes waft from your robes',† and
so forth, so that she may become 'the sweet scent
2 Co 2:15 of Christ'.† Then, turning back the cover at his
Rt 3:4 feet†—which means, feeling the nearness of Christ
from the mystery of his incarnation—she pleads to
be protected by that same cover. She has not yet
arrived, however, at the point of marriage, when
Sg 4:9 Christ will say to her: 'My sister, my bride',† until
Rt 3:12 another who seemed a closer kinsman†—namely,
free choice—first removes his sandal according to
See Rt 4:7–8 the specification of the law.† This is because no one
is redeemed by his own strength but only through
the grace of Christ.

52. How camp is to be moved. O Lord, I am
lazy and slow to move camp and follow the escort
of your tabernacle, because I have encamped on
See Nb 2:25 the north side,† where those who are the most
recent recruits to your army are located. Those
who are first in your battle line have pitched their
Nb 2:3 tents on the eastern flank.† The sun of justice† rises
Ml 4:2 upon them, as it were always new, so that they
2 Co 4:16 might be renewed each day† and pass from glory
†See 2 Co 3:18 to glory.† Those assigned to the south* follow them
*Nb 2:10 in line. They burn with desire and look constantly
to your love. After them are positioned those to
Nb 2:18 the west.† Their sins are disappearing every day.
The most recent recruits of all are those stationed
See Nb 2:25 to the north.† Moist with cold, they can barely stir
themselves to follow the others.

These four divisions all have three tribes, in
which can be discerned those who are perfect,

those of middling status, and those who are defi-
cient. Let your camp receive me among those who
are the most recent and laziest, the most recent and
least of them all,† so that I may follow all of the $\quad$ See 1 Co 15:7–8
others courageously leading your ensigns, Lord,
even though I am deformed! For what can I (who
corrupts your army with my filthy stench) reckon
myself among these others but a dead body? At
least let bandits thrust me into the tomb of Elisha,† $\quad$ See 2 K 13:21
because if only his bones touch me, at once will I
arise, alive and well, and, O Lord of hosts, hasten
swiftly into your army! For what should I refer to
as bandits except my sins, which have stolen me
from you—indeed have stolen me from myself—
and thrown me away, like a dead body, choked
and devoid of life? Would that through fear of my
sins I may at least be thrown into the tomb of the
true Elisha, who has been shaved† for my sake— $\quad$ See 2 K 2:23; 1 Ch
in order that I may be accepted and considered $\quad$ 19:4
the most lowly of all those who are in his house!† $\quad$ See Ps 84:10
Perhaps he may look upon my humility† and touch $\quad$ See Ps 31:7
my dead limbs with his powerful bones, and I may
rise up, alive again!

53. On the spiritual edifice. The house of God
is built primarily of three virtues, which are (as
it were) its foundation, its wall, and its ceiling.
Through three elements, moreover, it extends into
the three regions of the soul: through the cross
of true penance it extends into the memory, the
seat of faith; through spiritual poverty it extends
into the intellect, the seat of hope; and through
obedience it extends into the will, the seat of
charity. There are three things which strengthen
obedience and make it firm: humility, contempt
for the world, and patience. The first of these
pertains to faith, the second to hope, and the third
to charity. Because the devil strives to undermine

patience in three ways—namely, through insulting
language, loss of possessions, and bodily pain—the
three virtues—humility, contempt for the world,
and the hope of eternal reward—stand in front of
patience and defend her against them.

Obedience, moreover, is borne on four wheels,
through which the entire edifice of God is kept
firm and stable amidst the winds and waves. These
are prudence, temperance, fortitude, and justice,
which are to be understood in the human being,

the bull, the lion, and the eagle.† Likewise disobedience is borne on four wheels, and the whole
house of the devil rests on them and guards them.
They are lust, pride, gluttony, and anger, represented by the caterpillar, the locust, the grasshopper,
and the gnawer.⁴⁴† In this house of disobedience
are three offspring. The first of them takes the first
place; from him the entire apparatus of wickedness
arises. The three are represented by the flesh of
swine,† the mole, and the bat,* which are respectively the desire of the flesh,† the desire for worldly
things, and intellectual pride. These three steal the
site of God's house and reduce it to a desert where,
as the forest of vice springs up, beasts can take up
residence and birds build their nests. For the desire
of the flesh,† particularly fornication, destroys the
foundation of faith, and so the apostle writes: 'Can
I take parts of Christ's body and join them to
the body of a prostitute?'† The desire for earthly
things, which is the love of the world, eliminates
any place for charity, for as John says: 'Love of the
Father cannot exist in one who loves the world'.†
Likewise, intellectual pride removes any place for
hope, for as the Lord says: 'I watched Satan fall like
lightning from heaven'.†

See Ezk 1:10

See Jl 1:4

†Is 65:4
*See Is 2:20
1 Jn 2:16

1 Jn 2:16

1 Co 6:15

1 Jn 2:15

Jn 10:18

---

44. Compare to the foregoing III Sent 121 (at note 178).

There are, however, three things which admon-
ish and encourage us so that, once the kingdom of
the devil has been destroyed, we may restore and
rebuild the house of God. These are humanity's
fall, the threat of hell, and the promise of heavenly
glory. There are three things which aid in this
restoration: fasting, almsgiving, and prayer. Fasting
is related to a twofold cross: that of the breast,
which is taken up in Bethany,† and that of the back,   See Mt 26:6
which is taken up in Bethphage.† Almsgiving is   See Mt 21:1
related to the cross of the head, which is that taken
up on the Mount of Olives,† while prayer is related   See Mt 26:30
to the cross of the forehead, which is assumed in
the valley of Jehoshaphat.† Finally, there are three   Jl 3:12
things which in this world undertake to strengthen
and protect the kingdom of God, and in the future
world will perfect it and bring it to fruition: justification, peace, and joy in the Holy Spirit. Thus
the apostle says: 'The kingdom of God does not
mean food and drink; it means justification and
peace and joy in the Holy Spirit'.[45]†   Rm 14:17

---

45. A single manuscript offers the following mutilated
variant of this text:
'On the construction of the house of God and the chariot
of obedience. The house of God is principally built of three
virtues—as it were the foundation, the wall, and the roof—
in the three powers of the soul, namely the memory, the
intellect, and the will. The location is prepared through three
things: by the cross of true penance, the place is made ready
for faith; through poverty of spirit, it is prepared for hope;
and through obedience, it is made ready for charity. This
obedience is carried on four wheels. Of these each is needed
by the others, and through them the whole house of God
stands firm and strong amidst the winds and waves of the
sea. They are contempt of the world, the hope of eternal
reward, humility, and patience. Now contempt of the world
is needed for humility, and patience for hope. Since the devil
attacks our patience in three way—by insulting language, loss
of possessions, and bodily suffering—it is necessary that the
other three (namely humility, contempt of the world, and
the hope of eternal reward) precede patience and defend her
against these assaults.

54. On the four judgments. There are four judgments: one according to foreknowledge, a second according to cause, a third according to action, and a fourth according to retribution. We were judged according to foreknowledge before we existed. We are judged according to cause from that which we begin to be, when we are either good or evil. We are judged according to action when we demonstrate outwardly through our works what sort of persons we are inwardly, in our very being. We will be judged according to retribution when, in receiving reward for our good works, we will perceive what sort of persons we were foreseen to be by God from all eternity.

Of these four judgments, two are hidden—those according to foreknowledge and cause—and so in them human judgment is not involved. The two others—the judgments according to action and retribution—are public. In the first of them, judgment according to action, the power to judge is given by God to those in the present world. The second, judgment according to retribution, will be made not by other people but by God in the future. Judgment according to foreknowledge, moreover, is hidden and immutable. Judgment according to cause is hidden but can be changed. Judgment according to retribution is public and immutable. Judgment according to action is, after a fashion, a reflection and sign of the judgment according to retribution, because the former makes the cause clear and gives an indication of the divine

---

'There are, moreover, three other things which remove any place for God's house and reduce it to a desert where, as the dark forest of vice grows up, beasts take up residence and birds build their nests—namely, the desires of the flesh, the desires. . . .'

foreknowledge, while the latter will make the cause public and ratify God's foreknowledge.

55. There are two kinds of contemplation, one of love and the other of reason. These are wisdom and knowledge, which are sun and moon, day and night in the firmament of the Church. Of them the psalm says: 'Day gives word of it to day; night hands knowledge of it to night'.† Ps 19:2

56. 'Times will pass by and knowledge will grow manifold'.† Wisdom diminishes every day and al- Dn 12:4 most ceases to exist, while knowledge increases, grows, and spreads.

57. Knowledge for its own sake is curiosity. Knowledge which exists in order to be seen is vanity. Knowledge which exists in order to help one's brother is charity. Knowledge which aims at loving God and molding one's life is wisdom. This kind of knowledge is embraced, however, not with the help of writing or memory, but by the disposition of a pious mind and through a good conscience.[46]

58. A good and tranquil conscience is found in the perfect, a good but not tranquil conscience in those still imperfect, a wicked and not tranquil conscience in those just beginning to change, and a wicked but tranquil conscience in the obdurate.

59. In the Trinity, the Son is called the Word and Wisdom. He does not, however, become the Word for everyone, for not all are wise.[47] This fact is not imputed as a sin for anyone. But the will of the Father and the Son is understood in the Holy Spirit. This will is truly good, and one who is not a

---

46. Compare I Sent 19; III Sent 108 (at note 125); and SC 36.3 (SBOp 2:5–6).
47. Compare III Sent 62.

partner with it—that is, who is not of good will—
sins against the Holy Spirit.

60. Any desire for the good in us is God's will.
An inclination toward evil is our own will. A desire
for the good and an inclination not to want evil
represent both God's will and our own. A desire
not to want the good is entirely diabolic.[48]

61. The Father's power creates and sustains; the
Son's wisdom gives order and beauty to each creature; and the goodness of the Holy Spirit brings
more and more benefits. Certain things are useful
to some creatures, all things are useful to some,
and to some no things are useful; but there are no
things useful to no creatures, and no things useful
to all.

Certain things are useful to some creatures—
bread, for example. For some creatures, too, all
things are turned to the good.[†] To some creatures
no things are useful—to stones, for instance. There
are no things that are useful to no creature, and no
things that are useful to them all, because on the
one hand there exists nothing which cannot be
useful to some creature, and there exists nothing
which can be useful to all creatures. Usefulness is
found both in power and in wisdom, because the
Spirit proceeds from both the Father and the Son.

62. As long as a son is in the loins of his father,
he is not yet born, nor is he separated from his father except through a specific desire and temporal
action of the father. So too with the Son of God:
granted that his birth is eternal and always complete
in that it is in him, still he does not always become
that which he is said to be—namely, Wisdom or
the Word—nor does he become such for everyone,
because everyone is not wise, nor are wise people

Rm 8:28

---

48. Compare III Sent 21 (at note 17).

always so.[49] Nor for everyone, or any individual
person, does he always become that Word which
is called 'the word of God which was addressed
to Hosea',[†] or to Isaiah, or to Jeremiah. For that   Ho 1:1
reason is the Son said to be born.[†]   See Lk 2:11

The Holy Spirit, however, is believed not to be
born but to proceed, for he flows out always and
everywhere, pouring forth good things for everyone, the good and the bad alike, and raining down
benefits upon both the just and the unjust[†] —just   See Mt 5:45
like a perpetual, unceasing fountain of goodness.
For this reason he is called the goodness of God.
Thus it is written: 'The Spirit of God hovered over
the waters'.[†] This means that he offers himself to   Gn 1:2
every creature and, in a continuous act of goodness,
spreads himself out over each creature just like an
eagle on the wing. In this way he can show himself
by pouring out grace for everyone who desires
him, and by providing benefits even to those who
do not want him.

As a result it is written about Wisdom: 'She
reaches powerfully from one end of the world to
the other',[†] and about the Holy Spirit: 'The Spirit   Ws 8:1
of the Lord has filled the whole world'.[†] Note that   Ws 1:7
about Wisdom the word 'reaches' is used, while
about the Spirit the verb 'has filled' is employed.

63. 'That which contains all things has knowl-
edge of the word',[†] because he who embraces all   Ws 1:7
things—that is, both prosperity and adversity—
with the grace of God and strength of spirit, and
who makes all things come together for his good,[†]   See Rm 8:28
has an understanding of that word with which the
Holy Spirit speaks to the faithful soul. This is Ehud,
that most courageous and ambidextrous man who,

---

49. Compare III Sent 59.

See Eph 6:17
See Jg 3:20–21

with the sword of God's Word,[†] stabbed to death Eglon, the obese king (that is, the devil).[†]

64. God speaks to the faithful soul in three ways. One is through the natural law, of which it is written: 'Always do unto others as you would Mt 7:12 have them do unto you',[†] and 'Although the will to do good is in me, I cannot find the ability to Rm 7:18 accomplish it'.[†] Then he speaks through written law, with which all the books of Scripture are filled. And finally he speaks through the law of grace, by hidden inspiration.

Our ability to listen inwardly, however, is obstructed in three ways. As a result, we cannot hear See Ps 85:8 what the Lord God is saying to us.[†] It is obstructed by the noise and tumult of the world, by the storms of worldly affairs; by the noise and tumult of the flesh, by the storms of carnal temptation; and finally by the noise and tumult of the devil, by the storms of spiritual temptation.

Ws 9:15 65. 'A corruptible body presses the soul down.'[†] With the body and the soul, it is just like with a patient whom, at the order of his master, a servant undertakes to watch over and care for. If the servant does not lift him up, carry him about, feed him, and perform the other services which the exigencies of his illness and the restoration of his health demand, he incurs the wrath of his master. But he will no less anger his master if he responds equally to the sick person's requests for things that are both beneficial and harmful to him. On the other hand, if he serves the sick individual only with regard to his benefit and not his desire, he will find that his is a grumpy and burdensome patient.

So too the soul takes on the obligation of caring for and watching over the body from God. The body's miseries press down upon her and occupy her so much that she can hardly ever appear in the

Lord's sight. Moreover, if she does so, she is ordered by the Lord himself immediately to hasten back to her sick patient.[50]

66. The shepherd needs three things: a staff, a rod, and a dog. The staff and dog are for the wolf, the rod for the sheep. The staff signifies harsh, and the rod light, correction. The dog represents zeal on behalf of the Lord's flock. One should, however, keep this zeal tied down with the chain of reason and controlled by one's own hand, so that it cannot blindly rush out whenever it wishes. Otherwise it will bite sheep and wolves alike. One ought also to guard against using the rod on a wolf, or the staff on a sheep. The shepherd, moreover, should be very different from his sheep. Because of their weakness, they feed on the grass below with their eyes downcast, and they never look up. The shepherd should take his place in the middle of the flock, standing up straight. He should take nourishment from heaven—that is, with his eyes always turned upward, he should read in heaven the laws according to which he feeds his sheep on the earth. In his sack, moreover, he should always have bread—that is, he should always keep the Word in his memory, so that he may constantly be ready to explain, to anyone who asks, about faith and the hope which is in Christ.[51]

67. In response to the four facets of God, we owe two responses.[52] There are four facets in God: his power, wisdom, charity, and truth (or eternity, which is the same thing, for nothing truly is, unless it is unchangeable). It is appropriate for us to re-

---

50. Compare III Sent 36.
51. Compare III Sent 112 (at note 140); III Sent 118 (at note 164); and Div 100 (SBOp 6/1:367).
52. Compare to the following III Sent 82 and III Sent 93 (at note 100).

spond to these in two ways. To God's power, which
can punish us, and to his wisdom, from which
nothing can remain hidden, we owe true fear. By
this I mean the sort of fear which is hindered
neither by the sluggishness which comes of false
confidence, nor by the refuge afforded by pretense.
This sort of pretense arises either when we pretend
to work to fulfill God's commandment, or when
we imagine that God's mercy is beyond the bounds
of reason.

In response to God's charity and truth we owe
true love, the sort of love which is hindered neither
by lukewarm affection nor by any anxiety arising
from uncertainty. For what is owed for charity except charity? Moreover, truth removes any anxious
uncertainty from charity, and charity does the same
for truth. By uncertainty I mean any concern that
God's charity may not embrace one, or that his
truth may be deceptive, or that his eternity may
pass away, for as Paul says: 'You will be able to
grasp, with all the saints, the breadth and the length,
the height and the depth'.[†] In 'height', see God's
power; in 'depth', his wisdom; in 'breadth', his
charity; and in 'length', his eternity or truth. This
is the cross of Christ.[53]

Eph 3:18

68. Father, Son, and Holy Spirit. In the Father
God's power is denoted, in the Son his wisdom,
and in the Holy Spirit his generosity. Those who
sin do so by reason of either their weakness, their
ignorance, or their malice. Weakness is directed
against the Father, ignorance against the Son, and
malice against the Holy Spirit. This is what it
means to sin against the Holy Spirit.

69. About the soul's return to God, it should

---

53. Compare III Sent 74 (at note 57); III Sent 90; and Csi
5.13.27–29 (SBOp 3:489–92).

be noted that since it fell away from God in a particular order, it must be restored to him in that same order. First Adam's spirit sinned by falling in with, or obeying, the suggestion of the serpent or of the woman Eve; only then did his body sin by employing itself in the sin. For Adam was, as it were, midway between God and his wife. He was connected to God above by the twin bonds of fear and love, and to his wife below by the single bond of carnal love. The one which looked downward proved the stronger, and the two which looked upward were sundered. Through the power of the senses, this bond dragged carnal man down to his wife by the weight of its carnality. Soon he sinned bodily when he reached his hand out toward the fruit and readied his mouth to taste it.

Even if at this point some observation is interjected about Adam's charity or compassion toward his wife or about his longing for offspring, Adam cannot be excused on this account. For even if Eve had died in her sin, God could have provided for Adam a better, more beautiful Eve. If, moreover, Adam had desired so utterly to save her (since she was bone of his bone and flesh of his flesh[†]), had he remained innocent of sin and departed paradise with, and for, the sinful woman, perhaps through his assumption of hardships which he himself did not deserve, he could have made satisfaction to God on her behalf.   Gn 2:23

As it happened, however, Eve sinned at the serpent's suggestion, and Adam sinned at the suggestion of Eve. He sinned in the acquiescence of his spirit and in the decision he made,[†] causing his departure from God.[†] When his wicked servant[*] withdrew from him, the Lord laid claim to what belonged to him. On behalf of the spirit he imposed his legal right over the territory of his body,

See Gn 3:1–6
[†]Dt 32:15
[*]See Mt 25:26

instructing his ministers to take possession of it.[54]
Meanwhile the spirit of fornication, the spirit of
gluttony, and the other vices each claimed what

Ws 1:4

pertains to them in the body, given over† to sin as
it is. The wretched spirit, frustrated on all sides and
realizing the losses it has suffered above, below, and
everywhere, comprehends its misery and rushes
back to the font of mercy to seek pardon.

At once, as Solomon says, immediate mercy is

See Si 18:12

shown to the wretched spirit.† God is generous
with his forgiveness and sets his anger aside. For
the very day on which a sinner grieves, he will

Rm 10:13
See Ps 51:10
See Ps 51:13

be saved.† Although God turns his face from a
person's sin,† however, he nevertheless does not
restore to him the joy of salvation,† nor does he
permit him to look on his face, or return to him
rights over the possession which had been taken
from him. The human being does not give up. He
puts forth effort and serves God with deeds and
gifts, fulfilling what the apostle writes: 'I speak in
human terms, because of your weakness. As you
once put your bodies at the service of vice, to go
from wickedness to wickedness, now you must put
them at the service of justice for your sanctifica-

Rm 6:19

tion'.† He pushes his weak body. Although it is
lazy and rebellious, he urges it on until the Lord
has been placated and he comes back into the
fullness of grace, to the vision of God's face and
the recovery of his possession, and to his pristine
state, even with respect to the territory of his body.
He regains the condition in which his flesh will
obey the spirit without grumbling—so that that
which had served both the Lord and himself in
the beginning, and which after his sin had served
neither God nor self, and which in penance had

---

54. Compare SC 59.2 (SBOp 2:136).

served God but not self, now, after the reception of
grace, may serve both God and himself again. So
it is written in Hosea: 'I will love them willingly,
because my anger has turned from them',[†] and in
the psalm: 'My flesh has bloomed again, and I will
thank him willingly'.[†]

70. The arrogant angel claimed for himself a
likeness to God, saying: 'I will place my throne in
the north, and I will be a rival to the Most High'.[†]
Moreover the words which proved persuasive to
humanity were: 'You will be like gods.'[†] God the
Father asks: 'And is my Son, the splendor of my
glory and the image of my essence,[†] to have so
many rivals, so many equals, so many associates, in
his likeness to me?' Each of the pretenders was cast
down.

The true image of God, God the Son, saw that
the angel and the human being, who had both
been made in the same image of God[†] but were
not the image of God itself, had fallen through
an inordinate desire for likeness and equality to
him.[†] 'Alas', he said. 'Only misery escapes envy.
He whom justice does not forbid to do so must
offer aid. I will show myself to humanity as a
human being, the most despised and rejected of
men, a man of sorrow and familiar with suffering.[†]
As a result humanity can be zealous in imitating
my humility. Through humility they may come to
that glory after which they raced too hastily before.
And so let them hear my words: "Learn from me,
for I am gentle and humble of heart, and you will
find rest for your souls".'[†]

Thus the Son of God, as it were, readied himself,
and went forth to rescue through his humility the
one who had perished because of pride but was
able to be saved. He thereby made himself a mediator between God and humanity. Withdrawing

Ho 14:5

Ps 28:7

See Is 14:13–14

Gn 3:5

See Heb 1:3

See Gn 1:26

See Gn 3:5

Is 53:3

Mt 11:29

from God, he was taken captive and bound by
the devil. In this way he adopted both the person
and the role of the good mediator. He was made
human: 'A shoot has sprung forth from the stock of
Jesse, and a blossom ascends from his root; the spirit
of the Lord rests upon him, a spirit of wisdom and
understanding, a spirit of counsel and fortitude,
a spirit of knowledge and piety, and the spirit of

Is 11:1–3
fear of the Lord fills him'.† You should perceive
in these words our most courageous champion,
striding, as it were, onto the plain of the world to be
anointed for combat with the oil of the Holy Spirit,

Ps 19:5
exulting like a hero to run the race† for the ransom
of humanity. Note, moreover, that in the passage
quoted above the prophet Isaiah begins with the
higher things and proceeds downward to those that
are lower, because he was prophesying the descent
of the mediator from heaven. When we, through
the same gifts of the Holy Spirit, study the process
by which the mediator returns to the higher things,
we begin from the lower, that is with fear. Christ
had fear toward the Father, but it was pure and
filial fear through which he deferred to the Father's
honor in all things, saying: 'My nourishment is to

†Jn 4:34
do the will† of my Father who is in heaven'.* And

*Mt 7:21
in the psalm we read: 'My heart rejoices because it

Ps 86:11
fears your name'.† There are many other passages
in this vein. In these words it even seems that he
despised, humiliated, and defiled himself so that
the work which his Father had made through him,
but which had perished, could be restored to the
Father, renewed and made whole.

It was in this way, then—upwards, as it were—
that our mediator had fear toward the Father.
Downwards, as it were, he gave an example of
piety to wretched humanity, so that it might be
reconciled to the Father. Regarding both he had

knowledge, since he understood what he should show toward each. Although he had his good will from the Father from above, however, he had gotten nothing at all from humanity, lying below in its wretched state. Yet the reason for his ordination required that he should possess something from humanity in order to fulfill his ministry as mediator. He therefore exacted faith from human beings. He exacted faith from them by asking piety of himself. Nothing could have been more powerful than this demand, because it was not difficult for humanity, wretched as it was, to trust him, since it perceived that it had been preceded by the mediator in piety. But since human beings could not have put their trust in the mediator without hope—for who can believe in anyone in whom he does not have hope?—he gave them hope as well as faith; and to hope he added fear, because hope could not exist without it. He did all this so that humanity would not be deprived of so pious a mediator.

After his great pledge of salvation had been received by the guilty, the mediator returned to the Father. This occurred when he ascended alone onto the mountain to pray† and when in his anguish he prayed even more earnestly, when his sweat fell like drops of blood.† 'Father', he said, 'glorify your son.'† Behold what I have given up for you and what I have given up for humanity. Behold what I have from you and what from them. For indeed I am the mediator, and the purposes behind my mediating role now seem to rush together for their salvation. For they have been captured and chained. A powerful rival has bound them,† and if one stronger than he did not come, he could not snatch away his goods.† Only put your hand on me from on high† and I will snatch the captive

Mt 14:23

Lk 22:43–44

Jn 17:1

See Mt 12:29

See Mt 12:29

Ps 144:6

See Ps 18:17
from his powerful enemies[†] through the spirit of
fortitude—your fortitude and your strength. For
Lk 16:4
I know what I will do.[†] Though innocent, I will
die for the guilty, and my goodness will be incomparably more powerful than the wickedness of
the enemy. The suffering of one who is innocent
will be incomparably greater than that due for
humanity's disobedience.'

The Father replied: 'I have glorified him, and
Jn 12:28
will again'.[†] Now the brave mediator needs the
spirit of counsel, for if the prince of the world
understood what was happening, he would never
1 Co 2:8
have crucified the Lord of glory.[†] Through all the
events which followed, therefore, the mediator hid
the power of his divinity from the adversary, show-
See 2 Co 13:4
ing him only the weakness of his flesh,[†] although
Heb 4:15
it was without sin.[†] Through the justness of his
life he aroused the envy of the wicked enemy, and
through the weakness of his body he gave him hope
of victory over him. The miracles he performed
added to the devil's jealousy, while through them
he strengthened the faith of those to be reconciled
in him. The old deceiver was thus deceived himself, and he inflicted upon the mediator, who was
guilty of no sin, the most horrible kind of death,
which of course was the proper punishment for sin.
In this way the just one was unjustly slain, and for
the sake of justification he won over the enemy
a new kind of justice—specifically, that deriving
from a death unjustly inflicted upon him. That
which was in no way necessary for him to suffer
(since he was utterly without sin) he imputed to
the sinful. Through the punishment inflicted upon
his innocence he brought absolution to the guilty.
Placing his body and blood in humanity's hand, he
said: 'Eat of this, drink of this, and thereby live.'
And returning them to the Father's sight, he said:

'Behold, Father, the reward for my blood. If you require justice for their sin, accept my blood on their behalf. O Father, you have bestowed your favor, and the land of my body has brought forth its fruit.[†] Now justice will walk before you, and you will put your feet on the road of human salvation.[†] And in order that the one who justly fell might now justly be saved, you, O Lord, have shown the way, just as you demonstrated justice in your judgment toward Jacob.'[†]

See Ps 85:12

See Ps 85:13

Ps 99:4

It now remains to show how the spirit of understanding and the spirit of wisdom reside in Christ, the mediator. The body of Christ is the universal Church, that of the Old Testament as well as the New. At the head of this body—that is, at its first, or oldest, or highest part, which is the early Church—there are four senses—sight, hearing, smell, and touch. The eyes are the angels, so called because of the keenness of their contemplation. The ears are the patriarchs, because of the strength of their obedience. The nose, or power of smell, represents the prophets, because of their acquaintance with things not present. And the power of touch is the sense common to all of them. Now all of these senses were in the head prior to the coming of the mediator, but they were very weak in the lower portion of the body, which was nearly dead because of the absence of one other sense—that of taste. Without its aid the body was unable really to live, nor could any of the senses achieve the full force of their natural vigor. Just put anything which pertains to the nourishment of the whole body—to all the senses, to the entire body— before, under, or around the body, and what good will it do, if only the sense of taste is lacking? You can fill the ears with it, you can force it into the nostrils, or instill it in any other part of the body you choose; it will be able to enter, but it cannot be of any use. For the sweet flavor which the soul perceives in her innermost being comes only from the sense of taste, in a way which is unique, incommunicable to the other senses. Taste analyzes and judges all the things it takes up, nourishing and strengthening both itself and the other senses. The sense of taste, therefore, is positioned at the boundary-line of the head and the lower body (that is, the throat) so as to connect the two. It thus denotes him who, because of his carnality, is slightly less than,[†] or made lower than, the angels.[*] In a certain fashion, the mediator made himself less than and more humble than Moses, Elijah, and the other prophets, through his display of patience and humility. While they would cast down those who were enemies of God—and their own—through their mighty power, he rather taught his disciples: 'If anyone strikes your right cheek, turn the other to him as well'.[†]

Coming after the prophets and the patriarchs, and through the mysteries of his humanity, passion, and resurrection encompassing within himself—as if his mouth were tasting them—the limits of law and grace, of head and body, along with all that is helpful to salvation in the law, the prophets, and the psalms[†] and everything which gives life to the body or is useful to it, and through himself bestowing all the things to be comprehended by the body, Jesus Christ, by what may be termed the interior flavor of his divinity, was made for us through his savory wisdom the messiah, the wisdom of God.[†] He made all things beneficial to us. For living in himself, and through himself nourishing and sustaining the entire body, through the destruction of his body he brought joy to himself and to the angels. Through the appearance of his day he

†Ps 8:5
*Heb 2:9

Mt 5:39

See Lk 24:44

See 1 Co 1:30

brought joy to the patriarchs and prophets, for as
he himself said: 'Your father Abraham rejoiced that
he would see my day; he saw it and was glad'.† Jn 8:56
He brought joy and life to the whole body, so
that with general jubilation of mind, vivified and
strengthened by his spiritual touch, we can exclaim
'that we have seen and heard and touched, with
our own hands, the word of life'.† And so in all our 1 Jn 1:1
prayers we conclude by saying: 'Through our Lord
Christ'. We do so either because we direct all our
prayers and sacrifices to God the Father through
him, as through our mediator, or because whatever
we may hope for from the Father of lights—every
good and perfect gift†—we ask to be infused in Jm 1:17
us not through our ears or nose, but through him
who is our mouth and our power of taste and our
wisdom, so that it may be beneficial to the one
who takes it up.

71. As we read in Job, Wisdom 'is not found in
the land of those living comfortably'.† 'We heard See Jb 28:13
of it in Ephrath and found it in the fields of the
forest'.† 'We heard of it', meaning of its reputation, Ps 132:6
'in Ephrath'—that is, in a mirror, an imitation of
reality; but 'we found it' where it actually is, 'in
the fields of the forest', which means in the land of
those who do not live comfortably—in the hidden
places in the desert, in the recesses inhabited by the
holy. Such people live bodily in the fields of the
forest and are themselves the fields. This means
that in the midst of this world they are like level,
productive fields, fertile and flourishing with all
good things, who clear themselves through manual
labor in order to train the body, and who engage in
that work spiritually in order to instruct the spirit
too. For when the fields of the forest are cleared,
the trees are cut down. They are not, however,
simply flung away. Instead they are scattered over

the surface of the land in heaps (or, if there are very
few of them, they are collected), so that when a
fire is started it can have enough material to burn;
and the fire makes the old, infertile land fresh and
fruitful again. It is the same with those people.
When they hear the advice of Wisdom, which tells
us that 'the one who cultivates his land will be filled

See Pr 12:11, 28:19 with bread',[†] they cut down from the land of their
heart and body the old forest of their sins through
penitential labor and the exercise of holy discipline
and behavior. They do not, however, fling away the
remnants by forgetting them. Instead they scatter
across the expanses of their memory not only their
own sins, but those of others—indeed, those of the
entire world—and they ignite beneath them the
fire of the Holy Spirit, conceived in heaven above.
By completely burning up, down to the very roots,
everything which is or had been harmful or useless,
they make the land of their heart and body once
again fit and ready for the holy fruits of good works
through the plow of discipline and the seed of the
divine word. They are truly fields of the forest—a
company of saints in the towns, or rather of saints
living in the midst of the world as though in the
middle of a forest.

72. On the yoke which is easy and the burden
which is light. 'For my yoke is easy and my burden
Mt 11:30 light.'[†] There is a burden which carries the one
who lifts it up and makes him light. It is that light
burden of the Gospel, that yoke of Christ which
is easy for those who have turned to him. For one
who previously had been unable to shoulder the
commands of the law, afterward finds the precepts
of the Gospel light with the assistance of grace. A
person who had previously been unable to fulfill
Ex 20:13 the commandment not to kill[†] later finds it easy to

lay down his life for his brothers.[†] It is likewise with See 1 Jn 3:16
the other commandments. Thus, when a weighty
load is forced upon a beast of burden and he flees
from it as though it were impossible to carry, a swift
wagon is brought forward—that is, the Gospel,
which rushes through the whole world—and the
burden which the beast first refused as being too
heavy it afterward pulls easily, even if it is doubled.
It is the same with a little bird. Unfledged and
wingless, it cannot lift itself in flight, but when
the weight of feathers and wings is added, it easily
soars. Think too of hard bread. By itself it cannot
be swallowed, but when milk or some other liquid
is added to it, it becomes perfectly possible for it
to glide down the throat.

73. On the words of the apostle: 'Do not choose
to adapt yourselves to the world, but remake yourselves in accordance with the intent of your spirit,
so that you can recognize what the will of God
is, what is good, pleasing, and perfect'.[†] In these Rm 12:2
words we are shown that while through the bodily
senses we grow old and adapt ourselves to the
world, through the perception of the mind we are
renewed in the knowledge of God.[†] There are five Eph 1:17
animal or bodily senses through which the soul
endows its body with sensation. Beginning from
the lowest, they are touch, taste, smell, hearing,
and sight. Likewise there are five spiritual senses,
through which charity brings the soul to life. These
are the carnal love of one's parents, social love, natural love, spiritual love, and love of God. Through
the medium of life the body is joined to the soul
by means of the five bodily senses, while through
the medium of charity the soul is affiliated with
God by means of the five spiritual senses.

Love of one's parents is analogous to the sense of
touch, because the feeling is easy for everyone. It

might be described as thick and palpable, occurring and affecting everybody in so natural a way that you could not escape it even if you wanted to. The sense of touch is totally corporeal. It is engaged by the simple conjunction of any two bodies—as long as one or the other of them is alive, so that it can be touched. Just as your body cannot exist without a sense of touch whatever way you turn, so too your soul cannot be without this feeling. As a result, this kind of love is not much commended in the Scriptures; indeed there is emphasis on the fact that it should not be too strong, for the Lord says:

Lk 14:26 'If someone does not hate his father and mother',† and so forth.

Secondly, social love is comparable to the sense of taste. By social love we mean love of our brothers, love of the holy and catholic Church. Of this love it is written: 'How good, how delightful it is

Ps 133:1 to live together like brothers',† because just as life is conveyed to the body through the sense of taste, so

Ps 133:3 it is 'in this that the Lord confers his blessing'† and life. For even though the sense of taste is exercised bodily, it gives rise to an inner flavor by which the soul is affected. As a result this sense can be seen as primarily corporeal, but still in one respect it should be thought to be proper to the soul as well. It is the same with social love. Because it is effected through some sort of corporeal commingling—from a similarity in professions, or a likeness in interests, or other reasons of this kind—and is reared by such reciprocal arrangements, it seems to be primarily an animal sense. But still it is in great part spiritual, because just as flavor arises from tasting, so too the feeling of fraternal charity increases into that attachment about which it is written: 'Fine as oil on the head, running down the beard, running down Aaron's beard to the collar of his robe; and

copious as the dew of Hermon', that is, of a light
which has been raised up, 'falling on the heights
of Zion'.†

Ps 133:2–3

Thirdly, natural love is comparable to the sense
of smell. Natural love shows affection naturally to
everyone without any expectation of repayment.
It does so by reason of similarity in nature itself
and through cohabitation. Arising from the hidden
recesses of nature, and taking itself into the soul, it
considers nothing human to be alien to it.[55] The
sense of smell seems to pertain more to the soul
than to the body, because to bring it into being,
the interior of the body requires nothing but the
slightest inclination of its bodily organ, which is
the nose. While its influence is felt throughout the
body, moreover, its effect is nonetheless on the soul
rather than the body. So too natural love seems to
be more spiritual than animal, because, except for
the commonality of human nature, there is in it no
consideration at all of consanguinity, shared society,
or any other such prerequisite.

To the fourth bodily sense, hearing, may be
compared spiritual love—the love of one's enemies. For hearing does not operate at all with
respect to anything within, that is, inside the body.
Rather, it is concerned in its operation—that is,
in its pulsing at the ears—with things outside the
body. It summons the soul so that it can 'leave' the
body and hear. Similarly, no force of nature puts the
love of his enemies into a person's heart, nor does
any necessity sustain it; only obedience, which is
signified by hearing, does so. Thus this kind of love
is called spiritual. This is so, moreover, because it
is helpful in achieving similarity to the Son of God
and the status of sons of God, for the Lord says:

---

55. See Terence, *Heauton Timorumenos* 1.1, 77.

Mt 5:44–45

'Do good to those who hate you, so that you may become sons of your Father, who is in heaven',[†] and so forth.

Divine love is analogous to the fifth of the bodily senses, sight. Sight is, of course, the principal sense, just as among all the affections divine love holds pride of place. From the sight of the eyes the other senses are said to see, even though the eye alone sees. For we say: 'Touch and see, taste and see', and so on with the other senses. So too other things which are well loved are said to be loved from divine love. For it is clearer than light that nothing should be loved except because of God, and that anything which is loved on account of something else ought not to be loved, unless the thing on account of which it is loved is preferable to it. Thus it is written: 'From him every family, in heaven and on earth, takes its name'.[†] Sight is a certain pure, forceful, sheer power of the soul. Divine love is powerful, too, because it accomplishes great things if it is pure, and because, as it says itself, nothing impure can find its way into it.[†]

Eph 3:15

See Ws 7:25

For the love of God has no desire to be envious, since God does not deserve to be loved along with any other thing which is not loved on account of him. The power of sight, which is situated at the highest citadel of the body, at the most remarkable point on the head, keeps beneath it— according to the shape of the body itself, as well as according to proper order, worth, and strength— all the instruments by which the other senses operate. Regarding the other senses, those which are (as I have said) more spiritual are nearer to it in position, while those that are more corporeal are further from it. Of all of them the lowest is touch, less noble than the others. While it appears to be common to the entire body, it properly belongs to the hands. So too the mind, which can be called the head of the soul, and particularly the chief place in the mind, should be the seat of the love of God. This love should contain, rule, and illumine all the other kinds of love, and there should be none which hides from its light and heat.[†] Those sorts of love which are more spiritual, it should hold closer, while it should keep those which are more animal or carnal at further remove, since we should love the Lord our God with our whole heart, and with our whole soul, and with our whole strength, and then love our neighbor as ourselves.[†] Sight, as we have said, is located at the most worthy point in the body, and seems to exert itself somehow beyond the power of its animal nature. Insofar as is proper, it longs to mimic the power of the mind or memory, in a single moment of time darting through half the heavens and in a fraction of an instant traversing many miles of earth. It is likewise with the love of God. Taking its place in the christian soul, it draws the soul toward a certain likeness to the divine power. For while it demonstrates that every creature is limited and short-lived, and none is worthy of comparison to God, it still confesses that all which belongs to the Father belongs to it as well,[†] that all things cooperate with it for the good,[*] that Paul, Cephas, life, death, indeed everything belongs to it,[†] and that the whole world is part of the property of the faithful man.[56†]

Sight, in order to be sight, requires these elements: a beam of light, strong and pure, which can proceed from the pupil of the eye; pure, bright air which will not impede its passage; a body upon

See Ps 19:6

See Dt 6:5; Mt 22:37–39; Mk 12:30–31; Lk 10:27

†See Jn 17:10
*Rm 8:28
See 1 Co 3:22
Ws 17:4b, Septuagint version

---

56. On this addition to Ws 17:4, which occurs in the Septuagint but not in the Hebrew or Vulgate versions, see PL 184:393, n. 19. Bernard also alludes to the passage in V Mal 28.63 (SBOp 3:367).

which it can land; reason to which to report back; and memory, with which reason can consult. If any one of these is lacking, sight cannot be perfect. It is likewise with the love of God. In order for it truly to exist, certain things are required: a pure disposition, through which it loves God only for God's sake, and loves nothing else along with God except in God and on account of God; purity of life and conscience, which cannot impede love; spiritual discernment, which will not permit pure contemplation to wander, but will teach her to know God and not to accept anything else in God's place; reason, which can reach a decision on the basis of that discernment; and faith, which reason can consult concerning all its judgments and which will restrict reason within proper limits, not allowing it to cross over them. These are the spiritual senses about which it is said: 'Think about the Lord in goodness',[†] and 'Let what is thought by you be what is also thought by Jesus Christ'.[†]

Ws 1:1
Ph 2:5

74. On the cross of Christ and that of the devil. To know God is the highest form of knowledge, and it constitutes that blessedness for which we put ourselves in God's service, so that we may know him and Jesus Christ, whom he sent.[†] Jesus Christ cannot be known, however, except as he was hanging on the cross, when the thief on the cross beside him confessed his sins and exclaimed: 'Remember me, Lord, when you come into your kingdom'.[†]

See Jn 17:3

Lk 23:42

We are thieves who try to steal ourselves from God and desire instead to turn to nothingness, even though we are not able to be nothing. We wish to hide from God's sight,[†] even though it has been written of him: 'If I ascend into heaven',[†] and so on.

See Gn 4:14
Ps 139:8

Thieves also kill, and they bury the corpse in

the ground to conceal the murder. Likewise we too are murderers, since we kill our soul, which is far dearer than our body. We put earth over it by gazing longingly at earthly things to hide the fact that when we are occupied with earthly desires, we are actually dead. Nor can we come to our senses, so long as we delude ourselves by blaming what we do on the weakness of the flesh, or indulge ourselves by depending too much on God's mercy.

Putting aside our thievery, therefore, let us hang on the cross of Christ, confessing our wretchedness to him and, with full devotion of heart, begging his mercy.

We can, however, be on a cross in such a way as not to be on the cross of Christ at all. For while there is the cross of Christ, there is also a cross of the devil. The cross of the devil is truly a cross because it is an instrument of punishment. Like the cross of Christ, it has four aspects—depth, height, length, and width.[†] The cross of Christ is comparable to that of the devil in that it attacks contrary elements with contrary elements of its own, and likenesses with likenesses.

See Eph 3:18

The depth of the punishing cross is despair. One who nurses at the breast of despair rises up only with great difficulty. Its height is exaltation, and so the devil himself is called the summit of pride. Its width is the desire of the flesh, because wide is the road that leads to death.[†] Its length is obstinacy. Obstinacy is to be understood in two ways, for one person is so obstinate in his sin that he does not care to recover, while another returns to his vomit[†] after he has risen up from it.

Mt 7:13

See Pr 26:11

The cross of the Savior is opposed to this cross of the devil. Its height is hope, because through hope we are lifted up to those things that are unseen, judging those that we do see to be vile.

Its depth is fear of the Lord, because it is through this that we are afraid of the judgment of God and undertake to rein in the forbidden activities of the flesh. And so it is written: 'Fear of the Lord is the beginning of wisdom'.† Its width is charity, for it is said: 'Your command has no limit'†—and that command is charity, as in: 'I give you a new commandment, that you love one another'.† Its length is perseverance, for 'the man who stands firm to the end will be saved'.†

The height of the devil's cross is destroyed by the depth of Christ's, because the things which exalt themselves in us are repressed through fear of that true judge who repays each person according to his works.† The depth which is fear utterly splits the trunk of the other cross. Through hope, which is the height of Christ's cross, the depth of the devil's, despair, is undone. Because the true hope which belongs to citizens of the kingdom above presses an image of blessedness upon our mind, we sustain ourselves so as not to slip into despair. Thus are contraries destroyed by contraries—desperation by hope, and elation through fear.

The width of Christ's cross, which is charity, destroys the desire of the flesh, which constitutes the width of the devil's cross. For the more skillfully one binds himself to Christ with the chain of love, the more does he struggle to tame the flesh. Obstinacy, which is the length of the cross of the punisher, is conquered, meanwhile, by the perseverance of the Savior's cross. Even if he should fall, an individual who persists in his blessed goal of rising up will be crowned as victor. These are the two states which, in the life of a person, always struggle and alternate with one another; and each of us will be judged according to whichever of them he is finally discovered in. Thus we read:

Ps 111:10

Ps 119:96

Jn 13:34

Mt 10:22

See Ps 62:12

'Where I find you, there will I judge you'.[†] In these cases, then, likenesses are destroyed by likenesses.[57] See Ezk 18:30; Mt 24:40–41

The cross of Christ, in addition, is described in three ways, and each way has its own type of person. For there are three kinds of people: carnal, animal, and spiritual.

The cross of the carnal person is abstinence. One who restrains his flesh through abstinence truly crucifies himself. However, this cross is common to hypocrites as well, and they have already received their reward.[†] Mt 6:2

Lot represents the animal person: since he did not yet dare to approach the mountains (that is, the higher life), he remained in Segor (that is, in humility).[†] Such are certain monks who follow an indifferent way of life—their cross should be the fear of the Lord. Terrified by the fear of the Lord, they should banish secular concerns, which they have abandoned in body, from their spirits as well. For God looks into the heart, while a human being looks only on the face.[†] See Gn 19:19–23 1 S 16:7; see Ps 7:9

The cross of the spiritual person is charity. For on this cross—that is, in the heart of the spiritual individual—Christ hangs every day. Because he thought it proper to ascend the cross on our behalf, he invites us to the completion of his charity. Let us imagine him in this state—that is, hanging on the cross for us—when we fear that we might slip into despair. Let us, on the other hand, think of him coming in judgment, with his shoulder thrust forward, in accordance with the testimony of our conscience, whenever the devil's temptation entices us to the commission of some foul deed. And let us consider what the cross of charity means, so

---

57. Compare III Sent 67 (at note 53); III Sent 90; and Csi 5.13.27–29 (SBOp 3:489–92).

that, inflamed with the love of God, we can chastise
our bodies so as never to permit our hand to turn
to empty works or our foot to a deformed path.
This cross, just like charity, involves punishment
for the spirit, but it persists in glory, since it soon
becomes something other than a cross of punishment, proving glorious and delightful. Christ bore
this cross, and so it is written: 'Dominion is laid
upon his shoulder'.†

Is 9:6

About the cross of the carnal person, the apostle
says: 'Those who belong to Christ have crucified
their flesh, with its vices and desires'.† About the
second cross, it is said in the psalm: 'Pierce my flesh
with fear of you'†—that is, pierce with fear the lusts
of the flesh which we do not speedily abandon, as
well as the things after which we lust. Pierce with
fear, I say, the lusts of the flesh, from which I long
to be freed through my dread of your judgment
when you have whetted your sword like lightning
and set your hands to judgment† because 'I did not
fear your judgments'.† About the third cross, the
apostle says: 'There is nothing for me to glory in,
save the cross of our Lord Jesus Christ'.†

Ga 5:24

Ps 119:120

See Dt 32:41
Ps 119:120

Ga 6:14

75. There are two trails along which the soul
is drawn after Christ. One is that of compulsion,
as when we read: 'I will hedge in your ways with
thorns'.† The other is the voluntary path, indicated
in the words: 'Draw me after you'.†

See Ho 2:6
Sg 1:3

76. Two streams flow from the fountain of love.
One is the love of the world, or avarice, and the
other is the love of God, or charity. Between them
is the human heart, from which the fountain of
love bursts forth. When in its appetite it rushes
toward external things, it is called avarice, while it
is called charity when it directs its longing toward
things that are within. Thus, two streams flow from
the fountain of love: avarice and charity. Avarice is

the root of all evil† and charity the root of all good. $\quad$ 1 Tm 6:10
Thus everything which is good comes from the
one and everything evil from the other. Therefore
whichever of them is in us is of great significance
because everything which derives from us comes
from it. We have also discovered that this is nothing
other than our love which, since it is an impulse
of the heart, is singular and whole according to
its nature but nevertheless divided in its action.
When it moves itself beyond proper measure—
toward those things which it ought not to desire—
it is called avarice. When it is properly ordered,
it is called charity. In the one case your human
heart is evil and in the other case it is good. It all
depends on whether you love what is good well
or badly: if you love that which is good well, you
are good, but if you love that which is good badly,
you are wicked. For everything that exists is good.
But when that which is good is badly loved, that is
not good—it is evil. Thus it is not the person who
loves who is evil; nor is it what he loves which is
evil; nor is that love which loves, evil. Rather it is
the fact that one loves badly which is evil. Indeed,
this category comprehends all evil. And so order
charity rightly† and there will be no evil. $\quad$ See Sg 2:4

77. The soul has two walls, an inner and outer.
The inner wall is natural anger—that power of the
soul through which it grows angry at the vices and
is fortified against temptations. The outer wall is
the body; the soul is enclosed by it and kept, as it
were, imprisoned in it. Defended by its inner wall,
the soul wants to reject all the things that are of
the flesh, if it were possible to do so. Pressed in
by the outer wall, however, it sometimes descends
to the filthy regions marked by carnal enticements.
Nevertheless the soul is situated between the walls:
while of necessity it does not disdain the flesh,

neither does it love it passionately. There is, then, nothing wrong in drinking the water between the walls, but it is wrong to dig a lake between one

See Is 22:11 wall and the other[†] to gather up the waters— because there is nothing wrong with tending to nature's needs through the use of worldly goods, but it is wrong to allow avarice to take the place of necessity. Thus, you should not build a lake

See Is 22:11 between one wall and the other,[†] because that is wicked.

78. There are three trees of life. The first is that

See Gn 2:9 material tree which God made from the earth[†] in the beginning, when he planted it in the middle

See Gn 3:24 of paradise. Adam was expelled from paradise[†] so that after his sin he could not touch its fruit. The second is the Lord Jesus Christ who, by taking on human form, was 'planted' in the middle of his

See Gn 3:24 Church, just as the tree of life[†] was planted in the middle of paradise. Whoever has worthily eaten of

Jn 6:59 his fruit will live forever.[†] The third tree is the tree of life which was planted in the invisible paradise, and that is the wisdom of God. Its fruit is the food of the blessed angels.[58] The first, second, and third are all trees of life, but from the first humanity was ejected, by the second they were recalled, and for the third they were created. Thus the tree of life does not exist except in paradise—it cannot be found outside paradise, to paradise its roots tend, in paradise is its proper place, and there it puts forth its branches and bears its fruit.

79. There are three paradises. One is earthly, and its inhabitant was the earthly Adam. The second is spiritual. It is the Church of the saints, which the

See 1 Co 15:47 celestial Adam[†] founded and which he inhabits. The third is the celestial paradise, which is the

---

58. Compare III Sent 79.

kingdom of God, eternal life, and the land of those who truly live. God dwells in this paradise.

In the first paradise is the tree of life, a material tree. In the second paradise, the tree of life is the humanity of our Savior. In the third, the tree of life is the wisdom of God, the Word of the Father, the fountain of life, the origin of good. This is eternal life.[59]

Now let us proceed to draw a comparison. Most assuredly that tree of life which was in the earthly paradise could support the life of the body without any difficulty. But the tree of life in the spiritual paradise—that is, the Lord Jesus—promises eternal life to those who eat his flesh and drink his blood. The third tree of life not only restores one's original well-being, but adds to it greater strength. It not only repairs what had perished, but adds what had been lacking.

80. There are three states of holy souls. The first is in the corruptible body, the second apart from the body, and the third in the glorified body. The first consists in militant service, the second in rest, the third in the fulfillment of beatitude. Moreover, the first is symbolized in tabernacles, the second in altars, and the third in the house of God. 'How delightful is your tabernacle, Lord of hosts!'[†] Still, your altars are far more desirable, for further on is added: 'My soul yearns and pines for the altars of the Lord'.[†] Since, however, there is still something lacking in those altars, we read further: 'Blessed are those who live in your house, O Lord'.[†] — Ps 84:1 / Ps 84:2 / Ps 84:4

81. Three things preclude any lessening of effort on our part. One is fear of confusion, for as is written: 'And so they trembled with fear, where there had been no fear before'.[†] This sort of confusion — Ps 14:5

---

59. Compare III Sent 78.

invites punishment. Then there is lukewarmness in one's religion, as is depicted in the words: 'Would that you were either hot or cold!',[†] and 'When iniquity increases, in many people love will grow cold'.[†] Third is fear of pride, as in: 'Everyone who exalts himself will be humbled'[†] and other statements of this sort.

Firmness of discretion guards against any slackening of effort. When the eye of the heart, by which alone God can be seen, has been cleansed, this discretion constantly perceives that only our sins separate us from God. This leads to perseverance of effort, as though one were constantly hearing the words: 'Whatever your hand can do, do at once'.[†] There follows constancy in one's humility, the heart of which is found in the words of the apostle: 'Obey those put over you, and subject yourself to them'.[†]

82. On the two taxes. There are two taxes which God demands of us: fear and love. We truly owe these, being fully obligated for them as defendants before the highest majesty; and we will be utterly damned unless we pay them. The Scriptures speak in many ways about these two taxes.

There are, moreover, four characteristics in God to be requited. To them the two taxes of which we have spoken above pertain and are due. These are his power, his wisdom, his charity, and his truth.

God should be feared without dissimulation because he is powerful and because he is wise. You see, our fear responds to, is appropriate to, and befits two facets in God—his power and his wisdom. Truly he is most powerful whom no one can resist,[†] who dismisses the spirit of princes, terrible as he is among all the kings of the earth.[†] He is also most wise. For he knows all things,[†] and his wisdom penetrates all. He scrutinizes both minds and

Margin references:
Rv 3:15
Mt 24:12
Lk 14:11
Qo 9:10
Heb 13:17
See Est 13:9
See Ps 76:12
See 1 Jn 3:20

hearts;[†] he fathoms the deepest abyss[*] and every profundity. To these two facets of God we owe that true fear which pierces our very flesh,[†] restraining and keeping us from evil. True fear is that which is not obstructed by any sluggishness arising from a sense of security, or by any comfort provided by a false show of deference. There are some who are paralyzed by this kind of sluggishness. It is said of them: 'They are clever enough at doing wrong, but do not want to do right'.[†] Hypocrites likewise use the cloak which is such a false show of deference. They only want to seem devout and just among people. Of them the prophet says: 'This people honors us with their lips, but their heart is far from me',[†] and concerning such individuals it is written, not inappropriately: 'They do not have the fear of God before their eyes'.[†]

Moreover, we owe love, without any hint of doubt, to the two other facets which are seen in God, namely his charity and his truth (or his eternity, which is the same thing—for nothing truly is, except that which is immutable). And to his charity and truth what is more justly paid by us but sincere love? The Son of God showed wondrous charity toward us; although we were sinners, he died for us.[†] Because of this we are unable *not* to love him, as he himself asks it of us with the words: 'I have come to bring fire to the earth; and what should I desire except that it burn?'[†] It is as though he were saying: I have come to plant charity, which I have also come to make fruitful. For he promised us a heavenly fatherland,[†] and he is truthful in his promises. Indeed, he is truth itself, and he cannot deceive—in fact, he does not know how to deceive. He should, then, be loved in his truth. That love is true which is not impeded by any lukewarmness encouraged by harmful inclinations or any scruple

†See Ps 7:9
*See Dn 3:55
See Ps 119:120

Jr 4:22

Mt 15:8

Ps 14:3

See Rm 5:8–9

Lk 12:49

See Jn 14:6

Jn 14:15

See Jr 48:10

See Rv 3:16

Mt 6:24

Si 2:15–16

See Ps 145:13

See Eph 3:18

See Dt 6:5; Mt
22:37; Mk 12:30;
Lk 10:27

created by wicked doubts. 'If you love me', he says,
'keep my commandments'.[†] The lukewarm give
evidence of their harmful inclinations because they
do God's work[†] in a negligent fashion, and so are
spit out of God's mouth.[†] They seek God without
putting the world aside, but 'no one can serve
two masters'.[†] On the other hand, those exhibit
wicked doubt who show a lack of confidence in
God's future goodness. They accept only things
as they are at present—as though Christ, who has
made a definite promise, were not going to bestow
eternal bliss on us! But 'Woe to those who are
listless in heart, who do not trust in God, for they
will not be protected by him. Woe to those who
have lost the will to endure'.[†] Truly the Lord is
faithful in all his ways,[†] and so the truth of his
charity and the charity of his truth remove every
trace of doubt that his charity could cease to love
us, or his truth turn away from us, or his eternity run out. Paul therefore urges us to grasp the
height and depth, the breadth and length of God's
knowledge.[†] In 'height', understand his power; in
'depth' his wisdom; in 'breadth' his charity; and
in 'length', because of his eternal lack of change,
his truth. As such God deserves to be feared and
loved, because of the four qualities of which we
have spoken above.[60]

83. On the love of the world. The love of the
world consists of three elements: lust, curiosity,
and vainglory. What expels these three is love with
one's whole heart, soul, and strength.[†] Love with
one's whole heart drives out lust when one, recognizing that Christ has bestowed far more benefits
upon him than the things which he carnally loves
and in which he carnally delights, transfers the love

---

60. Compare III Sent 67 (at note 52) and III Sent 93 (at
note 100).

in his heart to him; but it still remains carnal to a certain extent. Love with one's whole soul drives out curiosity when the power of reason becomes interested only in those things which are God's. Love with one's whole strength drives out vainglory, so that a person no longer seeks to please others,† but rather God.

See Ga 1:10

The first of these loves is sweet, in that it is nurtured in the service of God and in his sacraments. The second is prudent, in that it is acquired through the Scriptures and meditation on them. The prudence of the second joins with the sweetness of the first, resulting, as it were, in a distinct flavor. The third of these loves is strong, in that it leads one to leave the mind behind† and to ascend to the contemplation of God.

See Ps 31:23; Ac 11:5

Let us see how these three types of love were demonstrated in Peter through the action of grace. The Lord foretold his passion to the disciples, but Peter, loving Christ sweetly as a carnal son loves his carnal father, said: 'May this not happen to you, Lord; may you never die'.† Then later, when the passion was at hand, he understood that it was appropriate for it to occur. Now, showing that he truly loved Christ with all his soul, Peter said: 'Even if all lose their faith, I will not'.† Still he did not yet love with his whole strength, for he denied Christ at the time of the passion. Afterward, however, endowed with strength from on high,† he confessed his sin freely, loving with his whole strength him whom he had previously denied.[61]

See Mt 16:22
See Mk 14:29
See Lk 24:49

84. 'I will come into your house with sacrifices.'† Christ is priest at the supper, both priest and victim on the cross. Every day he is each on the altar,

Ps 66:13

---

61. Compare III Sent 92 (at note 95) and SC 20.5 (SBOp 1:117–18).

and he is the highest priest in heaven and judge
everywhere. We will not show ourselves empty-
handed in his sight;[†] let us offer him most devoutly
not only what is ours, but especially ourselves, so
that if in making our offering we divide things up
badly, we might not be condemned along with
Cain.[†]

There are, moreover, three sacrifices which
should be offered not only by those who enter
the confines of the temple made by human hands[†]
and participate in the sacraments of the Church,
but also by those who strive to remain in union
with Christ and to be conjoined with the heavenly
Jerusalem. These are the sacrifices of pious contrition, of meritorious effort, and of praise or joy. Of
these, two are necessary in the present world. The
third is begun here but will be completed only in
the future world.

About the first of these the prophet says: 'My
sacrifice to God is this broken spirit';[†] it consists of
inner sorrow and outer penance. About the second
he says: 'You will accept the sacrifice of justice',[†]
and 'Sacrifice a sacrifice of justice, and trust in the
Lord'.[†] And about the third: 'Blessed is the people
who knows joy',[†] and 'The sacrifice of praise has
honored me',[†] and 'Blessed are those who live in
your house: they will praise you forever and ever'.[†]
God does not care for sacrifices, unless they are
rich and from the heart, and so it is written: 'Let
my soul be filled, as with soft, rich fat'.[†] The sacrifice of contrition draws out the curds of humility,
which consist of three elements. Specifically, each
person should first recognize how imperfect what
he possesses is in comparison to those who are his
superiors, as in: 'Would that I may realize what I
am lacking!'[†] Then he should consider how he has
nothing that is really his own, as in: 'What do you

See Ex 23:15

See Gn 4:3–12

See Ac 17:24

Ps 51:17

Ps 51:19

Ps 4:5
Ps 89:15
Ps 50:22
Ps 84:4

Ps 63:5

Ps 39:4

possess that you have not received?'† This element   1 Co 4:7
of humility is strengthened by reference to those
who are one's inferiors, for if a person had anything
of his own in what he possesses, surely others
would have it as well. Finally, he should reflect that
he has nothing in this life which he cannot lose.
He should reach this kind of humility by reference
to those who have gone before him—men such as
Adam, who lost paradise, and Solomon, who despite such profound wisdom, nonetheless erred.[62]
The sacrifice of just effort draws forth the oil of
discretion, and the sacrifice of praise demands the
wood of devotion.

Moreover, these three kinds of sacrifice have
vices opposed to them, off to their side. The wormwood of rage is opposed to the sacrifice of contrition, the vinegar of confusion to the sacrifice of
effort, and the poison of flattery or ingratitude to
the sacrifice of praise.

85. On the two flavors tasted by God's good
people. 'What advantage does one who is wise
have over a fool, except that he presses on as long
as there is life?'† A wise person is one who fears   See Qo 6:8
and loves God, for there are two flavors tasted by
God's good people—the flavor of his power and
the flavor of his goodness.[63] One who is lacking in
these disdains them, and he is a fool, for 'the fool
says in his heart: There is no God'.† The pauper† is   Ps 14:1   Qo 6:8

---

62. Compare III Sent 92 (at note 93).
63. This passage is based on the etymological connection
between 'sapientia' ('wisdom') and 'sapor' ('taste' or 'flavor'):
see Isidore, *Etymologiae* 10.s.240; III Sent 96; III Sent 126; and
SC 85.8 (SBOp 2:312), where Bernard says: 'Nec duxerim
reprehendendum, si quis sapientiam saporem boni diffiniat' ('I
would not find it inappropriate to define wisdom as a taste for
the good'). Here, Bernard says that fear is the proper response
to a taste of God's power and love the appropriate reaction to
a taste of his benevolence, and that together they constitute
wisdom.

Ps 116:15
Ps 34:21

Rv 14:13

Rv 14:13

See Ps 116:15

Ps 127:2–3

Jn 11:11

Rm 14:8

one who scorns worldly things—and himself. The
life of good people is God. In their departure from
the present life, they will be directed onto the road
leading to heavenly life, because regarding them
the prophet said: 'The death of his saints is precious
in the sight of the Lord'.† But of the wicked we
read: 'The death of sinners is the worst'.†

There are three things which make the death
of good people pleasing to God: sometimes their
life, sometimes the reason behind their death, and
sometimes both of these at once.[64] In those good
individuals who have lived well, their life makes
their death precious. About them it is said: 'Blessed
are those who die in the Lord'.† In some martyrs,
who in life had not lived justly but who died
for the Lord, the reason behind their death alone
makes their death precious—indeed, more precious. For if those who die *in* the Lord are blessed,†
are not those far more blessed who die *for* the
Lord? Whether someone dies in the Lord or for the
Lord, the death of his saints will, without a doubt,
be very precious in the Lord's sight.† Moreover,
whatever is undertaken on the Lord's behalf is more
glorious to the extent that it is more precious. Thus
the prophet emphasizes that the death of saints is
precious by saying: 'When he has bestowed rest
on those he loves, behold the Lord's inheritance'†
—you should supply the words—'will be at hand.'
And you must not think that he loves only martyrs, because we should remember the words: 'Our
friend Lazarus is asleep'.† All those who are truly
aware of what they are dare to say: 'Whether we
live or die, we belong to the Lord'.† Secure and

---

64. Compare II Sent 90 and Div 64.1–2 (SBOp 6/1:297–
98).

courageous, they await a death which they hold to be precious. For it is written: 'The just person, even if he dies an untimely death, will be at rest'.† Ws 4:7 The more faithfully those who truly burn to die for the Lord hope for death with sweet piety, the more devoutly do they embrace it. They therefore consider death to be very precious. Truly they are those who, keeping the blood of Christ constantly before their eyes, charge toward death for Christ, just like elephants at the sight of a mulberry tree or a cluster of grapes. In the most remarkable men, whose life and conduct were extraordinary and whose good and glorious death was undergone for Christ, their life and the reason behind their death both make their death most precious. They lived well, because they lived in the Lord. They die the best possible death and do so with honor, because they die in the Lord and for the Lord. They can joyfully sing, as a result of their pious confidence: For us, 'life is Christ, and death brings a gain'.† Ph 1:21 Thus the death of the just is good and precious. Through it they are granted rest from their labor, for from the Spirit they hear that they may rest after their work.† For the present life, along with Rv 14:13 whatever is in the world, is a burden and, as it were, a misery to a holy man, so that, along with the blessed Job, he may say: 'Why has light been given to the grief-striken, and life to those bitter of soul?'† And so death is better and more precious, Jb 3:20 because joy results from the change. Death is best and most precious, because it brings assurance of one's eternal life.

Again, there are three things which make the death of the impious individual dreadful: his life, during which the wicked person always lived un-worthily; the reason behind his death, when he dies or is killed impenitent as a result of some extraordinary crime or foul deed; or both of these at once, when he is punished with divine and human vengeance both for his lost life and for his immediate crime. Separation from the world makes the death of the impious wicked and bitter. They are as much disturbed by the loss of the world as they earlier rejoiced in mistreating any unfortunate person. Their putting aside of the flesh makes death even worse and more bitter because, since they cared for the flesh with excessive zeal, they are gravely saddened that it must now be handed over to the worms. Their eternal damnation makes their death the worst and most bitter of all. The grief that results is inconsolable, the punishment unending.[65]

86. 'What the caterpillar has left the locust devours, what the locust has left the grasshopper devours, and what the grasshopper has left the gnawer devours.'†

Jl 1:4

The caterpillar takes its name from the word for 'gnawing'. It is a worm which inhabits the vegetable-patch, and if it is even lightly touched it contracts, drawing itself into a ball. It is slow, and cannot dash about, but with its very slowness it utterly consumes healthy leaves. The locust jumps and flies, and does not completely devour whatever it chances upon; leaving behind leaves half-eaten, it moves on to others. The grasshopper, which according to some is the offspring of the locust, eats not only the fruits, leaves, and bark, but in its quite deliberate way drinks up the plant's very marrow, sucking it dry. The gnawer, which is also called 'blight', is extremely damaging; attacking the golden plants secretly, it turns the stalk and hay into a dark mass, rendering it useless not only

---

65. Compare I Sent 6.

as food but as fertilizer. Thus the Lord said in the Book of Amos: 'I struck you with a burning, scorching wind'.[66†]

Am 4:9

In these four we understand the four disturbances by which the health of souls is undermined. For there exist naturally in human beings four emotions—sadness, joy, fear, and hope—which are indicated by them. Sadness is a contraction of the spirit, joy an extending of it, fear a flight of the spirit, and hope (or greed) an increase in it. You are contracted in spirit whenever you are troubled. You spread out in spirit whenever you become joyful. You run away from your spirit whenever you are afraid. You grow larger in spirit whenever you hope for, or desire, something. Now truly those motions of the spirit which are the emotions reside in us as a result of our mortality, and we offend not in having them but in employing them badly. If these motions which are emotions occur in people, they are virtues in those who use them well, but passions or disturbances in those using them badly. It is then that they are properly compared to the caterpillar, the locust, the grasshopper, and the gnawer.

Now two of these emotions are opposed to one another with respect to present circumstances, and the other two differ with respect to the future. Those which relate to the present are sadness and joy. Those which pertain to the future are fear and hope. Either we are sorrowful and racked with grief, or we are happy and run riot with joy. The proper role for the just and strong man is neither to be broken by adversity, nor to become puffed up

---

66. Here 'aura' ('wind') is etymologically related to 'aurugerium' ('the gnawer'). See also the note below to III Sent 107 (at note 118).

in prosperity. In time of adversity, however, the
mind of the wicked contracts like a caterpillar;
that means that it is undermined by a consuming
sorrow. Thus the apostle warns us that a brother

2 Co 2:7

can be consumed by too much grief,† such as that
by which Judas perished. In prosperity the mind
of the wicked becomes like a locust. That means
that in its rampaging joy it cannot enjoy the goods
it has with moderation, but rather flies hither and
yon, flinging itself wildly about.

Thus far we have spoken about the disturbances
which relate to present matters. Let us now discuss those concerned with future affairs—fear and
hope. We fear adversity and hope for prosperity.
What sorrow and joy effect regarding the present,
fear and hope do for the future. In both what
he fears in adversity and what he hopes for in
prosperity, a wise person controls himself with the
reins of reason. The fool is troubled by an evil
like a grasshopper—that is, by terror over future
things which eats away the marrow of wisdom:
when he fears adversity more than is proper, he
becomes divorced from his mind, growing devoid
of reason and judgment. On the other hand, when
he hopes for good things, he is troubled by the
gnawer—that is, by ambitious longing for future
benefits—which harms him secretly through pride
(that is, through love of his own excellence). He
conceives such hope and exultation in his spirit that
he cannot hold to any proper limit. The illustrious
poet expresses these disturbances through a single
(but not absolutely complete) little verse:[67] 'Hence

---

67. The 'little verse' (*Aeneid* 6, 733–34, and not—as the
critical apparatus indicates—6, 734–35) is, of course, met-
rically correct and finished in terms of Vergil's meaning, but
Bernard apparently considers it incomplete because it does not
include the points he parenthetically adds. Alternately, 'pleno'

they fear and desire'—this about the future—'they grieve and rejoice'—this about the present; 'and, closed up in the darkness and their sightless prison, they cannot look upon the heavenly air'.[68] Those who are wrapped up in the darkness of these disturbances do not behold the clear light of wisdom and waste away within themselves.

The caterpillar is that passion which begins in the spirit and, while taking its time in deciding or forming a desire to sin, it sometimes contracts and sometimes stretches, striving to bring to fruition the wickedness it has initiated. When we nourish this vice and do not strike it down in us immediately, it grows and begins to fly about, becoming the locust, which erupts in evil activity. Then it rejoices in its evildoing and exults in wicked deeds.[†] When one becomes enslaved to this vice, See Pr 2:14 it becomes the grasshopper—that is, that sort of habit which is worst because of its slowness and deliberation. These vices corrupt the mind of human beings miserably, rip it to pieces, and suck it dry. If it should happen—a very rare occurrence— that after the emergence of the grasshopper some spark of spirit still lives in us, the gnawer, which is harsh necessity, destroys and obliterates it utterly. Thus does lust arise from wicked desire, and when habit serves lust and no resistance to this habit is forthcoming, it becomes necessity. The sinner is held fast by a chain made of these four, joined to each other as it were by links. In these four all the resultant kinds of wickedness can, not improperly,

---

might be emended to 'plano', which would then suggest that the meaning is not entirely clear, or needs amplification. By using the word 'versiculo', moreover, Bernard could be suggesting that the couplet resembles a liturgical versicle with its accompanying response.

68. Vergil, *Aeneid* 6, 733–34.

be discerned—and specifically the four types of punishments with which, as we learn through the authority of Holy Scripture, sinners will be tormented in hell. In the caterpillar which contracts itself, understand the cold; in the locust which jumps about, understand the fire,[†] of which we read in Job: 'From the cool waters it can pass to the height of heat';[†] in the grasshopper, which perches for a long time, understand wicked conscience, for as Isaiah says: 'Their worm will not die';[†] and in the gnawer, which does its damage secretly, understand the stench of hell, or the darkness outside.[69†]

See Mk 9:48

Jb 24:19

Is 66:24

Mt 8:12

87. King Solomon made a great throne of ivory and plated it with refined gold. The rear was rounded. There were two arms holding the seat on one side and the other, and two lions beside the arms. There were six steps up to it, and beside them were twelve lion-cubs. There was no such throne in all the other kingdoms.[†]

See 1 K 10:18–20

The sun's rays are sometimes hidden behind clouds, and a precious pearl[†] is extracted from muddy waters. So too divine mysteries are cloaked beneath these words, and they should not be read otherwise in the Church because they might seem to involve certain rather disagreeable, empty bits of finery.

See Mt 13:46

Solomon represents Christ, sometimes because of the meaning of his name, at other times because of the fame of his deeds. For it was he who ended the brutal war between humanity on the one side and God and the angels on the other.[†]

See Col 1:20

It was he who prepared the Virgin Mary for himself, so that he might reside in her womb, just as the spouse does in the marriage-bed,[†] Solomon

See Ps 19:5

---

69. Compare III Sent 107 (at note 119) and III Sent 121 (at note 182).

in his temple, a king on his throne, and God in
heaven. So we read: 'While the king was in his
chamber, my nard gave forth its scent'†—that is, Sg 1:11
when he was in the lap of the Father,† the sweetness Jn 1:18
of her chaste, virginal scent rose to his nostrils,
because alone among women was she so pleasing
to God. And deservedly so, for she is the pattern,
the standard, the image, and the model worthy of
life with God. In her that grace which is redolent
with the virtues and the dowry of all merits surely
shone forth in a remarkably privileged fashion.
God worked in her, contrary to nature on behalf
of nature. She was humble of heart, responsible
in speech, dignified in appearance, and praiseworthy in bearing. These are the indications of true
religion. She was the virgin without any stain of
wickedness, without any wrinkle of pretense.† See Eph 5:27
Eve was the sterile willow, Mary the fertile
olive-tree† whom God blessed. It is beyond our Ps 52:8
power to say anything worthy of her, because
whatever is said is less than her praise deserves.
She was shown to Moses in the burning bush,† to See Ex 3:2
Aaron in the sprouting branch,† to Gideon in the See Nb 17:8
dewy fleece,† to Isaiah in the maiden with child,* †See Jg 6:36–40
to Jeremiah when he says: 'The Lord will create *See Is 7:14
something new upon the earth: the woman will
embrace the man',† to Ezekiel in the eastern gate See Jr 31:22
which is never open,† to David in the daughter See Ezk 44:1–3
who hears and sees, and forgets her own people,† See Ps 45:10
and to Solomon in the throne made of ivory.† Ivory See 1 K 10:18
comes from the elephant, which is the most chaste
of animals. The coldest ivory is analogous to Mary's
chastity. Through divine power she was free from
both original and actual sin, and under the protection of the Holy Spirit† she felt no inclination See Lk 1:35
to lust at all. Pledging the purity of her virginity
to God, she did not fear the imprecation of the

law which holds that 'A woman who will not bear

See Ho 9:14–16 fruit'[†] will be cursed among her own people; she made no claim on her own behalf, nor did she fall under the sentence of any court, but rather she commended herself totally to God, who freed her

See Ga 3:13 from the stricture of the law[†] by giving her a son, so that she might be blessed among her people while also preserving her purity. This was so that she could remain a virgin while giving birth and become a mother though remaining untouched by man.

1 K 10:18 He plated it with refined gold,[†] that is with charity. So we read: 'A sword will pierce your

Lk 2:35 soul',[†] because the more tenderly she loved, the more sharply did she grieve. He plated the ivory with gold, just as is written in Ecclesiastes' words in praise of her: 'Oh, how beautiful is a chaste and

Ws 4:1 charitable people!'[†]

1 K 10:19 It was rounded at the rear.[†] There are two parts to human beings. There is the front—the soul, which is the more worthy, and the rear—the body. The rear of the throne, therefore, was rounded, because she was absolutely unflawed in body, despite whatever those heretics or Jews who denigrate her virginity might rant or chatter about, to the effect that 'if she gave birth, she must have had intercourse with a man'.

1 K 10:19 'Two arms held the throne, one on each side.'[†] These are the two kinds of lives, active and contemplative. They shone forth remarkably in blessed Mary.

See 1 K 10:19 Beside it were two lions.[†] These are the two guardians, the one heavenly and the other of earth —Gabriel, messenger of that most glorious birth, who, being himself a contemplative, assisted her in maintaining a contemplative mode of life; and the evangelist John, to whom, since he was him-

self chaste, the Virgin Mary was commended by
Christ as he hung on the cross. It was Christ who
supported her in the active life.

The six steps† are the six works of mercy,* or the
perfection of the virtues through the performance
of those six.

†See 1 K 10:19
*See Mt 25:42–43

The twelve lion-cubs† are the fathers of the
Old and New Testaments, who all, with a sense
of wonder expressive of both praise and honor,
stand in awe of the queen not only of earth and
humanity, but also of heaven and the angels, saying:
'Draw me in your footsteps; let us run after you in
the sweet scent of your perfume'.†

See 1 K 10:20

Sg 1:3

There was no such throne in all the other kingdoms.† There are many realms in heaven: that of
the celestial spirits, that of the apostles, that of the
martyrs, that of the confessors, that of the virgins;
but she was exalted even beyond all the choirs of
angels. 'So let us approach the throne of glory in
confidence.'† She is the star by whose guidance
and intercession we pass over to our homeland. She
made God the Father a brother to us. She beseeches
and prays to the Lord on behalf of his servants,
and approaches her son on behalf of his sons—her
natural son, that is, on behalf of his adopted ones.

See 1 K 10:20

See Heb 4:16

88. Naaman, the commander of the king of
Syria's army, was a great man and very rich, but
he was a leper. He had in his household a certain
young girl as a maidservant,† and so on.

See 2 K 5:1–2

What we have just covered, brothers, is the
historical narrative. History is the threshing-floor
of doctrine, on which able workers—learned and
wise masters—use the flails of diligence and the
fans of inquiry to separate the wheat from the
chaff.† Just as honey lies concealed beneath wax
and the kernel beneath the shell, so too does the

See Lk 3:17

sweetness of morality and wisdom lie hidden under
the bark of history.

Naaman means elegance or one who is elegant.[70]
He signifies the rich of this world, who, in their
own sight, seem powerful and outstanding.[71] Those
who are endowed with great wealth, who are
distinguished by their family name, who are lofty
because of the great pile of goods they possess,
who have a knowledge of letters or hold a position
requiring rhetorical skill—all of these truly seem
to be great in the eyes of people. Nonetheless they
are tainted by a wide range of crimes. They have

See Ps 4:7

grown rich with much wine and oil,[†] but a great
deal of money is also a cause of sin. For they are
more prone to vice and freer to do harm, just
like the profligate, like those tainted with leprosy.

Ps 102:13

When the time of their pitying[†] and the time of

Lk 19:44

their visitation[†] arrives, they receive the young
girl's advice.

See 2 K 5:2

That girl[†] is divine grace or wisdom; she is called
a virgin because of her purity—just like Abishag,[72]

See 1 K 2:2

who warms old men[†] but does not burn those who
are young. The girl is also a handmaiden, because
she is eager to serve everyone. Wisdom calls out
in the streets: 'How long, children, will you cling

Pr 1:21–22

to your youthful ignorance?'[†] She is Ethiopian,

See Eph 5:27

not because there is some blemish or flaw in her,[†]
but because she serves the Ethiopians—that is, she
restores those who are black with sin to a state of
shining brightness. This is the advice that she gives
to Naaman: 'Go into Samaria to the prophet El-

---

70. See Jerome, *Liber interpr. hebr. nom.*; in CCL 72:83.
71. To the following compare Res 3.1–6 (SBOp 5:103–109).
72. The critical text reads 'Abigail', though one manu-script. has the variant 'Abisac'. The reference, however, is to Abishag, the young woman who became David's companion in his old age (see 1 K 1:1–4).

isha, and he will cure you of your leprosy'.[†] Samaria   2 K 5:3
means 'protection',[73] and so 'Go into Samaria'
means: Return to that which protects you; watch
over your deeds. It was to shepherds keeping watch
over their flocks that the angels came and spoke.[†]   See Lk 2:8, 13
So too it was written on Apollo's tripod: 'Man,
know thyself.'[74] It has been said: 'Return to your
heart, you sinners'.[†] For when Dina goes wander-   Is 46:8
ing, she is corrupted by the prince of the earth.[†]   See Gn 34
That person does not go into Samaria who, driven
away from his own concerns, troubles himself with
those of others.

Following the girl's advice, Naaman proceeds to
Elisha and knocks at the door of his house.[†] The   See 2 K 5:9
name Elisha means 'the salvation of the Lord',[75]
and so this is Jesus, the Savior of the world, who
has saved his people from their sins,[†] and of whom   Mt 1:21
the prophet says: 'O Lord, your salvation has taken
me up'.[†] As Jesus said of himself: 'I am the salvation   Ps 69:29
of the people'.[†] His home is the Holy Scriptures,   Ps 35:3
the Church, and truly religious persons, in whom
he dwells through grace. The door is penance,
through which we enter to him and he to us. And
so when you go so far as to say: 'Here I am',[†] he   Is 58:9
replies: 'Return to me, and I will return to you'.[†]   Ml 3:7
We have been turned away from him and he from
us. Let us turn back to him, and he will turn back
to us. Elisha, sitting in his chair, sent his servant
to Naaman to say: 'Go, descend into the Jordan
and bathe seven times, and you will be cured'.[†]   2 K 5:10
Our Elisha was carried away from us in body, but
he sends his servant to us. That servant is pure

---

73. Jerome, *Liber interpr. hebr. nom.*; in CCL 72:148.
74. On this commonplace, see Jean Leclercq, *Études sur saint Bernard et le texte de ses écrits* (=ASOC 9/1–2) (Rome, 1953): 115, n. 22.
75. Jerome, *Liber interpr. hebr. nom.*; in CCL 72:111.

reason, made in the image of God.† This is the
servant who alone escaped the slaughter of Job's
sons and daughters, so that he could bring news

of the disaster.† Or the servant is the Holy Spirit,
because he makes us servants—that is, servants in
simplicity. Or again, the servant is Holy Scripture.
It says: Go out of Syria (that is, away from pride)
into the Jordan—into conformity to Christ.

The name of Christ means humility. He makes
himself the teacher of this subject when he says: I
do not summon you to the prophecies of the patriarchs; 'learn from me myself, because I am gentle

and humble of heart'.† I place myself before you
as a mirror. Outer humility is of little help, unless
internal humility is present. For true obedience
demands these three elements: that humility be
present in the heart, that patience be preserved in
the mouth, and that perseverance be maintained in
action. The words agree with this: 'Go down into
the Jordan.' The name Jordan means a 'descent',[76]
and this explains why the Lord chose this river in
which to be baptized.

'Wash seven times'—that is, perfectly. Still unworthy, Naaman replies: 'Are not the Abana and
the Pharphar, the rivers of Damascus, better, so that

I can wash in them and be cleaned?'† The name
Damascus means 'thirsting for blood';[77] this is the
world, which desires our eternal death. Pharphar
means a 'mole',[78] that deformed, blind creature
which inhabits the tunnels and hiding-places of the
earth, digging up gardens and crops from below
with the trail it burrows. It signifies lust for earthly
goods, which orders one to cast down his eyes

---

76. Jerome, *Liber interpr. hebr. nom.*; in CCL 72:67.
77. Jerome, *Liber interpr. hebr. nom.*; in CCL 72:64.
78. Jerome, *Liber interpr. hebr. nom.*; in CCL 72:115.

upon the earth.† This is that bent-over woman Ps 17:11
whom the Lord lifted up.† Abana signifies 'those See Lk 13:11–13
addicted to pleasure'. In order to despise the things
that can be seen, we must reply every day to those
who say: 'Is it not better to be wealthy, to feast
sumptuously and live in comfort, to recline on
soft couches, to go wherever one likes and enjoy
amusement, than to waste our days in troublesome
duties?' Which is to say: 'Are not the Abana and
the Pharphar, the rivers of Damascus, better, so
that I can wash in them and be cleaned?'† But 2 K 5:12
those around him said: 'If the prophet had enjoined
something difficult upon you, surely you would
have done it; all the more reason to wash and be
cleaned'.† Those at our side are the angels, assigned 2 K 5:13
to guard us, and men of religion who say: 'Even
if what was commanded had been beyond your
power, certainly you should have done it'—and
they offer us as evidence the blood of Stephen,
the cross of Peter, the sword of Paul, the rack
of Vincent, the gridiron of Lawrence, the skin
of Bartholomew,[79] and him who is our camel—
Christ,[80] who passed through the eye of the nee-
dle† (that is, through great distress) in undergoing Mt 19:24
his passion. If we contemplate him, we are commanded by events which must bear added meaning
for us, and we must acknowledge that 'whatever we
suffer in this life cannot compare with the future

---

79. The iconographic references are to the blood shed
in the stoning of Stephen; the cross on which Peter was
crucified; the sword held by Paul, with its hilt pointed upward
as reference to both his martyrdom and his preaching of 'the
sword of the Spirit, which is the Word of God' (Eph 6:17);
the gridiron on which Lawrence was roasted; and the skin
flayed from Bartholomew (which in some depictions is shown
draped over his arm).

80. See Gregory, *Moralia in Job* 1.15.21; in CCL 143:35–
36.

glory which will be revealed in us'.† For at the time Rm 8:18 of our original creation, he gave us to ourselves. In our rebirth he not only restored us to ourselves, but gave himself to us as well. What could we do great enough to respond to so enormous a price paid on our behalf? 'What can we repay to the Lord, for all that he has expended for us? Let us take up the cup of salvation'†—that is, let us die, if need be, for the love of Christ.†

See Ps 116:12–13
See Jn 11:16

On the seven washings of Naaman.[81]

Is 1:16

'Wash, and become clean.'† There are seven bathings or cleansings: a bathing of the outside of the body; a bathing around the body; a bathing in the body; two bathings in the tongue; and two bathings in the mind.

The bathing of the outside of the body is the renunciation of riches and possessions. These are called external because they are not attached to the body and are not part of its substance.

The second bathing is around the body. This is contempt for rich garments, because if there were no sin in precious clothing, the apostle would not 1 Tm 2:9 have said: 'Not in rich clothes'.† Moreover, if it were not praiseworthy to dress in poor garments, we would not possess so many testimonies, so many commendations by Christ of John the Baptist and See 2 K 1:8; Mt 3:4; Mk 1:6 Elijah, both of whom wore vile garb.† And Jacob says: 'If the Lord my God has given me bread to eat Gn 28:20 and clothing to wear'.† He did not say 'clothing in which I might pride myself', but rather clothing to cover his nakedness.

The third bathing is in the body. It is the mortification of the members, the punishment of the body itself. So we read: 'I punish my body and 1 Co 9:27 make it serve me'.† This is signified in Agar, who

---

81. Compare to the following III Sent 34 and Res 3.15 (SBOp 5:103–109).

spoke out against her mistress; from her Abraham suffered injury a second time, since she took on an insolent attitude.[†] Our flesh is a lustful beast, like an impudent ass. It must be chastened so that it will obey its mistress—the soul.

See Gn 16

There are two bathings in the tongue. The first is to beware boastful speech during time of prosperity (that is, whenever God bestows prosperity on either our flesh or our spirit); the second is to avoid any expression of impatience during time of adversity. He who is justly punished and is impatient about it is the companion of the thief who hung at Christ's left hand.[†] Anyone who is justly punished and accepts it patiently is like the thief who hung to Christ's right and entered paradise with him.[†]

See Mt 27:38

See Lk 23:43

There are two bathings in the mind: the setting aside of one's own will, and not presuming to defend one's own judgments.

These seven washings were seen in Christ. The bathing of the outside of the body is shown in him because although he was rich, he became poor on our behalf. The bathing around the body occurred in that when he was born, he was placed in a manger[†] and clothed in rags. The bathing in the body was that he fasted,[†] spent all night in prayer,[*] and endured hunger and thirst. In the tongue he gave no offense during time of prosperity, since when they wished to make him king, he fled.[†] Nor did he fail in time of adversity, because he kept his silence just like a sheep before its shearer.[†] He showed the washing in the heart as well, because he came not to do his own will, but that of his Father;[†] he put the divine judgment above the counsel of Peter, who said: 'Let this not happen to you, Lord'.[†] It can be seen again, when Joseph and his mother said to him: 'Son, why have you treated us in this

Lk 2:7
[†]See Mt 4:2
[*]See Lk 6:12

See Jn 6:15

See Is 53:7

See Jn 6:38

Mt 16:22

Lk 2:48
Lk 2:49
See Lk 2:51

Ex 15:9

Rv 13:1

See Lk 11:21–26

way?'† and he replied: 'Because I must be about my Father's business',† but still he followed them and submitted himself to them.⁸²†

Such is the sevenfold washing of Naaman in the Jordan. We can approach it as well under the guidance of Christ, who lives and reigns forever.

89. On the seven principal vices. 'The enemy said: "I will give chase and capture, I will divide the spoils and my soul will be filled" '.† He is truly the enemy of God who pursues his people, despoils him of his goods, and strives to absorb them into himself. This is that most wicked Pharaoh who wanted to keep the jewish people in Egypt, so that they could never make a proper sacrifice in the desert. This is the slippery slope, the destructive transgression—this is the beast of which we read in Revelation that it has seven heads,† which are the seven vices. Their names are negligence, curiosity, lust, acquiescence, bad habit, contempt, and malice. The devil leads forth these vices as though they were cherished, strongly-armed soldiers† to take human souls captive. God has entrusted the soul to humankind as a precious, unchanging treasure, to be protected with the utmost care. He also gave humanity three attendants—reason, anger, and desire—to keep watch over the soul continually, so that the most wicked enemy will not be able to alter or deceive the soul through the service of any of those soldiers mentioned above.

First, then, the enemy sends against the soul negligence, which attacks her by saying: 'Why are you so intent on prayer, why do you torment yourself with such vigilance? Stop this overzealous activity for a while, and let us finally enjoy a bit

---

82. Compare SC 19.7 (SBOp 1:113).

of pleasure.' Hearing this, the soul gives in, and in
the sluggishness brought about by negligence she
cools down from the fervor of her earlier delight.
After this curiosity follows; it encourages the
things which are of this world† to rush back and
forth, encircling the soul with sweetness on every
side. 1 Co 7:33

Lust comes next; it makes the soul cling to those
things which are seen,† and ardently to long for the
things she wants. See 2 Co 4:18

Then follows acquiescence, and the soul becomes as it were another Eve; she hears the words
'You will never die'† and has no fear of trying those
things which are forbidden to her. Behold a second
Dina, who is corrupted in her desire to visit the
people of other locales.† Gn 3:4 / See Gn 34

After acquiescence comes bad habit. What the
soul has tried, she now seeks out again and again.
But after habit has filled the soul with the stink
of vice, it casts her aside—as if she were dead and
buried.

At this point contempt arrives, because, now
desperate as a result of her indulgence in sin, the
soul cries out with Cain: 'My iniquity is greater
than any pardon I might deserve'.† You see this
also in Judas, who lost confidence in God's mercy
and hanged himself with a noose.† Gn 4:13 / Mt 27:5

At the end comes malice, as it were the mistress and conqueror. Malice strangles the soul and
plunges her into the pit of despair.

By all of these, as with a chain, the wretched soul
is bound: she is laid low by negligence, dragged
along by curiosity, taken over by lust, captured by
acquiescence, tied down by habit, imprisoned by
contempt, and choked by malice.

But God does not desire the soul which he had
made in his image to perish. He dispatches his own

See Mt 12:29 soldiers, who can tie up that proud, strong foe,† so that they may be able to crush all the things subject to him. These are the seven gifts of the Holy Spirit. The first of these is fear of the Lord. It approaches the captive soul, saying: 'Poor thing, why have you abandoned the God who created you, and become oblivious to the likeness to him which he impressed upon you? Undertake penance, then, so that you may find his forgiveness and come to merit the crown which has been promised to you.' Frightened at this, the soul pledges that she will obey God, saying along with the prophet: 'Pierce

Ps 119:120 my flesh with fear of you'.†

Next piety approaches the soul and instructs her fully in the worship of God, which, by looking after herself, she had abandoned in her wickedness and curiosity. Now recalled, she cries out with the prophet: 'It is good for me to be close to God, to

Ps 73:28 put my hope in the Lord'.†

In third place follows knowledge,[83] which inflames the soul with ardent desire. She who had been foul and blind in her lust now shows prudence. She sings out, exclaiming with the apostle: 'There is nothing for me to glory in, save the cross

Ga 6:14 of our Lord Jesus Christ'.†

Next comes fortitude, and she who, because of her acquiescence, lay sick, expelled from the celestial dwelling,[84] is now brought back inside. 'I will come into your house, and worship at your

Ps 5:7 holy temple',† and 'The Lord is my strength and

Ex 15:2 what I praise'.†

---

83. The critical edition here reads 'sententia', which I emend to 'scientia'.
84. The critical edition here reads 'lumina', which would give the meaning 'expelled from the celestial light'. I emend to 'limina', meaning 'a threshold', and, by extension, 'the dwelling to which the threshold belongs'.

She who had recently lain, as it were, dead
with the stench of evil habit—just like Lazarus,
dead for four days, foul-smelling†—is raised up   See Jn 11:39
through God's counsel, and freed by exclaiming
with the apostle: 'Who will rescue me from this
body, doomed to die?'†   Rm 7:24

Then comes understanding, which fills the soul
with the knowledge of God and illuminates her. In
this understanding she will shout, along with the
apostle: 'Send down your light and your truth'.†   Ps 43:3

Finally wisdom arrives. Wisdom is the perfection and culmination of all the virtues. She enlivens
and glorifies the soul so completely that she will
not stumble or lose confidence in the face of any
danger, but will shout in a vibrant voice: 'I will
proclaim your name to my brothers',† and so forth.   Ps 22:22

Thus the soul is bound by these seven gifts, as
by a chain. Through fear she is roused, through
piety recalled, through knowledge made cautious,
through fortitude snatched from peril, through
counsel made free, through understanding illuminated, and through wisdom revivified and encouraged to proceed to the kingdom above. May he
allow us to ascend to that kingdom, who has seen
fit to redeem us through his grace alone—our Lord
Jesus Christ.[85]

90. 'There is nothing for me to glory in, save
the cross of our Lord Jesus Christ.'† There are   Ga 6:14
two crosses—one of Christ and the other of the
devil. The cross of the devil takes its name from
the torture of crucifixion, because it crucifies. It
has four parts: depth, height, length, and width.
Its depth is despair, its height pride or elation,

---

85. To the foregoing compare III Sent 4; III Sent 19; III
Sent 20; and III Sent 98.

its width the desire of the flesh, and its length obstinacy and perseverance in sin.

Similarly, the cross of Christ has four parts: depth, height, length, and width. Its depth is fear of the Lord, and so it is written: 'The fear of the Lord is the beginning of wisdom'.† Its height is hope, for this hope does not deceive.† Its width is charity—love of God and neighbor—of which the psalmist says: 'Your command has no limit'.† Its length is perseverance in good works, for as we read in the Gospel: 'Anyone who has held fast to the end will be saved'.⁸⁶†

91. On the five regions.⁸⁷ The Lord says: 'Be about your business until I come back'.† The head of a great household loves those servants who are industrious and productive, but does not recognize those who are lazy, and disapproves of those who are indifferent. People are diligent in going about their business and deserve to be rewarded if, up to the very end, they do not cease to think about what is right and to do it. So it is pointedly stated: 'Be about your business until I come back'.† For at the death of each and every one of us, the Lord returns and is at hand either to condemn or to reward.

There are five regions which the Lord has designed for his faithful to 'go about their business'. Their names are the region of unlikeness, the southern region, the region of atonement, the region of hell, and the region of heaven above.

The region of unlikeness⁸⁸ is our present life. Certain men, loving it far too much, become very unlike God and, rather like beasts of burden, descend even to the place of death.† Now a person

Ps 111:10
Rm 5:5

Ps 119:96

Mt 10:22

Lk 19:13

Lk 19:13

See Ps 49:12

86. Compare III Sent 67 (at note 53); III Sent 74 (at note 57); and Csi 5.13.27–29 (SBOp 3:489–92).
87. To this passage compare Div 42.1–7 (SBOp 6/1:255–61).
88. See note above on III Sent 21 (at note 16).

who goes about his business prudently in this district is one who, by weighing matters carefully either before or after his conversion, discerns— even if the world has smiled upon him a bit— how deceptive the present life is, how brief and uncertain, and how vile and inconsequential are any temporal goods you can imagine. It is as evident as it can be with what stench and bitterness temporal goods can consume those who love and chase after them. About some such people, for instance, we can note that it is brutish and subhuman to be overcome by the desire for pleasure. It is also dangerous to be exalted and to lord it over others. And it is odious to be raised high by fame's heralds. It is also hard—though quite rare—to be puffed up by wealth. If we discern things properly and distinguish rightly among individual things, it becomes clearer than light that all temporal goods bring grief and hardship, since they are difficult to acquire and are retained only with fear, and their loss is accompanied by sadness. A deceptive happiness constitutes greater unhappiness. The goods of this world are not only deceptive because they are always in doubt, and insidious because they are sweet; they are also empty in that they bear no fruit, because they often change and are easily corrupted. Since they afflict us, they are harmful. They do not benefit those who hold them, and they disturb those who pursue them. They cannot be sought without effort, but can be possessed without any benefit. Blessed is anyone who does not go off after those things† which, once in hand, obstruct us, and when loved pollute us, and when lost afflict us. Such goods have wings, and cannot be retained.[89]

See Si 31:8

---

89. This section may be compared to Boethius, *Consolatio philosophiae* 1–3; III Sent 109 (at note 128); and Dil 7.18–21 (SBOp 3:134–37).

But one who is wise and a good merchant, so long
as the present market-days continue and there is an
opportunity to buy, acquires for himself a profitable
cargo—that is, contempt for the world.

The southern region is the cloister or the desert.
Here Christ hides those who are his own away
See Ps 31:20 from any conflict of tongues,[†] and afterwards he
will join them with the company of angels. In
the Scriptures the Holy Spirit is understood in
See Gn 13:1 'the south', and the 'southern plain'[†] represents the
communal life, a spiritual mode of living among
good people. The paradise of the cloister, facing
the sweet mildness of the favorable south wind,
flourishes, as it were, with as many flowers as it
abounds in virtues. In the cloister our profit is at
hand and the benefit of a holy kind of avarice lies
open to us. For there, through the generosity of
Christ, a person who seeks instantly finds, and one
See Mt 7:8 who knocks immediately obtains for himself[†] both
candidacy for the religious life and the gifts of the
virtues. There is situated the road by which one
can ascend to heaven. There is raised that ladder
See Gn 28:12 on which one can climb up.[†] There is unlocked
Ex 19:6 the gate through which the holy people[†] can enter
the holy city. Let, then, a person who is in the
world rush to the cloister to 'be about his business'.
Moreover, let one who is in the cloister not fall
asleep or grow sluggish in sloth like a lazy and
See Mt 25:26; Lk
19:22 worthless servant.[†] (It is one's way of life that brings
merit—a place alone does not make one blessed.)
Let such a person work as diligently as he can: let
him seek his own gain without penalty and freely
covet the delightful riches of the brothers—which
consist of humility, patience, gentleness, silence,
obedience, and many other treasures of this sort.
Anyone who, by a debt of honest charity, reveres
and esteems those qualities in one who possesses

them—whether he actually succeeds in imitating those virtues in action or proves unable to do so—will not appear empty-handed in the sight of his Lord.† He is engaged in acquiring for himself the most precious of all stocks, a model of right living. Conscious of the wonderful usefulness of this, the prophet said: 'I have chosen to stand at the fringe of the house of my God, which is better than living in the dwellings of sinners'.† And he adds: 'It is good and joyous to live together like brothers'.†

See Ex 23:15

Ps 84:10
Ps 133:1

The region of atonement is a place known not to humanity but to God. In it the souls of those who are going to be saved undergo punishment—just as their crimes require—in whatever fashion and for however long is pleasing to the highest judge. This is for their improvement, not their detriment. It is directed to erasing the blight which they have contracted and restoring the purity which they have lost, so that, fully cleansed, they can be joyfully united with that desirable purity which is God. Although they expect an end to them, the penalties they suffer are very harsh—beyond what can be described or imagined. Clearly one who does not hasten to ameliorate their punishments, insofar as he can, with the medicine of compassion denies his humanity and becomes like a beast. There the duties of fraternal charity, prayers, alms, and the very consecration of the Lord's body not only have a place but are a weighty obligation. These things and others like them bring great benefit to those who are there and themselves constitute atonement on their behalf, so that they may more quickly achieve the liberation from suffering which they sigh for. May those who hold the goods of deceased persons, even if by hereditary right, listen well to these words, but above all others let clerics and monks hear them, and let them tremble above all others; their provisions and stores derive from gifts made to churches! Wretched are those who abuse or traffic in what See Rm 6:23 they receive—that is the wages of sin,† commerce in souls! Surely they accept things in a way which points to judgment—and to their death—if they spurn paying out what they should for the purpose for which those things were entrusted to them. In that region, then, whoever assumes an attitude of compassion is securing a valuable commodity for himself, just like a good merchant.

The region of hell is the prison of the damned, in which and from which no redemption is possible. There is, however, another prison—this world, in which we are all held captive as exiles, but only for a time. The world, then, is a prison of captives, while hell is the prison of the damned. In that prison, under the command of inscrutable justice, crimes and foul deeds are punished with appropriate penalties if, during life here, they are not cured by the medicine of penance. It is remarkable but true, and it must not be heard without a thunder of fear for him who is above! The pains of hell have no conclusion, they allow for no hiatus, they know no remedy!

In that place is deathless death, failure which does not fail, an endless end! For each and every transgression, for all the bodily members which Rm 6:13 have served as weapons of iniquity† a particular punishment is due, relative to the character and repetition of each particular sin one commits. The sinner will be tormented the more heavily in whatever member by which the Creator was more wronged. For instance, because of his garrulity and gluttony, the rich man is punished more with See Lk 16:24 respect to his tongue.† Thus, whenever the devil offers his wicked temptations, whenever the flesh caresses a person and draws him to sin, he should, with keen consideration, rush back to this region, so that at least from terror at the punishments which the spirit encompasses with its spiritual gaze, he can resist the flesh and the devil, and be so frightened that he will be restrained from committing sin. The trading of a wise person occurs in this region. In it a cargo of great value is obtained— namely, hatred of sin.

The heavenly region is our mother Jerusalem,[†] the land of the living,[†] a truly beautiful work, a work worthy of its maker, God. Christ rules there. He reigns like an emperor in his kingdom, like the father in a household, like a spouse in the marriage-bed. There the conquerors of this world, setting aside their temporal military service, joyously serve the Highest King, who also ministers to them. They receive from him the gifts which they deserve. God himself, who was their goal and the director of their journey,[†] is the reward for their effort, the payment for their work, their crown of victory. There is complete and total assurance— life under God, life with God, life in God, life which is God himself. God is the single coin, the sole prize,[†] the same glory for all. He is participation without division, common to all yet utterly unique, not lessened by others' enjoyment of him and not growing old in time or decreasing because of their possession of him. Those who live there do not work, or plant, or grind, or cook; such are the works of necessity, and there no necessity exists. They do not steal, or plunder, or suffer corruption; for such are the works of iniquity, and there no iniquity exists. They do not give bread to the hungry,[†] or clothe the naked, or assist the stranger, or visit the sick, or bring peace to the quarrelsome, or bury the dead; for such are works

See Ga 4:26

Ps 27:13

See Ex 13:21

See 1 Co 9:24

See Is 58:7

See Mt 25:42–44   of mercy,† and there no misery exists from which
mercy may arise. Since necessity has passed away,
all the activities connected with necessity are done
away with. An eternal celebration exists for all.

See Gn 32:30; 1 Co   They look upon God face to face,† and are filled
13:12   with his sweetness without any feeling of being
stuffed. They eternally possess him whom they
always want to possess, enjoying union with him
without any loss to themselves. Our existence there
will have no fear of death, our knowledge there will
have no fear of error, our love there will have no

Is 35:10   defect; there is everlasting joy on all faces,[90]† and
See Tb 13:22   through all the streets and byways of Jerusalem†
the alleluia resounds. Blessed is the people who

See Ps 89:15   know that joy.† This is the business of those who
are at leisure, the labor of those who are free of
obligation, the activity of those who are at rest, the
concern of those who are assured—they will praise

Ps 84:4   you forever.† Their praise of you will be without
end, because their love of you will be without end.

One should long for this region and think about
it continuously, whenever the wicked serpent con-

Gn 49:17   fronts† those in the cloister, striking them with
storms of temptation and envying their perse-
verance, which he knows will be crowned with
glory—because the conclusion of the struggle,
rather than the struggle itself, brings the crown.
The forum and markets of this region bestow upon
those who do business there both a brilliant reputation and fruitful advantage. The stock acquired
here is far more precious than the others. It is love
of God. That love is as strong as death; floods of

See Sg 8:6–7   water cannot quench that charity.†

And so there are five regions, which are like
a merchant's stocks. They are contempt for the

_____

90. Compare to the foregoing III Sent 112 (at note 140).

world, a model for right living, a feeling of compassion, hatred of sin, and love of God. The servant
who has endeavored to acquire riches of this sort
deserves in future, having been put in charge of
many matters, to enter into the joy of his Lord.†   Mt 25:21, 23
92. On the six wings of the faithful.† 'Who will   See Is 6:2
give me the wings of a dove, so that I can fly
away and find rest?'† Here is another Peter, who   Ps 55:6
is shipwrecked in the sea.† Here is another Jonah,   See Mt 14:30
who ventures into the belly of the whale.† The   Jon 2
world is the sea; the world is the belly of the whale.
Anyone who loves the world and the things that are
in it† is comparable to the shipwrecked Peter and   1 Jn 2:15
the endangered Jonah, and one who is attracted
by a corpse can, not improperly, be referred to as a
raven.[91] All the things which exist under the sun—
honors, wealth, whatever worldly enticements you
may wish—are filth and carrion. So the apostle
says: 'I consider all things to be filth',† and so forth.   See Ph 3:8
It is ravens which circle around such things. Thus
does the stinking, polluted flesh strike and punish
the soul which, because of the excellence of her
own nature, is fine and delicate, aspiring to spiritual
pleasures. Like one who has eaten rancid food,
the soul is compelled, as the muck of vice grows
heavy upon her, to vomit out the stinking filth
at the coming of a ray from above. She earnestly
desires to lay aside the dark rapacity of the raven and
the whole old Adam† in order to be able to don   See Col 3:9–10
the whiteness of the dove's simplicity†—indeed,   See Mt 10:16

---

91. One might expect 'vulture' rather than 'raven' here,
but Bernard is introducing a comparison between the raven as
a symbol of iniquity and the dove as the symbol of purity. In
doing so he is echoing both Ovid, *Metamorphoses* 2, 534–632,
which includes the tale of the raven being transformed from
white to black as punishment for its treachery, and Gn 8:6–12,
where Noah uses both the raven and the dove to gauge the
circumstances of the flood, though with very different results.

See Rm 13:14 to put on Christ.[†] But because similarity makes
for attraction between things, with earth seeking
out earth, and because the flesh, being weighty,
is fastened by the indissoluble glue of heavy corruption to the things that belong to time, the soul
seeks wings for herself, so that through their help—
through pious desire, or even violent power—she
may be lifted up, or even forcefully pulled upward,
toward heavenly things. For as Job said: 'My soul
Jb 7:15 would prefer to be hanged'.[†] Then, through God's
mercy six wings are offered to the soul as she pleads
with desire. They are the six virtues. Thus it is
Rv 4:8 written: 'The animals had six wings',[†] and 'He
See Ps 104:3 walks above the wings of the winds'.[†] Because
they are good, those who are never tied down by
earthly concerns are rightly called nimble winds,
provided that their mode of life is truly directed
See Ph 3:20 toward heaven.[†] Christ watches over their virtues
and merits as the generous grantor of good things;
and he walks above them, higher and greater than
they. For it is written: 'He soared, soared above the
Ps 18:11 wings of the wind'.[†] There are, then, six wings of
the faithful. Two cover their sides, two their feet,
See Is 6:2 and two their heads.[†]

The wings on the sides are fear and hope. Fear
strengthens the soul, so that she will neither become careless nor grow arrogant. Hope preserves
and nurtures the soul, so that she will not fail
when confronted by adversity. These two benefits
are given to good people so that they may have
the weapons of justice in their right hand and in
2 Co 6:7 their left[†]—which means against the two things
that can impede them, namely worldly prosperity
and adversity. For the elect sometimes enjoy both
prosperity in earthly matters and joyful progress in
spiritual ones, which means that they have abundance both from the dew of heaven and from

the richness of the earth.† But in order that these   Gn 27:28
shining lamps† may not be snuffed out by the winds   Lk 12:35
of pride—may this not happen!—their brilliant
light is kept from harm through the protection
and concealment afforded by fear, just as though it
were in a lantern. They truly understand that the
judgments of God are like the great abyss,† that   Ps 36:7
he is greatly to be feared for his deeds among the
sons of men,† and that 'I, the Lord, will determine   Ps 66:5
justice'.† If this is written about the just, what of the   Ps 75:2
wicked? He says: 'The earth and all its inhabitants
will be destroyed'.† Of the hypocrites it is said: Ps 75:3
'A thousand will fall at your side, ten thousand
at your right hand'.† The elect also suffer worldly   Ps 91:7
adversity and endure storms of temptation, being
tempted as they are by the enticements afforded by
the vices. But in order that profound sadness may
not overwhelm them,† the anchor† of hope raises   See 2 Co 2:7
them up to those things that are everlasting. It is   See Heb 6:19
in this way that there will be great peace for those
who love God's name, and no stumbling-block for
them.† The elect advance through both honor and   Ps 119:165
disgrace.† They always walk the straight path, the   2 Co 6:8
king's highway.† Ehud, who, as we read in the book   Nb 21:22
of Judges, could use either hand equally well,† truly   See Jg 3:15
symbolizes the elect, because for them all things
work together for the good.† Thus, among the   Rm 8:28
various gifts that they receive, although they are
sometimes assailed by the vanity that is common
to us all, they never forget what they are. Paul
himself, while he was raised up through frequent
revelations, was still pressed down by the goads of
the flesh.† We read that Job and Joseph were like   See 2 Co 12:7
him. But of those who are themselves changed by
changed circumstances it is said: 'The fool is as
changeable as the moon'.†   Si 27:12

Fear, moreover, customarily has three elements.

The first is fear of hell, by reason of which God is feared as judge. It is as a result of this fear that we read in Job: 'I fear for all my deeds, since I know that you do not spare one who has committed a crime'.† Those who are just beginning have this fear. Next comes fear of slipping. Of it we read: 'One who stands should take care lest he fall'.† This sort of caution is needed by an individual who is climbing upward, so that he will not trip on some stumbling-block and, gravely wounded by it, fall back down. 'On the road I was walking', he says, 'they laid a trap for me'.† Those who are making progress possess this fear. Third is fear born of reverence. A good wife has it for a good husband. A good son has it—the son respects his beloved father. The soul, which is the bride of Christ, has such fear for her undying spouse. Those who are perfect possess this pure fear, which lasts forever.†

Hope also has three parts. First is hope of pardon, that our past deeds may be forgiven. Then comes hope of grace, that benefits may be granted to us. Finally comes hope of glory, that the crown which God has promised to those who love him† may come to us. It was in that hope that the martyrs poured forth their blood. Likewise, in their desire to demonstrate the disposition they had adopted— in order to rush forward more freely and achieve their goal more quickly—they unhesitatingly cast off the garb of their bodies.

However great just and spiritual people may be, food and other necessities must nonetheless be provided for their weak flesh—just as chaff must be provided for an ox, and hay for an ass, and bones for a dog, and a sty for a pig. For no one hates his own body.† The Lord fashions two wings to cover a human being's feet. These are those motions of the soul which, while paying

Jb 9:28

See 1 Co 10:12

Ps 142:3

Ps 19:9

Jm 1:12

See Eph 5:29

the required debt to bodily necessity, minimize the stain and uncleanness which derive from it. For it is written: 'Whoever touches pitch will be defiled by it'.† These wings on the feet are defined as penance   Si 13:1 in the heart and confession by the mouth. And so we read: 'My sacrifice to the Lord is this broken spirit',† and 'Confess your sins to one another'.† A   Ps 51:17 person who grieves over his past deeds in his heart   Jm 5:16 also confesses them with his mouth. Since the one recognizes the other as its comrade-in-arms, the second is not cast out or rejected because it does not enter without due preparation.[92]

There are, in particular, three elements to penance: contrition in the heart, confession of the mouth, and testimony in deed. Penance of the heart requires three things. First, worn down by his sins, one should grieve. Then, in his confusion, he should blush—this is a kind of confusion which leads to glory. Finally, in condemning what he has done, he should be displeased with himself. Confession of the mouth also demands three things, namely that one should disclose everything to a doctor; then that he should feel humbled, just like a defendant before his judge; and finally that he should show his obedience by making satisfaction. These are what the wings of the feet do.

But because the powers of air,† which are always   See Eph 2:2 jealous of our progress, set snares and traps for one who is flying toward heaven, the head of the person aloft is also covered by two wings—namely, humility and charity—so that one who walks with simplicity, walks also with confidence.† For of the   Pr 10:9 devil it is written: 'He envies the soul from on

---

92. The phrase Bernard uses is 'pedibus illotis' (literally, 'on unwashed feet'), which proverbially means 'without due preparation': see, for example, Macrobius, *Saturnalia* 1.24.12.

See Jb 41:25 high, for he is the king over all the sons of pride'.†
He fears to see humility, which is destructive of
pride, and he scorns it. Moreover, because he is full
of poison, he wastes away with hatred against the
Creator and jealousy toward humanity. Whatever
possesses the scent and flavor of the balm of charity strengthens the good and urges them forward.
Thus they triumph all the more gloriously over the
See Rv 12:9 old serpent.†

Humility, in addition, has three steps. The first
is for each person to assess what he lacks. Thus
the psalmist says: 'Oh, that I might know what
Ps 39:4 I do not have!'† This can easily be perceived by
reference to those who are better. The second
stage is to recognize what is not one's own. This
can be understood by reference to those who are
worse. The third step is to comprehend one's own
weakness and mutability—what he has and what
he can lose. This can be seen by reference to the
demons, or our first parents. In the first stage of
humility I see that I am flawed; in the second, I
find nothing that belongs to me; and in the third,
I am afraid of falling.[93]

Charity is threefold as well: it is carnal, wise,
and spiritual. It can also be called sweet, rational,
and strong. It is with regard to these three that it
is written: 'You should love the Lord your God
with your whole heart, your whole soul, and your
See Dt 6:5; Mt
22:37; Mk 12:30;
Lk 10:27 whole mind'.† With respect to the first, love with
the heart, it can be noted that God sometimes
gives us temporal benefits, so that we can cheerfully
keep his commandments. This can be seen in his
former people, about whom it is written: 'He gave
them the lands of the gentiles; they took possession
of what other people had worked, on condition

---

93. Compare III Sent 84 (at note 62).

that they keep his commandments and follow his law'.† Regarding the second, love with the mind, we can point to the promise of heavenly benefits. With respect to the third, love with one's whole strength,† it can be remarked that God should be loved for himself alone. So the prophet says: 'What else is there for me in heaven, and what, apart from you, do I desire on earth?',† and elsewhere he writes: 'Give thanks to the Lord because he is good',† not because he is good to you or to me, but because he is good in himself.

So there is first the person who gives thanks to the Lord because he is powerful. For it is he who ends the life of princes, terrible as he is among all the kings of the earth.† Then there is the individual who gives thanks to the Lord because he is good to him personally. Of such a person it is said: 'He gives thanks to you because you give benefits to him'.† Finally there is one who gives thanks to the Lord simply because he is good. The first of these is a servant who fears for himself, the second a merchant who desires a return for himself, and the third a son who shows deference to his father. The first two—the one who fears and the one who desires—both act in their own interest. It is only the son's love which does not seek things for itself.[94]†

Peter possessed the three types of love we have mentioned above. He exhibited carnal, or sweet, love when he said: 'May this not happen to you, Lord; may you not die'.† He showed wise or rational love when he said: 'I am ready to go with you to prison and to death'.† He showed spiritual or strong love when, after receiving the Holy Spirit,

Ps 105:44–45

See Dt 6:5; Mk 12:30; Lk 10:27

Ps 73:25

Ps 136:1

Ps 76:12

Ps 49:18

1 Co 13:5

See Mt 16:22

Lk 22:33

94. Compare III Sent 26; III Sent 121 (at note 179); and Dil 12.34–14.38 (SBOp 3:148–52).

See Ac 2:14–36

See 1 Co 13:8

Sg 8:6
1 Co 13:8

he preached the name of the Lord fearlessly before everyone.[95]† To put it another way, a person is first seized by a certain attachment to the sweetness of earthly things. That sweetness will not be expelled unless another surpasses it; and the sweetness of Christ exceeds it and does away with it. It is like a nail being removed with another nail. For a person is said to love with his whole heart the Christ who exhibited the grace of integrity in himself, both in his own character and in the renowned miracles which he generously performed while he was present on earth—curing the sick, expelling demons, eating and drinking with sinners, and so forth. By reason of these sorts of good works— and one could not deny them to be good even if he attributed them to a mere human being— a person with this kind of love embraces Christ affectionately. Such love, which comes from the heart (that is, from the human capacity for feeling), is termed carnal and sweet. This charity, however, can pass away,† and often does. The apostles appear to have loved Christ with this kind of charity prior to his ascension. Other persons love him with their whole soul, that is, with their reason, because their soul discerns and understands what every creature owes to its Creator, what everyone who has been redeemed owes to his Savior, and she serves and obeys him in accordance with that wisdom. This form of charity is higher and greater than the first and is said to be wise and rational. Its seat is in the soul, where reason is strong. Nonetheless it too passes away. There is, finally, that most worthy kind of charity which is called both strong and vigorous. So it is written: 'Love is as strong as death'.† This love never passes away.† A person should strive and

---

95. Compare III Sent 83 and SC 20.5 (SBOp 1:117–18).

struggle with his whole strength to possess it when
he realizes that God is the greatest of treasures and
the fountain of knowledge, of whom David says:
'My soul thirsts for God, the fount of life'.† Such a   See Ps 42:2
person strains to be united with God through the
conformity which he owes him, to cleave to him
in accordance with the words: 'It is good for me to
be close to God'.† And so the apostle says: 'Anyone   Ps 73:28
who cleaves to God is one spirit with him'.† He   1 Co 6:17
who has this kind of love is ready to die for his
brothers.[96]†   1 Jn 3:16

Through the first stage of charity the ignorant
person is initiated, through the second the initi-
ate is encouraged forward, and through the third,
already well advanced, he is firmly strengthened.
The first instructs, the second encourages, and
the third brings to fruition. Adverse circumstances
undermine the first kind of charity and prosperity
carries off the second, but the third has been built
upon a rock.† Neither life nor death can remove   See Mt 7:25
it.† So it is written: 'Who can separate us from   See Rm 8:38
God's charity?'† In another passage we read: 'You   Rm 8:35
will never remove from your care those whom you
have established securely in your love'.[97]

After pious creatures are covered on all sides
with these kinds of wings, they soar over the muddy places, seeking out the solitude of the desert
so that they may find rest. Some good people are
separated bodily from the wicked. Others are kept
among them by their duties and obligations; they
fly away only in their desire and from this they earn
merit, even if they are troubled by living together
with the wicked. Proceeding along the straight
path, therefore, they are raised to the court of

---

96. Compare III Sent 93 (at note 99).
97. *Prayer of the Mass for the Second Sunday after Pentecost.*

heaven up the ladder of contemplation. There they
see, taste, and drink the fullness of celestial wisdom,
which God reveals to children.[†] They obtain solid
food[†] for mature people. May he who lives forever
deem it proper to grant that food to us![98]

93. God should be loved with one's whole heart,
one's whole soul, and one's whole strength.[†] Carnal
love is not driven out unless something stronger
intervenes, such as death; because such love is
driven out through divine love,[†] just as a nail is
driven out with another nail.

This charity has three aspects. The first is that
Christ is loved because he is mild and generous—
when he sits down to eat with sinners and performs
miracles. This is, as it were, a carnal charity, and
it is of the heart. Christ is loved with the soul—
that is, with the reason—when one understands
what he owes to his Creator and in this wisdom
loves and obeys Christ. This kind of love, like the
first, falls away.[†] However, that love which is with
one's whole strength is powerful and cannot fall
away, since neither death nor life can divert such
love from Christ.[†] The first sort of love is sweet,
the second wise, the third strong. Adversity can
undermine the first and prosperity take away the
second, but nothing can destroy the third. The
first instructs, the second strengthens, and the third
completes.[99]

God should be loved perfectly by humankind,
and should be feared as well. He should be feared
because God is that power which no one can
resist[†] and that wisdom which no one can flee.

See Mt 11:25

See Heb 5:14

See Dt 6:5; Mt
22:37; Mk 12:30;
Lk 10:27

See Sg 8:6

See 1 Co 13:8

See Rm 8:38

See 2 Ch 20:6

---

98. Another recension of this text is edited from manuscripts at Paris and Lincoln by H. Rochais, 'Inédits bernardins
dans le manuscrit Harvard 185', *Analecta monastica* 6 (*Studia
Anselmiana* 50) (Rome, 1962): 124–32. Compare also I Sent
33; II Sent 134; III Sent 33; and Div 123.2 (SBOp 6/1:401–
402).
99. Compare III Sent 92 (at note 96).

Moreover, he should be loved because he is himself that charity† which loves us, and there should be no doubt about his love for us. God is the one who does not deceive anyone—he is truth, and so he loves truthfully. So one who fears and loves God perfectly can understand what is God's height and depth, breadth and length.† His height is his power; his depth his wisdom, which encompasses all things; his width his charity; and his length his truth—this is the same thing as his eternity, which is without either beginning or end, just like his truth.[100]

See 1 Jn 4:8

See Eph 3:18

94. On the three steps of descent. 'He has prepared ascents in his heart.'† A man who sinks as a result of sin takes three steps down to his destruction.

Ps 84:5

The first descent or fall was the decline or separation from the highest will, most perfect among all good things—which occurs when a person, imagining that the power of choice belongs to him, seizes it for himself. This is that estate of which the prodigal son says to his father: 'Give me the property which belongs to me'.† This is what belongs to him, and it is an extremely grave and dangerous thing. For such an individual, perverting the right order of things, desires in this act to mimic his Creator, so that just as though law itself existed for his benefit and under his power, he can in such things rule himself and make his own will the law for himself. But whoever makes bad use of his own will, without any regard for the yoke of obedience—like a young wild ass, freed† and loose—attempts to steal a likeness to God† and to deprive God of his rightful dignity and his unique excellence. Insofar as he does so, he is guilty of

See Lk 15:12

See Jb 11:12
See Ph 2:6

---

100. Compare III Sent 67 (at note 52) and III Sent 82.

wrongdoing. For if there exists any will which is subject to no one, then there can be no divine will which stands over all things; nor would it be the only will over which no other can stand. This, then, is the first step down. It is like flying into the heavens, which means toward a likeness to the devil, who said: 'I will put my seat in the north, and will rival the Most High'.[†]

See Is 14:13–14

See Rm 8:1

The second step down is to walk in the flesh.[†] This happens when the wretched person adapts himself to, and lives in accordance with, the law and dominion of the flesh, showing no regard for the highest good which is God or for the dignity which is proper to him. Like a beast he embraces the inducements of the eyes, the delights of sounds, the scents which lie outside him, the desire of the throat, the encouragements of lust, unbridled license, and other allurements of the flesh. This means that he wastes his property[†] consorting with prostitutes,[†] that is in carnal enticements. The apostle teaches us how harsh and dangerous this descent is when he says: 'If you live according to the flesh, you will die'.[†] Such is the second step down.

Lk 15:13

Lk 15:30

Rm 8:13

The third descent is when the wretched person never remains in the same place,[†] but is constantly slipping down to a worse one. In his pitiful collapse he sinks, striving to embrace those things outside him which are not his—possessions, riches, honors, and the like. All such things are said both to be outside us and not to belong to us. For as it is written: 'Woe to him who accumulates goods that are not his'.[†] One person excels in honors, holding the wealth of Croesus in his money-box. 'His barns are overflowing with varied crops'.[†] All these things are alien to us, all of them are outside of us and have no relevance to us. Whatever is not

Jb 14:2

Hab 2:6

Ps 144:13

in a person—whatever is outside him—is alien to him. To seek such things, to circle around them, means willingly to fill one's belly with the husks eaten by pigs.† This is the third step down.   See Lk 15:16

Through these wrong modes of living or descents which we have discussed, the son left his father and went to a distant country.† The first   See Lk 15:13 regimen or step involved the presumption of his own will, the second the ill-use of carnal enticements, and the third a blind desire for temporal goods. The first removes one from God, the second takes one even further away, and the third makes one very distant from him. Anyone who desires in his spirit to live free and unbridled, like a wild young ass,† moves away from God, but only to   Jb 11:12 the first place removed from him, that nearest to God. For the spirit is rational and immortal, since it approaches likeness to the divine more than our flesh or the things which are outside us do. Indeed the flesh, which after a while must dissipate into dust, is so much inferior to the spirit that it removes those who love it from God that much more. Still, it is significantly better and more worthy than the things that are outside us, because it is joined with the spirit in the unity of a single person, and together with the spirit it will be punished or glorified according to its deserts. So it makes a person less distant from God than do temporal goods, which place him at the furthest remove. And the less natural things are to human beings and the more extraneous they are, the more wretchedly do they imprison one in that distant region of separation from God. If, however, a person, even after he has fallen all the way to Babylon, wants to be freed, it is necessary that he arrange the ascents in his heart† and go up again along the same path   Ps 84:5 by which he came down. It is not necessary for

him to search out the route—a route that he does
not know. The route is known to him, since he
descended along it! The result is that by following
his own footsteps in retracing his path, he can rise
up, humbled, by the same steps by which, in his
pride, he descended.

So the steps of those ascending to the heavenly
city are the same as the steps of those descending
from it. There is but one door for those approaching God and those departing from him[†] and one
ladder on which the angels appeared to Jacob,
going up and coming down.[†]

The first step for one who is ascending should
be that which was last for him when he descended:
what was a road of iniquity[†] because of those descending on it can now be a road of truth[†] by
reason of those going up on it.[101] With every hint
of avarice removed, therefore, one should scorn
all temporal goods, not insofar as they have been
granted to us for our proper use, but because they
lead to ruin for many men. Those who are filled
up and heavily burdened do not run well. Those,
however, who are unburdened and free of hin-
drances proceed more swiftly and securely. One
must struggle naked against the naked foe—that is,
the devil, who has no load of earthly possessions.
See to it that you do not hold onto that by which
you will be held back. A person must throw off
his shoulders whatever can slow him down as he
hastens to his fatherland. For 'no one is able to
serve two masters',[†] and 'No one in God's service
entangles himself in secular concerns'.[†] Thus spiritual poverty must be embraced, so that the person
who wishes to live a pious life can judge whether
an enormous abundance of worldly goods is really a

See Jn 10:9

See Gn 28:12

Ps 107:17
See Tb 1:2

Mt 6:24
2 Tm 2:4

---

101. To the following compare III Sent 95.

comfort to our nature. The road is short; there is no
need for many provisions for the journey. Moreover, 'blessed are those who are poor in spirit'.[†] Mt 5:3
This is the first mode of life or ascent.

Secondly, it is appropriate that the enticements
of carnal desire should be more fully extinguished
by fasting, vigils, manual labor, frequent use of
sackcloth, and other mechanisms which the discipline of the Rule mentions and approves—indeed,
this should be a daily preoccupation.[†] Such sprouts See 2 Co 11:28
spring back quickly and are not easily uprooted,
just as it is only with difficulty that people acquire
the virtues, but they swiftly slip away. It is easy to
sink to the depths, but hard to progress to virtue.
So Peter, to teach us about caution, writes: 'Be
calm'[†] and 'Keep watch in prayer'.[*] And the chosen [†]1 P 5:8 [*]1 P 4:7
instrument[†] exclaims: 'Walk in the spirit, and you Ac 9:15
will not give in to the desires of the flesh',[†] because Ga 5:16
it is impossible for you not always to feel such desires, but it is not necessary that you give in to them.
So elsewhere he says: 'We should not permit sin
to reign in our mortal body'.[†] Moreover, he offers See Rm 6:12
himself as an example to us when he writes: 'I treat
my body harshly and force it into obedience, lest I,
who have preached to others, should be rejected'.[†] See 1 Co 9:27
And to others he said: 'Destroy those things in you
which belong to the earth'.[†] This is the second Col 3:5
regimen or ascent.

Thirdly, it is profitable that one should deny
himself and, having handed himself over to another's will, obey in imitation of our Head, who
was obedient to the Father even unto death.[†] He See Ph 2:8
himself said: 'I have come not to do my own
will, but that of him who sent me'.[†] Thus let one See Jn 6:38
say, like a domesticated animal tamed by the reins
of obedience: 'I was made a beast of burden in

Ps 73:22–23

your presence, and I will always be with you'.[†]
Obedience is the virtue of virtues. In the house

See Lk 10:38–42
See Mk 11:1

of Simon the sins of Mary are forgiven,[†] and in
Bethany Lazarus is raised from the dead.[†] The two
modes of life are represented by the two sisters
Martha and Mary. On Palm Sunday Christ began
his journey from Bethany, foreshadowing for us
the ethical road to the heavenly Jerusalem. Outside
Bethany neither the tears of a penitent, nor zeal for
good works, nor the quiet of holy contemplation
can be pleasing to God. Each and every person
must have his Moses, under whose guidance and
direction he may depart from Egypt—that is, turn

1 P 3:11
See 2 Tm 2:4

aside from evil[†] and serve worthily in God's army[†]
by fashioning himself in the desert through the
exercise of the virtues and good works. One who,
for Christ, subjects himself to and obeys those
placed over him is worthy to be raised up and rule
in heaven, where there will be loftiness without
any decline, and glory without any defect.

    Thus, there are three ascents. The first is to
despise the world, the second to mortify the flesh,
the third to deny oneself. This constitutes Jacob's

See Gn 28:12

ladder, on which he saw angels going up.[†] This
is the means by which the lost sheep is returned

See Lk 15:4–6
See Mt 12:42
See 2 S 11:4

to the fold,[†] the queen of the south is brought to
Solomon,[†] and Bathsheba is transported to David's
embrace.[†]

Ps 84:5

    95. 'He has prepared ascents in his heart.'[†] A
person experiences three steps going down to destruction. The first is the presumption of his will.
The second is his abuse of carnal enticements.
The third is the deceptive attraction of earthly
things. One should ascend by the same road along
which one has descended, with complementary
steps but in reverse order, so that the first step
of ascent becomes the renunciation of temporal

things, the second the mortification of the flesh,
and the third the setting aside of one's own will.
These are the three regimens through which we
return to Christ.[102]

96. There are three types of food which the human body naturally requires and in which it takes
pleasure. The first is the food which invigorates
our nature and strengthens it more and more from
day to day. The second type is that which simply
provides delight. The third is food which preserves
us in that state of good health which we need.

Likewise, the faithful soul naturally desires three
spiritual foods: justice, wisdom, and truth. Those
foods and their fruits can be found, all together, in
the wood of life† which is Jesus Christ. We must   Gn 3:22; Pr 11:30
see, however, how they work individually. Before
a person can love and embrace justice, he is weak
and ill, and can be shaken—like a reed—by love or
hate, by some favor of which he is deprived, by gifts
which he is promised, or by threats and menace.
After he becomes a cultivator of justice in these and
other respects, however, he can remain solid and
secure. He cares for no king, attends to no count,
and fears the visage of no powerful personage. For
the just person is as confident as a lion and will
be without fear.† He is one of those who can say: Pr 28:1
'We will walk the high road'† and 'I will come into   See Nb 20:17
your sight in justice'.† That food which provides   See Ps 17:15
courage is called justice.

Then, after the soul has been purified by the
regular practice of works of justice, she is at some
point drawn from the duty and responsibility of
Martha to the rest and tranquility of Mary.† She   See Lk 10:38–42
gives herself over to consideration of the Scrip-
tures and meditation on the law. Then, in a joyous

---

102. Compare III Sent 94.

prelude to charity, she begins to taste with the
throat and palate of the heart and is sweetened,
even if only a bit, by the rich wine of contemplation, whereupon she can freely say, along with
the prophet: 'How sweet are your words to my
throat; they are sweeter than honey in my mouth!'†
And just as is written: 'Let everyone who hears,
say: "Come" '† and sing, in pious encouragement:
'Taste and see how sweet the Lord is'.† This food
is called wisdom from its flavor[103] and because it
brings forth sweetness.

After consuming these two foods, however, one
must be careful lest he seem great in his own eyes;
lest, puffed up, he should look down upon others;
and lest he be pierced by the blade of insolence.
So the apostle asks: 'What do you possess that you
have not been given?'† Rather let him humbly
say everywhere† with the prophet: 'Give glory
not to us, Lord, not to us, but to your name!'†
Let him piously recall and faithfully observe the
Lord's injunction: 'When you have done all that
has been enjoined on you, say: "We are but useless
servants" '.† That admission is great and of great
merit. For evil things come from us, and good
things from God. That food which preserves our
health is truth.

Thus there are three types of spiritual food, as we
have said. Justice, which is shown in action, gives
us courage. Wisdom, which is found in the heart,
adds sweetness. Truth, which properly exists in
the mouth, preserves our well-being. Refreshed by
these three foods, the soul is nourished in her exile.

Ps 119:103

Rv 22:17
Ps 34:8

1 Co 4:7
See Ps 119:107
Ps 115:1

Lk 17:10

---

103. The connection is between 'sapientia' ('wisdom') and
'sapor' ('taste'), an etymological observation which cannot be
conveyed in translation. See also Isidore, *Etymologiae* 10.s.240;
III Sent 85 (at note 63); III Sent 126; and SC 85.8 (SBOp
2:312).

She is soothed and kept from harm, so that she will
not depart from unity with God and from his grace,
until at last she can, with great happiness, enjoy her
nuptials and the embrace of her Redeemer.

97. A fitting comparison to a wounded person.
'It is I who blot out the evil deeds and sins of
humanity',[†] says the Lord. These are the words   Is 43:25
of the Holy Spirit, for he is surely that ineffable
sweetness and goodness proceeding from the Father and the Son through whom the wounds of
sinners are healed. We should note, for instance,
how the restoration to health of one who is mortally wounded in body can also be fully applied, in
the moral sense, to the soul.

Let us say that someone is wounded by an arrow.
Its shaft and metal head have both pierced him
deeply. The doctor arrives with iron and fire. He
extracts both the shaft and the arrowhead. For if the
shaft alone is withdrawn and the head remains in
the body, no cure is effected. The patient is pained
by the operation and cries out in anguish. If the
physician is wise, he will act to lessen the pain by
treating the patient with salves and soft plasters.
Further, because of the considerable size of the
arrowhead, he must see to it that a pledget is fixed
over the wound. As the patient's health returns little
by little, this can be decreased in size, and when
health has been restored it is removed. Meanwhile
the patient is refreshed and strengthened with food,
and he takes a bit of wine, which improves his
disposition. After drinking he sleeps, so that he
may recover fully.

Now let us look at this from the moral perspective. Sin, knowingly committed, is an arrow
mortally wounding the soul. The Holy Spirit is
the physician of souls; he is called by various names
because of the different effects he brings about in

us. It is that physician who arrives, because God's
grace is truly abundant and available to everyone.
It does not turn away those who knock. It receives as sons—indeed, seizes—those who are not
looking for it, it waits longingly for those who are
negligent, and it draws the obstinate toward it. The
doorway which is the beginning of our conversion
is contrition of the heart. The Holy Spirit, then,
from whom all good things flow, comes to the sinner as though with fire and iron when he produces
the bitterness of contrition in him. Contrition
scrapes the land of our heart like a sharp stake;

Gn 3:18

like fire it burns away the brambles and thistles[†] of
the vices; and like a keen sword it lops away and
removes the enticements of the flesh. It is then,
under the rebuke of the Spirit, that a person reaches

See Ps 50:20–21

a judgment against himself.[†] He is marvelously
stricken and powerfully worn down. He staggers

Ps 107:27

and reels like a drunkard,[†] so that with the prophet
he may be able to say: Lord, 'you have shaken the

Ps 60:2

land and thrown it into confusion'.[†] How great that
pain is, and how the inner person reacts to the fire
and sword by dissolving in tears—for 'smoke rises

Ps 18:8

up from his anger'[†] —those who have experienced
it well know. See how the physician, coming to the
patient with fire and iron, burns and cuts away the
rotten flesh. The arrow's shaft is removed when the
sin is put aside, but the head remains imbedded in
the wound so long as the desire to sin persists. So
long as that desire is present, no cure is effected.
The arrowhead must, therefore, be extracted—the
will to offend again must be removed. Since this is
an effect brought about by the Spirit, he is called
fire, for it is written: 'Our God is a consuming

Heb 12:29

fire',[†] and Jeremiah says: 'He sent fire into my

See Lm 1:13

bones'.[†]
   After the cutting and burning which we have

described, the sinner is soothed by the Spirit with the oil of devotion, just as with soft plasters. This happens when, in good hope and a desire to obtain forgiveness, the sinner rushes toward the Church's keys, humbly confessing to a priest as Christ's vicar. For he has heard about, and trusts in, the fruit of confession—how all crimes are truly washed away through it. It is certainly of great benefit, showing how agreeable devotion to God is, that one person is subjected to another's judgment as though to God's, to be punished for his sin through the decision of a priest. For it is indicative of the mercy involved in heaven's plan that people should dismiss the sins of others, judging and distinguishing among them. Having themselves experienced the weakness that is common to all of us, they cannot help but show compassion, and they do not shrink from coming down from their higher positions and pitying others. David was a king, yet he fell. Peter was the head of the apostles, yet he offended God gravely. Each of them was humbled but rose up stronger than before, all as a result of grace. They learned—and each and every human being learns for himself—how great is our infirmity and how we should respond to the transgressions of others. If the angels were our judges, since they know nothing of sin from their own experience, they would be troubled at the very sound of the word and would not apply the medicine of compassion to us wretches. The devotion in making confession which the Holy Spirit bestows on a sinner is called oil, and so it is said: 'The yoke will rot away from your body as a result of the oil'.† Is 10:27

Following confession, one must demonstrate the fruit of good works. It is then that because of the size of the arrowhead a bandage is fixed on the skin: by reason of the pleasure that one

derived from his sins or because of their quantity,
the sacrament of penance is 'stretched over' the
sinner, as it were, for a long time and is strictly
observed by him. As time passes that austerity can
be tempered in accordance with the degree of
obedience and humility his superior observes in
the penitent.

These, then, are the indications of well-being
which gradually appear in the soul. The soul will
be fully recovered when those things will no longer

1 Jn 4:18 be necessary, when charity will drive out fear.† Fear
is the sackcloth which leads in that linen which is
charity. The fear of punishment is like the shade
afforded by a tree in the morning—it extends over
a great deal of territory. As the sun rises, however,
the shaded area contracts, and at midday one can
easily pass through it. The sun is the fervor of
charity, and as it ascends the fear of punishment
diminishes, so that it can easily be leapt over.

Note that these are the three results which we
have described penance as effecting. In addition,
when it is true penance—specifically, in that there
is a piercing contrition in the heart and devout
self-accusation in the mouth, which occurs when
one confesses or converses with another person—
and when the briefness of its duration does not
undermine it, then, as has been written, 'when you
have done all the things which were commanded

Lk 17:10 of you, say: "We are merely useless servants" '.†
Let there follow the holy mortification of the
flesh—we set limits to this because of hypocrites—
because it happens that when a person hangs on
the cross of penance, he is pierced by the nails
of justice. That mortification, which involves the
performance of good works, constitutes the act of
eating and restoring the patient. From this effect
the Holy Spirit is called bread, for it is written: 'He

has given him the bread of life and understanding to eat'.[†] Such a person as that now perceives in the See Si 15:3 Scriptures what pertains to the cloister, and he is thereby refreshed.

After this refreshment comes that drinking which disposes foods for swallowing, tempering their harsh elements. The drinking which cheers the soul is prayer. One who wishes to be with God ought to pray frequently. For when we pray, we speak with God; and when we read meditatively, God speaks with us. It is surely necessary that good work be supported by prayer and prayer by good work, for as Jeremiah says: 'Let us raise our hearts and hands to the Lord'.[†] One who engages in Lm 3:41 prayer along with his work lifts up his heart along with his hands. However, a person who prays but does not work lifts up his heart, but not his hands, while one who works but does not pray lifts up his hands, but not his heart.

Prayer, moreover, consists in purity and desire of the heart rather than in the quantity of words. Verbose speech is one thing and persistent disposition something entirely different. For it is written of the Lord himself that he spent the night in prayer[†] See Lk 6:12 and that, giving us an example, he prayed more urgently[†] at the time when it was proper for him See Lk 22:43 to do so in supplication; but he hearkens to the Father eternally. Old skins do not hold the wine of this sort of prayer,[†] for a person who is not See Mt 9:17 spiritual does not perceive those things which are God's.[†] There is another wine—one which is tart See 1 Co 2:14 and poisonous—on which those who are not of the spirit get drunk. Of the first wine it is said: 'The cup of unmixed wine is in the Lord's hand'.[†] It is Ps 75:8 truly the cup of that wine which makes the heart of each person glad.[†] Elsewhere we read: 'The See Ps 104:15

Ps 23:5

intoxicating cup of the Lord, how splendid it is!'†
But of the second kind of wine it is written: 'Their
wine is the gall of serpents, the venom of vipers

See Dt 32:32

which cannot be cured',† which is pressed from
the bitterest cluster of grapes and which Babylon

See Jr 51:7

quaffs from the golden cup† of her fornications.

There are, then, two kinds of intoxication. One
is from the wine of carnal lust, of which we read:

Lm 3:15

'Wormwood has made me drunk'.† The other is
from the wine of pure prayer, of which we read:

Ps 36:8

'You drink of the richness of God's house'.† The
former makes people mad, the latter sober. The
Holy Spirit is called wine because of this effect, and
so we read in Hosea: 'Your memory is as renowned

Ho 14:8

as the wine of Lebanon'.†

After food and drink, the patient is allowed rest
and sleep so that he may recover fully. This signifies
a taste of contemplation, through which there is

Rv 8:1

silence in heaven for about half an hour†—that is,
peace and the freedom of blessed tranquility in the
soul of the just. For Christ sometimes visits the
soul through contemplation—not in such a way as
to instill himself totally in it, but so as to offer a
taste of himself—not to fulfill the soul's desire, but
rather to prolong her love. He grants certain first-
fruits of his love, without bestowing the richness
of complete fulfillment. This is very much like the
earnest-money which is attached to a betrothal—it
indicates that in the future he will give himself to be
perceived and possessed forever. For the present he
discloses from time to time, through a slight taste
and a kind of foreshadowing, how truly blessed is
the saints' expectation of his glory and sweetness.
By reason of this gift of contemplation, the Spirit
is said to be our tranquility, for it is written: 'You

Mt 11:29

will find rest for your souls'.[104]†

---

104. Compare SC 18.5–6 (SBOp 1:106–108).

Thus we have treated of the means and manner in which the reborn soul is raised, through the steps of ascent, from the abyss of sin to the vision of God.

98. On the seven vices. 'The enemy said: "I will pursue and capture him, and divide the spoils; my soul will be filled" '.† These are the words of the ancient serpent;† they taste of the venom of diabolic perversity and reek with the gall and stench of his obdurate wickedness. Out of his unbearable envy and hatred, he does not cease to attack and pursue the human race, and before Christ's coming he had, in his assault, taken almost everyone captive. Today, he still takes many captive (though not so great a number)—and particularly those who are religious. For they are his chosen nourishment, and they assuredly are aware that the Jordan could flow into his mouth.† He has equipment quite capable of bringing this about: the seven deadly sins, which are the seven steps of descent—or more properly holes and horrible clefts through which one sinks down and falls until he is completely swallowed up in a pit of misery. Rescue from this pit comes either not at all or only with great difficulty.

There are, then, seven of these vices. Their names are negligence, curiosity, lust, acquiescence, bad habit, contempt, and malice.

The first fall—the first defection from the good —is negligence. This actually occurs when the soul begins to be weighed down by earthly concerns and attachments,† in accordance with what is written: 'They have ordered their eyes to look down upon the earth'.† Thus the soul shows no concern for the splendor of truth, upholds nothing, and loathes the precepts of justice as though they were burdensome and of no value. She neglects the observance of God's commandments, trampling them down with the feet of her mind as though they

Ex 15:9

See Rv 12:9

See Jb 40:18

See Lk 21:34

Ps 17:11

Jn 1:9

Jn 12:35

See Jn 12:40

Ps 49:12

See Sg 1:7

See Ws 2:24

See Sg 1:7

See Jr 9:21

See Ob 11

Lm 3:51

were but worthless mud. Having turned away from her God, from that light which truly illumines everyone coming into the world,† the soul experiences the darkness of her own falsehood, in which she wanders about as the Gospel says: 'She does not know where she is going',† for the darkness has blinded her eyes.† This indulgent slothfulness, this idle, listless weakness so saps a person's spiritual strength with an enfeebling languor, rendering it practically dead through its numbing cold, that the wretched individual no longer shows any concern for his own worth and what he has become. For as is written: 'When a person prospers, he loses intelligence'.†

The second pitfall is curiosity. This is the right order, because when the soul so foolishly departs from cautious attention to herself and grows indolent through carelessness about herself, it leads to curiosity about other things. For when the soul forsakes herself, she squanders herself on outside matters. Because she does not know herself, she is forced outside, so that she can take her kids to graze.† The kids signify sin, and are properly taken to mean the bodily senses, because just as death comes into the world through sin,† so too it enters into the mind through these windows. So we read in the Song of Songs: 'If you do not know yourself, O lovely one, go forth and graze your kids'.† One who is given to curiosity occupies himself in feeding his kids as long as he does not care to know what kind of person he is inside, or to what he has abandoned himself. The Scripture, however, cries out: 'Death climbed in through the windows',† and again: 'Strangers passed through the gates of Jerusalem',† and still again: 'My eye has plundered my soul'.† While, therefore, the soul directs herself to something else, the serpent steals in secretly, offers the fruit, and snatches paradise away. He speaks soothingly, he stifles reason with flattery and fear with lies, saying: 'You will never die'.[†]   See Gn 3:4

Lust follows curiosity. Behold Eve seduced by the serpent, wickedly placing her trust in him. She lusts after the fruit. And so the fruit is offered— beautiful to the eye and pleasing to the palate— to her desire. Her gluttony is aroused. Behold Dinah—when she goes forth to feed the kids, she is taken from her father, and her chastity is stolen from her.[†] The wretched soul, which in her   See Gn 34:1–2 curiosity had earlier gazed on things with wonder, now lawlessly grasps at them and presumptuously hopes to possess them.

Acquiescence comes next, which is actual consent. Eve eats the forbidden fruit, thereby breaking God's commandment and sinking into sin.

Lamentable habit follows this sort of acquiescence, with the result that one now stinks[†] as   See Jn 11:39 though having been in the tomb for three days, engaged in fashioning[105] for himself a whip made from cords, with which he may deserve—since he is unworthy—to be driven out of the Lord's temple.[†] This happens so as to agree with what we   See Jn 2:15 read: 'My iniquities covered my head'.[†] Therefore,   Ps 38:4 because he ignores, or cares little about, the riches of patience and heavenly goodness, through his frequent recourse to sin he treasures up for himself divine anger on judgment day.[†]   See Rm 2:4–5

When, moreover, his apparent impunity from the dreadful judgment of God leads him to engage

---

105. I emend 'conterendo' in the critical edition to 'conferendo' to give the image of a sinner, through habitual malfeasance, 'joining together' the strands which are his individual sins to form the whip with which he is ejected from the Church. This extends the allusion to Jn 2:15 ('et cum fecisset quasi flagellum funiculis omnes eiecit de templo').

readily in disgraceful actions over and over again,
the repeated lack of punishment draws him along
and entices him further. His reason is lulled to
sleep, bad habit ensnares him, and the poor person
becomes involved in contempt of God. For when
the impious individual has fallen into the depths,
he despairs and scorns God, with the result that,
oblivious to both his own reason and the fear of the
divine, the 'fool says in his foolish heart: "There is

Ps 14:1

no God"'.† Trapped in his prison—or his tomb—
he says: There is no salvation. For 'from the dead,
confession is impossible, just as from one who does

See Si 17:26

not exist'.†

Exposed to the tyranny of vice as a result of
his contempt, he falls just like a captive into the
abyss of that great pit which is called malice. This
step has to be thought not so much a fall as the
ruin of final damnation. It is when the visage of a
harlot is fixed upon the sinner, so that he will not

See Jr 3:3

know how to be ashamed,† but rather will hasten
to make wicked use of things that please him rather
than being satisfied with those that are allowed
him. Neither his spirit nor his hands nor his feet
are kept from such considerations. For whatever
enters his heart he contrives to use maliciously;
whatever comes into his mouth he chatters about
mendaciously; and whatever comes to his hand he
employs wickedly.[106]

We should, however, observe the properties of
each of these sins. Through negligence the soul

---

106. Bernard here uses a mode of expression similar to
poetic *versus rapportati*, in which normal sentence structure
is reconfigured into symmetrical grammatical groups. Thus
here Bernard's 'Quod enim in cor, in os, ad manus venerit,
machinatur, garrit, operatur malevolus, vaniloquus, facinorosus' would more conventionally be written: 'Quod venerit in
cor, machinatur malevolus; quod venerit in os, garrit vaniloquus; quod venerit ad manus, operatur facinorosus.'

is singled out. Through curiosity she is attracted. Through lust she is captured. Through acquiescence she is conquered. Through bad habit she is bound. Through contempt she is imprisoned. Finally, through malice she is choked, so that evil becomes sweet to her, rather than the good. These are truly the nooses of death; they are the nets which catch the christian soul. Battering-rams of this sort assault the walls of virtue and cast down the citadel of reason. Employing these ministers, Pharaoh every day kills our male offspring† and condemns us to work the clay and straw.† These are the weapons with which the strong man is armed for the fight, with which the father of darkness guards his palace. But one stronger than he arrives—the Son of God, coming down to us; and in order to plunder the strong man's spoils† he brought the seven gifts which expel and obliterate the seven vices.

Truly if, sighing, we call out to it, a sevenfold grace annihilates and carries off that sevenfold misery, making us once more sons of God and restoring in our hearts the temple of his glory.

The spirit of fear of the Lord thus arrives and approaches us. Of it is written: 'The fear of the Lord is the beginning of wisdom'.† This fear is the standard-bearer of the heavenly army. It is that wonderful forerunner, who rushes ahead among the other gifts to recall the soul[107] to her God, from whom she had departed through the enormity of her crimes. To carry off the vices it shouts into the ears of the wretched soul, like a terrible trumpet, like the thunder of reproach from above. As it is written: 'At your rebuke they will take to flight,

See Ex 1:16

See Ex 1:14, 5:10

See Lk 11:21–22

Ps 111:10

---

107. The reading 'animan' in the critical edition must be emended to 'animam'.

Ps 104:7

Eph 5:14
Pr 4:23

Si 19:1

See Jr 48:10

Ho 10:12, Old
Latin version

See Mt 10:28
See Pr 3:7

See 2 Co 5:10

Gn 45:26

Ps 13:4

Ps 119:120
Ps 60:2

Ps 21:3

and will tremble at the voice of your thunder'.†
Fear says: 'Wake up, you who sleep, and rise from
the dead'.† It adds: 'Above all else, keep watch over
your heart'† so that all of your senses will be vigilant
in guarding that from which life proceeds. It says
further: Be diligent and cautious in all things, even
the least. For as is written: 'The one who despises
trifles will gradually sink down',† and 'cursed is a
person who does the Lord's work in a negligent
fashion'.† Scripture also says, admonishing each
and every one of us: Know thyself,[108] and again:
'Shine the light of knowledge on yourselves'.† For
it is the most recent convert who does not know
his superiors. By advising that he should fear God,
who can destroy both body and soul in hell,† and
that he should depart from evil†—for each person will receive from the Lord according to what
he did in the body†—fear removes negligence in
judgment and puts it to flight. Then the soul, as if
waking from a deep sleep,† is returned to herself,
and, trembling, exclaims loudly: 'Illuminate my
eyes, lest I should sleep in death',† and 'Pierce
my flesh with your fear, for I am terrified of your
judgments',† and 'You have shaken the earth and
made it tremble'.†

Piety, which through its coaxing calls forth fear
and reverence for the worship of God, summons
us away from vain curiosity about things that are
outside us. It tells us that to be pious, a creature
which has everything from its Creator ought to
embrace and love him, and that it should fix its eyes
and the longing of its heart† upon him. The soul,
then, carefully weighing and faithfully determining
the things which are written on the tablet of the
heart through the spirit of piety, shouts out, saying:

---

108. See note above on III Sent 88 (at note 74).

'It is good for me to cling to God',[†] and 'I seek one thing from the Lord; this is what I ask'.[†] Ps 73:28 Ps 27:4

The spirit of knowledge destroys lust, for it teaches us that earthly things are destined to fall, that they are temporary and should become utterly worthless in our sight. It teaches us, moreover, that if we possess such earthly things in abundance, our heart should not be attached to them.[†] It instructs us, too, that they have to be assessed from the perspective of necessity and not indulged in out of cupidity: this is the highest form of knowledge. Thus the soul, moving forward through the spirit of knowledge, shouts out with the apostle, saying: 'I have come to consider all things as filth, in order that I may acquire Christ'.[†] See Ps 62:11

See Ph 3:8

Through the spirit of fortitude, acquiescence, or actual consent, is set aside. Each person who had been conquered by sin gains a triumphant victory over his enemy by turning aside from wickedness and putting evil to rest. Moreover, when the devil approaches—as he does quite often—he grieves over his losses and is confounded more day by day. Since there is no longer wickedness in her hands,[†] the soul, seeing this, shouts out, exulting and trembling;[†] she says: 'I will love you, O Lord, my strength; the Lord is my bastion and my refuge, he is my deliverer'.[†] Ps 7:3 Ps 2:11

Ps 18:1

The spirit of counsel is very powerful in doing away with bad habit. Monastic prelates have heard sufficiently about the stench and insufferableness of that wound. Among them it is neither new nor unaccustomed, and they have provided appropriate remedies through the spirit of counsel. However, it is necessary that, because of the enormity of that sin, the sinner should grieve more and be more confounded, and that he should subject himself to stricter and harsher discipline in order to make satisfaction. We do not doubt what was presaged in the raising of Lazarus by the distress, the tears, and the loud summons of Christ, and by the stone

See Jn 11:33–43

which had been put over the mouth of the tomb,[†] for it is written: Habit is overcome only with difficulty; those things which have grown up over a long time are corrected only slowly.[109] And so the poor soul is driven to shout out and say: 'My wounds stink and fester as a result of my foolish-

Ps 38:5

ness',[†] so that later she may, in her longing, say with the apostle: 'Who will save me from this body, doomed to die? The grace of God, through Jesus

Rm 7:24–25

Christ'.[†]

The spirit of understanding is surely required to do away with contempt. As it shines down from the heavens like the morning dawn, the soul shudders at the filth and the stinking pit into which she had fallen as a result of her contempt. Tearfully and with wondrous fervor she cries out to the Lord with the prophet: Lord, 'send forth your light and

Ps 43:3

your truth'.[†] For whenever the soul had shown contempt, she proved herself in her despair to be another Cain, another Judas, and, just as though shut up in a pit, she could never have beheld the extraordinarily bright rays of heavenly mercy. Yet she deserved to be delighted by the sight of these things, once the window of understanding had been opened for her by the Spirit.

Malice, which is the abyss of the final pit, cannot be done away with or expelled except 'with

Dt 5:15

a mighty hand and outstretched arm';[†] otherwise Pharaoh would not release the sons of Israel. And so the Son of God, who is the Father's wisdom, struggles against that vice—malice, the name of which might more truthfully be called 'death'—in

---

109. See Horace, *Epistulae* 1.2, 69–70.

spiritual combat. His triumph, which constitutes the overthrow of that vice, is his resurrection from death to life.† The prophet prayed against that vice when he said: 'Let not the waves of the sea wash over me, or the deep swallow me up, or the abyss close its mouth on me'.† Here two things join together, so as to be attended by infinite proclamations of celebration: the courage of the deliverer and the sweet pleasure of the one who has been freed.

Note the proper qualities of these gifts. Through fear the soul is roused, through piety she is called back, through knowledge she is instructed, through fortitude she is rescued, through counsel she is freed, through understanding she is enlightened, and through wisdom she is restored to life.[110]

Note too that in both the vices and the virtues we find a natural coherence in the succession of steps, a tightly-bound chain of effects. You see how we have shown two roads to you. The first is the road of iniquity†—a slippery road, a downward road, which draws one onto the precipice of destructive perversity, off which one tumbles from highest heaven down to an utter likeness to the devil. The second is the road of truth†—a road covered with brambles, a difficult road, which leads into the narrow passage of royal righteousness,† through which one rises from the gate of hell all the way to the loftiness of the angels through a proper sequence of ascents. May our Lord Jesus Christ, who lives and reigns forever, see fit to lead us to it! Amen.

99. 'Cleanse me of my secret faults, Lord':† from my faults in deed, my faults in thought, and my

Marginal references:
1 Jn 3:14

Ps 69:15

See Ps 107:17, 119:29 and 104, 139:24; Ws 5:7

Ps 119:30; Tb 1:2; 2 P 2:2

See Ps 45:6

Ps 19:12

---

110. To the foregoing compare III Sent 4; III Sent 19; III Sent 20; and III Sent 89.

Ps 19:13

See Rm 8:28

See Ps 119:112

See Gn 4:13

See Ex 13:21

See Zc 11:17

faults of association. We are freed from the first two of these in the present life and will be freed from the third in the future one. For it cannot happen that in the present life we are not touched at least by fault in thought. 'And spare your servant from the faults of others'.† You will be freed from the faults of others if you neither agree with them, nor forsake them, nor dissimulate about them, nor provoke them.

100. Christ is our foundation, the design through which we have been called to holiness;† a foundation is hidden. Our shelter, which is hope, rests on that reward which lasts forever.†

101. There are four kinds of people.[111] Two are classes of the wicked, with one of them worse than the other. The other two are classes of the good, with one better than the other. The members of each group, such as they are, devise a God akin to themselves. Those of the first class are called the desperate. They find it a part of their makeup that if anyone has offended them to some degree, they cannot pardon him at all. They also assess the sins they themselves have committed against God from the same perspective. Aware of the enormity of their crimes and God's singular justice, they despair over it, saying: 'My iniquity is too great for me to warrant forgiveness'.† These people understand themselves and God only in part—only in justice, without mercy—and they can better be said to exist 'in the light', that is in the contemplation of justice, which is signified by the pillar of fire.† They, however, fall into darkness as night wears on, just as one who fixes his eyes too intently on the sun goes blind.†

---

111. Compare III Sent 124 and Pre14.38–41 (SBOp 3:279–82).

The second kind of people, who can be termed the apathetic, exhibit this characteristic: they do not grieve over the sins of others, and if they fall into sin themselves, they retreat into negligence. As a result they believe that God will overlook sins rather than punish them. Such individuals are worse than the first, since they have regard neither for God's mercy nor for his justice.

These two kinds of human beings do not pray.

The first kind of good people are those who, even though they quickly become angry at one who sins against them, still find it in themselves to grant pardon to anyone who pleads for it. From this, perceiving that God is both just—that is, angered by sin—and merciful—that is, ready to pardon sins—they say: 'Although you will be angry, you will remember mercy as well'.† Such people as these, in accordance with the apostle's statement that 'Christ has become our justice',† temper mercy[112] with justice and justice with mercy, and walk the royal road.†

Hab 3:2

See 1 Co 1:30

Nb 21:22

The second kind of good people, who are more perfect, have, through the grace of God, such tranquility of heart in them that they are neither excited nor disturbed by joys or sorrows, prosperity or adversity. From this fact they perceive, even in this life to some extent, the simple, stable, changeless essence that is God's, and they take delight in it. Such people as these, even if they occasionally fall, do not think of God as wrathful. Rather, they believe that all things join together for the good† so that they may rise up stronger than before.

See Rm 8:28

To the first kind of good people is said: 'Perceive the Lord in goodness', and to the second: 'and seek

---

112. The reading 'misericordia' in the critical text must be emended to 'misericordiam'.

Ws 1:1

him in simplicity of heart'.† These two kinds of
good people pray.

There are, moreover, four steps in prayer, which
have four accompanying feelings. The first step is
when a person, setting foot on God's road, prays
like Job against his wicked habits and hopes to be
snatched from the snare of depraved practice in
which his foot is trapped. Second, the person who
has been freed from wicked habit now dares to
pray for pardon for his sins. Third, after pardon
has been granted, he prays with greater confidence
that virtue may be bestowed upon him. He prays
for this for others as well. Fourth, now that he has
become a friend of God, he prays in order to give
thanks for whatever should be sought rather than
to ask for it.

The first sort of prayer involves a feeling of
shame. For when one struggles in this way against
bad habit, he is often brought back into touch
with his earlier sins—gliding back into them, as it
were—and he is ashamed, not daring to approach

See Gn 3:8

the face of God.† So he comes from behind, along
with the woman who touched the hem of the

See Mt 9:20

Lord's tunic,† and he likewise touches its hem. The
hem is the thinnest part of the tunic, and when the
garment is moistened by rain, the hem becomes
wetter than the rest, since it absorbs the drops
trickling down to it. In this regard the apostles
can be called the hem; although they themselves
were without worldly renown, they were chosen,
and spurning all things, they followed Christ in
poverty. Even the least among us are called by the
Lord and receive the first-fruits of the Spirit. The
apostles are touched by those through whose alms
they are supported and honored, and who seek
their intercession. Alternately, the hem represents
those in monasteries, who are especially looked

down upon, because other people are frequently stung into a change of life by the sight of their humility and their abject state.

The second type of prayer is accompanied by a pure feeling. For when bad habit has been expunged, there is no artifice in the spirit of the one praying. He offers a pure confession, he does not speak with a double heart,† and he exposes himself totally, as a wounded person does to a physician in order to be cured. See Ps 12:2

The third kind of prayer comes with a feeling of fullness. For henceforth one extends his prayer, in order to pray both for himself and for others.

The fourth type of prayer involves a devout feeling. For because of the enormous attachment he has to God, one is now confident that what he had earlier prayed for is his, and so he begins with thanksgiving, just as the Lord Jesus did: 'Father, I give you thanks because you always hear me'.† See Jn 11:41–42

According to the apostle, the four of which we have spoken are oaths, prayers, petitions, and thanksgivings.† Each of them accords well with the others. For an oath involves swearing on holy objects; it occurs when a person does not trust in himself, but rather reaches out to things that are sacred because of the difficulty of his situation. Prayer, the 'reasoning of the mouth',[113] occurs when one 'has the word in his mouth' in order to seek forgiveness. A petition is an extension of the prayer; it is when one prays for virtues both for himself and for others. Thanksgiving has to do with both sins and things that one must receive. It consists of the praise and extolling of God.[114] 1 Tm 2:1

102. There are three things that obstruct confession—fear and shame, an expectation of earthly

---

113. See Isidore, *Etymologiae* 1.5.3.
114. Compare Div 107.1 (SBOp 6/1:379–80).

1 Jn 4:18
benefit, or despair. 'Perfect charity expels fear.'†
Note that charity is born, nourished, strengthened,
and brought to perfection.

103. 'Draw me after you; let us run in the scent
Sg 1:3
of your perfumes.'† When we are drawn along,
there is difficulty. When we run, there is freedom.
If we are drawn forward, there is effort for the
one doing the dragging. If we run, the labor is on
the part of the one who goes before us, namely,
on the part of the one who rejoiced like a hero
See Ps 19:5
to run his race.† He rushed on ahead in order to
speed us up; he put forth effort in order to draw
us on. God draws us on, and so do other people.
Other people do so through word and example
See 1 Co 3:6–7
and God by granting us increase.† Either kind of
progress—either of one just beginning the race or
of one well along—is nothing but an increase of
charity. For in some people charity is drawn forth,
while in others it both draws and is drawn forth.
When it does neither, it is not charity. Those who
are just beginning are drawn forward, while those
who are well advanced both draw and are drawn.
Sg 1:3
That person who said: 'Draw me after you',† was
being drawn forward. Thus it is written: 'No one
comes to me unless my Father has drawn him
Jn 6:44
to me'.† That person who said: 'Proclaim with
Ps 34:4
me the glory of the Lord.† Come to him and
Ps 34:5
be illuminated',†—implying further 'just as I have
been illuminated'—was drawing others forward.
In those who are being drawn forward, the Church
is charity; in them it is fiery and bright as it draws
them on. In those who make up the first group,
the one who draws others forward is like a mother.
In those making up the second, the one who is
drawn forward is like a son. One is like a mother
See Mt 23:37
when she takes the chicks under her wings,† when
she stretches out her wings and carries them on

her pinions,† feeding and looking after them.* One
is like a son when, because of his tenderness, he
prefers to be below rather than above, to be drawn
forward rather than to draw others on, to be taught
rather then to teach.

104. It makes a difference whether one says
'You will die' or 'You will die in death'.† Since
life and death are two things which are opposed
to one another, in ordinary language we just speak
of living from life† and of dying from death. If,
however, you double each of the terms, it is said
that one will live in life because life begets life,
and that one will die in death because death begets
death. This is not a pointless repetition, for there
is also a life that leads to death† and a death that
leads to life,† because whoever is alive is in process
of dying, and while he is dying he still lives. Thus,
four different possibilities arise: to live in life, to
die in death, to live in death, and to die in life.
We should reflect how this is so. To live in life
signifies a remarkable and blissful kind of life, and
points to a mode of living in which the gift of
physical breath is, as it were, joined together and,
through a kind of sharing, intermingled with the
grace of a blessed life. This is what is meant by
living in life and virtue—possessing the attributes
of a life of blessedness in the life of this body. On the
other hand, to die in death connotes the baseness
of the dying body at point of death, when its flesh
is denuded of the gift of life which is common
to all and the soul has no prospect of eternal life.
There is also the person who dies in life—one who
is alive in bodily terms, but who is dying by reason
of his deeds. Such are those who descend, though
living, into hell,† and the widow who, while still
alive, is already dead.† Fourth, there are those who

†See Dt 32:11
*See Eph 5:29

See Gn 3:4

See Si 3:7

See 1 Jn 5:16
See 1 Jn 3:14

Ps 55:15
1 Tm 5:6

live even in death, such as the holy martyrs, who truly die in order to live.

105. The soul naturally possesses three powers or capabilities. The first is reason, the second desire, and the third anger. Reason by its nature distinguishes between good and evil, and even between that which is more and less good, and between that which is more and less evil. What reason perceives to be good, desire by its nature wants and longs for, but it is weighed down by the burden of the flesh and hindered by the heaviness of the body. Anger is required against these difficulties; it is incited against the tribulation and weightiness we have mentioned. For by its nature it is aroused against things that are wicked, turning away from them.

Upon these three powers are founded the three principal virtues—faith, hope, and charity. First, faith is founded upon reason, because what the soul perceives through reason, faith believes in. By that act of believing faith strengthens reason, for when that which is perceived is believed, it is strengthened. Moreover, through faith reason is even raised toward those things that are eternal and invisible. Secondly, hope is founded on desire. Hope is engendered toward things that are invisible and lie in the future. With respect to them hope encourages and strengthens desire, so that our desire will not slip down toward lesser things. Charity is founded upon anger, so that it will not become thoughtless anger or pride. The salve which assuages this is charity, which anger thus rouses and strengthens. These three virtues are both one and varied. They are one because they derive from one source and aim toward one end, but they are varied in their roles and in the effects which they have. Because they derive from one source and are one, they have one servant in common—namely, fear—who does the bidding of each and readies a place for them all. Since, however, they are also varied, each has its own servant as well. Nonetheless, the servant who is common to them all holds pride of place and has command over those that are proper to each.

106. Fear, the servant of faith. Fear prepares a place for faith by cleansing the memory, which, once purified, is the seat of faith. The particular servant of faith, however, is true penance, through which the memory is cleansed a second time. For faith has confidence in the Lord's passion, and when one reflects upon the great charity with which he suffered for us, he grieves over his wickedness and becomes obedient to God. He grows penitent and blames himself, and so his memory is purified. Thus, a place is made in it for faith. It is fear that commands this penitence, for repentance is born of fear.

Fear, the servant of hope. Likewise, fear serves hope, cleansing the understanding in order that hope may reside in it. The understanding is the seat of hope. Hope has reference to things that cannot be seen, toward which the understanding is lifted through hope. Fear acts just like a servant by purifying the understanding: it prepares a mansion for its mistress, who is hope. Now unless the memory is first cleansed, the understanding is not lifted up. Rather, it is pressed down to the depths through memory. The particular servant of hope is poverty of spirit. For when a person loves earthly goods, how can he hope for eternal things? One who is poor in spirit, however, spurns earthly goods and, by placing his hope in eternal things, lifts up his understanding. Once again, fear commands this sort of poverty as if its master, and with it fear cleanses the understanding so that it may provide a place—an elegant dwelling—for hope.

Fear, the servant of charity. The will is the seat and home of charity, because charity is voluntary and resides in a good will. Fear prepares a place for it when it purifies the will, which cannot be cleansed unless the memory and understanding are purified first. The particular servant of charity is obedience. For one who obeys, loves, obeying out of love. Fear is the master of obedience. It orders obedience to purify the will, in order that charity can take its place there.

107. 'Why did I not die in the womb, or perish immediately as I came forth from it? Why did I find two knees to receive me, two breasts to nourish me?'† My dear brothers, if the material food by which the body is nourished is taken within us but not properly digested, it not only benefits us nothing, but actually does us harm. Similarly if the divine word, on which the soul feeds for its life, is heard outwardly and understood within us but not observed, it is more to our injury than our good. If kept, to be sure, it brings great sweetness, but if not kept it brings bitterness. Thus, when David exclaimed: 'How sweet to my throat is your word',† he immediately added: 'and so your servant keeps it'.† The sweetness derives from keeping the word. While all things have their time, there must be no delay in observing God's commandments. They must be kept continuously, without any interruption, because a person who does not observe them today will be less able to do so tomorrow. Why should today's redemption await tomorrow's uncertainty? Nothing is more certain than death, but nothing more uncertain than its precise hour. The holy man weeps over these unfortunate circumstances, saying: 'Why did I not die in the womb?'† These words must be taken in the spiritual sense, something far different

See Jb 3:11–12

Ps 119:103
Ps 19:11

Jb 3:11

from what they appear to say. We must not allow that the holy man desired that he had been aborted or had died just as he came forth from the womb, when he knew that this would have been harmful to himself and, worse, contrary to God's will. The fact that the words must be taken in the spiritual sense is made clear from what follows, when he says: 'May the day perish on which I was born, and the night on which it was said: "A child has been conceived"'.† There is one day of light, and another of darkness. On the day of light Adam was created, while on the day of darkness Cain was born. Thus, Job did not say: 'May the day perish on which I was created', but 'on which I was born'.† Now, there is a carnal birth or conception, and a spiritual one. The carnal is when we are made human—that is, the sons of men—and the spiritual is when we are made sons of God. The latter is that good birth of which the prophet says: 'We have conceived of your spirit, and we labor to bring the spirit forth'.† About the latter birth we are not going to say anything at present, but we must deal with the former—the one caused by sin—because as often as we sin, we are born completely of the devil. This is our wicked birth. Just as an infant is brought into existence through four steps—being first conceived, then born, then tended, and finally fed with milk—so too sin is effected by four steps in human beings. It is effected through four steps in the heart and four steps in action.

First comes temptation, pleasure follows, then the mind is dragged into consent, and finally there is either prideful hope or despair, depending on whether one excuses his sin or sobbingly admits to it. For just as the fetus is conceived in the womb, so sin begins in temptation and is brought forth when pleasure is added. It is tended, as it were, when

Jb 3:3

Jb 3:3

See Is 26:18

consent follows, and it is nourished at its mother's breast when the sinner either expects too much of God's mercy or gives in to despair. Believing that he cannot be forgiven, he either admits his sin sobbingly or makes some excuse for it.

A similar comparison can be drawn about sin's consummation in action. The first step is when one sins secretly, the second when one makes his sin known, the third when he proceeds to make the sin habitual, and the fourth when he gives way to presumption or despair—either giving his allegiance to the one who encouraged his wickedness or making excuses for his sin. In the name of the human race the holy man Job wept over the fact that sin is brought to fruition through these four steps when he said: 'Why did I not die in the womb?',[†] and so forth. That is to say: When the temptation to sin first occurred, why was that initial inclination not suppressed before it proceeded to the stage of pleasure? For we ought to trample the head of the serpent under foot— that is, to suppress the first inclination of sin in ourselves. 'For blessed is the one who will take and dash your babies against the rock',[†] which is as if to say: 'Why did I not die in the womb'[†] so as not to be drawn on to sinful pleasure? And if I have gone on to enjoyment, why have I then progressed all the way to consent? This is what follows: 'Why did I not perish immediately on coming forth from the womb?'[†] If, moreover, I have consented to sin, why further have I been led into despair or false hope, either making excuses for my sin or going on to anoint my head with the oil of a sinner?[†] This is what is meant by the words: 'Why have I found breasts to nurse me?'[†]

In the same way, all of these words can be referred to the stages of action in sin, because if one

Jb 3:11

Ps 137:9
Jb 3:11

Jb 3:11

See Ps 141:5

Jb 3:12

sins in secret, why does he make his sin known? If he makes his sin known, why does he turn it into a habit? If he has even made it habitual, why does he despair or presume on God's mercy? This is what is meant when he says: 'Why have I found breasts to nurse me?'[†] For Cain nursed at the breast of desperation, saying: 'My iniquity is greater than any pardon I can deserve'.[†] One should not despair over sin, because God 'leads to courage those who have been defeated, and calls forth those who lie in tombs'.[†]

Jb 3:12

Gn 4:13

Ps 68:6

The occurrence of sin in our first parent may be compared to these same steps and processes in ourselves. First came the devil's temptation in the form of the serpent. Then followed the temptation of Eve, which represents the delight of the flesh. Then came the consent of the man himself, who after his sin offered an excuse for himself and turned his own failing back against the Creator, saying: 'The woman whom you gave me tricked me'.[†] Moreover, although he said: 'I was afraid',[*] we should not think that he was afraid out of any humility—he was afraid out of pride! For when one does not love God's face[†] but rather fears his punishment, that fear comes not from humility, but from arrogance. Yes, he was afraid, but he was also puffed up with pride.[115] As a result he made excuses for his sin as is written: 'to offer explanations for one's sins'.[†]

[†]See Gn 3:12–13
[*]Gn 3:10

See Gn 3:8

Ps 141:4

These, then, are the four winds that destroy and annihilate everything. Against them the Lord rouses four skilled craftsmen—the four cardinal virtues—who repair and restore the things which have been torn down and destroyed. These are also

---

115. The Latin 'Timuit enim, sed tumuit' involves a play on words that cannot be captured in the translation.

the four pestilences which the prophet specifies
when he writes: 'What the caterpillar has left <the
locust devours, and what the locust has left>[116]
the grasshopper devours, and what the grasshop-

See Jl 1:4

per has left the gnawer devours'.† Diabolic temptation is symbolized by the caterpillar, which is
quite properly compared to the devil since it is a
foul creature, ugly in appearance and moving in
a winding course; all of this conforms well to the
devil. Pleasure is comparable to the locust, because
one whose enjoyment is insufficient whether he
engages in this sin or that is just like a locust flying
from one spot to another. The grasshopper is like
the offspring of the locust, because a grasshopper
devours more than either a caterpillar or a locust.
It always clings to the stalks of crops and perches on
them, not springing about so much.[117] It is properly
compared to the habitual consent one gives to sin.
Prideful hope or desperation is comparable to the
gnawer, because whatever is consumed by a tossing, devastating wind[118] is devoured and laid waste
by God, since there is nothing left afterward which
is of use. Similarly, when a person sins until the end
of his life either through presumption (when he
hears that the mercy of God is greater than the sins
of humanity, and that God will redeem Israel from

See Ps 130:8

all her iniquities†), or through despair (when he
hears that God is just and that there is no salvation
in hell), then nothing can be hoped for from him
which is of use either to himself or to anybody

---

116. The bracketed words are omitted in the critical text
and restored here.
117. I emend 'magis consumit locusta quam eruca vel
bruchus' of the critical edition to 'magis consumit bruchus
quam eruca vel locusta' for reasons of sense.
118. The etymological connection is between 'aura gente'
(a 'tossing wind') and 'aurugo' (a plague or, here, 'the gnawer').
See also note above on III Sent 86 (at note 66).

else. If there is anything left in an individual in whom temptation has triumphed, the grasshopper which is consent devours it. If there is anything left after the action of consent, then prideful hope or despair consumes it. In truth, then, nothing is left by these.[119]

Thus the Lord raised three persons from the dead, and it was announced to him that a fourth had died. He did not raise this fourth person. Rather he said: 'Let the dead bury their dead'.† He See Mt 8:22 raised one in her house (specifically the daughter of the chief priest†) and the second outside his See Mt 9:25 house at the town gate,† and the third when he was See Lk 7:12–15 already rotting in his tomb.† One is raised up in his See Jn 11:39–44 own home when he restrains the first inclinations to sin in himself and does not take temptation to pleasure. One is raised up at the gate when he does not take pleasure to consent. And one is raised up in the tomb when he does not take consent all the way to prideful hope or desperation. Or to put it another way, one is raised up in his home when he grieves over the sin which he has committed in private, but does not sin publicly. One is raised up at the gate when he repents the sin which he has committed either privately or in public, but is not drawn to sin habitually. And one is raised up in the tomb when he repents his private and public sins, which he has taken—all for nothing—to the state of habit, but is not dragged into despair or presumption.

Christ raised the first individual in her house with only a few witnesses, saying that the girl was not dead but only sleeping,† and thereby indicating See Mt 9:24 through such a dead person one who can rise easily

---

119. Compare to the foregoing III Sent 86 and III Sent 121 (at note 182).

because he is not really dead, that is, one who has restrained the first inclinations to sin in himself or who has not made his sin public. He raised the second person at the gate in the sight of a great many witnesses and did not say that the man was sleeping, showing that one signified by this dead person—one who has taken pleasure from sin or made his sin public—is more difficult to revive than the first. In the third instance, he even wept over the man who was bound with cloths and already beginning to rot in his tomb, in order to indicate that one who has assented to sin and carried his sinning through to the point of habit can rise up again only with much hard effort, heartfelt contrition, and a great outpouring of grief. For habit is another nature. The fourth person Christ does not raise at all, because one who in his despair or presumption dies impenitent is not revived by the Lord. For when a sinner sinks into the depths of iniquity, he spurns Christ. May he who lives and reigns forever preserve us from this fate!

108. 'If you rest within your allotted portions, you will be like the wings of a dove covered with silver',† and so forth. My dear brothers, we have constructed a religious house, a gathering of bodies, but it is far more important to create the kind of assembly which represents a joining of souls. For it is not particularly praiseworthy to collect our bodies together if we remain separated in our minds, and there is no benefit in assembling in a single place if we have disagreements in spirit. Nor does any locale, however sacred it may be, bring advantage to those who are not marked by harmony of spirit, for as the prophet says: 'I will not attend their bloody assemblies, nor will their names pass my lips'.† On the other hand, where

Ps 68:14

Ps 16:4

two or three gather together, God is in their midst:† See Mt 18:20
by the same token, living together is good† for See Ps 133:1
people, if they live in Jesus' name—that is, with
love of God and neighbor. Only to such as these is
it said: 'Rejoice, Jerusalem, and all of you who
love the Lord, come together!'[120]† The prophet See Is 66:10
teaches and admonishes them to lie down and rest
within two inheritances—within the present and
the future, or the two Testaments—when he says:
'If you rest within your allotted portions',† and so Ps 68:14
forth. In the allotted portions we should understand the two Testaments, or our present and future
inheritance—that is, both the portion which is
promised and those to whom it is promised. For an
allotted portion means a share chosen by lot, and
so a cleric is one chosen by lot whose inheritance
is God alone.[121] Thus the prophet says: 'The Lord
is the substance of my inheritance'.† This is that Ps 16:5
wonderful inheritance of which David says: 'The
measuring lines have fallen in excellent places for
me; indeed, my inheritance is wonderful!'† An Ps 16:6
inheritance of this sort, moreover, does not lie in
the land of the dying, but in that of the living,
and so the prophet says: 'Lord, may my property
be in the land of the living'.† These words allude See Ps 142:5
briefly to what human beings must do and what
they must undertake, meaning the command we
should follow and the prize we should strive to
obtain—a reward which is not merely a reward,
but a reward that is earned. The words, 'If you
rest', specify what human beings must do, while

---

120. See Is 66:10, as in *Introit of the Mass for the Fourth Sunday in Lent*.

121. See Isidore, *Etymologiae* 7.12.1–2. The reference here is to an etymological relationship between the Greek 'cleros', which Isidore defines as 'sors vel hereditas', and 'clerici', who are so called, he says, 'quia de sorte sunt Domini, vel quia Domini partem habent'.

what they must strive to obtain is indicated when
the text says: 'and the tail feathers on the dove's
back' will have the sheen, the splendor, 'the color
of gold'.† The reward is referred to in the words:
You will be 'the wings of a dove covered with
silver'.†

We should rest, therefore, within the two Testaments, in order that we may believe that what
was prefigured in the Old has been fulfilled in the
New. There is, however, the rest of sleep, of death,
of sluggishness, and of repose and tranquility. Of
the rest of sleep the Lord said to his disciples: 'Sleep
now, and take your rest'.† Of the rest of death
the apostle says: 'Those who have slept in Jesus,
God will lead forth with him'.† Of the rest of
sluggishness it is written: 'Rise up, you who are
asleep, and Christ will shine upon you'.† About
the rest of tranquility and repose it is written: 'If
you rest within your allotted portions',† and so on.

Moreover, he does very well to say 'within your
allotted portions' rather than 'in between' the two
portions, thereby demonstrating more precisely
the harmony and unity of the two Testaments.
For the most profound unity and harmony exist
between the Old Testament and the New, because
everything that was prefigured in the Old is fulfilled in the New—and, as we can say more explicitly on Bede's authority,[122] the New Testament is
nothing other than the Old Testament understood
in the spiritual sense. Although they might seem to
disagree in certain particulars, in truth they agree
in everything. Thus two cherubim with their faces
turned toward one another attend upon the throne
of mercy,† because the two Testaments, which are
symbolized by them, are in harmony with each

Ps 68:13

Ps 68:13

Mt 26:45

1 Th 4:14

See Eph 5:14

Ps 68:13

See Ex 25:18–20

---

122. Bede, *De tabernaculo* 1; in CCL 119A:19.

other. One should rest, then, with faith and knowledge to this effect within the two. In addition, one should repose within the two inheritances, so that the one may be held in contempt while the other is embraced with overwhelming desire and feeling. This circumstance is not a good which one seeks, but a necessity to which one assents. We possess the one inheritance for our use and the other for our enjoyment—one to employ, the other to delight in; the one for our support, the other for our glorification; the one for our consolation, the other for our reward. We must, therefore, sleep within these two inheritances, so that we may possess the one for our sustenance on the journey and hope for the other as our reward in the heavenly fatherland. If we rest in this way within the two inheritances, we will be changed from the one to the other. This is the transformation wrought by the right arm of the Most High.† There are those, however, who See Ps 77:10 do not rest in this fashion. For they give attention to, and love, only the goods of the present life, and do not strive after their future inheritance. As a result, the wretches will be cut off from it. Thus Solomon said: 'An inheritance to which one hastens too quickly at the beginning will not be blessed at the end'.† See Pr 20:21

This is why it is recorded that the Philistines, after capturing the ark of God, placed it beside their idol Dagon. The next morning they found Dagon lying on the ground before the ark, and they raised it up again. The next day they again found it thrown down on the ground; once more they picked it up. On the third day, however, they found it with its head and hands cut off. As a result the Philistines were struck by a horrible plague: rats crawled out of the ground and attacked them, and large tumors rotted away their flesh.† The name See 1 S 5:1–9

See Jr 51:7

See Mt 25:41

Ps 76:5

See Ps 39:6

See Ex 16:20ff.

'Philistines' is translated as 'those who fall through drink'.[123] They worship riches as if they were God, which is what is meant by putting Dagon beside the ark. Those who make Dagon, meaning riches, their god grow drunk on the golden chalice of Babylon.†

Yet there are also some who, while intoxicated by higher wisdom, still put riches before the Lord, savoring only those things which belong to the world and none of those which are God's. Others consider riches and God to be of equal worth, while still others judge riches to be beneath God, but not as far beneath him as they ought to—those who, when they lose their temporal goods, do not endure the loss with patience but rather murmur against God. All such people will be struck by a shameful blow to their back when, at the end, with everyone looking on and listening, they will hear the words: 'Begone, accursed ones, into the eternal fire'.† Of such people David says: 'They have enjoyed their sleep, and none of them find any riches in their hands'.† They hoard up their treasure, but they do not know to whom it will pass next.† Such people are symbolized in those who stored up manna, but not for the Sabbath.† Those who keep manna for a day other than the Sabbath represent those who use earthly goods not within the bounds of necessity, but to excess. They seek glory in a surfeit of temporal possessions. As a result they do not use possessions so as to be sustained by them as they serve in Christ's army, in order that they may at length be rewarded on the Sabbath of souls. Manna hoarded by such persons brings them death, just as an excess of riches does to those who abuse them. It generates rottenness,

---

123. See Jerome, *Liber interpr. hebr. nom.*; in CCL 72:66.

which gives birth to the worms that will not die.† See Is 66:24
Truly, if we rest within these two inheritances, so
as to possess the one to meet our needs and to seek
the other as our reward, we will be, in the present
life, the wings of the dove that are covered with
silver, while in the future, the tail feathers on the
dove's back will possess the sheen or color of gold.† See Ps 68:14

The wings of the dove, that is of the Church,
are those who in their good work lift up others
toward higher things through their teaching and
example. The Church is compared to a dove because of numerous similarities between them. For
the dove is without gall, nourishing chicks which
are not its own, living beside streams, building
its nest in the apertures of rocks, and sighing its
song. In a similar fashion, the Church is without
the gall of envy. She too nourishes those who
previously had been someone else's sons—namely,
the devil's. She too resides beside the streams of
the Scriptures and makes her nest on the rock
which is Christ. For this rock which is Christ† See 1 Co 10:4
is a refuge for hedgehogs—those who are hairy
by reason of sin. Moreover, she sighs amidst the
toils of the world over the postponement of the
kingdom. Of her the Song of Songs says: 'My dove
is unique'† and 'Your eyes are those of doves'.† Sg 6:8 Sg 1:14
And the tail feathers on the back of the Church
have the sheen of gold. It should be pointed out
here that one thing is signified by the back and
another by the tail feathers, just as gold is one thing
and the sheen of gold something different. In the
back we should understand patience. Thus David,
desiring to indicate Christ's patience, says: 'The
wicked have wrought their work on my back'.† In Ps 129:3
the tail feathers should be understood beatitude,
which we acquire through patience. There will not
exist for us the kind of tail feathers as there are for

See Is 66:24

See Ps 68:14

See 1 Jn 3:2

See Jn 17:3

1 Co 8:1

See 1 Co 8:1

Ezk 3:12

the Philistines, because theirs are the worm that does not die,† while ours are gold and the sheen of gold.† Through gold is understood the fullness of wisdom, which we will possess in the future when we see God as he is,† for such knowledge as this will constitute our glory. Thus the apostle says: 'This is our glory—to know you and Jesus Christ, whom you sent'.† Charity is understood in the sheen of gold, for in the future life perfect charity will accompany perfect knowledge. For the more perfectly we know, the more perfectly will we love; and the more perfectly we love, the more perfectly will we know. For in the present life, unless knowledge is accompanied by charity, it is useless, because as the apostle says: 'Knowledge puffs one up'.† If, however, knowledge has charity as its companion, it becomes useful, because charity builds.† Note, moreover, that some people simply seek to know, which is curiosity; others gain knowledge in order to become known, which is vanity; and still others gain knowledge in order to sell it, which constitutes the crime of simony. Some, however, use their knowledge to build up themselves and others, and that is pious charity.[124] Note as well that our future beatitude is well represented by the tail feathers on the back, because just as behind them nothing is accessible to our power of sight, so too we cannot now comprehend the extent of the happiness we are going to enjoy in the future. May God, who lives and reigns forever and ever, see fit to grant this felicity to us! Amen.

109. 'The Spirit lifted me up, and behind me I heard a tumultuous shouting: Blessed be the glory of the Lord in his dwelling-place'.† The prophet

---

124. Compare I Sent 19; III Sent 57; and SC 36.3 (SBOp 2:5–6).

Ezekiel, strengthened by the Spirit of God, is praising in a wonderful fashion grace, through which we become Christians. He blunts the presumption of those who boast of what they deserve and believe that what comes from themselves suffices for them, even though the apostle says: 'We are not qualified to believe that any good which is in us comes from us; rather, every qualification we possess comes to us from God'.[†] Indeed it is he who brings about within us both the desire and the ability to do good;[†] from him comes every outstanding and perfect gift.[†] The mouths of such people, therefore, are stopped up by these words of the prophet, since he says that he had been raised up by the Spirit in order to hear the tumultuous shouting.[†] For he would not have been able to hear it at all, had he not been raised up by the Spirit. And by what spirit? Not by the spirit of wickedness, but by the spirit of kindness—not by that spirit by whom Judas was seized[†] in order that he could become a master of betrayal,[125] nor by that spirit who raised up Christ and placed him on the parapet of the temple[†] so that he could hurl him down headlong. For that malicious spirit seizes and lifts up persons in order to cast them down after they have been exalted. The Spirit of the Lord, however, exalts those whom he lifts up in order to make splendid those who had been humbled.[†] This is the upright Spirit of the Lord,[†] guiding us on the straight road.[†] He is the Lord of knowledge,[†] toward whom our thoughts are directed. Where that Spirit is, there is freedom.[†] It is to this that the prophet says he was lifted up.

See 2 Co 3:5

See Ph 2:13

See Jm 1:17

See Ezk 3:12

See Lk 22:3

See Mt 4:5

See Mt 23:12
See Ps 25:8
See Ps 107:7
1 S 2:3
See 2 Co 3:17

---

125. I thus translate the reading 'ut proderet magister' of the critical edition. One manuscript offers the alternate reading 'ut proderet magistrum' ('so as to betray his master'), which might be preferable.

The Lord, moreover, raises one up in a variety of ways: by summoning, by justifying, by glorifying, and by illuminating—that is, by bestowing knowl-

See Ps 19:8 edge.[†] For he bestows knowledge, but by teaching his children what is good, in accordance with what is said in Micah:[126] 'O humanity, I will show you what is good and what the Lord requires of you— to do justice, to love mercy, and to walk humbly

Mi 6:8 with your God'.[†]

What the Spirit teaches humanity[127] is great indeed, for one cannot know what is good unless he has been taken up and instructed by the Spirit. There are some things which, while good in themselves, become evil for those who make use of them. Such are riches, the goods of the world. In their nature things like this are surely good, but it is wicked to misuse them. Moreover, they do not have the power to bring about what they promise, and so they are false goods.[128] Knowledge can even sometimes be counted among these, because

See 1 Co 8:1 without charity it puffs itself up.[†] True goods are spiritual; they are never capable of not being good. The Holy Spirit shows these goods to each person, teaching him what God expects of him—such as that he should freely make the sacrifice which he

Mi 6:8 owes, and should do justice,[†] and so forth.

Everyone, therefore, ought to render judgment beginning with himself, as is written: 'At the beginning of his speech, the just person is his own

See Pr 18:17
1 Co 4:3 accuser',[†] although the apostle says: 'I will not pass judgment on myself'.[†] Who would dare to judge

---

126. The critical text reads 'Malachiae' here, but this must be emended to 'Michae'.
127. The reading 'hominem' in the critical text should probably be emended to 'homini'.
128. This section may be compared to Boethius, *Consolatio philosophiae* 1–2. Compare also III Sent 91 (at note 89) and Dil 7.18–21 (SBOp 3:134–37).

himself? But while one who had been compelled
to do everything he had done might not have
passed judgment on himself, the apostle did not
pass judgment on himself in the sense that he
offered no opinion about his own justness, since
he did not pride himself on any merits. Assuredly,
no one should judge himself in this way. There is,
however, another sort of judgment of self according to which each person should pass judgment
on himself, whereby one ascribes all his evil characteristics to himself and all his good ones—if he
has any—to God. We ought to pass judgment on
ourselves in this fashion. And so the apostle says:
'If we judged ourselves, surely we would not be
judged'[†]—that is, damned by the Lord. See 1 Co 11:31

We ought to pass judgment on others as well,
that is, make judgment for the benefit of others,
in accordance with the passage: 'Give judgment
for the destitute and the orphan'.[†] God demands a Ps 82:3
twofold judgment from us, for he expects us to
love mercy, and not merely to do it. For there
are those who perform works of mercy but do
not love them. Rather they do them in order to
be seen doing so by others.[†] Thus the prophet Mt 6:5
explicitly said: Love mercy, so that you will not
only act mercifully, but will love it, beginning with
yourself, in accordance with the words: 'For you
to take mercy on your soul is pleasing to God'.[†] Si 30:24
For how can you show mercy to another, if you
will not be merciful toward your own soul? You
will be merciful by loving justice, just as, on the
contrary, you will be cruel if you love wickedness.
For 'he who loves wickedness despises his own
soul'.[†] A person ought to shower mercy—that is, See Ps 11:5
the works of mercy—upon others, so that he may
rightly do justice and love mercy. But because it
is not enough for this to be done only once, this

Mi 6:8 text follows: 'And walk humbly with your God'.[†]
This is in agreement with the statement of James:
'Pure, unspoiled religion in the eyes of God the
Father is this: aiding widows and orphans in their
troubles, and keeping oneself uncontaminated by
Jm 1:27 the world'.[†] While he says there 'aiding widows
and orphans in their troubles', we have here the
Mi 6:8 injunction 'to love mercy'.[†] While he there writes
'keeping oneself uncontaminated by the world',
we have here the words 'to walk humbly with your
Mi 6:8 God'.[†] A person cannot do or understand these
things unless he has been illuminated by that Spirit
by whom the prophet testifies that he was lifted up
See Ezk 3:12 to hear a tumultuous shouting.[†]

This tumultuous shouting is the turning of the
sinner to justice. By crucifying the flesh, with its
Ga 5:24 vices and desires,[†] he despises his previous error
and, as if transformed from himself into someone
else, he says along with the apostle: 'I live; now not
Ga 2:20 only do I live, but in truth Christ lives in me'.[†] This
shouting is tumultuous indeed. This is the change
See Ps 77:10 in the right arm of the Most High.[†]

There are four types of positive change in life,
just as there are four opposite types of negative
change through which a soul flees from God:
worldly joy, uncontrolled grief, empty hypocrisy,
and swollen arrogance. Worldly joy consists of two
elements: the succession of temporal goods and the
satisfaction of wicked desires. In the succession of
temporal goods, when the things one hopes for
in temporal affairs actually come about, a person
becomes arrogant and rejoices when he should
be saddened. Since he does not have knowledge,
See Qo 1:18 however, he does not feel grief.[†] It is another, more
damaging sort of pleasure when one rejoices in the
worst sorts of things—when he is not only eager to
do evil deeds, but later enjoys having done them.
In such a circumstance laughter will be joined with

grief,[†] while mourning will seize the last stages of   See Pr 14:13
such joy as this.

Uncontrolled grief customarily arises from two
causes: the loss of temporal things and despair arising from the huge numbers of one's sins. Judas was
swallowed up by this kind of grief; going away, he
hanged himself with a noose.[†] So too was Cain,   See Mt 27:5
who said: 'So great is my wickedness that I cannot
deserve forgiveness'.[†] In order that a brother who   Gn 4:13
had been rebuked would not be swallowed up in
such grief, the apostle commanded the Corinthi-
ans to take him back, telling them to do so 'lest he
be swallowed up by such great grief'.[†]   2 Co 2:7

Third is empty hypocrisy. False Christians operate under this vice. They do not really seek to
be that which they want to seem, and while they
feign an outer appearance of holiness, they are
hungry wolves in sheep's clothing.[†] These are the   See Mt 7:15
whitewashed wall,[†] the tombs filled with nothing   See Ac 23:3
but the bones of the dead.[†] In their house is one   See Mt 23:27
weight here, another there, one scale here, one
there,[†] both abominable in the Lord's sight. The   Pr 20:23
number of such individuals is not small, for this
whole people is hypocritical. As the prophet says:
'This people honors me with their lips, but their
heart is far from me'.[†]   Mt 15:8

Fourth is swollen arrogance—when a person
boasts of having some good quality which he does
not possess, or believes either that he has a good
quality which he does possess on his own, or that
it has come to him from God as a result of his own
merits, which demand it. Such a person also taunts
those who do not possess such qualities.

These are the four forms of flight through which
the soul is drawn away from God.

If we reverse these four, four types of conversion to God are discernible. These are heavenly

joy, the sadness which derives from remorse, true
piety, and devout humility. Thus it is said four
times in the Song of Songs: 'Return, return, O

Sg 6:12

maid of Shulam,[129] return, return!'.† The maid
of Shulam refers to the lost soul, who wanders
in the region of unlikeness[130] either because she
lies captive under the weight of sin or because
she is at odds with truth. So the prophet says:

Jr 3:14   Is 13:2

'Turn back, my children,† hoist the signal'† in Zion.
Zion indicates the image which is in our mind,[131]
where the signal of the victory of Christ's passion
is raised. Through this sign we are defended against
that spirit who subverts our courage of mind, so
that we will not surrender our place at his assault.
Therefore, faithful soul, if the spirit who has power
should rise over you, you should not abandon your
post to him. That spirit comes over us when he
inflicts troubles upon us or suggests wicked deeds
to us. Indeed, the lion rises up from its lair, and
the destroyer of nations has raised himself up, in

See Jr 4:7

order to reduce our land to desert.† The lion's lair
comprises the hearts of those who are of the flesh
and hypocrites, in accordance with what Job said:
'He rests hidden in the shade of the reed, in the

Jb 40:16

swamps'.† For the shade and the reed are the hearts
of hypocrites, since they seem to be what they are
not, outwardly seeking the brightness of justice but
inwardly having only illusions born of pretense.
The swamps are the minds of those who indulge
in pleasure. They not only do evil, but even glory
in their vices. The lion, which is the devil, is said
not to depart from this lair, but to rise up from it,
because he always carries himself about pridefully,

129. The critical text reads 'of Shunam' rather than 'of
Shulam'.
130. See note above on III Sent 21 (at note 16).
131. Jerome, *Liber interpr. hebr. nom.*; in CCL 72:108.

as in the verse: 'I will rise above the high clouds and place my throne to the north'.† He rises up in order to turn our land into desert. Do not fear. Raise up the signal of Christ in Zion. Through it you will be able to defeat this spirit, this lion, this destroyer of nations; and the bride from the lairs of lions and the mounts of panthers† will be crowned when the soul passes from the vices to the virtues. For the crown of the Church is said to consist in this, that it effects the sinner's return to a life of virtue, because 'the one who has made a sinner turn away from the error of his life will save his soul from death'.† Therefore, faithful soul, be strong lest you lose your place and the land of your inheritance, that land to which the Lord exhorted Abraham to go, saying: 'Leave your land, your family, and your father's house, and come into the land which I will show you, and you will be blessed'.† Our land is the lust of the flesh, our family is curiosity, and the house of our father is pride, which is the first vice for those departing from God, but the last for those returning to him—for in the first case one puts down his foot and in the last he removes it. In this house congregate all the sons of despair, under him who is king over all the sons of pride.† The land is evil, the family perverse, the house profoundly wicked.[132] We are all ordered to depart from here with Abraham, to leave behind these three so that we can enter into three others.

To these is the bride in the Song of Songs said to be brought—namely into the garden,† the wine-chamber,† and the marriage-couch.* The garden signifies action because of the great quantity of one's deeds. There we pick the lilies of everlasting hope. The wine-chamber is contemplation,

See Is 14:13–14

See Sg 4:8

Jm 5:20

See Gn 12:1–2

Jb 41:25

See Sg 5:1
†See Sg 1:3
*See Sg 1:15

---

132. Compare III Sent 114 (at note 147).

through which the soul becomes so intoxicated with joyfulness of mind that she sets aside all earthly things and, forgetting what has gone before, along with the apostle strains ahead for what is still to come.[†] Its sweetness is so great that no one can know unless he has tasted it. The prophet invites us to this with the words: 'Taste and see how sweet the Lord is'.[†] The marriage-couch is eternal bliss, the land of the living, the land which was promised to Abraham. This couch is laden with flowers, and takes to itself nothing which is not in bloom. It is positioned between two eyes, of which it is written: 'If you rest within your allotted portions',[†] and so on. For the two allotted portions are the two inheritances, the left and the right. The left inheritance is the humanity which was taken on by the Word, while the right is the divinity which took humanity unto itself. These two natures are properly referred to as though they were two inheritances, indeed an inheritance and a land of beatitude together, because it is blessedness to see God both in his humanity and in his eternal divinity. Nevertheless the left inheritance is beneath the right, in accordance with the words: 'His left arm lies under my head, and his right will embrace me'.[†] Humanity lies under the head of divinity, because it was created by divinity, and can be seen by the body's eyes. Divinity, however, can only be perceived spiritually and for now only through a glass, and then only obscured.[†] This beatitude is God's dwelling-place, in which the Lord's glory is blessed; for 'blessed be the glory of the Lord in his dwelling-place'.[†] He is blessed by us, because he blesses us. He blesses us each time we keep the Sabbath, in truth with a double robe. We bless him in turn by believing that all our goods are from him and that they are all everlasting. May he who lives

See Ph 3:13

Ps 34:8

Ps 68:13

Sg 2:6

See 1 Co 13:12

Ezk 3:12

and reigns, God forever and ever, see fit to bestow
them upon us.

110. 'When all things lay in quiet silence',[133†] See Ws 18:14
and so on. There are three silences. The first runs
from the time of Adam up to Moses. The second is
from the pronouncements of the prophets until the
coming of the Lord. The third is from that point
up to the time when Christ will come to judge the
living and the dead, and the world through fire.

In the first period of silence, the carnal law
recognized, as it were through its own power of
perception, that thanks were due to God, and so
there lived many holy men such as Abel, Noah,
and so forth. In the second period the spiritual law
existed, given through Moses but actually by God.
In this era the jewish law prevailed, but the law
of benefits and charity remained unspoken. Those
who lived in the first period were silent, sinned
wickedly, and perished in their silence. Yet they
did have some slight excuse: sin was not imputed
to them in cases where there was no law. Still,
woe to Cain and the like! Those who remained
silent in the second epoch sinned worse in that
they persevered in their darkness by abandoning
the good commandments; but blessed were those
who kept them, like the prophets. Woe to those
who were quiet then:[†] by remaining silent how See Is 6:5
wickedly they perished! Nonetheless they still had
some defense, for there had not yet come the
second Adam, who opened the road which the first
one had so evilly closed; there had not yet appeared
the one who would shatter the gates of hell—the
one whom those who had arrived at those gates[†] Is 38:10
in the middle of their days were awaiting—he who

---

133. See Ws 18:14, as in *Introit of the Mass for the Sunday
Within the Octave of Christmas.*

See Ws 7:30

is that wisdom which can overcome evil.† We in the third period are silent when we ignore the merciful, ineffable divine law. Alas, we fall worst of all and with the greatest peril—for us there is no excuse whatever! What can we respond to the words: 'Away with you, evildoers'?† 'With their hands and feet bound', let them be thrown 'into the darkness outside',† which is the reverse of eternal life.

See Mt 25:41

See Mt 22:13

During the first period of silence Noah built his ark of incorruptible beams of wood, beams which had been squared. They were joined together with pitch, inside and out,† so that no one within would perish. During the second period of silence, Christ built the ark which is the Church—he built it of those who are going to triumph in eternity; and, just like the first ark, it floats on the waves of this world. In the third era of silence the justice of God will appear, because 'then he will reward each person according to his deeds'.† And so woe to those who exercise silence now because, as their charity grows cold, they will be under the horns of Babylon! The apostle John instructs us about this through a vision in the Book of Revelation, passing over everything up to this time: 'Come, I will show you the condemnation of the great whore'†—that is, the cause of the damnation of the wicked. That great whore Babylon—that is, confusion—is the Antichrist and the wicked who will exist in his time. Now 'she is enthroned over many waters'†—that is, she rules over the many wicked people of today, over all of whom she is the head. Or, 'she is enthroned over many waters', meaning that she rules over many peoples whom she attracts to herself through lust. Thus, the Lord says to Job: 'What strength there is in his'—that is, the devil's—'loins!'† whenever he ensnares men,

Gn 6:14
See Mt 16:27
Rv 17:1
Rv 17:1
Jb 40:11

whose sexual power lies in their loins, 'and what
power there is in his stomach muscles't whenever
he deceives women, whose power of procreation
lies in their stomach. So too does the prophet say
to Jerusalem, as though to a harlot: 'On the day
you were born', which is to say in this age of the
world, 'your umbilical cord was not cut't—that
is, you did not restrain your lust. 'The kings of
the earth', who are the rulers of these dark places,
'have committed fornication with her, and those
who live in the world have become drunk on the
wine of her adultery',† which is the wine of her
manifest fornication. Just as a drunken person fears
nothing, so those who cling to earthly things are so
blinded by love of them that they fear neither God
nor eternal punishment. Such people are subject
to the worst kind of fear and remain silent.

An angel took John into the desert in spirit,
and he saw a woman seated upon a scarlet beast.†
He uses women to represent those soft people who
resemble Eve, from whom sin came. They embrace
the devil as their foundation, and he is bloody both
in himself and in his followers. Either because they
spill the blood of the saints or poorly understand
God's words, they are full of blasphemous titles,†
since they allege that the evils they do are not
displeasing to God. They have seven heads†—that
is, the five senses, to which are afterward added
first their own sin and then the Antichrist—and
through these seven heads the devil leads people to
death. Or the seven heads are the seven criminal
sins—perjury, adultery, murder, false witness, and
the rest. Or the seven heads are pride, through
which Adam exhibited his haughtiness in the first
place when he said: 'I will never be shaken in
my prosperity',† and the daughters of pride—envy,
anger, lust, lechery, greed, discord, and idolatry.

Jb 40:11

Ezk 16:4

Rv 17:2

See Rv 17:3

See Rv 17:3

See Rv 17:3

Ps 30:6

See Jn 4:7

The Samaritan woman† was possessed by these
seven heads—namely, by the five senses, which she
abused, and by error, which had blinded her; but
Christ, passing by, at once converted her with his

See Jn 4:7–30

message.† She did not have the seventh head, the
Antichrist. It was as if she were not dead, for at
the sixth hour Christ said to her: 'You have had
five husbands'—that is, the five free senses, which
you have abused—'and the man whom you have
now'—that is, the error which blinds you—'is not

Jn 4:18

your husband'.† Or, to give another interpretation,
the seven heads represent all the crimes which we
commit over the seven days in which our entire
life is encompassed. Alternately, the seven heads are
the seven demons which Christ drove out of Mary

See Mk 16:9; Lk
8:2

Magdalene† —that is, the five wicked senses which
he turned to good, and error and the Antichrist,
which is faithlessness.

How does this happen? For now, the free spirit
has a secure defense against these seven heads,
specifically the eight[134] virtues—humility, faith,
hope, charity, patience, sobriety, chastity, harmony
—and it employs the seven gifts of the Lord's

See Mt 6:9

Prayer, namely 'Our Father',† and the seven gifts of

Mt 5:9

the Gospel 'Blessed are the peacemakers',† and so
forth; to these another is added to effect blessedness by making it derive from the gifts that one

Mt 5:8

possesses—namely, 'Blessed are the pure in heart'.†
So there are eight beatitudes. To put it another way,
people work for seven days; as the authoritative
text of Genesis says, on the sixth day the earth

See Gn 1:24

brought forth a living soul.† When our flesh re-
frains from works that bring death—which it does
by emulating the life of the saints—it brings forth,
according to its kind, living shafts of the virtues.

---

134. The critical text reads 'duodecim' ('twelve'), which
I emend to 'octo' ('eight'), as given here.

On the seventh day it enjoys rest, for it is written that on the seventh day the Lord rested from all the work he had been doing.[†]   See Gn 2:2

We should, then, to be purified as many times as there are pronouncements to be added up. The result is that we should be bathed not only seven times, but as many as seventy times seven,[†] and we should say: 'When all things lay in deep silence'[135†]   See Mt 18:22   See Ws 18:14
—which is to say: we were all silent, we said nothing—'and night had journeyed along her course',[†]   Ws 18:14
which indicates that this life is truly dark when it covers our hearts with silence, with the blackness of sin and the blindness of ignorance. Then the divine message is sent forth from the ark of the Father—the true Paraclete (which means counselor). He taught us prior to his passion that we should undergo seven cleansings against the seven heads of Babylon, and after his resurrection he left us just as many forms of nourishment.[136] Our Elisha instructed the leper Naaman to be washed seven times in the Jordan,[†] which means 'descent'.[137] May   See 2 K 5:10
God, who lives and reigns forever, lead us to the possession of these benefits. Amen.

111. On the Assumption of the Blessed Virgin. 'She was made mine: she was bathed with water, cleansed of blood, anointed with oil, and clothed with robes of many colors'.[†] My brothers, the   See Ezk 16:8–10
tarnish must be removed from the silver for it to shine more brightly. The covering of rust must be scraped away, so that the silver may glitter more splendidly when brought into the light. Silver symbolizes divine eloquence. If I were to pass over

---

135. See Ws 18:14, as in *Introit of the Mass for the Sunday Within the Octave of Christmas.*
136. The reference is to the gifts of the Holy Spirit: compare Res 3.6 (SBOp 5:109).
137. Jerome, *Liber interpr. hebr. nom.*; in CCL 72:67.

this point in silence, you would be no less aware
of it through your own power of discernment.
That is why we read in the psalm: 'The words
of the Lord are pure; they are silver refined by

Ps 12:6

fire'.† The tarnish coating this silver is the surface
of the text, the historical sense. Set it aside if you
wish to extract the kernel which lies hidden within
Sacred Scripture, and the spiritual sense which can
restore you will shine forth. Thus Solomon says:
'Remove the tarnish from silver, and it emerges as

Pr 25:4

a vessel which is utterly pure'.† One removes the
tarnish from the silver if he does not hold simply
to the surface of the text, but rather embraces the
spiritual understanding, which does not consist of
that surface but lies hidden beneath it. Through it
the soul is joyously renewed, and, raised in love of
God, it is nourished with pious refreshment.

The words with which we began come from
Ezekiel and as given they refer to a woman on
whom gifts are bestowed by her spouse so that
she may be found all the more worthy of union
with him. The words also befit a congregation;
in this case the line becomes a recollection of
the gifts granted to it by the Lord in his gracious
mercy. They apply just as well to the blessed Virgin,
whom, showered with gifts by God, the heavens

Ps 96:11

rejoice in and the earth exalts.† For if these words
appropriately refer to a woman and to a congregation, much more can they be applied to the
glorious Virgin. Now, raised above the choirs of
angels, she has become the mistress not only of
humanity, but also of the angels. And so the line

Ezk 16:8

which we have quoted—'You were made mine',†
and so on—applies properly to her.

Note too that we should recall four things which
show the grace of the gifts granted to her. For it
is said that she was bathed with water, cleansed of

blood, anointed with oil, and clothed in robes of many colors.† Through these four are understood See Ezk 16:9 the four cardinal virtues, more fully showered upon her than on any other person; and so she must be joined to her spouse through his embraces, since she becomes ever more pleasing to him as his perception of these gifts in her increases.

The water symbolizes wisdom or prudence; as a result of its being granted to her, the blessed Virgin is raised among the prudent bridesmaids, indeed above the prudent bridesmaids,† by reason See Mt 25:2 of her extraordinary prudence. Water refreshes the outer person by removing thirst. This prudence sustains our inner humanity. It directs us to perform good works, destroying within us the thirst for fleshly enticements. Then it is asserted that she was cleansed of blood.† This passage gives us to See Ezk 16:9 understand that she possessed the virtue of temperance. She was anointed with oil,† in which See Ezk 16:9 fortitude is implied. She was clothed in robes of many colors,† which signifies that she was endowed See Ezk 16:10 with justice: she does nothing except what she ought to do, nothing beyond what is permitted to her; she is engaged only in worthy occupations. So David writes: 'Let your priests be clothed with justice and your saints exalt'.† These signs of the Ps 132:9 virtues the bride receives from her spouse, the handmaiden from her lord, the mother from her son, the daughter from the Father—the Virgin Mary. These are the four columns in front of the entrance to the tabernacle.† Through them one See Ex 38:19 departs from the discord of this world and ascends to the vision of God. They are the columns which hold up the house of our Job.† For our Lord Jesus See Jb 1:19 was so resplendent with these virtues even in the infirmity of our flesh that no inclination to sin existed within him, and none of the weakness of sin

See Is 53:9

which results from having sinned. For he is the one
who committed no sin, and no guile was found in
his mouth.† It is not inappropriate, then, that the
four virtues, bestowed on the blessed Virgin by
God, can be understood through the words which
have been discussed here.

Because her glorious assumption compels us to
say something in her honor, it is proper for us to
go over again the points we have raised, explaining
them more fully from the beginning onward. But
how can we be worthy to say anything in praise
of her? Is not whatever the human tongue can say
less than what the Virgin Mary deserves? If we
truly appreciate the dignity of the woman whom
we are attempting to praise, whatever our human
weakness can proclaim in her honor is meager
and insufficient! How could a human being, a
sinner, do justice in praising the woman by whom
the Creator of humankind and angels chose to
be born? It is the mother of God, the queen of
heaven, the pledge of our hope, whom we are
endeavoring to praise. What we have begun is not
in our power—it is beyond us!

Ezk 16:8

What is written applies well to her: 'You were
made mine'.† For she did not create herself. She
was made by God, who desired the mystery of the
Incarnation, the secret of our redemption, to be
fulfilled in her womb. And so it is said: 'Then the
Creator of all things spoke and instructed me; he
who created me rested in my tent'.† This is the
city of God, of which wondrous things have been
spoken.† God is the maker of this tabernacle. God
dwells in it. God makes it holy. The Word of the
Father sanctified this tabernacle and entered it once
it was made holy. Going forth from it, he preserved
it in holiness. It is written: 'He is my God; his way

Si 24:12

See Ps 87:3

is pure'.† Thus it is properly said: Woman, you were made by me.† Ps 18:30

See Ezk 16:8

'She was bathed with water.'† There is good water and bad water. The bad water is that which was turned into blood for the Egyptians. Of it the psalmist says: 'He turned their water into blood, and killed the fish'.† Elsewhere: 'Some go down into the sea in ships, plying their trade on the wide ocean'.† This water represents that empty, useless knowledge which does not build, but puffs up.† It does not educate, but destroys. It does not incite one to good, but hurls one down into evil. This water babbles† because it is not deep. In truth, the waters of Shiloah flow silently.† For that true knowledge which aims at instruction, at building things up, does not swell up with literary charm or showiness. Those who follow her she teaches kindly, raises up securely, and brings to a splendid end. The glorious Virgin was bathed in this water, becoming the temporal mother of him to whom belong the treasures of knowledge.†

See Ezk 16:9

Ps 105:29

Ps 107:23
See 1 Co 8:1

See Pr 7:10
See Is 8:6

See Col 2:3

'She was cleansed of blood.'† In this passage, the stain of original sin is indicated through the image of blood. The divine mercy banished it from the blessed Virgin so that it remained in her in terms of neither act nor guilt. The Son of God so sanctified his tabernacle that no inclinations to lust remained in her, no inducements to vice. For he who stopped the flow of blood from the woman with a hemorrhage through a mere touch of his robe† kept from his mother all stain of original sin.

See Ezk 16:9

See Mt 9:20–22

'She was anointed with oil.'† There is both good oil and bad oil. The bad oil is that of which David speaks: 'They grew in number from the fruit of their grain, wine, and oil'.† Further: 'For the oil of the sinner will not moisten my brow'.† There

See Ezk 16:9

Ps 4:7

Ps 141:5

is also good oil—the grace of the Holy Spirit—
and he who is anointed with it will be free, not
enslaved. So it is written: 'And the yoke will rot off

Is 10:27
your neck because of the oil'.[†] David writes: 'Just
like the oil on his head, which runs down Aaron's

Ps 133:2
beard'.[†] The Son of God was anointed with this oil
See Heb 1:9
beyond all his fellows,[†] and the blessed Virgin was
anointed with it as well. She was worthy to hear
the words spoken by the angel: 'The Holy Spirit
will come upon you, and the power of the Most

Lk 1:35
High will cover you with its shadow'.[†]
See Ezk 16:10
'She was clothed with robes of many colors.'[†]
In the robes of many colors should be understood
the diversity of the virtues. It is proper that these
should be mentioned after the oil. For once one has
charity, a family of many virtues follows. Charity
does not exist in isolation in anyone; so powerful
is its connection to the other virtues that where
charity is, the other virtues must be present as well.
Without charity the other virtues are of no benefit
to salvation. As the apostle says: 'If I have the gift
of prophecy and know all the mysteries and possess
all understanding and all faith, so that I can move
mountains, but do not have charity, I am noth-

1 Co 13:2
ing'.[†] This is the damask tunic, the ankle-length
See Gn 37:23
robe of Joseph.[†] It is the garment about which
the Book of Wisdom says: 'She made a striped
cloak for herself and gave a sash to the Canaanite

Pr 31:22, 24
merchant'.[†] This garment is properly referred to as
ankle-length, to show how essential perseverance
in the virtues is. This tunic ought to be ankle-
length, so that we may achieve the crown to which
we are raised through the virtues—namely, perseverance in virtue. For it is the outcome, not the
struggle, which gains one a crown. It is because of
this that it is ordered that the loin, along with the

See Lv 3:9
tail, of the ram be offered to the Lord.[†] One offers

both the loin and the tail to the Lord when his
abstinence from carnal desires shows how fruitful
his perseverance is. This perseverance bestows a
crown upon the good person. The blessed Virgin
was dressed in robes of many colors,† for in her   See Ezk 16:10
none of the virtues was lacking. Each was brought
to its state of perfection, and so the maidens all
loved her.† These are the robes from which waft   See Sg 1:2
sweet odors. Thus David says: 'Myrrh and aloe
and mezereon waft from your robes, from ivory
palaces'.† Myrrh signifies the mortification of the   Ps 45:8
flesh. Aloe, which is also called ammoniac and
which soothes tumors, indicates humility. Mezereon, which grows to a great height, quite appropriately symbolizes sublime hope. The prophet
instructs us about the order of our progress: first he
mentions myrrh, then aloe, and finally mezereon.
God's champion should first restrain carnal urges in
himself through fruitful penance. Then, so that he
will not grow arrogant as a result of his good deeds,
he must install humility as a guard over himself.
Finally he should embrace the things of heaven
with firm hope.

Moreover, the matters which we have discussed
can, not inappropriately, be referred to the faithful
soul. Anyone who denies that the soul was made
by God disavows the very name of a Christian.
The soul is bathed in water when knowledge is
instilled in her through divine generosity. She is
cleansed of blood when original sin is remitted in
her. She is anointed with oil when she is filled
with the dew of the Holy Spirit. She is clothed
in robes of many colors when, enveloped by the
various virtues,† she becomes inflamed with desire See Ps 45:9
for God. May our Lord Jesus Christ who lives
and reigns with the Father and the Holy Spirit,

deem it proper, through the intercession of the most blessed Virgin, to increase this desire in us.

112. 'Who, in your judgment, is the wise and faithful servant the Lord has placed in charge of his household, to supply them with food at the proper

See Mt 24:45

times?'[†] These words of our Redeemer carry great weight and deserve the most intense examination. The manner of presentation itself indicates this fact. For the Lord did not ask the question because he did not know the answer, but rather to show us that hardly anybody can be found worthy to be put over his household. Paul indicated the same thing with these words: 'Now, what is required

1 Co 4:2

in stewards is: who may be found trustworthy?'[†] 'Who' is employed here to imply that it is difficult, because the word is often used to indicate difficulty.

Mt 24:45

In the passage 'Who, in your judgment?',[†] and so forth, Christ suggested that, just as a true judgment

See Mt 18:16

should depend on the evidence of two witnesses,[†] there are two elements which make someone worthy to be placed over Christ's household and indicate his suitability to assume the office of prelate. The two things to which he referred are prudence and love; these are so essential to a prelate that without them no one should be found worthy of the office. Neither of them suffices without the other, because if someone is prudent but does not have love, he will work not for the benefit of those placed under him, but in order to fulfill his own desires—either to gain financial profit, or to win general recognition, or to grow important as a result of his splendid reputation. On the other hand, if one is a loving person but lacks prudence, he does not have the temperament to clamp down on the heretics who arise from time to time, and it is possible that he will frequently be unable to foresee what is beneficial for those under his care. In order that prelates may possess these two characteristics, Christ instructed them: 'Be prudent like serpents, and innocent like doves'.† Mt 10:16

  Christ clearly demonstrated that he wants individuals of this sort to serve as prelates in his Church when he committed his one and only spouse, redeemed from the devil's yoke by his own blood, to Peter, whom he recognized as stronger in these traits than the other disciples. On Peter, after his threefold confession of love†—by which See Jn 21:15–17 he removed the stain of his threefold denial†—he See Mt 26:69–75; enjoined the responsibility of feeding his sheep Mk 14:69–72; Lk 22:54–62; Jn 18:25–27 three times. 'Feed my sheep',* Jesus said. Even earlier, when the Lord had asked his disciples who *Jn 21:17 they would say the Son of Man was, it was Peter who responded with prudence to the query, before the others: 'You are the Christ, the son of the living God'.† Just as he showed fervent love in the con- Mt 16:16 fession mentioned above, so here he demonstrated the highest prudence in that answer.[138]

---

138. A single manuscript adds the following:
  'And so it is properly said: "Whatever you bind on earth" and so on (Mt 16:19). Such is that vicar, my dear friends, whose feast is celebrated today by the whole Church, and for whose guidance a chorus of all the faithful gives thanks. The Lord gave him the duty of governing when he said to him: "And I will give you the keys to the kingdom of heaven" (Mt 16:19), so that as the gatekeeper of heaven he could admit those whom he perceives to be suitable but keep out those worthy of such treatment. For the keys represent the knowledge and power of discernment, through which he can admit the worthy and exclude the unworthy from God's kingdom. Indeed, there should be great power of discernment in a pastor, so that he may know whom he should loose and whom he should bind, to what person he should preach profundities and what person he should instruct in rudimentary things. For the apostle says: "I became weak for the weak, so that I could save them all" (1 Co 9:22). This is the sort of discernment which is meant in the keys granted to Peter. For the pastor conferred his own name upon his vicar when he said: "You are Peter." He said: "You are Peter", so called after me, for I am the rock; you will be a marble column, "and upon

Although prelates of the Church should be of
this sort, many prove quite different from the ideal
—indeed, many are profoundly contrary to that
ideal. For some prelates are wolves, some are mercenaries, and some are just, holy shepherds. We
call those wolves who appropriate the properties
of those subject to them. In order to do this, they
condone crimes, giving their charges license to sin.
We call those prelates mercenaries who serve those

---

this rock"—that is, upon myself—"will I build my Church"
(see Mt 16:18). He who was the rock did not desire that his
Church should be founded on the man Peter, but upon the
rock. For all the Church's power to free people comes from
God, not from other people. Indeed, a powerful heresy grew
up in the corinthian Church, whose members boasted about
who had baptized them, saying: "I am of Paul, I of Apollo, I of
Cephas" (1 Co 1:12). In this fashion these people attributed
their salvation to other people rather than to God, and so chose
to found it upon humanity. Paul replied to them: "Was Paul
ever crucified for you? Or were you baptized in the name
of Paul?" (1 Co 1:13). God, therefore, determined that an
extraordinary prince should be established above the others
(although there were also other leaders in the Church, for as
the psalmist says: "You make them princes over the whole
land" [Ps 45:16]), so that the unity of the Church's faith may
be protected, and if any disharmony about the faith were to
spring up among the disciples, the authority of the one pastor
could bring them back to one position. For if there were two
prelates of differing schools of thought, sometimes the faith
might be torn asunder.

    'And because he was the true prince, he apportioned to
Peter a certain part of his own princely power, for the sick
positioned themselves in the streets, and all were cured by
his shadow (see Ac 5:15–16). On Peter this power—whereby
his shadow would cure the sick—was more fully bestowed,
for this ability pointed to something special in the highest
pastor. There are two Churches, the present Church and the
heavenly one. In the present Church sins are washed away, so
that those who have been so purified can be brought together
in the Church above. The present Church is the shadow of
the future one. These two Churches are symbolized by Peter.
His shadow signifies the Church of the present, and his body
the heavenly Church. His shadow cures the sick, because the
present Church washes away sins.'

    I have emended 'noluit', at line 18 of the critical apparatus
here translated, to 'voluit' for reasons of sense; 'fides', at line
21, should probably read 'fidei'.

put under them zealously during prosperous times, in return for wool and milk; but when a time of adversity arrives, when the wolf approaches, they desert their sheep. These kinds of prelates—the wolves and the mercenaries—are falsely referred to as shepherds. Those who shape the persons placed under their care through their own good life and true teaching and do not refuse to lay down their life for them if the occasion demands it can, however, truly claim the title of shepherd for themselves.

These shepherds necessarily ought to have four things as part of their pastoral office: a rod, reed-pipe, a dog, and a staff. They must have the rod and the pipe for the sake of the sheep, the dog because of the wolf, and the staff because of the dog and the wolf. They should have a rod in order to control and correct the sheep by gently striking them, and the pipe in order to soothe them. They should have a dog to ward off the wolf, and the staff to strike both the dog and the wolf from time to time. The rod signifies that gentle, paternal correction administered to those in their care, and the pipe that sweet, attractive teaching which comes from the hope of eternal life. One other thing must be added to the items that have been mentioned already: the pastor should have a leash for his dog, to allow the animal only such space to perform its function as is appropriate to the place, time, and person involved. This is to insure that, should these circumstances be ignored if someone who is subject to him commits some offense, the pastor can make the harsh rebuke of the dog, which is suitable against heretics, yield to his own judgment through the application of his staff, and to assure that the dog will not in any case go beyond its role of keeping the flock together or its responsibility to anathematize those who persistently do evil.[139]

Such are those who are worthy of being placed over God's family, the Church, so that they may provide food for her at the appropriate times— that is, administer her temporal goods and reveal the mysteries of the Scripture in time, meaning in this present life. For in the future life we will all be taught by God,[†] since God will be all in all[*] when we all can read in the book of life.[†] This will happen, under God's direction, in our eternal bliss, to which may he who reigns forever lead us.[140]

†See Jn 6:45
*See 1 Co 15:28
See Ph 4:3

113. 'Fear God and keep his commandments; this is the whole duty of humanity.'[†] This is the heavenly, profound advice of the wise man—that we should fear God and love him with our whole heart.[†] In this passage two things are enjoined upon us: fear and love, which make up the road by which one proceeds, or as it were the ladder by which one

Qo 12:13

See Dt 6:5; Mt 22:37; Mk 12:30; Lk 10:27

---

139. Compare III Sent 66; III Sent 118 (at note 164); and Div 100 (SBOp 6/1:367).

140. A single manuscript adds the following:

' . . . in the celestial fatherland, where Christ presides and rules like an emperor in his kingdom, like a father in his household, like a groom in the marriage-bed. There the victorious, after completing their temporal service in the world, joyfully support their king. He in turn ministers to them, since they receive what is to be given them because of their merits. God, who was their goal, is now the leader of their journey (see Ex 13:21) and the reward of their effort— the prize of their labor and the crown of their struggle. There is complete security, life under God, life with God, life which is God himself. God is the one coin (that is, the one reward) (see Co 9:24)—the same glory for all, neither divided nor separated, common to all and yet utterly unique, neither failing through repeated use nor growing old over time, and not decreasing by reason of their enjoyment of him. There our existence will have no fear of death, and our knowledge will have no fear of error, and our love will have no defect, because eternal joy will rest upon our heads (Is 35:10) under the leadership of our Lord Jesus Christ.'

Compare to this passage III Sent 91 (at note 90).

ascends† to the God of gods, the Lord of lords.* Fear is indicated where he says 'Fear God', and love in the words 'and keep his commandments'.† He aptly said: 'Fear God and keep his commandments'. He did not say: 'Fear God and love him', putting the effect before the cause or what follows before what proceeds. He knew with certainty that 'the proof of love lies in one's deeds'.[141] After the sage, speaking with the spirit of God, enjoined these two, 'Fear God and keep his commandments', he added without any break the cause of each when he said: 'This is the whole duty of humanity';† that is, through this every person becomes similar to, and to some extent comes close to, the one who, possessing true being, does not know alteration— who said of himself: 'I am who I am'.† Of him the prophet wrote: 'But you are always the same, and your time never runs out'.† The philosopher says the same thing in the words: 'Maker of heaven and earth, you who command time to pass over the ages, you remain changeless while giving motion to all things'.[142] He is the one who is not removed by the construction 'he was', or eliminated by the phrase 'he will be'—in other words, he is subject to no temporal alteration,[143] and to him every person of faith owes fear and love during this earthly service of ours.

Now six characteristics of God should be taken into account, to which these two duties are easily related: his power, justice, wisdom, charity, patience, and truth (or eternity). Fear responds to the first three, while love or affection relates to the latter three. It should be noted, of course, that

†See Gn 28:12
*See Dt 10:17
Qo 12:13

Qo 12:13

Ex 3:14

Ps 102:27

---

141. Gregory, *Homiliae in Evangelia* 30.1; in PL 76:1220C.
142. Boethius, *Consolatio philosophiae* 3.M. 9, 1–3.
143. Compare SC 31.1 (SBOp 1:219–20).

although we speak of God in human language, we should not entirely pass over the fact that whatever mode of explanation we may use, the things that we say of him must not be understood in merely human terms. When we say there is power in God, we do not mean that we are locating some property in him in a human way. Rather through these words we are indicating, in some fashion, what God is, because it is no different to say 'The power of God is in God' than to say 'God is power'. Our judgment about similar expressions must be the same, not different.[144] That God is powerful, indeed most powerful of all, is shown by the effects of his power and proven by frequent authoritative remarks in the holy writers—for ex-
Ps 115:3 ample, in the words: 'He does whatever he wills',[†] or elsewhere: 'He looks down upon the earth and makes it tremble; he touches the mountains and
Ps 104:32 they pour forth smoke'.[†] But lest you say: 'Yes, he is powerful, but he has no concern for justice', hear too what the prophet says through the Holy
Ps 7:11 Spirit: 'God is the just judge'.[†] Elsewhere he says:
Ps 94:1 'God is the lord of vengeance'.[†] Again, the prophet writes: 'When I choose the time, I will dispense
Ps 75:2 justice'.[†] And this as well: 'You wrongly thought that I was like you, but I will rebuke you and
Ps 50:21b accuse you to your face'.[†] Perhaps you will still say: 'While he may be powerful, and while he may be just, nonetheless he does not see all things, nor can he know everything.' Foolish person, what can remain hidden from him to whom even the most undisturbed passage between two undivided pieces of property is obvious, for whom every dark thing

---

144. Compare Csi 5.6.13–14 and 5.7.15–17 (SBOp 3:477–81).

shines brightly, to whom every silence speaks? For
'the Lord is great, his strength is great, and there is
no limit to his wisdom'.† Ps 147:5

Fear responds to these three, because God
should be feared most of all because of them; this
is not just any fear, but the true fear of which
the psalm speaks: 'The fear of the Lord is the
beginning of wisdom'.† Those in whom is found a Ps 111:10
sluggishness born of false confidence or a shroud of
pretense do not possess such fear. To one drugged
by false confidence these words are spoken in
the Book of Revelation: 'Would that you were
either hot or cold! But since you are lukewarm,
I will spit you out of my mouth'.† One is hot if See Rv 3:15–16
he is profoundly inflamed by the fire of charity
to perform good works. One is cold if he is so
removed from God by the chill of the vices that
he cries out from the depths: 'Take pity on me,
God!'† The lukewarm person is one who assures Ps 51:1
himself that, by virtue of God's great patience, he
will escape punishment for his sins. To him the
apostle says: 'Are you unaware that God's patience
should draw you to repentance?'† To those clothed See Rm 2:4
in pretense the Lord says in the Gospel: 'Beware
of false prophets who come to you',† and so on. See Mt 7:15
Elsewhere he says of them: 'They claim in their
words to know God, but they deny him in their
deeds'.† These are the people about whom the Tt 1:16
Lord said: 'This people honors me with their lips,
but their heart is far from me'.† Elsewhere we Mt 15:8
read: 'The Lord is near to their lips, but far from
their hearts'.† On the outside such people feign See Jr 12:2
the simplicity of the dove, but in their breast they
house the bitterness of the serpent and the rage of
the wolf. Bodily they reside among the good—in
appearance but not in mind, in bearing but not

in disposition, in name but not in will.[145] Of such people it has been said: 'They went forth from us, but they were not of us.' People such as this do not possess true fear; only those do in whom there is no weakness born of harmful affection, in whom there lies no anxiety deriving from evil mistrust. Evil mistrust means the suspicion that God may not be able to do all things, or may not be just, or may not know everything.

Enough about these matters. Let us now deal briefly with the three other characteristics which we have posited of God, and, since talking about it at this point will help to kindle true love in us, let us first say summarily of charity: God's charity is God. John writes: 'God is charity, and whoever lives in charity lives in God, and God lives in him'.† God loves us with that charity which he himself is—not merely after we had been justified, but even when we were still sinners, and not however much one may imagine, but to the extent that he even handed over his only-begotten Son to suffer death for us. The fact that he loved us is demonstrated not only by the result, but also by the fact that scriptural authority declares it. For John says, in his letters: 'God's charity for us was shown by the fact that he sent his only-begotten Son into the world, so that we may live through him'.† Further: 'Because God loved us first, and sent his Son as a sacrifice for our sins, we should also love one another'.† The Son of God came down and took on flesh. He endured the passion and redeemed our bondage. He glorified humanity. Paul attests that God loved us not only when we had been justified but even while we were sinners and that he handed over his own Son to death on own behalf, when he writes:

1 Jn 4:16

1 Jn 4:9

See 1 Jn 4:10–11

---

145. There is a play on words here: 'nomine non numine'.

'God proves his charity toward us by reason of the fact that if Christ died for us at a time when we were still sinners, all the more will we be spared his wrath now that we have been justified by his blood and saved through him. For if, when we were God's enemies, we were reconciled to him through the death of his Son, how much more, now that we have been reconciled, will we be saved through his life'.† Again: 'If God is for us, who is against us? See Rm 5:8–10 He did not even spare his own Son, but turned him over on our behalf'.† Although innocent, he See Rm 8:31–32 died for us, even though he found nothing in us he could love; for it had to be attested that he loved us so that we would not fall into despair. But how did he love us? In such a way to prevent us from growing proud. How much did he love us? Enough to inflame us powerfully with love of him. God must be loved because he created us, but he should be loved all the more because he restored us. God must be loved because he made us exist, but he should be loved all the more because he redeemed us through the death of his Son, so that we could live forever in bliss. We love God because he loves us. We ought to love him because he draws us to himself with long-suffering patience. For although we are sinners, he does not condemn us at once, but, like a merciful father, patiently awaits our turning to him.[146] For the truth impresses his love upon us when he whom we know to be truthful promises us eternal life. So we should love him with our whole heart, with our whole mind, with our whole strength,† so that we may be worthy to See Dt 6:5; Mt 22:37; Mk 12:30; Lk 10:27 attain what he promises to us.

114. 'Daughters of Jerusalem, come and see King Solomon, wearing the diadem with which

---

146. Compare Dil 5.15 (SBOp 3:131–32).

See Sg 3:11
See RB 48:24–25

See Mt 26:48–50

Mt 26:48

See Ps 114:1
See Jon 3:3

See Gn 12:1

his mother crowned him'.† This saving exhortation is directed to those who are still weak and tender.† This world embraces such people as though they were dear to it, kissing them as the deceitful Judas did Jesus. Indeed, the kisses of the world are like those of Judas. For with his kiss Judas betrayed Christ into the hands of the Jews,† and that spiritual Judas which is the world turns its followers over to the power of demons. Judas said to those with whom he was conspiring: 'Whomever I kiss is the one; take hold of him'.† The world says to the devil and his angels: 'Whoever follows me is the one; damn him.' The fact that this exhortation is addressed to the weak is clearly indicated by his use of the word 'daughters'. For the writer did not say 'sons', in the masculine gender; instead, by utilizing the word 'daughters' he shows that the people he is exhorting are those encumbered by feminine frailty. We to whom this saving exhortation is directed, and for whom it is intended, are all 'daughters'—we are all weak. Let us come to see King Solomon in order to set aside the stench of the stable in favor of the sweet smell of the marriage-bed, or, to speak allegorically, the crimes of Egypt in favor of the manna of the desert.

Let us go from the filth of vice to the heaven of the angels, from the degradation of wretched slavery to the exaltation of angelic freedom. Let us go forth as the sons of Israel did from Egypt,† escaping Pharaoh through a three-days' journey.† Allow us to explain this briefly: one escapes Pharaoh through a three-days' journey if he commits no offense in either thought, word, or deed. So let us go forth in the sort of departure or exodus experienced by the patriarch to whom God said: 'Leave your country and your family and your father's house'.† By 'land' he means that curiosity

of spirit with which we rush wantonly about—
now here, now there—as though through various
locales. By 'family' he signifies those desires of the
flesh which, after a fashion, are our close relatives;
for the flesh is clearly related to the soul and the soul
to the flesh, and regarding carnal desires the apostle
says: 'Have no concern for the cravings of the
flesh'.† Elsewhere he adds: 'If you walk in the way [Rm 13:14]
of the flesh, you will die'.† These carnal desires, [See Rm 8:13]
then, must be thrown off at once. By 'father' he
is signifying the devil, who is called the father of
those who emulate him. So it is written in the
Gospel: 'You come from your father, the devil'.† [Jn 8:44]
By 'your father's house' is meant one's old way of
life,† and so the text reads: 'Leave your country [Eph 4:22]
and your family and your father's house'†—that is, [See Gn 12:1]
take charge of your spirit, which wanders about
with decided curiosity, and direct it toward your
Creator. Then do away with fleshly cravings and
leave your old way of life behind.[147] It is as if to say
that for you to be able to become a new person,† [See Eph 4:24]
utterly set aside your old self with all its deeds.† [See Col 3:9 and]
[Eph 4:22]

We can call these things by other names, too—a
prison, a cage, and fetters. That curiosity of ours
which we have mentioned is a prison, in which we
are locked up to no purpose amidst the transitory
things of this world. The desires of the flesh are the
cage in which the soul is confined so that it can
taste nothing besides earthly things,† and cannot [See Ph 3:19]
work to any other purpose but to satisfy those
fleshly cravings like a beast of burden. Our old
way of life is called fetters, because we are chained
down by it so that we cannot go forth to see King
Solomon.[148]† [See Sg 3:11]

---

147. Compare III Sent 109 (at note 132).
148. Compare III Sent 7 (at note 6).

The sight we have of Solomon is threefold.[149] The first view is during our exile here, the second will come at the time of judgment, and the third will be in the kingdom of heaven. Of the first it is written: 'You believe because you have seen me; blessed are those who have not seen and yet believe'.† Moreover: 'Many kings and prophets wanted to see what you see, and never saw it'.† Surely they beheld, insofar as it can be seen here, the majesty of his divinity, but what they desired to behold was the face of his humanity. Of the second view it is written: 'All flesh shall see the salvation of God'.† The wicked will see the one whom they despised, and the good will see the one in whom they believed. Of the third vision, that which will occur in heaven, it is said: 'Let the wicked one be taken away, so that he will not see the glory of God'.†

In his first appearance he appeared as a gentle person. In the second he will appear as the just judge, for as is written: 'When I choose the time, I will dispense justice'.† In the third vision he will appear in glory, because 'you have crowned him with glory and honor',† O Lord. In the first appearance he gives sight to the blind,† in the second he sets free those who are in chains,† and in the third he lifts up the just.† In the first vision he appeared as an object of affection, in the second he will be terrifying—because the good will fear him out of reverence and the wicked by reason of their terror of hell, since their own bad conscience will prejudge them—and in the third he will be wondrous, for 'the angels long to look upon him'.† The first sight of him gives rise to hope, the second elicits fear, and the third increases charity. The first

Jn 20:29
Lk 10:24

Lk 3:6

See Is 26:10, Old Latin version

Ps 75:2

Ps 8:5
Ps 146:8a
Ps 146:7
Ps 146:8a

1 P 1:12

---

149. To what follows compare Div 50.1 (SBOp 6/1:270–71); Epi 2.2–3 (SBOp 4:302–403); and OS 5.9 (SBOp 5:368).

brings hope, so that we will not be cast down in adversity. The second elicits fear, so that we will not be elated in prosperity;[150] for we should neither be consumed in the fire of tribulation nor be washed away by a flood of prosperity. The third vision, as we have said, increases charity, because charity will be perfected when we will see God face to face.† In his first appearance he was the corrector of conduct, for he said: 'Learn from me, for I am gentle and humble of heart'.† In the second he will be the judge of merits. In the third he will be the grantor of rewards.

1 Co 13:12

Mt 11:29

The three names Solomon, Ecclesiastes, and Jedidiah† relate well to one another with reference to these three appearances of Christ. Solomon means 'peaceful', as Christ surely was in his first appearance; for as we read: 'I was peaceful toward those who despised peace',† and so on. Ecclesiastes means 'preacher', which is what Christ will be in his second appearance, when 'he will summon the heavens from above and the earth to witness the trial of his people',† and when he will tell the wicked: 'Depart, evildoers, into eternal fire'† while saying to the good: 'Come, you whom my father has blessed, and receive the kingdom'.† In his first appearance both the good and the bad saw him, though not all of them. In the second all will see him, the bad as well as the good, for while he says to the bad: 'Depart, evildoers',† he will speak to the good in a gentle voice: 'Come'.† In his third appearance only the good will behold him, because, as is written: 'Let the wicked one be taken away so that he will not see the glory of God'.†

See 2 S 12:15

Ps 120:7

See Ps 50:4

See Mt 25:41

Mt 25:34

See Mt 25:41

Mt 25:34

See Is 26:10, Old Latin version

Now we see Christ in his first appearance, in which he is gentle, longingly inviting sinners; in

---

150. See *Prayer of the Mass for Ember Saturday in Spring.*

which he is lovable, since he brings us benefits; in which he is the corrector of behavior, offering us instruction through his deputies. Scripture encourages us to this view of him when it says: 'Come and see King Solomon'.[†] 'See'—that is, know—'the king', the one who governs all things and reigns over all things—placing yourselves under his dominion and patterning yourselves after him in your way of life. Since many often become arrogant because of their good deeds, the Scripture adds the name 'Solomon', as if to say: 'so that you will not grow proud of your good works, but will maintain peace[†] within yourselves as much as you can, and show peace to others.' We maintain peace within ourselves when the flesh does not struggle with the spirit, or the spirit with the flesh,[†] but our sense power is obedient to reason and our reason to its Creator. We show peace to others if we do not create a stumbling-block for a brother,[†] if we love those who hate us,[†] if we assist our enemies with the necessities of life.[†]

'See him', I emphasize, 'wearing the diadem with which his mother crowned him',[†] and not the one with which his stepmother crowned him. For the true Solomon was crowned by his stepmother, by his Father, and by his mother. His stepmother crowned him with a crown of misery, his mother with the crown of justice,[†] and his Father with the crown of glory.[†] The stepmother of Solomon is that faithless synagogue which crowned him with a crown of thorns,[†] a crown which pierced him both outside and inside. It pierced him outwardly with its physical thorns and inwardly with its spiritual ones. He was pierced within not for his own sins—because he had none—but for ours. If the one who was without sin was pierced on our behalf, what

See Sg 3:11

See Is 26:3

See Ga 5:17

See Rm 14:13
See Mt 5:44
See Rm 12:20

Sg 3:11

See 2 Tm 4:8
Is 28:5 and 62:3

See Mt 27:29

else remains but for us to be pierced for our sins
along with him?[151]

It is for this reason, according to some, that compunction is so called, because in suffering remorse
we are pierced along with the pierced Christ, just
as we are crucified with Christ crucified.[†] There
are others who say that compunction takes its name
from the fact that we feel remorse not only for our
own sins, but also for those of others, or by reason
of the fact that we are pierced not only for our
fleshly offenses, but also for our spiritual ones.

The mother of the true Solomon is the blessed
Virgin, who crowned him with the crown of justice.[†] That crown consists of four precious jewels.
We call them the four customary and principal
states of mind—joy, love, sadness, and fear. Christ
experienced all these states of mind, but under
proper control. They are, therefore, appropriately
referred to as a crown of justice[†] because, as Augustine says: 'Justice is nothing but a properly ordered state of being'.[152] His mother is said to have
crowned him with this diadem, therefore, because
he experienced these states only as a result of what
he inherited from her. He felt joy, for it is written:
'And my heart will rejoice',[†] and so on. In the
psalm it is said: 'My soul will rejoice in God'.[†]
He was our fellow-man, and so it was appropriate
for him to rejoice with those who were glad.[†] It

See Ga 2:19

See 2 Tm 4:8

See 2 Tm 4:8

Is 66:14; see Jn
16:22
See Ps 33:21, 34:2

See Rm 12:15

---

151. The Latin is confused here. 'Si qui fuit sine spina,
punctus est pro nobis, quid aliud restat nisi compungi sibi pro
nostris spinis' would be translated: 'If he who was without
thorn was pierced on our behalf, what else remains for us but
to be pierced for our *thorns* along with him?' I have emended
'spina' to 'peccato' (or 'erratu') and 'spinis' to 'peccatis' (or
'erratibus') to translate as given in the text.
152. See Augustine, *De Genesi contra Manichaeos* 2.14; in
PL 34:204.

is clear that he had love for everyone, because he
See Jn 15:13 loved us so much that he laid down his life for us.†
See Rm 5:6–9 Though innocent, he died for us,† even though he
found nothing in us worthy of his love. If the Lord
See Ph 2:6–7 died for his servant,† what should the servant do
for his Lord—the one who has been redeemed for
his Savior? Let them take up the cup of salvation
See Ps 116:13 and invoke his name.†

Christ experienced fear, for as we read in the
Mk 14:33 Gospel: 'He began to be afraid and distressed'.† But
he felt this fear willingly, rather than because of his
condition. He felt sorrow because he chose to, not
because as a Jew he was able to do so. Thus it is
Mt 26:38 written: 'My soul is sad, even unto death'.† In this
fear of Christ we should take note of three things:
the will of the Father, the desire of Christ's spirit,
and the inclination of his flesh. The will of the
See Eph 1:10, 3:9 Father was to complete the work of redemption,†
and specifically to redeem the human race through
Christ's death. The desire of Christ's spirit was
to obey the Father. The inclination of his flesh,
however, was to avoid death, since it is natural for
the flesh to be terrified of death. The will of the Father was honored, the desire of the spirit crowned,
and inclination of the flesh properly controlled.
So although Christ said: 'Father, if it is possible,
let this cup pass from me', he immediately added:
Mt 26:39 'but let it be not as I wish, but as you will'.[153]† The
Father of Christ is God, who crowned him with
the diadem of glory. And so we read: 'O Lord, you
have crowned him with glory and honor, and made
See Ps 8:5–6 him ruler over all the earth'.† A full understanding
of this crown is prepared for us, but it will be
granted only in the future life.

When he wore his first crown Christ was despised. He can be emulated when wearing the

---

153. Compare Gra 3.8 (SBOp 3:172).

second. Wearing the third, he will be the object of our love. He is offered to us wearing the second crown, and so we hear: 'Come, daughters of Jerusalem, and see King Solomon wearing the diadem with which his mother crowned him',† as Sg 3:11 if to say: 'You ought to emulate King Solomon wearing this crown, so that you may direct all your affections in the way proper to them, in order to deserve attaining a full understanding of the third crown.'

115. 'Among all those born of women, none greater than John the Baptist has appeared.'[154]† The See Mt 11:11 angel of the Lord announced his coming to his father Zechariah with the words: 'Do not be afraid, Zechariah, for your prayer has been heard and your wife Elizabeth will bear you a son; his name will be John, he will bring joy and delight to you, and many will rejoice at his birth'.† The Holy See Lk 1:13 Spirit said to John: 'And you, child, will be called the prophet of the Most High; for you will go

---

154. One manuscript adds the following here:
'My friends, see the magnificent commendation of blessed John the Baptist which is offered by the mouth of Truth, the enormous praise of the precursor acclaimed by the tongue of the Creator. Behold the high renown of Christ's herald, to which the distinction of the Judge itself bears witness. God the judge is thus speaking about his own herald. Christ is speaking about John! "Among all the those born of woman" (see Mt 11:11), and so on. It is as though he were saying: "Could any woman, any corrupt female, any woman at all conceive a son greater than John by man alone?" For Elizabeth, who conceived a holy son from a man, still gave birth to him—even though he was holy and pure—of a man. The blessed Virgin Mary, however, conceived by the Holy Spirit and gave birth to both God and man—who is altogether greater than John, just as the brilliance of the sun cannot be compared to a lantern. So John himself, speaking of Christ and himself, said: "He must grow greater, and I smaller" (Jn 3:30). Christ grew greater, because he spoke to us as God and Lord. John grew smaller, because while he is praised as the herald of the highest Judge, still he is a son without issue. Let it, therefore, be said: "Among all those born of woman" (see Mt 11:11), and so forth.'

Lk 1:76

before the Lord to prepare his way'.† John is the
one about whom the Holy Spirit said, through
Malachi: 'Behold, I am sending my messenger
before you, who will prepare your way before

Mt 11:10; see Ml
3:1

you'.† As elsewhere we read: 'This is the voice
crying in the desert: "Prepare the way of the Lord,

See Is 40:3

make straight the path of our God" '.†

    John cried out in three deserts: first in the desert
of momentary vanity, then in that of humblest
simplicity or simple humility, and finally in the
desert of complete purity.[155]

    John was in the desert of momentary vanity
before he was sanctified, in his mother's womb.
For prior to that he was subject to sin, which is
called not merely vanity, but the vanity of vani-

Qo 1:2

ties.† Sin is properly called a desert because it is
rightly deserted by the holy. Although it would
be incorrect to say that John was in the desert of
vanity itself, nonetheless whatever he did before
emerging from his mother's womb he is said to
have done in the desert of vanity. Thus he is said
to have cried out in the desert of vanity when, at
the approach of Mary, the mother of the Lord, to
Elizabeth, he was filled with the Holy Spirit and

See Lk 1:39–41

leapt in the womb.† His mother Elizabeth, filled
too with the Holy Spirit, exclaimed prophetically:
'Who am I, that the mother of my Lord should

Lk 1:43

come to me?'†

    John cried out in the desert of humblest sim-
plicity or simple humility when, as people began
to make judgments about him and everyone came
to believe that he was the messiah, he replied:
'I baptize you with water, but there will come
another more powerful than I; I am not worthy
to loosen the strap of his sandals. He will baptize

---

155. Compare what follows to II Sent 11.

you with the Holy Spirit and fire'.[†] Our Lord Jesus   Lk 3:16
Christ taught this humility in words and sanctified
it by his example. He taught it verbally when he
said: 'Learn from me, for I am gentle and humble
of heart'.[†] He sanctified it by his own example,   Mt 11:29
since he showed himself humble in everything he
did. This humility is referred to as a desert because
few seek it out, and it is shunned by many.

John also cried out in the desert of complete
purity when, powerfully moved with a zeal for justice and the fire of charity, he openly condemned
Herod for his adultery. 'It is not lawful for you
to have your brother's wife',[†] he said. This desert   Mk 6:18
has three elements, and it bestows three benefits
on us. It encompasses the beauty of holy behavior,
the innocence of honest speech, and the purity
of good action. It bestows simplicity of intention,
rightness of will, and fullness of charity. This sort
of absolute purity is properly termed a desert, since
it is sought by almost no one.

The first desert is a parched, impassable land,[†]   See Ps 63:1
the second a flourishing and delightful territory,
and the third a productive farm. So it is written:
'What is this coming up from the desert like a
column of smoke, with the aromas of myrrh and
frankincense and every powdery spice?'[†] In these   Sg 3:6
three deserts John celebrated three marriage feasts.
In the first of these he was reconciled to God, in
the second he was adopted as a son, and in the third
he was rewarded. The first is called reconciliation,
the second adoption, and the third reward. At the
first banquet there were three dishes—the first the
washing away or removal of original sin, the second
the bestowal of grace, and the third the reform of
nature to the end that just as one had been deformed through Adam, he could now be made like
Christ. Similarly, there are three dishes at the sec-

ond banquet. The first of these is the consolation of God's word and the second is an immediate—and long-desired—vision of the Savior, whom John identified by pointing him out with the words: 'Behold the lamb of God who takes away the sin

Jn 1:29

of the world',† and so on. The third dish at this feast is a foretaste of that sweetness which is eternal. At the third banquet, the same number of dishes are found. The first is eternal incorruption, the second true glorification, and the third the endless vision of God.[156] So John proceeded from the feast of reconciliation, through that of adoption, to that of reward. May God, who lives and reigns, grant this to us.

116. When the Son of the highest king wished to take a bride, he sent his servants out to find one

See Mt 22:2–3
See Mt 21:35

for him.† However, they were murdered.† These were the prophets. Then, after receiving his Fa-

See Mt 21:37

ther's permission,† he went forth himself and redeemed the bride whom he desired by his own

See Rv 5:9

blood;† cleansing her with the water which flowed

See Jn 19:34; Ezk
16:9; Eph 5:26

from his side,† he made her beautiful and worthy of his embrace. Moreover, he adorned her with

See Ezk 16:13

gold and silver†—that is, with divine wisdom and the word of God—and with clothes, which are the virtues, and with possessions, which represent

1 Co 12:4

the division of gifts.† Later, wishing to return to his Father, he committed her to the care of his strong, vigorous soldiers—the apostles. They were to lead her to his Father's throne. As they were doing so, the king of Babylon, who is the devil, obstructed them, wanting to carry the bride away. But the apostles spilled their own blood resisting him and defending her, and in this way they made

---

156. Compare to the foregoing II Sent 65.

a path for her. The king of Babylon, seeing that he could not prevail by force, sent down heretics to tear the bride to pieces and despoil her by guile, under the appearance of a proper husband. But those good confessors who took up the defense of the bride after the apostles and martyrs—Jerome, Augustine, Gregory, and others—struggled against the heretics, expelled them, and disclosed the path through their teaching.

Once the path was cleared, however, the servants and workers of the bride, who ought to guide her—even though they could follow the grand, easily discernible footprints of their predecessors—fall subject to the king of Babylon and instead pursue her, rip her apart, and trample her. Such are the clerics of our time, who should be the salt of the earth and the light of the world.[†] People like these abuse God's wisdom and his words. They steal the garments and cloaks of the bride—that is, the properties with which the Church could clothe and feed her poor—and turn them to their own purposes. By weakening the bride and befouling her as much as they can, they pierce Christ's side,[†] which was wounded on the Church's behalf. Despising their duty and their rank, they take upon themselves the roles of others. By waging battles and acting in a military fashion, they assume the office of soldiers. By engaging in business, they take on the job of merchants; by accumulating fields, they unworthily affect and adopt the role of farmers.

Those clerics who have professed a monastic rule and delight in the communal life have the responsibility of the Levites, who were selected from their brothers to offer the sacrifices

See Mt 5:13–14

See Jn 19:34

See Nb 1:48–53,
3:5–10

See Lv 1:2–2:16

in the tabernacle;† for 'Levi' means 'one who is
chosen'.[157] These clerics are singled out from all
others to offer a special sacrifice in the Church.†
    This sacrifice has five parts. First, one must offer
a bull—that is pride, which is the root of sin. One
burns this as a sacrifice to God when he kills and
destroys it in himself. For pride puts piety to flight,
and as such dissolves and severs the life of the
community.
    Second, a ram must be sacrificed. The ram sym-
bolizes anger, which rushes backward and makes
See Si 10:14
one an apostate from God.† When provoked, a ram
runs backward so that it can strike more forcefully.
In the same way, anger abandons proper order and
departs from God, so that it can strike and drive
an adversary back. This too should be sacrificed to
God, because it obstructs communal life and is opposed to social well-being. It destroys agreement.
    If these two sacrifices are required for the sake
of communal life and harmonious society, the goat
must be burned next. This is an animal which
butts, and as such it represents the base, forbidden inclination of our appetite.[158] Its sacrifice is
essential to a wholesome lifestyle and purity of
conscience. Now when a goat feeds, it climbs the
crevices of mountains and cliffs. By supporting
itself on the ground with its two hind feet, it raises
and lifts the other parts of its body upward. Those
two hind feet represent food and clothing. It is
necessary to regard these rightly, and therefore to
look down upon mundane things while raising our
other members to the heights.
See Lv 1:14
    Fourth, a dove or pigeon† should be sacrificed.
It is pure and simple, and its song is a sigh. So too a

---

157. See Jerome, *Liber interpr. hebr. nom.*; in CCL 72:68
158. Compare III Sent 10 and III Sent 121 (at note 177).

just person who is innocent and upright does not
cackle like a bird, but rather sighs at the corruption
of his sins and wails out of his desire for eternal
bliss. He lives beside pools of water,† that is the   Sg 5:12
four Gospels. Through foresight he is on guard
against the falcon and the hawk,† which represent   See Jb 39:13
greater and lesser[159] persecution (for he is tempted
from both within and without). He drinks those
waters and is washed clean in them.

The fifth sacrifice is of bread, which is of three
types.[160]† One kind is simply unleavened bread on   See Lv 2:1–8
a gridiron. It can be seen from any angle. A second
kind is bread which is covered with oil in a frying-
pan and cannot be seen. The third is bread which
is in an oven. It cannot be seen at all—it too is
covered with oil, and it also has incense poured
atop it. These three kinds of bread represent the
three modes of perceiving wisdom—the historical,
the mystical, and the moral. Historical understand-

---

159. I emend the reading 'minorum' in the critical text
to 'minorem'.
160. One manuscript gives the following alternate version
of this passage:
'Fifth, bread is offered, which is of three kinds, as above:
there is bread baked on a gridiron, bread baked in a frying-
pan, and bread baked in an oven. These are the three modes
of understanding—the historical, the moral, and the mystical.
Bread baked on a gridiron can be seen from every angle, and so
the historical sense is obvious. Moreover, such bread should be
without leaven: thus, history is without deception (otherwise
it would not be history). Bread baked in a frying-pan can
be seen on one side. This is the moral sense: it is clear only
to those who submit themselves to norms of right conduct,
for not all people obey the Gospel (Rm 10:16). The bread
baked in an oven cannot be seen from any angle. Thus the
truth about Christ, the Church, and the Trinity is not fully
comprehended. One can only possess an inkling of it from
afar. We do not grasp through knowledge the truth about the
Trinity, because it is incomprehensible; to know the Father
and Jesus Christ, whom he sent, constitutes eternal life.
'The first type of bread is flavorful to the sensual palate,
the second to the palate of a pure will. The power of reason
apprehends the third type, glimpsing it from afar.'

ing is obvious and perceptible from all angles. The mystical sense is clear to some extent, but it is partially concealed. It is covered with oil, which means with the works of mercy, which shine with charity and the brilliance of right action. Moral understanding is still more hidden. The disposition which it creates works in the soul, involving not only the oil of mercy and charity along with the brilliance of right action, but also incense, which signifies devout prayer. An alternate exposition is that the three types of bread represent the three classes of those who are going to be saved: the married, the chaste, and the prelates.[161] Who lives and reigns.

117. 'The Lord lives; his fire is in Zion and his

See Is 31:9

furnace in Jerusalem.'[†] Just as we ask for a few coals from another's house to build a larger fire in our

See 2 Co 5:1–3

own,[†] so in this world, just as in a home not our own, we kindle the flame of charity so that we may possess it in full in the fatherland above. Here we are in Zion, when we look upon God from afar.[162] There we will be in Jerusalem, when we will see him up close. Paul says that in Zion 'we see now in a mirror', but in Jerusalem, we will see

---

161. Bernard makes a similar tripartite division of Christians elsewhere: compare Div 9.3 (SBOp 6/1:119); Abb 1 (SBOp 5:288–89); and Nat 1.7 (SBOp 4:249–50). In all instances the categories are the prelates of the Church (either 'prelati' or 'rectores'), the chaste (meaning both secular clergy and monks), and the married. Writing of this bernardine classification scheme, Georges Duby, *The Three Orders: Feudal Society Imagined*, trans. Arthur Goldhammer (Chicago-London: University of Chicago Press, 1980): 223, notes its dependence upon Augustine and Jerome, and adds: 'He [Bernard] thereby expressed his wholehearted acceptance of the Gregorian program, his conviction that all the servants of God should, under the direction of the bishops, "follow chastity and the virginal way of life and scorn the pleasures of the world," and that the married estate constituted the layman's rule of life.'

162. See the *Response for the Mass of the Fourth Sunday in Advent*.

'face to face. Now I understand only in part; but
then I shall know fully, just as I am known'.[†] Here
there is a little blaze, there a furnace. Here there
is a part, there fullness. Then we will see perfectly,
exchanging what is imperfect for what is whole,
our hope for our reward, the appearance for the
reality.

    118. Christ and the Church constitute a single
body. Christ is the head and the Church the body,[†]
for just as the vital power and vigor of the entire
body lie in its head, so too the life and foundation
of the Church are in Christ; and if she wishes
to become like her head[†] and serve him, she will
put aside her diversity of persons and functions to
become one with him for all eternity.

    The eyes of this ecclesiastical body are the bish-
ops, who should look after the lower members.
They are not only eyes but shepherds, and those
subject to them are not only referred to as members, but in their relation to the bishops they should
also be called little sheep.[163] The relationship between a shepherd and his sheep has much in common with that between a prelate and each member
of his flock. The one rules and the other is ruled.
The one nourishes, and the other is nourished. Just
as the shepherd presides over his sheep by reason of
the dignity of his created nature[†] and authority—
because as a rational being he stands erect and
looks to heaven—so too bishops should be found
especially reasonable and prudent in comparison
to those beneath them. They should have a dog,
a leash to restrain the animal, a staff to ward off
wolves, a rod to guide the sheep (who cannot
endure the heavy staff), and a bag for carrying

1 Co 13:12

See Eph 4:15–16;
Col 1:18

See Rm 8:29

See Heb 9:11

---

163. The play on words between 'oculi' ('eyes') and 'ovic-
ulae' ('little sheep') cannot be conveyed in translation.

their bread. In God's Church there are ravenous wolves, against whom one must have the dog— that is, the barking of harsh correction and the threat to bring the temporal sword to bear if the spiritual one is not sufficient. The dog, however, must be controlled with a leash to prevent him from rushing about impulsively, since stays must be granted and summonses issued with proper regard for the deed and the dignity of the individual involved. Wolves should be attacked with the staff of excommunication, but can a prelate hand over to the likes or dislikes of the dog what pertains to the love of God and the benefit of one's neighbor, and that which involves justice? He must use the staff, which means that he must be sparing not even of himself, because 'in beginning a presentation, the just person accuses himself'.† The sheep—that is, the common people—are to be controlled with the rod of gentle admonition, so that they will not stray. In his bag the bishop should store the bread which is God's word, so that he will always be prepared to offer a reasoned answer to anyone making a request.[164]

See Pr 18:17

The archdeacons are the nose of this body. With their well-honed power of smell they should grasp the scent of others' mode of life and pass along their perceptions to the bishop.

The deans are the ears. They should hear legal cases and render judgment according to what they have heard. For it is written: 'I judge in accordance with what I hear'†—not according to what I hate, or what I love.

See Jn 5:30

The priests and deacons are the mouth and tongue of the body. They are preachers of God's word.

---

164. Compare III Sent 66; III Sent 112 (at note 139); and Div 100 (SBOp 6/1:367).

The arrangement ought to be as I have described, but lately all the elements of the ecclesiastical body are reversed and confused. The eyes do not look upward. They look down for gifts. They look to love and hate. What is written is evident in them: 'There was darkness over the deep'.† In them are the face of Lazarus bound in cloth,† the eyes weighed down with sleep,† and Saul with scales on his eyes.† The nose, too, has lost its sense of smell. It mistakes the wicked for the good and the reverse,† protecting and oppressing those whom it chooses. The ears twist their judgments. The mouth and tongue remain silent.

Gn 1:2
See Jn 11:44
See Mt 26:43
See Ac 9:18
See Is 5:20

The chest, the back, the arms, and the hands of the Church are the knights. The heart is in the chest; courage resides in it. These members should courageously protect the ministers of the Church. In human beings, the back is suited for carrying, the arms for lifting, and the hands for touching. These members should, then, diligently bear, take up, and handle the Church's burdens. All of these things, however, have been altered. How wicked are hands which chatter and tear out the eyes which they ought to dry,† or cut off the nose which they ought to wipe, or lop away the ears which they ought to wash, or close themselves to one whom they ought to serve! They exchange words about the life of clerics at their banquets and engage in debates on the subject in the public squares.[165]

See Rv 7:17

165. One might note the literary effect Bernard achieves here with the phrase 'litterae in conviviis, disceptationes in triviis', especially the allusion the latter words might suggest to the educational trivium, home of both literature and disputation. Compare too the complaint which Bernard makes regarding the dissemination of the works of Peter Abelard: 'Would that his poisonous writings were still kept in boxes, and not being read in the public squares!' ('cuius virulenta folia utinam adhuc laterent in scriniis, et non in triviis legerentur'): Ep 189 (SBOp 8:13).

See 1 Co 12:22

The belly, which is often dismissed as of little value because of its weakness,[†] is just the receptacle of food. It is, nevertheless, the source of nourishment for the body. It digests what we eat, providing vital sustenance to the higher and lower members. Monks and hermits constitute the stomach of the Church. The world looks down on them, but they are the receptacle of spiritual food, the nourishment of doctrine. They represent the foundation of the Church, and are prefigured in Moses praying on the mount;[†] in Samuel lying in the temple;[†] and in Elijah tarrying in the desert.[†] The monks and hermits provide spiritual sustenance to the higher and lower members of the Church. What is written is applicable to them: The human race lives but a short time, but if it were not for them, the earth would perish in lightning or earthquake.[166]

See Ex 17:1–7
See 1 S 3:3
See 1 K 19:1–18

The feet, which carry the entire body, are the farmers. On their labor live all the others we have mentioned.

Such is the proper ordering of the Church, if she wants to become one with her head.

Jn 12:24

119. 'Unless the grain of wheat',[†] and so forth. It is a pious and holy undertaking to recall how many benefits Christ's death bestowed upon us. It brought us release from our own death and a cure for eternal death. It also represents an example and pattern for our present life and is both cause and effect of our heavenly glory. For the Son of God brought us God's grace and removed God's wrath toward us. Christ drank of death, so that death could not consume humanity. He shared God's anger with us, as has been written, so that we may share God's grace with him.[167] For we

---

166. See Ps.-Rufinus, *Vitae patrum* 3, Prol.; in PL 73:739.
167. John Chrysostom, *In Iohannem tractatus* 14; in CCL 36:150.

were sinners, and because of our sins they pierced[†] an innocent young person, so that through the incalculable devotion that he freely showed toward us he could offer us an example of the most fervent kind of charity, dissolve our guilt, obliterate our disgrace,[†] put an end to our punishment, open heaven, and restore to us himself and all things through him.[†] These are the fruits which the precious death of Christ brought forth. Through his death the death of his saints has become precious in the Lord's sight.[†] For our death was of no value whatever prior to Christ's death, since even the elect descended to hell. Even for the just death was bitter, because even though they were at rest, they were nonetheless cast into a cloud of darkness and enjoyed none of the sweetness of the vision of the divine. Through the death of Christ, therefore, we receive—as we have said—relief from our death, because now we are brought together not in hell, but in heaven.[†]

Thus the Word is the moisture, the Virgin is the earth, and Christ is the fruit. He was made human and transformed our hay into grain when, through his death and resurrection, he provided us with the never-failing spiritual bread of life and salvation at a time when, like beasts and animals, we recognized and longed for only perishable things. How good is the bread made from this grain! Even the angels feed upon the sight of it and are filled on it in the heavenly fatherland. It nourishes us through faith, so that we will not fail along the way.[†] It feeds each of us, but always remains whole. The one who gives himself to the angels to perpetuate their joy has also given himself to human beings in order to restore their well-being. Likewise, the one who is the food of the angels[†] has become our medicine.

See Zc 12:10; Rv 1:7

See Lk 1:25

Col 1:16

See Ps 116:15

See Ph 3:20

See Mt 15:32

Ws 16:20

See Jn 12:24

This grain of wheat,† therefore, is the preaching of the word, and the ground is the faithful soul.

See Jn 12:24

For unless the grain of wheat falling upon this ground†—that is, the teaching of the word which penetrates the human soul—were dead (meaning that it effects a recollection of the Lord's death and a desire to emulate it), so as to mortify the soul in a way that is salvatory and (as I might say) life-giving, then that grain of wheat which is God's word would remain isolated in the strength and value which belong to it alone, without benefit or usefulness to the soul. 'If, however, it has died'— that is, has done what we have just outlined—'it

Jn 12:25

yields much fruit'.† This means that it not only rips out the vices by the roots, but even brings forth shoots of the virtues and of good character through its seasonable growth.

Indeed the recollection and emulation of the death of Jesus Christ are the waters of Siloam,

See Jn 9:7, 11
See Ezk 36:25

in which we can wash† and be cleansed of our sins.† From these two derive the charisms of grace, the waters of paradise, the draughts of tears, the gifts of charity, the inducements to virtue, true means of consolation, the remedies provided by God, and those joys which are always new. These are waters that are sweet and suitable for drinking. Those who have tried them know that they descend from the fountain above. They flow down

†Sg 4:15
*Is 8:6

from Lebanon,† moving softly,* and they make places fruitful down to the lowest regions. They moisten the dryness of our heart and cause the city

Ps 46:5

of God to rejoice.† Would that these waters might flow freely into the pond which is our heart, with the assistance of that grace through which the Son of God, on our behalf, descended from the lap of

See Jn 1:18

the Father† to our land, put on the garment of our mortality, and died on the cross. We ought to suffer with him who suffered, be crucified with him who was crucified,[†] and die along with him who died by remembering this lovingly and imitating it devoutly, if we wish to reign in glory with him;[†] for the joy of ruling comes only after a time of pain. One reaches the glory of majesty[†] through the cup of suffering, and no one can achieve that through which he will possess eternal bliss, unless he first drinks of that whereby he will endure temporal grief. This is that famous cup which brims over,[†] that cup held by the Lord in which there is foaming wine, richly spiced.[†] All the faithful drink from it, each according to his own share.[†] 'You have made us drink copious tears', the psalmist said.[†] But the Lord does not allow anyone to suffer more than he can endure.[†] However often we suffer something painful for Christ,[†] therefore, we should do so with great joy, as though we were drinking from a cup offered to us by the Lord. Christ was also the greatest teacher of patience, for when Peter unsheathed his sword to defend him,[†] he said: 'Put your sword back in its place.[†] Am I not to drink the cup that the Father has given me?'[†] David, draining this saving cup with complete love, said: 'I will take the cup of salvation and call on the name of the Lord'.[†] When he fled from Absalom, therefore,[*] and Shimei cursed him in the worst possible fashion,[†] Abishai wanted to take vengeance but David angrily forbade it,[†] saying: 'What has this to do with me and you, sons of Zeruiah?[†] The Lord has ordered him to curse David.[†] The Lord can give me a blessing in place of this curse.'[†] It is as though he were speaking the words our Lord used during his passion: 'Am I not to drink of the cup which my Father has given me?'[†] The disciples were intoxicated by this cup when they left the Sanhedrin rejoicing because they were deemed worthy to

See Ga 2:19

See Rm 8:17

See Is 2:10, 19

See Ps 23:5

Ps 75:8
See Eph 4:7
Ps 80:5

See 1 Co 10:13
See Ph 1:29

See Jn 18:10
See Mt 26:52; Jn 18:11
Jn 18:11

†Ps 116:13
*See 2 S 15:14; 1 K 2:7
1 K 2:8
See 2 S 16:10–14
2 S 16:10
2 S 16:11
See 2 S 16:12

Jn 18:11

See Ac 5:41
suffer humiliation in Jesus' name.[†] Stephen drank
from this cup when he prayed for those who were
See Ac 7:59
stoning him.[†] Lawrence, placed on the gridiron,
taunted his executioners. Vincent, taken to the
pillory, complained about his persecutors' delays.
Whoever has become intoxicated by drinking from
this famous cup, therefore, will be unable to feel
either fleshly delights or bodily pains. One must
drink, then, from this cup—I say one must drink
from it, just as the Lord commanded: 'Drink of
Mt 26:27
this, all of you'.[†] Indeed no one is excepted. We
are all ordered to drink from it, because the route
to the heavenly fatherland is not open to anyone
who does not patiently drink from the stream of
See Ps 110:7
suffering as he goes.[†]

That wheat, moreover, is flavorful, sweet-
smelling, and nutritious. It has the taste of faith,
the aroma of hope, and the strength of charity.
The flavor of faith nurtures and refreshes us, the
sweet smell of hope delights and touches us, and
the firmness of charity strengthens us and leads
us to perfection. Nonetheless the grain of wheat
has chaff—the vanity of arrogance and the perversity of heretical doctrine—from which it must
be separated through saving discretion. It must be
See Lv 2:14
heated and dried in the fire of tribulation,[†] so that it
can be ground more efficiently when it is crushed
and milled between the two stones of obedience
and poverty. Truly, when the word of God—or a
commitment to life under a rule—is situated in
the heart of an honestly poor, perfectly obedient
person between the harshness of poverty and the
strong discipline of obedience, it elicits keen perceptions of divine and spiritual understanding—
like tiny grains of pure-white, ever-increasing flour
—with which it refreshes the souls of the faithful.
To prevent the winds of pride from scattering

this flour, however, the water of humility binds it together, reducing it to a single mass. From it bread is made of three ingredients—fear, sorrow, and work.

Fear, moreover, looks to three things, while sorrow arises from three and work is composed of three. The three to which fear looks are the wisdom of God, from which nothing is hidden; the power of God, through which he can do whatever he wills; and the justice of God, which allows no sin to go unpunished. It is by reason of these, then, that the fear arises which cleanses the human's heart. Sorrow grows out of three circumstances: first, because we have not done what we should have; second, because we have done things we should have shunned; and third, because in these two ways we have offended God. Work consists of three elements: austerity in food and clothing, manual labor, and devotion to nightly vigils. From these three—fear, sorrow, and work—is made that bread of expiation which, like a saving potion, cleanses us of our foul crimes.

There follows the bread of consolation, which is also composed of three ingredients—faith, hope, and charity. Each of these three ingredients has three elements, too. Faith earns forgiveness of sins, obtains the talents which belong to the deserving,[†] and rejoices greatly[†] in the fact that it has been illuminated by the Father of lights.[†] Hope aims at daily progress in improving oneself, the recollection of the benefits of heaven, and an expectation of the good things to come. Charity encompasses a delight in justice, a desire for increased innocence, and a thirst for God.[†] Charity also calls out to him for whom it desires to lay down its life.[†] Because all of these are given to console us after our tribulation, the bread which follows that of expiation

See Mt 25:14–30
Jn 3:29
Jm 1:17

See Ps 42:2
See Jn 15:13

is called that of consolation, in order that joy may replace sorrow.

The third bread is that which consolidates. Only a few people possess it, and then rarely, as a sort of foretaste or prelude in the tabernacle of this life. It is to be obtained to one's full satisfaction only in the palace of heaven. This bread also consists of three elements: the vision of God, love, and praise. That vision of God which in this life we call contemplation will there be easily achieved, and our love will enjoy full bliss, while our praise will be unchanging. In other words, our vision of God there will be unobstructed by the presence of anything else, our love will be utterly unimpeded, and our praise will involve no effort or weariness.

We refer to these three as types of bread because it is God who refreshes us, and he in turn is refreshed by the goods we possess.

We who are of the Lord's portion ought, therefore, to think about the points which have been raised and, above all, attend to things that are most worth doing, so that in feeding the pigs in this region of unlikeness[168] we may not be fed on husks ourselves.† For now we are seated at the wedding feast of the Lamb† in God's Church. Now we are wearing a wedding garment† and taking part in the first resurrection.† Now the robe and ring have been restored to us, along with our father's forgiveness and his kiss.† Now the fatted calf has been slaughtered for us,† and from on high the music and dancing resound.† This is the praise of the saints in God's Church.† This is truly the grace which has been given freely to us! Let us, therefore, give glory to the one† who has bestowed grace on us. Let us, without servile fear, serve him, freed

See Lk 15:15–16
Rv 19:9
Mt 22:12
Rv 20:5

See Lk 15:20–22
See Lk 15:23
See Lk 15:25
See Ps 150:1

See Rv 19:7

---

168. See note above on III Sent 21 (at note 16).

from the grasp of our enemies.† Let us obey him Lk 1:74
in all things. Finally, let us, with fervent desire and
a strong spirit, rush forward into heaven, so that
we may behold God's benefits in the land of the
living† and our joy may be complete.† See Ps 27:13

120. 'The Lord will reward his saints for their See Jn 16:24
labors, and will lead them along a marvelous road'.† Ws 10:17
One labor is that of the flesh, a second that
of compunction, and a third that of charity. Carnal labor is burdensome, that of compunction is
affective, and that of charity is effective. Of the
burdensome character of the first, it is written:
'Their heart is humbled by their labors',† and so Ps 107:12
on. Elsewhere we read: 'Come to me, all of you
who labor and are burdened, and I will refresh
you'.† In his kindness the Lord calls out to those Mt 11:28
who are laboring under a burden. Surely everyone
is laboring, because Adam was told when he was
expelled into the world: 'You will eat your bread in
the sweat of your brow'.† But some people—those See Gn 3:19
who serve the devil, whose yoke is unbearable
and whose burden cannot be borne—labor and are
burdened, while others—those who serve God—
labor and do not find it onerous, but rather are
honored by it.[169] Thus we read: 'God, your friends
are much honored'.† They are not burdened, be- Ps 139:17
cause the Lord's yoke is easy and his burden light.† See Mt 11:30
Of the work of compunction it is said: 'I am exhausted by my grief',† and so forth. This labor Ps 6:7
is truly affective, because a person who starts to
repent truly conceives within himself a beneficial
disposition which leads him to the desired result.[170]

---

169. The play on words is between 'onerati' ('burdened')
and 'honorati' ('honored').

170. There is a play on words here between 'affectum'
('disposition') and 'effectum' ('result').

The work of charity is said to be effective because it brings to completion what compunction has started.

Moreover, carnal work punishes, while that of compunction brings remission and that of charity bestows reward. The first punishes because those who are lost in the pleasures of the flesh are tormented in this world by their search for enjoyment. As the apostle writes: 'The Lord has abandoned them to their heart's desires, through which they punish their own bodies with affliction'.† They will be punished for all eternity, unless they recover their senses. The second labor brings remission, because those who are pierced by repentance earn forgiveness of sins; for at the moment a sinner expresses regret, he will be saved.[171]† The third labor is said to be rewarding, because it merits reward; for 'you will eat through the effort of your hands'.† Since this labor bestows reward, the psalm adds: 'You are blessed, and things will be well for you'.†

Each of these labors has a cross peculiar to it. Carnal labor has a cross of punishment, because it punishes both in this world and in the future one. The labor of compunction has a cross of abstinence, because repentance requires abstinence. The labor of charity has a cross of glory, because he who loves God crucifies his flesh, with its vices and desires.† This crucifixion constitutes glory, for it is written: 'Let me boast of nothing but the cross',† and so on. The first cross is extremely demanding, since it is exacting down to the last penny.† The second cross is necessary, because one who sins must abstain from doing so. The third cross is

Rm 1:24

See Rm 10:13

Ps 128:2

Ps 128:2

See Ga 5:24

Ga 6:14

Mt 5:26

---

171. On this locution see Jean Leclercq, *Recueil d'études sur saint Bernard et ses écrits* 1 (Storia e letteratura 92) (Rome: Edizioni di storia a letteratura, 1962): 308.

voluntary, for it is written: 'I will willingly sacrifice to you'† not out of fear, but because it is sweet and good to do so.

Ps 54:6

In addition, each labor has its own kind of death. The first death is that which damns, because anyone who is a friend of the world is deemed an enemy of God,† and death is the wages of sin.* The second death is common to all, because while some mortify their members† with their vices and passions† as do the good, others mortify the flesh[172] with its vices and desires† in the way that hypocrites do. The third death is precious, and it deserves reward. As is written: 'The death of his saints is precious in the Lord's sight'.†

†See Jm 4:4
*Rm 6:23
See Col 3:5
Ga 5:24
Ga 5:24

Ps 116:15

We may also say that the impenitent thief hangs on the first cross, the penitent thief on the second, and Christ on the third.† Note well that when Adam sinned in paradise, the Lord began to look for him, asking: 'Adam, where are you?'† For a considerable time he called out in paradise, but he did not get the response he desired. Adam, moreover, attempted to turn the fault against the Creator himself.† It was for this reason that he was expelled.† So God shouted 'Adam, where are you?'† for a long time but was not able to find him in paradise. So, too, when God came down to earth and, at the end, looked upon the thief as he was hanging on the cross, it was as if he were calling out: 'Adam, where are you?' 'Lord', the thief replied, 'I am on the cross, receiving what I truly deserve.† I make no excuse. I earned what I am suffering. I ask you for your mercy: "remember me, Lord, when you enter your kingdom".'† Because he repented, the one to whom he confessed did not inflict a

See Lk 23:39–43

Gn 3:9

See Gn 3:12
See Gn 3:23–24
Gn 3:9

See Lk 23:41

Lk 23:42

---

172. The critical text reads 'eam', which I take as the equivalent of 'carnem' in Ga 5:24.

judgment based on vengeance, but restored him
to his fatherland with the words: 'Today you will

Lk 23:43 be with me in paradise'.[†]

By indicting yourself, you will ascend to the
place from which you have fallen by making excuses. For when God approaches and a person
offers his confession, the mercy of God who is
drawing near meets the honesty of the one who

See Ps 85:11 confesses his sin.[†] Because mercy recognizes truth,
she does not allow justice any place to undertake
a prosecution. Indeed, when mercy gives her

Ps 85:10 consent, justice and peace embrace,[†] because
through the effort of mercy and the allowance of
justice, reconciliation is effected between God and
wretched humanity.[173]

Furthermore, each kind of labor has three elements. In carnal labor, one part lies in delight
(the point at which consent joyfully joins with
temptation), the second in actual performance, and
the third in making the action habitual.

It is similar with the labor of compunction.
One part lies in gloom, the second in sorrow, and
the third in turbulence. The gloom drives away
delight, the sorrow prevents action, and the turbulence removes the habitual character of sin. We
read of these three elements in the Book of Job. Of
the first we read: 'May gloom obscure that day'; of
the second: 'May it be swallowed up in sorrow';
and of the third: 'May dark turbulence take hold

Jb 3:5–6 of that night'.[†] The work of gloom is shame. For
if one delights in thinking about sin, he needs to
become ashamed of what he thinks. The work
of sorrow consists of prolonged weeping. For the
disclosure of one's evil action brings about not only
internal shame, but tears of sorrow as well. Since

---

173. Compare III Sent 23 (at note 22).

one sins more gravely when it becomes habitual,
turbulence—meaning that wondrous pain of grief
which constitutes profound shame—is required.
For one should suffuse his whole mind with sorrow, and instill that sorrow in his body through
abstinence as well. That turbulence is the violent
wind of which David said: 'You will obliterate the
ships of Tarshish'—that is, the search for pleasure—
'with a raging blast'.† For as ships float in the sea,   Ps 48:8
people float in the abyss of the world. The violent
wind of penance strikes them, so that the curiosity
which in some people takes joy in wicked delight
or evil action can be destroyed by the blast of harsh
penance and suitable shame.

One labor of charity is to love oneself, a second
is to love one's neighbor, and a third is to love
God. One who loves himself carnally does not
love himself at all, because 'one who loves iniquity
despises his own soul'.† The fact that it takes effort   Ps 11:5
to love oneself is clear, because the flesh wars
against the spirit and the spirit against the flesh.†   See Ga 5:17
It also takes effort to love one's neighbor, since it
brings a burden which must be borne. So we read:
'Each of you should carry the other's burden'.†   Ga 6:2
Similarly, it takes effort to love God, because 'we
are being destroyed for your sake the whole day'.†   Ps 44:22; Rm 8:36
Since we are outside, we do not easily come inside,
where one loves God.

The first labor of charity initiates, the second
moves one ahead, and the third brings one to fulfillment. The labor which begins is that of which
Solomon says: first 'take pity on your soul, you
are pleasing to God',† for how can a person who   Si 30:24
despises himself love anyone else? The labor that
moves one forward is undertaken when one looks
out for the benefit of his neighbor. The third labor is that which completes, because the word of

Rm 9:28

God is a summary and final sentence,[†] and 'I have seen that there is a limit to every perfection, but your commandment'—that is, charity—'is without limitation'.[†] For whatever compunction takes up, charity brings to completion.

Ps 119:96

The first labor of charity, moreover, is sober, for after a person loves himself, he resists twofold drunkenness with a double sobriety. Outer drunkenness lies in the flood of desire, and internal drunkenness in an obsession with worldly concerns. Outer sobriety consists of the restraint of desire, and inner sobriety means the elimination of curiosity.[174]

The labor of charity toward one's neighbor is just. For justice consists of two elements: being kind and doing no harm. We ought to do no harm to our neighbor, because 'what you do not want done to you, you should not do to another'.[†] We should also be kind to our neighbor: 'Treat others as you wish to be treated yourself'.[†]

See RB 61.14; Tb 4:16

See Mt 7:12

The labor of charity toward God is pious. Piety consists of two parts: a lack of trust in ourselves, and confidence in God. A person ought to have no faith in himself and to trust in God.[†]

See Si 11:22

The first labor of charity is constructive, since it is sober. The second labor of love justifies, because it is just. The third saves, because it is pious. Love of self raises up Lazarus,[†] because it does away with evil habit. Love of neighbor raises up the young man near the gate,[†] because it precludes our acting in such a way as to injure our neighbor, either in deed or by bad example. Love of God raises up the young girl in her house,[†] because it removes sin even from one's own will. To raise that girl Jesus took along with him John, who

See Jn 11:1–44

Lk 7:11–17

See Lk 8:49–56

174. Compare Div 54 (SBOp 6/1:279).

represents prevenient grace; James, who represents the grace which works in conjunction with prayer; and Peter, who represents grace which is well-established and enduring. The girl's father and mother are brought in as well.[†] They represent the severe reproach characteristic of a father and the pious consolation characteristic of a mother.

See Lk 8:51

A young person who has been lifted beyond himself through his sense experiences is lying on a bier—meaning that he is dependent upon his conscience. One is carried away from his conscience when his reason surrenders to the flesh so fully that he either does not realize that his conscience is eating away at him or cannot feel its pangs.

There are four feet on this bier. The first foot is the force of threats, the second the enticement of promises, the third the deceit of ignorance, and the fourth a delight in evil. It is in these four ways that one enters the counsel of the wicked,[†] which means to put earthly things before those of heaven, transitory things before those which remain the same, changeable things before those which cannot be altered. Four remedies, however, have been prepared against them. The first is courage, needed by those under pressure from threats. The second is temperance, essential for those seduced by promises. The third is prudence, which aids those misled by deceit. The fourth is justice—that is, rightness of will—which is needed by those who are struck by the foulness of their evil behavior. These are the four cardinal virtues, which obliterate every wicked and worthless counsel.

See Ps 1:1

Four peasants carry this bier. These are the four states of mind—fear, hope, anger, and joy. Fear carries the first foot, the force of threats, because unless a person is afraid, he will not be moved by threats. Hope props up the power of flattery, because if one is not hopeful, he will not give ear to flattering words. Anger buttresses a lack of prudence, for the impetuosity of anger eliminates discretion. Joy supports a taste for evil, for if one does not rejoice in wickedness, he will not incline toward evildoing.

There are two ends to the bier, one at the head and the other at the feet. The one at the head represents overconfidence in God's mercy, and the one at the feet a foolish lack of trust in it. These are the two breasts of which Job asked: 'Why did I nurse on these breasts?',[†] for some are so confident of God's mercy that they abuse it, while others put the savagery of their sin beyond God's mercy and do not trust in it at all. The ends have lattices to the right and the left,[†] so that those on the bier will not slip off. On the one side they have the depraved habit of doing evil and on the other a connection with parents and friends. For one lies on the hard wood because he does not appreciate how foul and bitter sin is—since his bitter pleasure prevents him from feeling it. Thus Jeremiah says: 'He made me drunk on wormwood'.[†] The very hardness of the wood signifies how harsh the bitterness is, and over it is placed hay—that is, a coating of false happiness. A lid is put over the bier—hypocrisy in monks, flattery in secular persons. It compels them to continue embracing sin by preventing them from raising their eyes to heaven.

Three rewards follow from the three labors of charity. Love of self brings pardon as its reward, love of neighbor brings grace, and love of God brings glory. Thus God gives himself as a reward to his saints, leading them along a marvelous road.[†] But before he can lead them onto the marvelous road, he must lead them away from the road of misery. The way of misery is the road of iniquity,

Jb 3:12

See 2 Co 6:7

Lm 3:15

See Ws 10:17

while the marvelous road is that of truth.[†] The road of iniquity, which represents misery piled upon misery, is delightful at first, but it becomes harsh as one proceeds, and in the end it brings damnation. It defiles those who enter upon it, takes hold of those walking along it, and destroys those who reach its end.

See Ps 119:29–30

At the beginning of this road pride, which is the root of all evil, is set up as a gate. It is the first vice for those who are departing, and the last for those returning. Temptation lies in front of the gate, pleasure in the gate itself, and consent in the road. Temptation offers access, pleasure gives entrance, and consent brings progress along the path. Temptation occurs when perverse thoughts fly by the soul, but none enter it. It is in this sense that Christ could possibly be tempted,[†] because this sort of temptation does not constitute sin. Pleasure occurs when some of those thoughts fly into the soul, and the soul enjoys their remaining there, although it does not choose to carry them into action. Consent occurs when the soul assents to such pleasure and does not shun acting on it, if an opportunity arises. Pride beautifies the exterior of her gate with whitewash, so that entering it may appear attractive to those who approach it through temptation. The road starting from the gate of pride and proceeding to the east has a precipice to either side. As a result, no safe exit from the road remains for anyone who sets foot on it, nor is there any way back. So unless one leaves it by the same gate through which he entered, there is no place where he can find escape.

See Mt 4:1–11

If, therefore, one steps upon this road beyond the gate and chooses to follow its path forward, he comes upon a first dwelling at the place of vainglory, a second at envy, a third at anger, a fourth

at sorrow, a fifth at greed, and a sixth at gluttony.
Here he is enclosed in a tomb, with his hands and
See Jn 11:44 feet bound and his eyes closed,[†] because as he gets
See Ps 35:6 lost in his desires, his way grows dark and slippery.[†]
Thus he is shut up in this tomb, and unless Jesus
See Jn 11:38 should come to Lazarus,[†] he falls to eternal ruin.

If, however, the traveler elects to veer off into
See 2 Co 6:7 any of the earlier dwellings to his left or his right,[†]
he finds disaster all around him, because—as we
have said—he will come upon the precipice on
either side. At the gate of vainglory is hypocrisy, in
the house itself disobedience, and in the bedchamber empty boasting. Presumption makes a new
arrival fickle, while disharmony and strife make
him worldly and obstinacy renders him unyielding.
As one approaches envy, there first arises mutter-
ing; then slander introduces hatred; and then joy
at his excesses becomes his companion on one
hand, while pain over others' successes accompanies him on the other. At the gate of anger sits
indignation, in the house resides insult, and further
within is blasphemy. Arrogance has its domicile
there, shouting is nearby, and strife ruins the place.
Weakness takes hold of anyone who approaches
sorrow's home. Indifference to God's commandments surges up in him. Despair directs him to
the bedchamber. The wandering of his mind leads
him astray. As one approaches greed, fraud greets
him first; then perjury smiles at him; intoxication leads him on; betrayal urges him onward; and
hardness of heart obstructs his return. There are
two types of gluttony: one of the stomach and the
other of the genitals. On approaching gluttony one
finds himself joined first by a dulling of his sense;
then unsuitable joy smiles upon him. Buffoonery
has its residence there, drunkenness sits beside it,
and impurity suffuses the place. Pleasure urges on

the person who approaches luxury, fickleness surrounds him, and thoughtlessness surges up in him.
Blindness of mind puts a bolt on the door and self-
love stands at her side—along with hatred of God,
attachment[175] to this world, despair of forgiveness,
and the misuse of God's mercy. As a result, the
sinner rots in the tomb we have mentioned, de-
composing in the foulness of his vices; and with
the stone of love of the world placed over him, he
cannot rise up.[†]   See Jn 11:38–39

Now first God looks intently upon this person,
and in response he blushes, because he knows that
he is foul in God's sight. After God shows his
face,[†] the person trusts in him. When God puts   See Ps 80:3, 7, 19
out his hand, the person arises.[†] Then God takes   See Lk 7:14–15,
the wretch off the road of iniquity and leads him   8:54–55
away from it. In leading him away, God unites the
person with himself through confession, draws the
person to him through good works, and joins the
person to him through his cooperation. Thus does
God lead an individual onto the good road, guide
him along it, and bring him to its end.

There are three aspects to the good road: its
edge, its approach, and its path. The edge is narrow,
the approach steep, the path level. At the edge
are those who repent, on the approach those who
serve God, and on the path those who persevere.
We enter across the edge, proceed by means of
the approach, and rush forward along its path. In
entering we are led onto the road, in proceeding we are guided along, and in running we are
brought to our destination. God shows himself
stern at our entrance, propitious as we progress, and
friendly as we rush forward. His sternness brings
fear, his kindliness instills love, and his friendliness

---

175. I emend 'effectus' of the critical text to 'affectus'.

elicits devotion. He gives law to those who are just beginning, instructs those who are on the way, and brings to perfection those who are well along. So we read in the psalm: 'I will give you understanding', namely, by establishing law for those beginning the journey, 'I will instruct you about the way you should take'—this is spoken to those on the journey—'and I will keep my eyes firmly on

Ps 32:8

you'.† At first, then, he turns his eyes away, as if in wrath, when he instills shame over one's sins. Then he turns his eyes back, showing his face so that the sinner, who was at first terrified, is soothed. Finally he sets his eyes firmly, ordering the sinner to remain uninterruptedly in his gaze in order that the person can behold his visage, so that judgment

See Ps 17:2

can proceed from his face.†

Perfection follows from this process. For the law that has been established convinces one to take

See Ps 119:33

the road of justification,† in order that, through fear of the law, the sinner may make satisfaction. Then God's instruction discloses the road of the

See Ps 119:32
See RB Prol.

commandments, along which one runs† after his heart is freed through charity.† Perfection leads us to the road of truth. We enter upon that road so that we may reach the truth. For to the statement: 'I am

Jn 14:6

the way and the life' is added: 'I am the truth'.† The psalmist already sensed this because he said: 'Lead

Ps 86:11
See Ps 86:11

me, Lord, along your way'.† To what end? 'So that I may walk in your truth'.† Justice brings about the road of justification; charity disposes the road of commandments; and the overflowing goodness of God directs the road of truth.

Thus God leads his saints along a marvelous road, a road which is delightfully wondrous and wondrously delightful. At first that road is the way

See Sg 5:1

of justification, leading to the garden.† Then it becomes the way of the commandments, bringing one into the wine-chamber.[†] Finally it becomes the way of truth, which takes one to the bed-chamber[†] of the king.* That road is truly marvelous which is at first bitter, then sweet, and finally devout.

See Sg 2:4

†See Sg 3:4
*See Est 2:13

121. 'My yoke is easy and my burden light',[†] says the Lord. Oh, words sweeter than honey, sweeter than the honey dripping from the comb,[†] words steeped in heavenly nectar! Oh, words brimming with profound meanings, blooming with the sheen of soothing eloquence! Heaven is amazed; the earth stands in awe.[†] Oh, how joyous is this passage! The more often you read it, the more completely it attracts your spirit; the more exhaustively it is analyzed, the sweeter it tastes!

Mt 11:30

See Ps 19:10

See Is 49:13

For Christ says: 'My yoke is easy and my burden light'.[†] Now in the yoke and burden are indicated the two stages of obedience. For a yoke is one thing and a burden another—first in their actual substance, then in their distribution among individuals, and finally in their different qualities. The yoke of God, in terms of its actual substance, is 'to love those who love us, and to do good to those who do good to us'.[†] If you cannot pay someone back by actually giving him something, you can still do so of your own free will by prayer. The burden of God is 'to love our enemies, and to do good to those who hate us'.[†]

Mt 11:30

See Lk 6:32–33

See Lk 6:27

In terms of their distribution among individuals, the yoke is imposed on some people, the burden on others. The first is given to those who are undisciplined and imperfect, the latter to those who are persevering in their good work and to the perfect.

With respect to their different qualities, the yoke is easy and the burden is light.[†] In the yoke is great easiness, and in the burden not only great or greater

See Mt 11:30

See Lk 6:32–33

lightness, but the greatest possible lightness. For to whom would it not be easy to love those who love you,† and so forth? But it is altogether unknown to the imperfect how light the burden is. Those beginning their journey hear of its lightness and those making progress catch its scent from afar, but only those well along partake of it directly.

Holy Scripture, the divine text, embraces and comprehends both of these elements under the single word 'obedience'. Obedience is the virtue which is mistress over the other virtues, holding primacy among them. Holy Scripture often commends it above the rest. So we read: 'Obedience is

1 S 15:22

better than sacrifices'.† Elsewhere it is written that obedience is the key of David, and what it opens,

See Is 22:22; Rv 3:7

nobody can close.† Truly it is a key, for obedience brings the friends of the spouse into the three treasuries of the Lord, reveals to them the deepest mysteries of God, and makes them actual kinsmen

See Sg 5:1
†See Sg 2:4
*See Sg 3:4

of God. Obedience leads them into the garden,† the wine-chamber,† and the bedchamber.* The garden is the historical sense, the wine-chamber the moral understanding, and the bedchamber the spiritual or mystical sense.[176] Those to whom the key discloses history, it makes God's kin in the first degree. Those to whom it makes known the moral sense and those to whom it reveals the spiritual sense, it joins to God in the second and third degrees, while uniting them each to the others.

The garden, moreover, is divided into three periods of time: a time of planting, a time of growth, and a time of harvest. The time of planting is described in Genesis, where the author deals with the creation of heaven and earth and of male

---

176. Compare what follows with III Sen 123; SC 23 (SBOp 1:138–50); and Div 92.1–3 (SBOp 6/1:346–48).

and female—that is, of Adam and Eve. The time of growth is referred to in the Gospel: 'You have heard that people of old were told: "An eye for an eye, a tooth for a tooth." I tell you: refrain from evil, and if someone strikes you on one cheek, offer him the other as well'.† The time of harvest is described See Mt 5:38–39 elsewhere in the Gospel: 'Those who have done good works will enter eternal life. Those who have done evil† will go into the eternal fire.'† All of these Jn 5:29 things are written in accordance with history. See Mt 25:46

Similarly, the wine-chamber, which is said to be the moral sense, is divided into three smaller chambers. The first of these is the attitude one has toward those set over him, the second his attitude toward his confrères or peers, and the third his attitude toward those subject to him. Subordinates who love their superiors out of charity and obey them humbly in God's place enter the first chamber. So we read: 'Servants, be subject to your masters with due fear, even to those who are ill-tempered'.† Those who love their confrères See 1 P 2:18 or peers out of charity and anticipate them in showing mutual respect enter the second chamber. For we read that we should 'anticipate one another in exhibiting mutual respect'.† Prelates who love Rm 12:10 those under them with paternal love, diligently instructing them in word and deed, enter the third chamber. In the first chamber obedience is signified; in the second, justice; and in the third, true charity.

Blessed Job entered all three of these chambers. He entered the first by being humbly obedient to God, enduring calmly whatever he suffered. As he said: 'The Lord gave, the Lord has taken away',† and Jb 1:21 so on. See his obedience! Job entered the second chamber when he tolerated with equanimity his friends' quarrels and their disorderly ways. Behold his justice! He entered the third chamber when he wisely guided his foolish wife and their children in word and deed, for he said: 'You are talking like a foolish woman'.[†] See his true charity!

Jb 2:10

Besides all these reasons why obedience is so worthy of commendation, Holy Scripture also says that it is a bronze altar,[†] beneath which is a pit housing a constant fire, and before which animals are sacrificed.[†] Obedience is a bronze altar, because however much someone fasts and prays or wastes himself in excessive effort, handing over his body to burn in the fires for God's sake, none of this will be of any benefit to his salvation[†] unless he offers that sacrifice upon the altar of obedience. That altar is made of bronze,[†] because our obedience should be so strong that not even death can separate us from it,[†] or any other bodily hardship. Behold that bronze altar, beneath which is a pit housing a constant fire![†] By the pit, humility is signified, and by the fire, charity. Those two are beneath the altar because obedience is founded upon both of them, as though on firm rock, so that it can always remain immovable and unshaken against the winds and the waves.[†] Before this altar animals are sacrificed—specifically the proud bull, the wanton ram, and the foul kid. The bull symbolizes pride, the ram anger, and the kid lust. We sacrifice the bull before this altar when we trample down pride through our humility, as is always necessary in a soul before perfect obedience can be given to it. We sacrifice the ram when we restrain our anger through patience, as must always happen in a soul before perfect obedience can be given to it.[177]

Strengthening this obedience and keeping it firm are three things to one side and three to

Ex 38:30

See Ex 27:2–8 and
Lv 6:12–13

See 1 Co 13:3

See Ex 38:30

See Sg 8:6

See Ex 27:28 and
Lv 6:12–13

See Mt 7:24–25

---

177. Compare III Sent 10 and III Sent 116 (at note 158).

the other, which turn their heads around so as to reflect upon one another in turn.[178] The first three are humility, contempt for the world, and patience. Of them the first relates to faith, the second to hope, and the third to charity. For how can obedience be found in someone in whom there is no humility, contempt for the world, or patience? How can faith exist in someone in whom there is no humility? How can there be any hope of eternal life in a person who does not disdain the world? How can true charity exist in a person in whom patience is not found? Behold the six precious columns, solid and firm, upon which obedience supports itself on one side and the other!

Moreover, this obedience is borne upon the four cardinal virtues as though in a carriage or chariot with four wheels. These are prudence, temperance, courage, and justice, which are understood in the figures of the human being, the bull, the lion, and the eagle.[†] The Lord himself emphasized the power of this kind of obedience in the images of the yoke and the burden when he said: 'My yoke is easy, and my burden light'.[†]

See Ezk 1:10

Mt 11:30

Now, the yoke or burden of God has three forms. The first is regular discipline, the second the fear of hell, and the third loving grace. The first of these is borne by those who keep their hands from evildoing only through fear of temporal punishment. The second is carried by those who preserve their hearts from wicked thoughts through fear of the pain of hell. The third is possessed by those who shun evil and do good[†] solely through their love of God. Those who bear the first are slaves, those who carry the second are hired workers, and those who have the third are sons; the first rouses

See Ps 34:14

---

178. Compare what follows to III Sent 53 (at note 44).

slaves, the second encourages hirelings, and the
third strengthens sons. Slaves are those who are
just beginning, hired workers those who are on
the way, and sons those who are persevering.[179]

If someone wants to know how sweet honey
is, he could not do so better than by first experi-
encing the bitterness of wormwood. Similarly, if
one wishes to understand more fully how good
obedience is, he can do so best by understanding
its opposite—that is, by recognizing the evil of
disobedience. So let such a person realize that there
are two masters, utterly opposed and contrary to
one another—God and the devil. 'Can there be
any agreement between Christ and Belial?'† Be-
longing to these are two cities, completely different
from one another both in character and in name—
Jerusalem and Babylon. Jerusalem means 'vision
of peace',[180] while Babylon means 'the disorder of
sin'.[181] As many citizens as these cities have, all of
them are dissimilar and deeply unlike one another.
For the citizens of Jerusalem are Abel and every
other just person, all of them predestined to life.
The citizens of Babylon are Ham and every other
reprobate, all of them foreseen as destined to die.

Just as the four cardinal virtues provide the
means of transport for obedience, the four principal vices constitute the chariot of disobedience.
They are lust, pride, gluttony, and anger, which
are symbolized in the caterpillar, the locust, the
grasshopper, and the gnawer.[182]† And just as Christ's
yoke has three forms, so too the devil's yoke is
found to have three. The first yoke is that of

2 Co 6:15

See Jl 1:4

---

179. Compare III Sent 26; III Sent 92 (at note 94); and
Dil 12.34–14.38 (SBOp 3:148–52).
180. Jerome, *Liber interpr. hebr. nom.*; in CCL 72:121.
181. Jerome, *Liber interpr. hebr. nom.*; in CCL 72:62.
182. Compare III Sent 86 and III Sent 107 (at note 119).

wickedness and disgrace, which is lust. Solomon gave offense in this respect.† The second yoke is that of prosperity and wealth. The rich man who dressed in purple gave offense in this.† The third yoke is that of pain and misery. Achaziah gave offense in this manner when he consulted the god of Ekron after he had fallen through his porch railing and, as it were, was in pain.†

See 1 K 11:1–13

See Lk 16:19–31

See 2 K 1:1–2

Besides what we have already noted, if one diligently considers what Bethany means and how Scripture describes it, he can appreciate how manifold the value of obedience is. Bethany means 'the home of obedience'.[183] So it is said that outside Bethany neither tears of repentance, nor zealous good works, nor the holy repose of contemplation can be pleasing to God. For it is in Bethany that Lazarus is raised after four days;† and there, in Simon's house, Mary is released from the burden of sin.† Finally, one comes from Bethany to Jerusalem,† that is to the 'vision of peace',[184] because it is through obedience that the one sheep lost out of a hundred is carried back to the flock on the shoulders of the loving shepherd,† that the drachma which has been found is restored to the treasure of the highest king,† that the queen of the south is led to the real Solomon,† and that Bathsheba is returned to the embrace of the true David.†

See Jn 11:39

See Lk 7:36–50

See Mt 21:17; Mk 11:11

See Lk 15:2–5; RB 27

See Lk 15:8–9

See 1 K 10:4; Mt 12:42

2 S 11:2–27

122. 'My beloved went down into his garden, to the bed of spices, to pasture his flock in the gardens and gather lilies.'†

Sg 6:1

This is the enclosed garden,† refreshing in its lively waters† and filled with sweet-smelling flowers. This is the garden of delights, in which the

Sg 4:12

See Is 58:11

---

183. Jerome, *Liber interpr. hebr. nom.*; in CCL 72:135.
184. Jerome, *Liber interpr. hebr. nom.*; in CCL 72:121.

fruits of all the virtues are found and where the
tree of chastity, the wood of life,† and all the other
trees of paradise† are located. In this garden our
beloved planted four kinds of herbs brought from
afar, specifically from paradise: unblemished bodily
purity, which is like the lily;† the loveliness of
spiritual innocence, which is like the hyssop; the
truthfulness of honorable speech, which is like the
violet; and consistent justness in action, which is
like the rose.[185]† A bed of spices* is said to exist here,
because, since the discipline of right belief has been
taught on one side and the other, it is laid out as
it were with equal borders, is frequently turned
over as if with the spade of charity, and is planted
with many seeds of grain. Behold, what formerly
had been a Pantheon—a reflection of all the gods,
heresies, and schisms—now has been transformed
into the bed of all the spices! Our beloved pastures
his flock and refreshes them with these sorts of
spices, so that ultimately he can gather lilies,† which
means to give a reward to each according to what
he deserves.

Our beloved desired to go down into this garden of the Church, because wicked Pharaoh had
already usurped it for himself and filled it with slips
of the kinds of plants that are native to his own
realm—that is, of the vices. The bride of Christ
was being held captive under his control, serving
him in making bricks from mud,† having been sold
as a slave to sin.† Pharaoh's heart was hardened,* and
his hand lay heavy upon her.† He would not release
her except through the intervention of a strong
hand.† In order that our beloved could rescue her,
therefore, he went down into Egypt with a strong
hand and an outstretched arm.† In order to close

Gn 2:9; Rv 22:2
See Gn 2:16

Si 39:19; Is 35:1

†Si 39:17
*See Sg 6:1

See Sg 6:1

Jdt 5:10
†See Rm 7:14
*Ex 7:13, 22
See Ps 32:4

Dt 6:21

Dt 5:15

---

185. Compare II Sent 147.

the mouths of those who speak lies[†] and rescue her from the slanders of people,[†] he weighed her delight in sin—based on the price for which she had been sold into slavery to sin[†]—on a scale[*] against the value of his own blood,[†] and it was found to be the lesser of the two.[†] Thus she secured victory in his court.[†]

But since marriage law requires the consent of the bride, he sent messengers to ask it of her. He located, therefore, a servant after his own heart[†] and sent him with a harp[†] to speak to her heart[*]— to call her[†] to him, soothing her spirit, accustomed as it was to the mud of Egypt and made filthy by it. It was David who was sent. He entered Egypt with a nuptial song already composed and poured forth this splendid passage from his heart:[†] 'Hear me, daughter, look and listen closely: forget your people and your father's house. The king will desire your loveliness, because he is the Lord your God'.[†]

At that instant, Isaiah arrived, and seeing her in the chains of captivity he called out: 'Rouse yourself, raise yourself up, Jerusalem.[†] Remove the chains from your neck, captive daughter of Zion.'[†] When many other bridesmen of the celestial court approached as well—namely the patriarchs and the prophets, saying all the same things—she finally appreciated the nature of her spouse's favor. Rising from the dust, she said: 'You have been mindful of me',[†] O Lord my God, for 'you lift me up from the gates of death, so that I may declare your praises at the gates of the daughter of Zion'.[†] She continued, just like Abigail: 'Who can give me as a maidservant of my Lord, so that I can wash the feet of my Lord's slaves?'[†] Quickly lifting herself up, this Abigail climbed up on a donkey—that is, she made her flesh submissive to her—and followed the king's servants.[†]

See Ps 63:11

Ps 119:134

†See Lv 27:14; Rm 7:14   *Jb 31:6
Mt 27:6
See Dn 5:27
See Jb 23:7

See 1 S 13:14

†See 1 S 16:23
*See Ho 2:14
See Is 40:2

See Ps 45:1

Ps 45:10–11

Is 51:17

Is 52:2

Dn 14:37

Ps 9:13–14

See 1 S 25:41

See 1 S 25:42

The spouse met her, cheerful and joyous. He took her right hand, guided her with his advice,

See Ps 73:24

and received her in glory.[†] He brought her into

See Sg 3:4

his mother's bedchamber,[†] placing her in the bed of his charity. Clothing her with the ornaments of his grace and putting his left arm beneath her head

See Sg 2:6, 8:3

while embracing her with his right,[†] he said: 'I charge you, daughters of Jerusalem, do not awaken

See Sg 8:4

or rouse my bride until she herself desires it'.[†] Then he stationed sixty of Jerusalem's strongest men to stand watch around her bed. They were skilled in battle, and each had his sword at his side against the

See Sg 3:7–8

night's terrors.[†] He kissed her with the kiss of his

†See Sg 1:1
*See Ac 20:1
See Lk 19:12

mouth.[†] Then he bid her farewell,[*] going off to a distant country to become king and then return.[†] He gave his bride an order through the prophet Hosea: 'You will await me a long time, and you

See Ho 3:3–4

will have no priest, no sacrifice'.[†]

Pharaoh sensed beforehand that the husband would be gone, and bringing his army together he told them: 'Come, I will give chase and overtake; I will divide the spoils, and my soul will be filled. I will draw my sword, and my hand will

Ex 15:9

destroy them'.[†] At once he attacked the husband's

See Ac 12:3–4

camp: he took Peter captive[†] and crucified him

See Mt 4:18

along with his brother Andrew;[†] he beheaded Paul,

See Ac 7:58–59

exiled John, stoned Stephen,[†] tore the skin from Bartholomew, and put Laurence and Vincent to

See Is 40:2

the fire, taking his malice to its full scope[†] in employing such varied and horrible methods of persecution. 'And they left the corpses of God's servants as food for the birds of the air, the flesh of his saints for the beasts of the earth; they shed their blood all over Jerusalem, and there was no

See Ps 79:2–3

one to bury them'.[†] The bride groaned to see

Ps 44:11

her defenders set up like sheep for the slaughter,[†] and she suffered bitter grief. The earth, however, is irrigated with the blood of the martyrs of the Church. The field of the faithful becomes soaked with that abundant moisture, and as a result of the cutting of a single branch a thousand more grow back! So she was victorious through that by which it was hoped she would be conquered. She gains the victory by dying. She rises up by falling. Her triumph is achieved!

When her enemy, savage in his cunning, perceived this, he growled, and fleeing back to those weapons of stealth† for which he is famous, he refrained for the time being from persecution. Husbanding his strength, he called back his sword and took counsel. Finally he said: 'No plague does more harm than an enemy who was one's friend. I will therefore sow dissension among their leaders, causing them to wander in a trackless waste rather than remaining on the right road.† They will say "Peace, peace", but there will be no peace.† I will incite heresies and schisms, turning everything into internecine civil war. It will be easier for me to get their own forces to attack them than mine.'

This is what he said, and soon they were making their words more soothing than oil while actually preparing their weapons.† Then they attacked one another, inflicting mutual wounds† and angrily cutting themselves down on both sides. As a result, the bride's grief became far more bitter than previously, since she was now weeping over the fact that her entrails were being torn apart by her own sons. But the distinguished soldiers of the christian army, perceiving that their cunning enemy was prevailing, took up the service of the Spirit once more, sharpening the weapons of faith. With courage and prudence they expelled the enemies from the Church's camp—Augustine drove out the Manichaeans; Jerome expelled Jovinian and

Margin notes:
See Gn 3:1

See Ps 107:40
Jr 6:14

See Ps 55:21
See 2 Ch 20:23

the Ebionites,[186] along with many others; and other figures drove out the remaining dangerous heretics and schismatics as they arose—and thereby restored peace and joy to the Church.

The ancient foe saw this and, jealous over the peace that had been revived in the Church, ground
Ps 112:10
his teeth and wasted away.[†] Planning renewed war-
See Jg 5:8
fare,[†] he returned to the weapons of spiritual combat. Summoning the great leaders of his army— the spirit of fornication, the spirit of gluttony, the spirit of greed—he said: 'Come now! We are accomplishing nothing; the whole world has already
See Jn 12:19
followed after them.[†] Although they are glorying in the fact that they have escaped and eluded our cunning traps, they still have to test our strength.' He thereupon sent them against the Church's camp. They found their enemy inebriated and sleeping
See Mk 14:37
during the night.[†]

Their opponents, thrown into disorder, staggered like drunkards. All of their skill had dissi-
Ps 107:27
pated.[†] As a result they suddenly begin to seek things for themselves, rather than showing con-
See Ph 2:21
cern for the property of Jesus Christ.[†] They claim God's sanctuary by hereditary right, lay claim to
See Ps 74:7
the tabernacle of his name,[†] and drag away from the Church, as she struggles and cries out against them, the seamless tunic of charity, woven from end to
†See Jn 19:23
*See Jn 19:5
See 1 P 1:19
end,[†] and the purple robe[*] of faith, moistened with the precious blood of the lamb,[†] with which the spouse had covered his bride's nakedness, as well as the other ornaments of religion. They leave the
See Ezk 16:39
Church utterly nude.[†] She cries out in lamentation. Disgraced by her nakedness and bare buttocks, she

---

186. Augustine wrote numerous works against the dualistic Manichaeans, with whose thought he had once affiliated himself. The Ebionites were a jewish christian sect opposed to certain elements of pauline thought. Jovinian's teachings on virginity were attacked by both Augustine and Jerome.

bewails the fact that all of her hidden, shameful members have been exposed to ridicule. She beseeches the sons of her own womb for help, but they show her no pity.† She begs them for aid, but they jeer at her. Using both her hands and all her strength, she manages to pull around her breast and vital parts the few tatters of the monastic and canonical religious life which had just barely evaded the hands of the plunderers.† She begs that these at least be left to her, but they do not listen to her.

Nonetheless they occasionally pretend to take pity on her and try to persuade her to put on a garment which gives the appearance of virtue by concealing vice. She, however, curses it with loathing. She will not take it up or acknowledge it unless it is that robe, woven by the hands of wisdom and imbued with the blood of the lamb,† which was left to her by her spouse but carried off by her sons. She clothes herself in no other, but rather flings anything else down in disgust. So she too is thrown down, rejected, attacked, and reproached by everyone. These are the dangers which beset us and our Church; because of them her sorrow has become very bitter indeed.†

Although three woes have come and gone, one still remains† —the messenger of Satan,* who transforms himself into an angel of light† and will sit in God's temple, presenting himself as though he were God.† He is already using the hidden power of wickedness† in his taunting predictions: 'Look, here he is; look, there he is!' But, O bride of Christ, do not believe it;† restrain yourself! Your beloved has already gone down into his garden, to the bed of spices, so that he can feed his flock in the garden and collect the lilies.†

See Jb 19:17

See Jg 2:14

See Rv 7:14, 22:14

See Is 38:17

†See Rv 9:12, 11:14
*2 Co 12:7
See 2 Co 11:14
See 2 Th 2:4
See 2 Th 2:7

See Mt 24:23

See Sg 6:1

See Sg 1:3

123. 'The king has brought me into his chamber.'[187]† In the 'chamber' understand the word in the moral sense, according to which three dwellings are distinguishable. The first is said to be fragrant and the second fruitful, while the third is related to wine. In the first reside those who submit humbly to those placed over them.† In the second are those who have learned to endure, with remarkable patience, the disorderly behavior of their confrères. In the third are situated those who know how to preside over those committed to their care wisely in both word and deed.

See Heb 13:17

If one wishes to ascend to the summit of perfection, therefore, he must first enter the cell of discipline. The word 'discipline' derives from the verb meaning 'to learn',[188] since it is on the path of the disciple that one must learn to restrain his animalistic inclinations, set aside perverse habits, and amend his disorderly conduct. In this cell one should become small and foolish, since God chose what is foolish in the eyes of the world† and no one will enter the kingdom of heaven unless he has become like a little child.† In this cell the one who has for some time been turned away must turn himself around. As the apostle says, it is when one is turned back to the Lord that the veil is lifted† from him.

See 1 Co 1:27

See Mt 18:3

See 2 Co 3:16

Perhaps you cannot appreciate how one is turned back unless you first understand how one has been turned away. Everyone who occupies himself in nonsense and trifles during the time that the rule stipulates should be devoted to God

187. Compare the following to III Sent 121 (at note 176); Div 92.1–3 (SBOp 6/1:346–48); and SC 23 (SBOp 1:138–50).
188. The verb is 'discere'. See Isidore, *Etymologiae* 1.1.1. and 10.66.1–2.

is properly described as turned away. Everyone who worries about worldly matters,[†] or money, or earthly profit when the word of God is preached, is turned away. Every person who is tied up in anxiety over his possessions and distracted by lust for wealth, or who strives after the recognition of our age and the honors of this world, is turned away. Moreover, one who appears to be detached from such concerns—who stands up and hears the words of the law[†] with an attentive face and eyes, but who is actually rambling about in his heart and thought—is also turned away from God, not turned back toward him. From such a person the veil has not yet been lifted.[†] He is blinded in mind.[†] If he searches for the door of Lot's house, he will never find it.[†] If he climbs the mount with Abraham and Isaac, he will always stay back in the valley with the donkey, never to behold the rites.[†] The one who, after entering the cell of discipline, has been instructed and armed with all these examples and others like them, now appears worthy to proceed to the second cell, which is the cell of nature.

Just as the word 'discipline' is derived from the verb meaning 'to learn', so the word 'nature' is derived from the verb meaning 'to be born'.[189] On the scales of nature a poor person weighs the same as a rich one, a knight the same as a lord, a priest the same as a bishop, a monk the same as an abbot, a slave the same as a king. For in nature no one is higher or lower, first or last, noble or of obscure birth. Nature always creates all of us equal. The fact that someone is set over someone

Margin notes:
See 2 Tm 2:4; RB 2 and 27

See Ne 8:9

See 2 Co 3:16
See Mk 8:17
See Gn 19:10–11

See Gn 22:1–19

---

189. See Isidore, *Etymologiae* 11.1.1. Isidore reads: 'Natura dicta ab eo quod nasci aliquid faciat': 'Nature is so called by reason of the fact that it causes everything to be born.'

else or under someone else should be ascribed not
to nature, but to the one who ordains all things,
who is believed to distribute and allocate the gifts
See Eph 3:7; 1 Co
12:4 of his grace† justly. Once one has entered the cell of
nature, therefore, he should, upon being situated
in that second cell, exhibit to his confrères how
much progress he made in the first. For it is just
See 1 P 4:10 that anyone should strive to share† with others the
See Tb 4:9 gift which he receives.† As a result, this cell can
be called fruitful: the one who speaks well and
lives well, and shows himself consistently righteous
See Jn 12:25, 15:5 among his brothers, surely brings a rich harvest.†
For any person who is wicked and reprobate will
be indicted through his character, while a good
person will, once singled out by his goodness, grow
even better. Sometimes a bad person will, because
of him, desist from his perversity. A good one will
always become better because of him.

After one has corrected his behavior, abandoned
his depraved habits, restrained his wild urges, and
lived for a time among his confrères without be-
See Ph 2:15; 1 Th
2:10 ing quarrelsome,† he is now clearly worthy to be
brought into the third chamber, which is that of
grace. Further, the one who has learned how to
govern, support, and correct both himself and others should hold a position of authority. The one
who presumes to teach, however, before he has
been taught is likely to direct his rudderless ship
into the rocks and waves rather than to rescue it
from them. Is a person who never had a teacher,
or had only a poor one, ever going to mold his
student into a good person?[190]

Moreover, the one about whom we have been
speaking—the one whom we have brought into
the cell of grace because of his diligence in acting

---

190. Compare Circ 3.7 (SBOp 4:287–88).

well—is numbered among those who know how
to feed the flocks committed to their care both by
word and by example when, entering the field of
the Scriptures and gathering various flowers redolent with heavenly sweetness, he nourishes those
entrusted to him and, through that nourishment,
leads them all the way to the tree of life, which
stands at the center of paradise.† For he teaches   See Gn 2:9
them at what time the cherub who holds the
flaming, revolving sword to guard the path to the
tree of life† can be moved or placated. The angel   See Gn 3:24
holds the sword so that it can strike; it flames so
that it can burn; and it revolves so that it can turn
around. This is the sword which Jesus came to send
upon the earth—the sword which divides son from
father, daughter from mother, husband from wife
and children.† Its blade cuts down all the desires of   See Mt 10:34–35
the flesh† and its flame consumes inner vice with   See Ga 5:16; Eph
fire, but its revolving motion turns it aside from all   2:3; 2 P 2:18
the things which can be kept within bounds.

It is through these three means—burning, cutting away, and conversion—that the path to the
tree of life is laid open. The cherub, who signifies
complete knowledge,[191] is mollified, so that one
may approach the tree of life. This is the tree
which is described as being situated in the middle
of paradise.† What this means and how it may be   See Gn 2:9
understood, can be explained—with God's help—
as follows.

Paradise is the place of delights.† A middle refers   See Ezk 28:13
to something which has at least two ends. Now
the tree represents that wisdom or understanding through which the faithful soul possesses real,
certain knowledge of the distinction between her
Creator, herself, and every other material creature.

---

191. Jerome, *Liber interpr. hebr. nom.*; in CCL 72:63.

For when the soul is, through contemplation, sufficiently raised up, she sees that the heavens and the
earth—indeed, all corporeal being—is beneath her
and of less worth than she. She also sees that only
her Creator is above her and of greater worth than
she. It is at this point that the soul, now perfected,
arrives at the tree which is in the middle of paradise.
She is now situated at the middle, because she
regards only herself as being midway between the
Creator and corporal creatures. She is in a place
of delights, because she perceives that she stands
above every bodily creature and is inferior only
to the Creator. For what greater delight can there
be than for the human soul to be superior to the
sun, the moon, the stars, and every other material
creature?[†] This explains what that tree represents
and why it sits in the middle of paradise.[†]

See Gn 1:28
See Gn 2:9

We do not yet actually possess the tree of life.
This happens in the following way. When the soul
sees herself brought to this point, as if through a
kind of meditation, and considers with the eye of
discernment the things which are beneath her and
the one who is above her, it becomes necessary
for her to calculate the intensity of her love for
individual things by appropriate degrees of comparison. This can surely be achieved if she loves
only her Creator more than herself, and more than
the things that are beneath her by as much as she
understands that he is of greater worth than she
and of still greater worth than the things below
the spiritual realm. This is the first stage. Then the
soul comes to love herself more than the things
that are beneath her by as much as she perceives
herself to be above them. Thus she ascends to the
second stage. On the other hand, should she love
temporal things—which were created by God's
goodness because of her and were arranged by

him with wondrous beauty—in such a way as to
give no offense to the fount of life† in her love of   See Ac 3:15
them, she has reached the third stage. Now free
of care, she can employ the things of the world in
accordance with necessity and busy herself in the
work of expiation, serving her Creator lovingly.
This, then, is the tree of life. The one who tastes
its fruits teaches and acts not for himself or for the
world, but comes into being and lives† for God   See Ga 2:20
alone. May he protect you everywhere, and lead
you into his kingdom for all time!

124. 'Think about the Lord in goodness and
seek him in simplicity of heart.'† 'A person who   Ws 1:1
is like an beast does not accept the things which
belong to the spirit. A spiritual person can judge
the value of everything, but will not be judged
by anyone.'† The human soul does not perceive   See 1 Co 2:14–15
the things which lie beneath her except by rea-
son of her own lowliness, nor can she experience
God—or think about God—except through her
own being. However great the soul may be, she
cannot perceive God except through a mysterious
reflection in a mirror† so long as she remains a   See 1 Co 13:12
pilgrim in this world.† Although the mirror can   See 2 Co 5:6
never be eliminated, the mystery can be mitigated
to some extent: since the soul is the image and
likeness† of God, she can—with her face unveiled,*   †Gn 5:3
if she is not immersed in a dark fog—behold the   *See Co 3:18
glory of God. It happens that she can see God in
the same state with respect to her as that in which
she perceives herself: since she is uncovered, she
will experience him as uncovered. If, however, the
soul is shrouded in fog, whirling about constantly
in darkness, she experiences God such as she is
herself: being confused, she will perceive him in
confusion. God, therefore, appears holy to one
who is holy, and distorted to one who is distorted.†   See Ps 18:25–26

See Ps 10:13

Ps 73:11

See Ws 5:6

See Pr 2:14

Ps 50:21

See Ps 50:21
1 Co 15:52

There are, then, four kinds of human beings: the bad, the worse, the good, and the better.[192] Each type experiences God according to the way they think about themselves. Let us first consider the bad. They are persons who sin without fear, who say in their heart: 'He will not make me pay.† What do our sins matter to the Most High?' 'And they asked: "How does God know? Does the Most High have such knowledge?" '† Because they have no fear, they cannot have any zeal for justice. (On the other hand, the sun of justice can rise† over those who fear God.) Such people are all wrapped up in the darkness wrought by their deep blindness. Having forgotten, through their negligence, the actions they should condemn, they recognize that they are negligent, and so they perceive God as negligent too. Almost all worldly people are infected by this vicious practice. They are those who, putting aside the fear of God and zeal for justice, rejoice when they do evil, exalting in their horrible deeds.† Confident, although they actually have no grounds for the confidence which derives from hope, they fearlessly delude themselves. But they will, at some point, hear from the Lord these words: 'Did you really think I would be like you? I will accuse you and convict you to your face'.† The bad person believes that the Lord is like him: being negligent himself, he thinks that God is negligent as well. But he will be accused and convicted in his own sight† when he beholds in front of him, instantaneously, in the blinking of an eye,† those deeds which he had forgotten. Now, however, this will work not to his correction, but to his damnation.

---

192. Compare III Sent 101 and Pre 14.38–41 (SBOp 3: 279–82).

There is another category of wicked persons—those who are called the worse. They labor under the reverse disease, for they are the ones who draw out their sins like a long cord. When they have accumulated a huge pile of wrongs, they begin to judge themselves for their crimes. The result is that as they approach the sun's rays from out of the thick darkness, they encounter a light so incredibly pure that because of their judgment of themselves they despair of receiving God's forgiveness. For they feel that if others had inflicted upon them so many savage cruelties as they have thrust upon God, they could not forgive them. They are held back by the light's remarkable splendor: judging themselves without mercy and forgetful of Lord's dignity and piety, they do not approach the word in the flesh, the sun in the cloud, that judgment which is tempered with mercy, the light inside the clay jar.[†] Along with Cain, they moan: 'So great is my iniquity that I cannot deserve forgiveness',[†] and along with the traitor they cry: 'I have sinned by betraying innocent blood'.[†] In their despair they find it easier to rush to the noose than humbly to ask pardon. They conceive of God as cruel and merciless, and in their impiety they slander his compassion, failing to perceive that his mercies are many[†] and that he is patient and exceedingly forgiving.[†]

See 2 Co 4:7
Gn 4:13

Mt 27:4

See 2 S 24:14
Ps 145:8

Those whom we described first do not ask for a doctor, because they do not feel themselves to be ill. Those we spoke of second recognize that they are sick, but have no faith in the power and kindness of the physician. The bad perceive God as negligent and those who are worse see him as cruel. Since they both think of the Lord as a reflection of their own attitudes, they fall victim to the same destruction, though as a result of two different diseases. Neither of these kinds of people See Ws 1:1 think about the Lord in goodness,† for it is equally horrible to hope without fear and to fear without hope.

Another class of person exists—those who are called the good. These people frequently grow angry and fall into sin, but when angered they quickly calm down. If they sin they confess their wrongdoing; moreover, they forgive those who sin against them, believing that God is offended by crime but placated by repentance.[193] Just as they forgive those indebted to them, so do they perceive See Mt 6:12; Lk 11:4 that God pardons them,† although he actually is neither offended nor placated, since he judges all See Ws 12:18 things calmly and arranges all things agreeably.† Such persons are prepared to take pity on others and to make satisfaction to God however often they sin. Such people as they are, they also perceive God to be: because they are merciful to others, they are certain that the Lord will show mercy to them. Such people, then, think about the Lord in See Ws 1:1 goodness,† but not in true knowledge or in simplicity, because they perceive him as changeable, deeming it proper to multiply his simplicity as a reflection of their own mutability. It is truly a rare bird on this earth[194] which can progress to this point, but God must be sought in simplicity—in such simplicity that we recognize him to be utterly simple, neither offended by our sins nor placated by our penance, but simply desiring our repentance. This is why holy men like David and Peter get up easily even after serious falls, because they seek See Ws 1:1 God in simplicity of heart.† They do not perceive

---

193. See *Prayer for the Mass of the Thursday after Ash Wednesday*.

194. See Juvenal, *Saturae* 6, 165.

him as changeable, but see him as simple in his timelessness.

It is difficult for people of our time, however religious or powerful they may be, to have the ability to attain this level, because they can barely hope, after so great a fall, to find a God so kind as to restore them to their original condition. Those great souls who abound in prophetic spirit restore themselves at once and immediately say: 'I have sinned; you will cleanse me, and I will shine whiter than snow',† and 'You will give me to hear joy and gladness, and my bones, which were crushed, will rejoice again'.† Note, moreover, that one thinks about the Lord in goodness and seeks him in simplicity of heart†—he is sought but is not yet found, because at that point we are only beginning the journey.

'But he is found by those who do not test him.'† Testing the Lord means to walk with him† with duplicity of heart. The duplicity occurs when we undertake God's work, but with the understanding that we will persevere in our service only to a point which we fix for ourselves beforehand, at which we will see if it is going well for us. If not, we will give it up. A soul which dismisses the consolation of God will at once be drawn to some other form of comfort. Cain is a good example— when he lost the Lord, he immediately sought some worldly consolation. The Lord is found by those who walk with him† with their whole heart* —which means with a perfect heart† —and who look upon each kind of fortune with an unbowed head, not knowing how to stray from the Lord's commandments.

'For the Lord will show himself to those who have faith in him.'† For the just person lives as a result of his faith,† and he trusts in God. Anyone

Ps 51:7, 10

Ps 51:8

See Ws 1:1

Ws 1:2
See Gn 6:9

†See Gn 6:9
*See Mk 12:30; Dt 6:5
See Jos 24:14

Ws 1:2

Rm 1:17; see Hab 2:4

See 1 Jn 3:2

who trusts in God will not be confounded. The
Lord manifests himself in this world through faith,
but in the next through his actual appearance, and
there we will be like him.†

125. A soliloquy involving a fourfold meditation
on his own condition.

When I can free myself from official duties and
engage in a kind of soliloquy with myself, thinking about my being, I consider three aspects of
myself—three aspects which are quite clear and
immediate. I reflect on the fact that I am a human
being, a monk, and an abbot—a human being by
nature, a monk as a result of my repentance, and an
abbot with respect to the requirements of obedience. Yet I add a fourth aspect which is a matter of
grace, specifically that I am also a Christian. This,
I emphasize, is a matter of grace, not of nature. If it
were a matter of nature, there would be no pagans,
no Jews. I remember that these four aspects of
myself are matters respectively of nature, of grace,
of repentance, and of obedience: I am a human
being by nature, a Christian by grace, a monk by
reason of my repentance, and an abbot in terms of
the requirements of obedience.

I reflect on the fact that I am a human being—
that is, I meditate upon the great privileges that
God considered humanity worthy to receive. He

See Gn 1:28

set humankind over all earthly things,† and while
all other animals stoop forward toward the earth,
'he gave each human being an upturned face, so
he could look up to heaven'.[195] 'You crowned him
with glory and honor, Lord, and placed him over

Ps 8:5–6
See Ph 3:19

what you have made'.† Animals he permitted only
to taste earthly things,† but on human beings he
bestowed the capacity to enjoy the eternal things

195. Ovid, *Metamorphoses* 1, 85.

of heaven. It is properly written that things which are visible last but for a time, while things which are invisible are eternal.† Surely this represents a great honor given me by God! He gave me reason with which to judge myself and examine all my deeds, so that I will not be judged by anyone else.† For as the apostle writes: 'If only we examined ourselves, we would certainly not be subject to the judgment† of anyone else.'† Brute beasts are not damned, therefore, because the power to judge themselves and to examine everything has not been given to them. It has been granted, however, to human beings. 'Judgment is now being passed upon the world'— that is, the judgment of humanity—'and now will the prince of the world be expelled'.† I give thanks to you, Lord Jesus, for you gave me myself as a good judge, a kindly judge, a sufficient judge. 'For a spiritual person can judge the value of everything, but can be judged by no one'.† If I prove a spiritual person in judging the value of things, surely that is enough. For the Lord will not judge the same matter twice.¹⁹⁶†

126. On the seven gifts of the Holy Spirit and the beatitudes of the Gospel.

The first gift is fear of the Lord. A person who possesses this gift despises every kind of wickedness, in accordance with the psalm: 'I despise and loathe evil, but I love your law',† and 'I hate every manner of wickedness'.† For it is written: 'To fear the Lord is to hate evil',† and 'Fear the Lord and withdraw from wickedness'.† It is also said of Job that he was 'a man who feared God and shunned evil'.† Without this gift—the first of the gifts—

Margin notes: See 2 Co 4:18; See 1 Co 2:15; 1 Co 11:31; 1 Co 2:15; Jn 12:31; See 1 Co 2:15; See Na 1:9, Septuagint version; Ps 119:163; Ps 119:128; Pr 8:13; See Pr 3:7; Jb 1:1

---

196. This dictum, of course, became, later in the twelfth century, the cornerstone of Archbishop Thomas Becket's opposition to the treatment of criminous clerks proposed by King Henry II in the Constitutions of Clarendon of 1164.

which is the beginning of all piety, no good can spring up or survive. For just as false confidence or apathy is the source and mother of all crime, so is fear of the Lord the root and guardian of all good things. Thus it is written: 'If you do not maintain yourself firmly in the fear of the Lord, your house will quickly be overthrown',[†] because every enterprise undertaken by the virtues tends to collapse suddenly if it ignores the protection of this gift. So Solomon says: 'Remain in fear of the Lord every day, and you will have hope for the future, and your expectations will not fail you'.[†] So too the apostle says: 'Work for your salvation in fear and trembling'.[†]

What more should I say? Fear and piety are interconnected. One cannot exist without the other. Simeon, therefore, was described as a man who was just and full of fear.[†] This is why it is written: 'You will worship the Lord your God and serve only him, clinging to him'.[†] So Solomon says: 'Fear the Lord and keep his commandments'.[†] We should have this kind of fear, just as blessed Job proclaimed that he had it with the words: 'I have always feared God—the feeling is like waves swelling over me'.[†] As a result of this fear of God, we set aside all things, we renounce the world, we even deny ourselves. As the Lord says: 'If anyone wishes to follow me, let him deny himself'.[†] This, then, is divine fear: it subjects to poverty any person whom it completely fills, setting him apart from wickedness. It is, therefore, first among the gifts, just as poverty is first among the beatitudes. For the Lord specified poverty as the foundation of the other virtues when he said: 'Blessed are the poor in spirit, for theirs is the kingdom of heaven'.[†]

The second gift is the spirit of piety, which is like the beatitude that occurs second in the Gospel,

Si 27:4

Pr 23:17–18

Ph 2:12

Lk 2:25

See Dt 10:20
Si 12:13

See Jb 31:23

Mt 16:24

Mt 5:3

of which the Lord says: 'Blessed are the gentle, for they will possess the earth'.[†] Concerning such Mt 5:4 people the Lord says in the Book of Isaiah: 'The spirit of the Lord is upon me; he has sent me to speak to the gentle'.[†] Moses, moreover, was the See Is 61:1 mildest[†] of all those who lived upon the earth. Nb 12:3 About the gentle, Job also said: 'The Lord puts the humble on high, and he raises up the sorrowful through his saving power'.[†] Solomon, therefore, Jb 5:11 adds: 'Humility comes before glory'[†] and 'Glory Pr 15:33 will come to the person who is humble in spirit'.[†] Pr 29:23 Moreover, it is written of the Lord: 'He will save those who are humble in spirit'.[†] Ps 34:18

On the other hand, of the proud it is said: 'The Lord stands opposed to those who are proud',[†] and Jm 4:6 'The spirit is exalted before it falls'.[†] Pride thrusts Pr 16:18 a person from a high point to a low one, while humility raises him from the depths to the heights. For the angel who was proud in heaven fell to the infernal regions, while the person who humbles himself on earth will ascend to heaven. So the humbler anyone should be, the loftier he actually is. Thus it is written: 'The greater you are, the more you should humble yourself in all things, and you will find grace in the Lord'.[†] The Lord also says in Si 3:20 this vein: 'Anyone who wants to be first among you must be your servant',[†] and 'When you have done Mt 20:27 everything you have been ordered, say: "We are but useless servants" ',[†] and again: 'Learn from me, See Lk 17:10 for I am gentle and humble of heart'.[†] Without Mt 11:29 the virtue of humility, the other virtues cannot advance. This is why blessed Gregory wrote: 'The person who brings together virtues without humility is like a person who carries dust into the wind'.[197] Just as dust is dispersed by the force of a

---

197. Gregory, *In evangelia homiliae* 7.4; in PL 76:1103.

strong wind, so every good which lacks humility
will be torn away by the blast of vainglory. It is
far better to be a humble sinner than to be just
but arrogant. This was demonstrated clearly by the
Lord when he adduced the example of the publican

See Lk 18:10–14   and the pharisee.† Also, just as a wise person has
said: 'A person's humble confession of his wicked
deeds is better than proud preening about his good
ones'.[198]

    The third gift is the spirit of knowledge, of
which Solomon says: 'Whoever adds to his knowl-

See Qo 1:18   edge adds to his sorrow as well'.† For true knowledge is the recognition that we are mortal, frail,
and destined to fall; that we should weep and moan
in this exile, this place of misery, this workhouse,
this pilgrimage, this valley of tears. So it is said
in the third beatitude, which corresponds to this
third gift: 'Blessed are they who mourn, for they

Mt 5:5   will be comforted',† and it is also written: 'Woe
to those who are laughing now, because you will

See Lk 6:25   mourn'.† On this point Solomon also said: 'Laughter is joined to grief, and sorrow will take the place

Pr 14:13   of great happiness'.†

    The fourth gift is the spirit of fortitude, which
is like the fourth beatitude in the Gospel, where
it is said: 'Blessed are those who hunger and thirst

Mt 5:6   after justice, for they will be filled'.† For one who
hungers and thirsts after justice will be strong, fearless, and unconquerable in the face of any adversity.
Solomon, therefore, says: 'The just person will be

Pr 28:1   as bold and fearless as a lion',† and 'Nothing that
Pr 12:21   befalls a just person will make him sad'.† It was
all those endowed with this spirit of whom the
apostle said: 'Some good people were subjected
to being pilloried and flogged, some were put in

---

198. Defensor, *Liber scintillarum* 8.39; in CCL 117:38.

chains and in prison, some were stoned or dis-
membered or captured and put to the sword. They
went about in the skins of sheep or goats—hungry,
distressed, ill-treated. The world was not worthy
of them. They went out to live in the wastelands,
in mountains and caves and ravines'.† The apostle Heb 11:36–38
also says this: 'What can separate us from Christ's
love? Trouble?',† and so on. That spirit sustains and Rm 8:35
guides the whole Church, equipping and defend-
ing her against all the wiles of the enemy. So the
husband cries out to his bride: 'You are beautiful,
my beloved, as sweet and lovely as Jerusalem, but
as terrible as a line drawn up for battle'.† Sg 6:3

The fifth gift is the spirit of counsel, which
encourages one to show compassion to others and
take pity on them. It corresponds to the fifth beatitude, of which it is written: 'Blessed are the merciful, for they will obtain mercy'.† On this point Mt 5:7
Solomon also says: 'A person who is inclined to
be merciful will be blessed'.† We act upon this Pr 22:9
beatitude in three principal ways: when we perform those six works of the beatitude of which
we read in the Gospel;† or when we strive to See Mt 25:35–46
correct those who have committed some fault and
to lead them back to the good; or when we show
ready patience over injuries that are inflicted upon
us. It is the second type of compassion—or the
spirit of counsel—which led Jesus, though God,
to empty himself and take on the condition of a
slave,† in order that he could thereby reform every See Ph 2:7
transgressor and bring him back to his sheepfold.
So the apostle writes: 'He sacrificed himself for
our sins, to rescue us from the wickedness of this
world'.† One must, then, emphasize this kind of See Ga 1:4
counsel, so that he may conform to the apostle's
injunction: 'Press on, both in season and out; be
ready to argue and rebuke'.† 2 Tm 4:2

There is another type of counsel, the virtue of discretion, through which we can distinguish true virtues from those that are pretended or false; through it we recognize Satan as the fount of hypocrisy. For as the apostle says: 'Satan disguises himself as an angel of light',[†] and, as blessed Cyprian puts it, he equips his minions[199] like ministers of justice,[†] but they turn day to night,[*] bringing destruction instead of salvation. Truly that virtue is the mistress and teacher of the other virtues, prudently keeping all the others within proper limits and guiding them from above. She maintains them all forcefully and with discretion, so that they will not wander without restraint either too little or too far. Boethius notes that the virtues hold a middle position. If one goes beyond what is appropriate, or does not go far enough, he departs from virtue.[200]

The sixth gift is the spirit of understanding, which is aligned with the sixth beatitude: 'Blessed are the pure in heart, for they shall see God'.[†] For unless the mind's gaze has been carefully purified, it will not be able to comprehend the divine mysteries clearly. As is written: 'The holy spirit of instruction shuns deceit and keeps herself apart from ideas which lack understanding'.[†] Solomon says: 'Wicked thoughts are an abomination to the Lord.[†] Perverted ideas keep us distant from God.'[*] One who desires to possess clear and genuine understanding, therefore, should strive to shun the deceptive clouds of wicked thought, guarding his heart prudently and diligently. So Solomon says: 'Watch over your heart very firmly, because life comes from it'.[†]

2 Co 11:14

†2 Co 11:15
*See Am 5:8

Mt 5:8

Ws 1:5

†Pr 15:26
*Ws 1:3

Pr 4:23

---

199. Cyprian, *De catholicae ecclesia unitate* 3; in CSEL 3:211.
200. Boethius, *De persona et duabus naturis* 7; in PL 64:1352.

The seventh gift is the spirit of wisdom, which is kind of an inner flavor,[201] an extraordinarily sweet taste. Of it the psalmist says: 'Taste and see how sweet the Lord is',† 'Wait and see',* and 'Come to him, and you will be illumined'.†Through this inner draught of the divine wisdom we enjoy a foretaste of the things which are above; we contemplate how delightful it is to sit among the denizens of heaven, where nothing can happen to displease us, where nothing pleasant is absent. This seventh gift corresponds to the seventh beatitude, of which the Lord says: 'Blessed are the peacemakers, for they will be called the children of God'.† Those who keep their mind peaceful and calm taste of heavenly things with greater sweetness, and behold them more acutely. For the more patient one is, the more he is shown to be wise. Solomon, therefore, says: 'A man's learning is demonstrated through his patience'.† Of persons such as this it is also written: 'There is overwhelming peace for those who love your law, and there is no stumbling-block for them'.†

These seven gifts are the seven women who struggle over a single man,† the seven spirits who rest upon the flower,† the seven lamps glowing on the lampstand,† the seven eyes on the stone,* the seven spirits in front of God's throne.†

127. 'My soul proclaims the greatness of the Lord.'† It proclaims his glory through its voice, its action, and its disposition. It proclaims his glory with its praise, its love, and its testimony. It proclaims his glory by offering both the form and the substance of praise, love, and testimony to his

†Ps 34:8
*Ps 46:10
Ps 34:5

Mt 5:9

See Pr 19:11

Ps 119:165

See Is 4:1
See Is 11:1–3
†See Ex 25:37
*See Zc 3:9
See Rv 4:5

Lk 1:46

---

201. Bernard again draws the etymological link between 'sapientia' ('wisdom') and 'sapor' ('taste', 'flavor'). See also III Sent 85 (at note 63); III Sent 96; SC 85.8 (SBOp 2:312); and Isidore, *Etymologiae* 10.s.240.

greatness. 'My soul proclaims the greatness of the Lord' because it has been made marvelously great by the Lord, who is himself great. First of all, my soul was wonderfully created by the Lord in

Gn 1:26

the image and likeness† of God, but afterward it became miserably deformed in Adam. Now it has been restored, even more greatly and gloriously and splendidly, by the Lord. 'My soul proclaims the

Lk 1:46

greatness of the Lord'.† Every creature proclaims the greatness of the Lord, but my soul does so more completely than any other creature, for in no other creature has God created anything so wondrously as my soul. But he is the Lord: as he wished, so has it been done. 'My soul proclaims the greatness of the Lord'. Proclaim the greatness of the Lord, not your own! A person who proclaims his own greatness dishonors God, and, to the extent that he does so, he has not raised himself up but thrust himself down. Your duty is to humble yourself and to exalt the greatness of the Lord.

Lk 1:47

'And my spirit exults.'† Note the order. First she strokes the harp, then the psaltery: she puts the soul first, then the spirit. For what belongs to the spirit does not come first, but rather what pertains to the soul does, and only then what relates to the spirit. 'And my spirit exults' beyond every creature. Indeed it rejoices even beyond itself because of the enormity of its joy. In what does it rejoice? Not in me but in God my maker, through its enjoyment of his knowledge and love. It does so not through me, but through the intercession and saving work on my behalf by my savior Jesus, my son—mine in a quite singular sense. He is my God, my savior, and my son! He is the maker of all things and of me too, but he is the son of me alone, and, with me as mediator, he becomes the salvation of all!

'Because he has looked upon the humility of

his handmaiden.† His handmaiden would not have Lk 1:48 dared even to raise her eyes toward him, unless he had first deemed it proper to look upon his handmaiden. His mercy looked down upon us first, because our wretchedness had left us far too contemptible to behold him. Among all persons he looked down particularly upon me—to whom, beyond all others, he gave a special privilege. Note too that she was not content to say that 'he looked upon me', or 'he looked upon his handmaiden', or 'he looked upon my humility', but rather she humbled herself thoroughly, thereby establishing the firmest possible foundation for her to receive and securely keep gifts of such greatness and beauty. 'He has looked upon', she said, 'the humility of his handmaiden'. The individual words are balanced in their weight. For there are handmaidens who are not at all humble. Hagar was a handmaiden, but she was arrogant; she looked down upon her mistress.† Many women are humble, but Gn 16:4 they are not handmaidens of the Lord. Humility, therefore, demonstrates a disdain for self, and the handmaiden expresses her servitude through her devotion. 'He has looked upon the humility of his handmaiden.' By looking upon me through his grace, he made me both humble and his handmaiden. He made me his handmaiden, she said— his own handmaiden—by performing his special work in me and through me.

'For behold, from this day all generations shall call me blessed.'† Oh, exalted heart, with what Lk 1:48 bright eyes have you seen every creature suddenly brought together in true bliss! 'Behold', she says. This is an injunction used by one who both perceives and shows. Behold, I now see what is going to be done through me, what fruit is going to derive from me, how many enormous benefits are

going to come through me, not for myself alone,
but for all generations! 'All generations shall call
me blessed.' They would not call me blessed unless
they enjoyed something of the same bliss that I
possess. For how can one vomit if he does not
eat? 'They shall call me blessed' because they will
take possession of my blessed fruit. All generations
will be blessed through my fruit, and since they
all will be blessed, they all will call me singularly
blessed—all generations, the generations of heaven
and the generations of earth, all the angels and
all the elect. For there are generations among the
angels, too; and as a result the one from whom

Eph 3:15   every family in heaven and on earth takes its name†

        is called the father of spirits. For some are fathers
to others in heaven—they are fathers to those over
whom they preside with paternal charity, and in
whom they engender and bring forth the affection
due to true fatherhood. So every family among
them takes its name from the highest father, because he loves them, instructs them, and guides
all of them like the highest and true father he is.
In response they love, instruct, and guide those
who have been made subject to them paternally,
in accordance with the gift of fatherhood which
they have received. In the same way, those who
are good fathers on earth receive the gift of their
fatherhood from the highest father, according to
how much more or less they achieve a knowledge
and love of the highest form of fatherhood. 'All'

Lk 1:48   of these 'generations shall call me blessed.'† For the
number of generations among the angels will be
restored through the one begotten through me,
and the human race which had been condemned
in Adam will be reborn to eternal bliss through

See Lk 1:42   the blessed fruit of my womb.† Within these and
indeed beyond all these generations, 'all genera-

tions shall call me blessed'.† Deservedly, therefore,   Lk 1:48
O Queen, will all generations call you blessed.
You have given birth to true eternal bliss for all
generations!

'Because he who is powerful has done great
things for me.'† I emphasize that I do not attribute   Lk 1:49
to myself the fact that all generations will call me
blessed.† I do not ascribe it to my own merit, but to   See Lk 1:48
the one who has done great things for me.† For I am   See Lk 1:49
called blessed by all generations as a result of the fact
that I have been blessed by him and revealed to all
in a kind of mirror of blessedness. 'Because he has
done great things for me.'† He has done not some   Lk 1:49
single great thing for me, but many great things.
One of the great things accomplished by him is that
I am a virgin, another is that I am a mother, and
another is that I am at once both virgin and mother.
And whose mother? The mother of the only-
begotten God, creator and savior of all! 'He has
done great things for me.' The greatness and variety
of the good things he has done for me cannot be
described or imagined! Who is it who has done
such great things for you? 'He who is powerful, and
holy is his name.'† Do not wonder about this. Do   Lk 1:49
not ask how these things could happen. The one
who has done them is powerful—he is powerful.
Indeed he is all-powerful. Mark his power well:
he has the power to do everything that he desires.
Great are those things which you perceive in me,
but great indeed is the power which has done such
great things in me! From the great and marvelous
things he has done in me, consider how great and
marvelous his power is. Why has he done these
great things for you? Because 'his name is holy'.
This is the only reason why he has done such great
things for me—his holy name. It is because of his
name, not because of any merit of mine, that he

has done such great things for me: he wished to reveal his name, which is wonderful and holy and inexpressible, in me. What is this name? The good, See Mk 10:18 because no one is good save God alone.† So it is because of his unique goodness that he has done such great things for me—because he wished to reveal in me both his power and his goodness, for Lk 1:49 he is singularly powerful and holy is his name.† But just as his name is holy in itself, so too is it made holy in us. As it was predestined in him for all eternity, so too should it be brought to fulfillment in us.

'And his mercy will reach from generation to Lk 1:50 generation.'† Behold his name! What is it? His mercy. Where is it? His mercy extends from generation to generation—from the Jews to all peoples, from the beginning of the world to its end— but not indiscrimately, only to those who fear See Lk 1:50 him.† There is no distinction among individuals for God. Jew and Greek, barbarian and Scythian, See Col 3:11 slave and free,† man and woman in every race and generation—so long as a person fears God and does justice, he will be welcomed to God's presence. Lk 1:50 'His mercy extends to those who fear him.'† One begins from fear of him so as to proceed to love of him. Those who are still afraid by reason of their sins should not despair, because his mercy is shown to those who fear him. His mercy forgives sin for those who fear him, and that remission of sin nourishes the love of those who thirst after him. Those who love him know his name. The love itself constitutes that knowledge.[202] However far we still are from knowledge of him, so much the less do we love him. Nonetheless, if we cannot yet love him perfectly because we do not yet know

---

202. See Gregory, *In evangelia homiliae* 27.4; in PL 76:1207.

him perfectly, still we can fear him lovingly. For
one who fears without love is a slave, not a son.
Such fear as this brings punishment, not mercy.

'He has used the power in his arm.'[†] By nature Lk 1:51
we were truly sons of anger,[†] but by the redemp- See Eph 2:3
tion of Jesus Christ we have been made sons of
mercy, because he used the power in his arm,[†] Lk 1:51
tying up the strong man and stealing his goods.[†] See Mt 12:29
To put it another way, if the Son had not freed us
and reconciled us to God through his death, that
comforting mercy would not exist for those who
fear him, but there would rather stand over those
fearful persons that justice which punishes, because
'he has scattered those who are proud in mind and
heart'.[†] Since 'all of the Lord's ways are truth and Lk 1:51
mercy',[†] just as earlier he acted from that merciful Ps 25:10
attitude through which he redeemed the humble,
he is acting now out of the sense of justice with
which he judges the proud. He has built, as it were,
a twofold wall from both of them by using each
in turn. 'He has scattered the proud.'[†] From the Lk 1:51
beginning of the world, the proud—human beings
and angels both—have been scattered. 'The great
dragon'—Satan—'was hurled down from heaven'[†] Rv 12:9
and driven into this gloomy atmosphere because he
did not choose to remain united with the truth, for
one who is not joined to God's truth is scattered
in his own vanity. The proud people who built the
tower of Babel were scattered, since their unity in
language was dissolved into a plethora of tongues.[†] See Gn 11:1–9
Every proud person is scattered to the very extent
to which he is proud. For what is pride but dust
thrown into the air and scattered by the wind? 'He
has scattered those who are proud in mind and
heart'[†]—meaning those who pride themselves on Lk 1:51
their intellect and their courage. How clearly has

Mary here revealed the secret hiding-place inhabited by this worst kind of pride!

There exists, after all, a sort of pride which is bestial and vile. This pride is obvious to everyone, even foolish people, because it wallows most of all in the pleasures of the bodily senses. It rejoices in a sleek body, or beautiful clothing, or fulfilling a longing for food or some other foul object of desire. There is another kind of pride, which seems more splendid but nonetheless is far baser. It occurs when one is raised over others because of his knowledge, or his power, or the acuity of his talent, and then treats the others as though they were cattle in his eyes, while showing great concern for the important figures of this world. There is also a third kind of pride—the foulest of all—which arises when people exult over their virtues, or over marvels they have performed, or over their understanding of the eloquence of the angels or of the celestial mysteries.[†] Those people surely are proud in their mind and heart[†] who, on the outside, keep their eyes cast down but inside raise them up high. For what does it mean to be proud in mind and heart? The word 'mind' refers to keenness of understanding, while the 'heart' symbolizes a feeling of vainglory. So it is appropriate to add that they are proud in 'their' mind and heart, because even if they possess some knowledge bestowed on them by God, their pride derives only from themselves.

God has dispersed those who are proud in each of these three senses of pride—the beasts of the field, the birds of the air, and the fish of the sea.[†] The fish are those people who probe and tear finely-woven nets—who, among the faithful (as though among the waves), seem to be humble, but in truth are creatures not of sweet clear streams, but

See 1 Co 13:1–2
See Lk 1:51

Ps 8:7–8

of the bitter sea. They are fish of the sea, and so they travel along the ocean paths[†] rather than those of heaven. For although they grasp a bit of heaven when, as it were, they leap into the air, they still plunge back totally into the deep sea. The birds of the air, on the other hand, are those who are raised up in their obvious arrogance, since, out of a desire for temporal glory (as though in a whirlwind) they imagine that they are touching the stars. The sacred history describes Antiochus as such a man[†] and Herod as well,[†] and nowadays one can not just read about many others like them, but see and weep over them. The beasts of the earth are those who are given over simply to gluttony and lust. They recover their senses and escape the devil's snare more easily than do those who are prudent in their own eyes. So 'he has scattered those who are proud in their mind and heart',[†] because he disperses those suffering from every kind of pride. Some, however, he oppresses so that they will perish in eternity, while others he humbles so that they can come back to life.

'He has deposed the powerful from their thrones.'[†] First of all, he deprived the demons, the rulers of these dark regions[†] who were strong in their evildoing, of their power. After expelling the Jebusites from Jerusalem, he placed the seat of his realm there.[†] 'He has deposed the powerful from their thrones'[*] when his word reached the king of Nineveh[†]—meaning the rulers of this world— who came down from his throne, and, clothed in sackcloth and ashes,[†] humbled himself in order to turn aside God's wrath. God deposed Saul[†] and raised up David.[†] He also deposed proud Ahab from his throne. He said to his prophet: 'Have you not seen how Ahab has humbled himself before me?'[†] But since Ahab did not persevere in

Ps 8:8

See 1 M 1:11–67

See Ac 12:20–23

Lk 1:51

Lk 1:52

Eph 6:12

See 2 S 5:6–10;
1 Ch 11:4–9
*Lk 1:52
See Jon 3:1–10

See Jon 3:6

See 1 S 13:8–15,
15:10–35
See 2 S 2:1–4

1 K 21:29

See Lk 1:52

his humility, God did not exalt him as a humble person[†] but condemned him as a proud one. Every day he deposes the powerful of this world, some to eternal punishment and others to the kingdom of humility. He holds his scale in his hand, showing mercy to a person when he wishes while hardening

See Rm 9:18

a person's heart when he so desires.[†] Why, then, does he condemn one who has been deposed while saving another who was faltering? He keeps his reasons to himself, hidden among his treasures. Only one thing can be known for certain: if we are not humbled, we cannot be saved.

Lk 1:53

'He has filled the hungry with good things.'[†] First he humbled them, then he nourished them. The spirit of prophecy here speaks of future things as though they were past. For the hungry are not yet filled with good things. If they were filled with good things, how could they be hungry? If they were hungry, how could they be filled with good things? We should perhaps speak in accordance with the idea that 'the angels long to

See 1 P 1:12
Mt 18:10

catch a glimpse of him'[†] although 'they always behold the face of the Father'.[†] They are both hungry and filled with good things. They possess their desire abundantly, but also have an abundance of desire. That kind of abundance, however, is utterly devoid of any sense of nausea, and that kind of hunger is totally without pain—indeed, it is a blissful hunger which itself always satisfies them. This is so not only in the heavenly fatherland, but also along our way. On the road they hunger and

See Mt 5:6

thirst for justice,[†] and in the fatherland they will be satisfied when his glory is made manifest. Still, even here, along the way, the hungry are filled with good things, because God bestows nourishment

See Ps 145:15

upon them at the proper moment.[†] They are filled with good things and denuded of wicked ones.

They are filled with good things—with the gifts of the Holy Spirit. The hungry are filled, not those who have feasted to the point of disgust. The poor are satisfied, for 'he sends the rich away empty-handed'.† Esau was rich; he had no care for his brother's presents, merely telling him: 'I have plenty; keep what is yours'.† Jethro, the priest who was a kinsman of Moses, was rich, and so he did not agree to accompany him to the good things which God had promised to Israel.† King Hiram of Tyre was rich, and so he thought that the towns which Solomon had ceded to him were of little value.† Thus you should never be rich and satisfied in your own eyes, lest you be left to yourself, empty and vain. Always say to the Lord your God: 'I am hungry and poor'.† O Lord, the bread and clothing for my soul are in your hand. If you will give me food to eat and clothes to wear, you will be my God, and this stone will be a sign of the fact.† For if we have held out our hand to Egypt and the Assyrians to get sufficient food,† we have stretched out our hands to a foreign god.[203]† God feeds and

Lk 1:53

See Gn 33:11

See Nb 10:29–30

See 1 K 9:12–14

See Ps 70:6

See Gn 28:20–22

See Lm 5:6
See Ps 44:20

---

203. One manuscript adds the following here:
' "And that stone will be a sign" (see Gn 28:22). What stone is that, except the stone which the builders rejected (see Ps 118:22; Mt 21:42; Mk 12:10; Lk 20:17)? The builders are the wealthy and the proud, who said: "Leave us! We do not choose to know your way" (Jb 21:14), "We have no king but Caesar" (Jn 19:15), and "We do not want this man to rule over us" (Lk 19:14). That stone, I say, is a sign: and of what is it a sign to those who are pilgrims in this world, and are humble and thirsting? It is a sign of the divine mercy, which does not abandon those who keep hope in it, but rather fills the hungry with good things (see Lk 1:53) until it takes up its son, Israel (see Lk 1:54). But he was still called Jacob when he anointed the stone and put it up as a sign. Later, after a considerable time, he was made Israel. So long as he was struggling with the man who altered his pay ten times (see Gn 31:41), he was not worthy to be called Israel. It was not until his soul returned to its land with all its possessions, and he struggled not with a human being but with an angel (refusing to release

clothes us on this road, therefore, filling the hungry
with the benefit of his consolation in order that we
may at last become Israel—that is, we may become
contemplatives.[204]

For it is then, in contemplation, that God received Israel, his servant.[†] For as long as he was
called Jacob, he worked in the sweat of his brow,
on another's land, although he served faithfully. But
when he came back to his father with everything
he had, he was at once allotted another name—
Israel—because the Lord aided his servant Israel.[†]
He received him as he was returning from Syrian
Mesopotamia, exhausted by his labors and toil,
longing to behold his father's face. He took him up
in order to nourish him; he took him up in order
to bring him to perfection and lead him all the
way to his face. 'He received his servant Israel',[†]
who was not proud but humble, not hairy but
smooth,[†] not a hunter but a shepherd. Why did he
accept him? Because he is 'mindful of his mercy'.[†]
This is the solitary reason why he received him—
'so that he could reveal the richness of his glory
to those vessels of mercy which he had prepared
for glory'.[†] For God might have seemed forgetful
of how to show pity, if he had delayed sending
his Son until the very end of the world. He was
mindful, however, of what he had never forgotten,
so that we may always remember God's mercy and
sing of it forever.[†] 'He received his servant Israel.'[*]
He accepted his nature. He took up his cause.

Lk 1:54

See Gn 35:10

*Lk 1:54

See Gn 27:11
Lk 1:54

See Rm 9:23

†See Ps 89:1
*Lk 1:54

---

him until the break of day) (see Gn 32:24–28), that he changed
his name and was called Israel.'
   I have emended the reading 'peregrinus', at line 7 of the
critical apparatus here translated, to 'peregrinis'.
   204. See Jerome, *Liber interpr. hebr. nom.* [in CCL 72:75]:
'Israel est uidere deum siue uir aut mens uidens deum': 'Israel
means "to see God", or "a man or intellect which beholds
God." '

He assumed his duty. The Father welcomed his
son. At last, he received his servant Israel in his
true Son—all the descendants of his body, from
the first just human being to the most recent of
them. He received him in a sweet odor,† like the   Lv 2:9
evening offering.† He will also receive him into 'an   Ps 141:2
inheritance which is spotless and unsoiled, reserved
for him in heaven'.† Note that the final word of this   See 1 P 1:4
canticle is 'mercy'. It begins with mercy, it ends in
mercy, and throughout it deals with mercy.

'Just as he promised to our ancestors.'† This   Lk 1:55
last verse is that which completes the decalogue
and which finishes the tabernacle made up of ten
curtains.† In this verse the truth of God's promises,   See Ex 26:1
the authority of both Testaments and the unity of
the faithful are all proven, and it properly refers
to each and every one of the words previously
spoken. It is as though Mary were saying: the one
who is powerful, merciful, just, and truthful in all
his words and deeds has done this and that for
me, and so he has completed all things through
his work, 'just as he promised to our ancestors'.†   Lk 1:55
Indeed God, who brought all things into being,
spoke only once, but that which was done once
in him for all eternity cannot be shown in a single
instant to those who live their lives in the passage of
time. So he spoke to our ancestors 'at various times
and in various ways',† but still only infrequently   Heb 1:1
and allusively. As a result very few recognized him
from his message, until more recently 'he spoke
to us through his Son',† who revealed himself far   Heb 1:2
more clearly. Yet that word was seen only as a dim
reflection in a mirror† and by very few people,   1 Co 13:12
until finally in recent days he was brought forth
from the lap of the Father in the splendor of his
saints before the dawn,† to be recognized by the   See Ps 110:3

elect. From the beginning,[205] therefore, he spoke
to our ancestors that which began to be made
clear only at the world's end, so that one and the
See Gn 28:22 same stone† may join both the ancient fathers and
us new sons in a union of one faith and charity,
See Sg 6:8 and so that there may be a single dove,† a single
See Sg 2:13 lovely one†—she who trusted that he was going
to come and who received him when he arrived.
Among those patriarchs the most distinguished,
the first, the greatest was Abraham, in whose seed
See Rm 4:1 are numbered all the faithful† to whom, even now,
God speaks in a column of smoke during the day
See Ex 13:21 and a column of fire during the night,† and to
whom he will speak in the ages yet to come—
not in a mirror or through a vision or in a dream.
Rather, he will speak himself, in a single instant to
1 Co 13:12 all, face to face.† That happens when he hands over
1 Co 15:24 the kingdom to God his Father,† and God will be
1 Co 15:28 all in all.† Amen.

---

205. The critical text reads 'itinio' for 'initio.'

TABLE OF ABBREVIATIONS

GENERAL ABBREVIATIONS

ASOC	*Analecta Sacri Ordinis Cisterciensis; Analecta Cisterciensia.* Rome, 1945-.
CCL	*Corpus Christianorum, Series latina.* Turnhout, Belgium, 1953-.
CF	*Cistercian Fathers* series. Spencer, Massachusetts; Washington, D.C.; Kalamazoo, Michigan, 1970-.
Cîteaux	*Cîteaux in de Nederlanden; Cîteaux: Commentarii cistercienses.* Westmalle, Belgium; Nuits-Saint-Georges, France, 1950-.
CS	*Cistercian Studies* series. Spencer, Massachusetts; Washington, D.C.; Kalamazoo, Michigan, 1969-.
CSEL	*Corpus scriptorum ecclesiasticorum latinorum.* Vienna, 1866-.
PL	J.-P. Migne (ed.), *Patrologia latina.* 221 vols. Paris, 1844–1864.
RB	*Regula monachorum s. Benedicti.*

THE WORKS OF BERNARD OF CLAIRVAUX

SBOp	Jean Leclercq, C.H. Talbot, and H.-M. Rochais (eds.), *Sancti Bernardi opera.* 8 vols. in 9. Rome: Editiones Cistercienses, 1957–1977.
Abb	*Sermo ad abbates*
Apo	*Apologia ad Guillelmum abbatem*
Ben	*Sermo in natali s. Benedicti*
Circ	*Sermo in circumcisione Domini*
Conv	*Sermo de conversione ad clericos*
Csi	*De consideratione*
Dil	*Liber de diligendo Deo*
Div	*Sermo de diversis*
Ep	*Epistola*
Epi	*Sermo in epiphania Domini*
Gra	*Liber de gratia et libero arbitrio*
Nat	*Sermo in nativitate Domini*
O Pasc	*Sermo in octava paschae*
OS	*Sermo in festivitate Omnium Sanctorum*

Par	*Parabola*
Pre	*Liber de praecepto et dispensatione*
PP	*Sermo in festo Ss. apostolorum Petri et Pauli*
QH	*Sermo super psalmum Qui habitat*
Res	*De resurrectione*
SC	*Sermo super Cantica canticorum*
Sent	*Sententia*
V Mal	*Vita s. Malachiae*

BIBLICAL ABBREVIATIONS

Ac	Acts	Jm	James
Am	Amos	Jn	John
Ba	Baruch	1 Jn	1 John
1 Ch	1 Chronicles	2 Jn	2 John
2 Ch	2 Chronicles	3 Jn	3 John
1 Co	1 Corinthians	Jon	Jonah
2 Co	2 Corinthians	Jos	Joshua
Col	Colossians	Jr	Jeremiah
Dn	Daniel	Jude	Jude
Dt	Deuteronomy	1 K	1 Kings
Eph	Ephesians	2 K	2 Kings
Est	Esther	Lk	Luke
Ex	Exodus	Lm	Lamentations
Ezk	Ezekiel	Lv	Leviticus
Ezr	Ezra	1 M	1 Maccabees
Ga	Galatians	2 M	2 Maccabees
Gn	Genesis	Mi	Micah
Hab	Habakkuk	Mk	Mark
Heb	Hebrews	Ml	Malachi
Hg	Haggai	Mt	Matthew
Ho	Hosea	Na	Nahum
Is	Isaiah	Nb	Numbers
Jb	Job	Ne	Nehemiah
Jdt	Judith	Ob	Obadiah
Jg	Judges	1 P	1 Peter
Jl	Joel	2 P	2 Peter

Ph	Philippians	Si	Ecclesiasticus
Phm	Philemon		(Sirach)
Pr	Proverbs	Tb	Tobit
Ps	Psalms	1 Th	1 Thessalonians
Qo	Ecclesiastes	2 Th	2 Thessalonians
	(Qoheleth)	1 Tm	1 Timothy
Rm	Romans	2 Tm	2 Timothy
Rt	Ruth	Tt	Titus
Rv	Revelation	Ws	Wisdom
1 S	1 Samuel	Zc	Zechariah
2 S	2 Samuel	Zp	Zephaniah
Sg	Song of Songs		

CISTERCIAN TEXTS

Bernard of Clairvaux

- Apologia to Abbot William
- Five Books on Consideration: Advice to a Pope
- Homilies in Praise of the Blessed Virgin Mary
- Letters of Bernard of Clairvaux / by B.S. James
- Life and Death of Saint Malachy the Irishman
- Love without Measure: Extracts from the Writings of St Bernard / by Paul Dimier
- On Grace and Free Choice
- On Loving God / Analysis by Emero Stiegman
- Parables and Sentences
- Sermons for the Summer Season
- Sermons on Conversion
- Sermons on the Song of Songs I–IV
- The Steps of Humility and Pride

William of Saint Thierry

- The Enigma of Faith
- Exposition on the Epistle to the Romans
- Exposition on the Song of Songs
- The Golden Epistle
- The Mirror of Faith
- The Nature and Dignity of Love
- On Contemplating God: Prayer & Meditations

Aelred of Rievaulx

- Dialogue on the Soul
- Liturgical Sermons, I
- The Mirror of Charity
- Spiritual Friendship
- Treatises I: On Jesus at the Age of Twelve, Rule for a Recluse, The Pastoral Prayer
- Walter Daniel: The Life of Aelred of Rievaulx

John of Ford

- Sermons on the Final Verses of the Songs of Songs I–VII

Gilbert of Hoyland

- Sermons on the Songs of Songs I–III
- Treatises, Sermons and Epistles

Other Early Cistercian Writers

- Adam of Perseigne, Letters of
- Alan of Lille: The Art of Preaching
- Amadeus of Lausanne: Homilies in Praise of Blessed Mary
- Baldwin of Ford: Spiritual Tractates I–II
- Geoffrey of Auxerre: On the Apocalypse
- Gertrud the Great: Spiritual Exercises
- Gertrud the Great: The Herald of God's Loving-Kindness (Books 1, 2)
- Gertrud the Great: The Herald of God's Loving-Kindness (Book 3)
- Guerric of Igny: Liturgical Sermons Vol. 1 & 2
- Helinand of Froidmont: Verses on Death
- Idung of Prüfening: Cistercians and Cluniacs: The Case for Cîteaux
- Isaac of Stella: Sermons on the Christian Year, I–[II]
- The Life of Beatrice of Nazareth
- The School of Love. An Anthology of Early Cistercian Texts
- Serlo of Wilton & Serlo of Savigny: Seven Unpublished Works
- Stephen of Lexington: Letters from Ireland
- Stephen of Sawley: Treatises

MONASTIC TEXTS

Eastern Monastic Tradition

- Besa: The Life of Shenoute
- Cyril of Scythopolis: Lives of the Monks of Palestine
- Dorotheos of Gaza: Discourses and Sayings
- Evagrius Ponticus: Praktikos and Chapters on Prayer
- Handmaids of the Lord: Lives of Holy Women in Late Antiquity & the Early Middle Ages / by Joan Petersen
- Harlots of the Desert / by Benedicta Ward
- John Moschos: The Spiritual Meadow
- Lives of the Desert Fathers
- Lives of Simeon Stylites / by Robert Doran
- The Luminous Eye / by Sebastian Brock
- Mena of Nikiou: Isaac of Alexandra & St Macrobius
- The Monastic Rule of Iosif Volotsky (Revised Edition) / by David Goldfrank
- Pachomian Koinonia I–III (Armand Veilleux)
- Paphnutius: Histories/Monks of Upper Egypt
- The Sayings of the Desert Fathers / by Benedicta Ward
- Spiritual Direction in the Early Christian East / by Irénée Hausherr
- The Spiritually Beneficial Tales of Paul, Bishop of Monembasia / by John Wortley
- Symeon the New Theologian: TheTheological and Practical Treatises & The Three Theological Discourses / by Paul McGuckin
- Theodoret of Cyrrhus: A History of the Monks of Syria
- The Syriac Fathers on Prayer and the Spiritual Life / by Sebastian Brock

CISTERCIAN PUBLICATIONS

TITLES LISTING

Western Monastic Tradition

- Anselm of Canterbury: Letters I–III / by Walter Fröhlich
- Bede: Commentary...Acts of the Apostles
- Bede: Commentary...Seven Catholic Epistles
- Bede: Homilies on the Gospels I–II
- Bede: Excerpts from the Works of St Augustine on the Letters of the Blessed Apostle Paul
- The Celtic Monk / by U. Ó Maidín
- Life of the Jura Fathers
- Maxims of Stephen of Muret
- Peter of Celle: Selected Works
- Letters of Rancé I–II
- Rule of the Master
- Rule of Saint Augustine

Christian Spirituality

- The Cloud of Witnesses: The Development of Christian Doctrine / by David N. Bell
- The Call of Wild Geese / by Matthew Kelty
- The Cistercian Way / by André Louf
- The Contemplative Path
- Drinking From the Hidden Fountain / by Thomas Spidlík
- Eros and Allegory: Medieval Exegesis of the Song of Songs / by Denys Turner
- Fathers Talking / by Aelred Squire
- Friendship and Community / by Brian McGuire
- Gregory the Great: Forty Gospel Homilies
- High King of Heaven / by Benedicta Word
- The Hermitage Within / by a Monk
- Life of St Mary Magdalene and of Her Sister St Martha / by David Mycoff
- Many Mansions / by David N. Bell
- Mercy in Weakness / by André Louf
- The Name of Jesus / by Irénée Hausherr
- No Moment Too Small / by Norvene Vest
- Penthos: The Doctrine of Compunction in the Christian East / by Irénée Hausherr
- Praying the Word / by Enzo Bianchi
- Rancé and the Trappist Legacy / by A. J. Krailsheimer
- Russian Mystics / by Sergius Bolshakoff
- Sermons in a Monastery / by Matthew Kelty
- Silent Herald of Unity: The Life of Maria Gabrielle Sagheddu / by Martha Driscoll
- The Spirituality of the Christian East / by Thomas Spidlík
- The Spirituality of the Medieval West / by André Vauchez
- Tuning In To Grace / by André Louf
- Wholly Animals: A Book of Beastly Tales / by David N. Bell

MONASTIC STUDIES

- Community and Abbot in the Rule of St Benedict I–II / by Adalbert de Vogüé
- The Finances of the Cistercian Order in the Fourteenth Century / by Peter King
- Fountains Abbey and Its Benefactors / by Joan Wardrop
- The Hermit Monks of Grandmont / by Carole A. Hutchison
- In the Unity of the Holy Spirit / by Sighard Kleiner
- A Life Pleasing to God: Saint Basil's Monastic Rules / By Augustine Holmes
- The Joy of Learning & the Love of God: Essays in Honor of Jean Leclercq
- Monastic Odyssey / by Marie Kervingant
- Monastic Practices / by Charles Cummings
- The Occupation of Celtic Sites in Ireland / by Geraldine Carville
- Reading St Benedict / by Adalbert de Vogüé
- Rule of St Benedict: A Doctrinal and Spiritual Commentary / by Adalbert de Vogüé
- The Rule of St Benedict / by Br. Pinocchio
- The Spiritual World of Isaac the Syrian / by Hilarion Alfeyev
- St Hugh of Lincoln / by David H. Farmer
- The Venerable Bede / by Benedicta Ward
- Western Monasticism / by Peter King
- What Nuns Read / by David N. Bell
- With Greater Liberty: A Short History of Christian Monasticism & Religious Orders / by Karl Frank

CISTERCIAN STUDIES

- Aelred of Rievaulx: A Study / by Aelred Squire
- Athirst for God: Spiritual Desire in Bernard of Clairvaux's Sermons on the Song of Songs / by Michael Casey
- Beatrice of Nazareth in Her Context / by Roger De Ganck
- Bernard of Clairvaux: Man, Monk, Mystic / by Michael Casey [tapes and readings]
- Bernardus Magister...Nonacentenary
- Catalogue of Manuscripts in the Obrecht Collection of the Institute of Cistercian Studies / by Anna Kirkwood
- Christ the Way: The Christology of Guerric of Igny / by John Morson
- The Cistercians in Denmark / by Brian McGuire
- The Cistercians in Scandinavia / by James France
- A Difficult Saint / by Brian McGuire

- A Gathering of Friends: Learning & Spirituality in John of Ford / by Costello and Holdsworth
- Image and Likeness: Augustinian Spirituality of William of St Thierry / by David Bell
- Index of Authors & Works in Cistercian Libraries in Great Britain 1 / by David Bell
- Index of Cistercian Authors and Works in Medieval Library Catalogues in Great Britian / by David Bell
- The Mystical Theology of St Bernard / by Étienne Gilson
- The New Monastery: Texts & Studies on the Earliest Cistercians
- Nicolas Cotheret's Annals of Cîteaux / by Louis J. Lekai
- Pater Bernhardus: Martin Luther and Saint Bernard / by Franz Posset
- Pathway of Peace / by Charles Dumont
- A Second Look at Saint Bernard / by Jean Leclercq
- The Spiritual Teachings of St Bernard of Clairvaux / by John R. Sommerfeldt
- Studies in Medieval Cistercian History
- Studiosorum Speculum / by Louis J. Lekai
- Three Founders of Cîteaux / by Jean-Baptiste Van Damme
- Towards Unification with God (Beatrice of Nazareth in Her Context, 2)
- William, Abbot of St Thierry
- Women and St Bernard of Clairvaux / by Jean Leclercq

MEDIEVAL RELIGIOUS WOMEN

edited by Lillian Thomas Shank and John A. Nichols:
- Distant Echoes
- Hidden Springs: Cistercian Monastic Women (2 volumes)
- Peace Weavers

CARTHUSIAN TRADITION

- The Call of Silent Love / by A Carthusian
- The Freedom of Obedience / by A Carthusian
- From Advent to Pentecost
- Guigo II: The Ladder of Monks & Twelve Meditations / by Colledge & Walsh
- Halfway to Heaven / by R.B. Lockhart
- Interior Prayer / by A Carthusian
- Meditations of Guigo II / by A. Gordon Mursall
- The Prayer of Love and Silence / by A Carthusian
- Poor, Therefore Rich / by A Carthusian

- They Speak by Silences / by A Carthusian
- The Way of Silent Love (A Carthusian Miscellany)
- Where Silence is Praise / by A Carthusian
- The Wound of Love (A Carthusian Miscellany)

CISTERCIAN ART, ARCHITECTURE & MUSIC

- Cistercian Abbeys of Britain
- Cistercians in Medieval Art / by James France
- Studies in Medieval Art and Architecture / edited by Meredith Parsons Lillich
  (Volumes II–V are now available)
- Stones Laid Before the Lord / by Anselme Dimier
- Treasures Old and New: Nine Centuries of Cistercian Music (compact disc and cassette)

THOMAS MERTON

- The Climate of Monastic Prayer / by T. Merton
- Legacy of Thomas Merton / by P. Hart
- Message of Thomas Merton / by P. Hart
- Monastic Journey of Thomas Merton / by P. Hart
- Thomas Merton/Monk / by P. Hart
- Thomas Merton on St Bernard
- Toward an Integrated Humanity / edited by M. Basil Pennington

CISTERCIAN LITURGICAL DOCUMENTS SERIES

- Cistercian Liturgical Documents Series / edited by Chrysogonus Waddell, ocso
- Hymn Collection of the...Paraclete
- Institutiones nostrae: The Paraclete Statutes
- Molesme Summer-Season Breviary (4 volumes)
- Old French Ordinary & Breviary of the Abbey of the Paraclete (2 volumes)
- Twelfth-century Cistercian Hymnal (2 volumes)
- The Twelfth-century Cistercian Psalter
- Two Early Cistercian Libelli Missarum

STUDIA PATRISTICA

- Studia Patristica XVIII, Volumes 1, 2 and 3

CISTERCIAN PUBLICATIONS

Editorial Offices & Customer Service

• **Cistercian Publications**
  WMU Station 1201 Oliver Street
  Kalamazoo, Michigan 49008   USA

  Telephone 616 387 8920
  Fax   616 387 8390
  e-mail   cistpub@wmich.edu

Canada

• **Novalis**
  49 Front Street East, Second Floor
  Toronto, Ontario M5E 1B3

  Telephone 416 363 3303
             1 800 204 4140
  Fax   416 363 9409

U.K.

• **Cistercian Publications UK**
  Mount Saint Bernard Abbey
  Coalville, Leicester LE67 5UL

• **UK Customer Service & Book Orders**
  Cistercian Publications
  97 Loughborough Road
  Thringstone, Coalville
  Leicester LE67 8LQ

  Telephone 01530 45 27 24
  Fax   01530 45 02 10
  e-mail   MsbcistP@aol.com

Website & Warehouse

• **www.spencerabbey.org/cistpub**

• **Book Returns (prior permission)**
  Cistercian Publications
  Saint Joseph's Abbey
  167 North Spencer Road
  Spencer MA 01562-1233   USA

  Telephone 508 885 8730
  Fax   508 885 4687
  e-mail   cistpub@spencerabbey.org

Trade Accounts & Credit Applications

• **Cistercian Publications / Accounting**
  6219 West Kistler Road
  Ludington, MI 49431   USA

  Fax   231 843 8919

Cistercian Publications is a non-profit corporation. Its publishing program is restricted to monastic texts in translation and books on the monastic tradition.

A complete catalogue of texts in translation and studies on early, medieval, and modern monasticism is available, free of charge, from any of the addresses above.